KV-610-084

Managing Human Resources in North America
Current Issues and Perspectives
Edited by Steve Werner

Global Leadership
Research, Practice, Development
Edited by Mark Mendenhall, Gary Oddou, Allan Bird and Martha Maznevski

Global Compensation
Foundations and Perspectives
Edited by Luis Gomez-Mejia and Steve Werner

Performance Management Systems
Edited by Arup Varma, Pawan S. Budhwar and Angelo DeNisi

Managing Human Resources in Central and Eastern Europe
Edited by Michael J. Morley, Noreen Heraty and Snejina Michailova

Global Careers
Michael Dickmann and Yehuda Baruch

Global Leadership (Second Edition)
Research, Practice, Development
Mark E. Mendenhall, Joyce S. Osland, Allan Bird, Gary Oddou, Martha L. Maznevski, Michael J. Stevens and Günter K. Stahl

Forthcoming:

Manager–Subordinate Trust
A Global Perspective
Edited by Pablo Cardona and Michael J. Morley

Managing Human Resources in Asia-Pacific (Second Edition)
Edited by Arup Varma and Pawan S. Budhwar

Managing Human Resources in Asia-Pacific

Second Edition

Edited by Arup Varma and Pawan S. Budhwar

Routledge
Taylor & Francis Group

NEW YORK AND LONDON

Please see the series website at:
http://www.routledge.com/cw/globalhrm/

Second edition published 2014
by Routledge
711 Third Avenue, New York, NY 10017

Simultaneously published in the UK
by Routledge
2 Park Square, Milton Park, Abingdon, Oxon OX14 4RN

Routledge is an imprint of the Taylor & Francis Group, an informa business

© 2014 Taylor & Francis

First edition published by Routledge 2004

Library of Congress Cataloging in Publication Data
Managing human resources in Asia-Pacific / edited by Arup Varma &
Pawan S. Budhwar. —2nd Edition.
pages cm. — (Global human resource management ; 20)
Includes bibliographical references and index.
1. Personnel management—Asia. 2. Personnel management—Pacific Area.
3. Human capital—Asia--Management. 4. Human capital—Pacific Area—Management.
I. Varma, Arup. II. Budhwar, Pawan S.
HF5549. 2.A75M36 2013 658.30095—dc23
2012043798

ISBN: 978–0–415–89864–5 (hbk)
ISBN: 978–0–415–89865–2 (pbk)
ISBN: 978–0–203–15705–3 (ebk)

Typeset in Times New Roman and Franklin Gothic
by Swales & Willis Ltd, Exeter, Devon
Printed and bound in Great Britain by
TJ International Ltd, Padstow, Cornwall

Managing Human Resources in Asia-Pacific

Given the enormous economic and developmental changes in nations in the Asia-Pacific region, and the related movement of people between and across countries, it is critical that we better understand the HRM policies and practices of these nations. The latest instalment in the Global HRM series, *Managing Human Resources in Asia-Pacific* (Second Edition), presents the HRM situations in a number of southeast Asian and Pacific Rim countries, highlighting the growth of the personnel and HR function, the dominant HRM system(s) in the area, the influence of different factors on HRM, and the challenges faced by HR functions in these nations. This edition extends its coverage to Cambodia, Fiji, Indonesia, and the Philippines, and discusses HR research challenges in the region.

Arup Varma is Professor of Human Resource Management at Loyola University Chicago's Quinlan School of Business. From 2002–2007 Varma was Director of the HRER Institute and Chair of the HRM department at the School of Business Administration. Varma earned his Ph.D. from Rutgers University, an M.S. in Personnel Management & Industrial Relations (with honors) from XLRI Jamshedpur (India) and a B.S. in Economics (with honors) from St. Xavier's College, Calcutta, India. Dr. Varma's research interests include performance appraisal, expatriate issues, and HRM in India. He has published over 40 articles in leading journals including *Academy of Management Journal*, *Personnel Psychology*, *Journal of Applied Psychology*, *Human Resource Management Review* and the *Journal of World Business*. He is also co-founder and President-elect of the Indian Academy of Management.

Pawan S. Budhwar is a Professor of International HRM and Associate Dean Research at Aston Business School, UK. He is a Co-Founder and first President of the Indian Academy of Management. Budhwar has published over 75 articles in a number of leading journals on International HRM/OB related topics with a specific focus on India. He has also written and/or co-edited nine books on HRM-related topics, including Asia-Pacific, the Middle East, Performance Management, India, Developing Countries, Research Methods, Major Works in International HRM, and Doing Business in India. He is on the editorial board of over ten journals and is an Associate Editor of *Human Resource Management*. Budhwar is also an advisor to the Commonwealth Commission for scholarships and fellowships, a Fellow of the Higher Education Academy and the British Academy of Management and an Academician of the Academy of Social Sciences. He is also a Chartered Member of the Chartered Institute of Personnel and Development.

Routledge Global Human Resource Management Series

Edited by Randall S. Schuler, Susan E. Jackson, Paul Sparrow and Michael Poole

Routledge Global Human Resource Management is an important new series that examines human resources in its global context. The series is organized into three strands: content and issues in global human resource management (HRM); specific HR functions in a global context; and comparative HRM. Authored by some of the world's leading authorities on HRM, each book in the series aims to give readers comprehensive, in-depth and accessible texts that combine essential theory and best practice. Topics covered include cross-border alliances, global leadership, global legal systems, HRM in Asia, Africa and the Americas, industrial relations and global staffing.

Dedications

To my mother, Leelawati (AV).

To my mother – Daya Kaur – and my sisters – Shakuntala and Kamlesh (PSB).

To those who have an interest in the management of human resources in the Asia-Pacific region.

Contents

Figures

Tables

Contributors

Johngseok Bae is a Professor of Management, teaching human resource management and business philosophy at Korea University Business School, Seoul, 136–701, Korea. Email: johngbae@korea.ac.kr

Pawan S. Budhwar is a Professor of International HRM and Associate Dean Research at Aston Business School, Aston University, Birmingham, B4 7ET, UK. Email: p.s.budhwar@aston.ac.uk

Andrew Chan is Associate Professor in the Department of Management at the College of Business, City University of Hong Kong, 83, Tat Chee Avenue, Hong Kong. Email: mgandrew@cityu.edu.hk

Anand Chand is an Associate Professor in the School of Management & Public Administration, Faculty of Business and Economics, The University of the South Pacific, Suva, Fiji Islands. Email: chand_a@usp.ac.fj

Wan-Jing April Chang is an Associate Professor of the Department of Educational Psychology and Counseling (Industrial and Organizational Psychology Area) at the National Hsinchu University of Education, Hsinchu City, 300, Taiwan. Email: aprilchang0408@gmail.com

Marilyn Clarke is a senior lecturer in Human Resource Management (HRM)/ Organizational Behaviour (OB) at the Business School, University of Adelaide, 10 Pulteney St, Adelaide, Australia 5005. Email: marilyn.clarke@ adelaide.edu.au

Fang Lee Cooke is a Professor of Human Resource Management and Chinese Studies at the Department of Management, Monash University, Melbourne, Australia, VIC 3145. Email: fang.cooke@monash.edu

Anne Cox is a senior lecturer at the School of Management and Marketing, Faculty of Commerce, University of Wollongong, Australia. Email: avo@uow. edu.au

Philippe DeBroux is a Professor of International Management and International Human Resource Management at Soka University, Tokyo 192-8577 Hachioji-shi Tangi-cho 1–236, Japan. Email: debroux@soka.ac.jp

Noelle Donnelly is a senior lecturer, School of Management, Room 1009, Rutherford House, 23 Lambton Quay, Pipitea Campus, Victoria University of Wellington, Wellington 6140, New Zealand. Email: Noelle.Donnelly@vuw.ac.nz

Ann Hutchison is a lecturer in Human Resource Management at the business school at the University of Auckland, Private Bag 92019, Auckland, New Zealand. Email: a.hutchison@auckland.ac.nz

Naresh Khatri is an Associate Professor of Strategic Human Resource Management and Transformational Leadership in the Department of Health Management and Informatics, School of Medicine, at the University of Missouri, Columbia, MO 65212, USA. Email: KhatriN@health.missouri.edu

Marlin Abdul Malek is a senior lecturer at the Department of International Business, School of International Studies, Universiti Utara Malaysia 06010 Sintok, Kedah, Malaysia. Email: marissa@uum.edu.my

Derek Man is a Teaching Fellow at the School of Business, the University of Hong Kong, Hong Kong. Email: dman@business.hku.hk

Suwastika Naidu is a teaching assistant in the School of Management & Public Administration, Faculty of Business and Economics, The University of the South Pacific, Suva, Fiji Islands. Email: naidu_s@usp.ac.fj

R. D. Pathak is a Professor of Management, the Head of the Graduate School of Business as well as the Director of the MBA Program at The University of the South Pacific, Suva, Fiji Islands. Email: Pathak_R@usp.ac.fj

Margaret Patrickson is an Adjunct Associate Professor with the International Graduate School of Business at the University of South Australia, City West Campus in Adelaide 5000 Australia. Email: margaret.patrickson@unisa.edu.au

Chris Rowley is a Professor at the Cass Business School, City University, London, UK and Director of Research and Publications and the Centre for Research on Asian Management, HEAD Foundation, Singapore. Email: C.Rowley@city.ac.uk

Debi S. Saini is Professor and Chairperson of the HRM area at the Management Development Institute, Mehrauli Road, Gurgaon, Haryana–122007, India. Email: debisaini@mdi.ac.in

Sununta Siengthai is an Associate Professor of the School of Management at the Asian Institute of Technology, Klong Luang, Pathumthani 12120, Thailand. Email: s.siengthai@ait.asia

Klaus J. Templer is an Associate Professor and the Head of Psychology at SIM University (UniSIM), 461 Clementi Road, Singapore 599491, Republic of Singapore. Email: kjtempler@unisim.edu.sg

Arup Varma is a Professor of HRM at the Quinlan School of Business, Loyola University Chicago, 1 East Pearson Street, # 406, Chicago, IL 60611, USA. Email: avarma@luc.edu

David T. W. Wan is an Associate Professor and the Head of the Human Resource Management Programme at SIM University (UniSIM), 461 Clementi Road, Singapore 599491, Republic of Singapore. Email: davidwantw@unisim.edu.sg

Preface

Since the last edition of this book was written in 2004, a number of changes have taken place in the Asia-Pacific region. Key among them include the enhanced economic contributions of economies in the region towards the global economic growth, the further emergence of significant emerging markets in the region (including China becoming the second-largest economy of the world and India becoming the third most important destination for global foreign direct investment [FDI]), the rapid emergence of multinational companies from emerging markets in the region (such as India and China), a strong resilience of the Asia-Pacific region against the present global economic crisis, rapidly growing centres of excellence in business and management education and research in the region (for example, in Hong Kong, Singapore and Australia), rapidly emerging management institutions in India and China, and the ever-increasing contributions of the regional economic and trading blocs (such as the Association of Southeast Asian Nations [ASEAN], the Asia-Pacific Economic Cooperation [APEC], the South Asian Association for Regional Cooperation [SAARC] and the Asia-Europe Meeting [ASEM]). Consequent to such developments, it is becoming clear that the global economic, strategic and political influence is now rapidly shifting to Asia-Pacific and the region has become the world's centre of gravity.

As a result of such developments, understandably the number of publications related to the region over the last decade or so has considerably multiplied. In particular there has been a surge in the literature on management in general in the Asia-Pacific region. Lately some scholars have initiated a move to highlight the indigenous constructs and models (ahead of the established Western management models) that can be considered more valid and suitable for the region. Indeed such work is in its infancy. Also, there is still a scarcity of robust literature about the nature of HRM system(s), factors affecting the same, the challenges faced by HRM and the future of HRM in the Asia-Pacific region. Such a resource will contribute both to better theory and practice development. This book attempts to fill this gap in the literature.

Given the strong heterogeneity among the nations in the region based on differences in economic development, as well as socio-cultural, political and institutional differences, and the influence of such factors on HRM policies and practices, one can safely assume significant cross-national variations in the HRM systems of Asia-Pacific nations. Further, due to the context-specific nature of HRM, it is important for concerned policy makers and researchers to be aware of such differences, to expect HRM strategies to vary significantly across countries and realise that the strategies used to manage human resources (HR) in one country can be ineffective or irrelevant in another. There is then a strong need to seriously consider the evolving business and management concepts and practices in order to develop relevant management systems for firms operating in the Asia-Pacific.

Consequent to the strong state of flux in the region, the challenges regarding the management of HR are expected to be both complex and demanding. In order to help provide both policy makers and researchers with reliable information, an attempt has been made in this book to highlight in detail how national HRM systems across the countries covered in this volume are unique and deeply rooted in their national socio-cultural and institutional context. Thus, the objective of this book is to provide the reader with an understanding of the nature of HRM systems in 13 countries in the Asia-Pacific region – China, South Korea, Japan, Hong Kong, Taiwan, India, Thailand, Vietnam, Malaysia, Singapore, Australia, Fiji and New Zealand. It is intended that the reader not only acquires an understanding about the HRM functions in these countries, becomes aware of the diverse and unique configurations of national factors (cultural, institutional and business environment) that dictate HRM in cross-national settings, but also understands the key challenges faced by HRM in each country and the future of the HR function in each country. Such information will allow the readers to develop a comprehensive understanding of HRM in the region.

To achieve the set objective, all the contributions have been written around a set framework. It highlights the historical developments of the HRM function, the influence of key factors (that is, the national culture, national institutions and a dynamic business environment and business sector) on HRM policies and practices, the key challenges facing the HRM function and the future of the HRM function. The book also provides a mini-case relevant to the contents of a given chapter and useful websites for each country. This book then consolidates in a single source the dynamics of management of human resources in the Asia-Pacific countries and addresses questions pertaining to the past, present and future of HRM in these countries. All of the chapters in this volume are original contributions to the field and were specially commissioned for the book. It is hoped that this volume would serve as a catalyst to the development of further theoretical insights and appropriate techniques of HRM in this area.

The subject area of the book is suitable for both undergraduate and postgraduate HRM and international management courses. In addition, this book will be of interest to cross-national HRM researchers and practitioners. There were two main reasons behind the birth of this book: first, is the scarcity of a single volume that highlights the scenario of HRM in the Asia-Pacific context that can be used on relevant courses and second, the first edition was a great success and there followed long discussions with the series editors and the publishers to create this edition of the book.

We would like to thank all those who have in various ways helped to make this project a success. In particular we would like to thank John Szilagyi and Sara Warden at Taylor and Francis for all their patience and help with the development of this volume. Thanks are also given to Randall Schuler and Susan Jackson for their encouragement and guidance to do this second edition. Lastly, a big thanks to all the contributors who did a great job in responding to our various review- and submission-related requests.

Arup Varma
Loyola University Chicago
Chicago

Pawan S. Budhwar
Aston Business School
Birmingham

Foreword

Global HRM is a series of books edited and authored by some of the best and most well-known researchers in the field of human resource management. This series is aimed at offering students and practitioners accessible, coordinated and comprehensive books concerning global HRM. To be used individually or together, these books cover the main areas in international and comparative HRM. Taking an expert look at an increasingly important and complex area of global business, this is a ground-breaking new series that answers a real need for useful and affordable textbooks on global HRM.

Several books in the series are devoted to human resource management policies and practices in multinational enterprises. Some books focus on specific areas of global HRM policies and practices, such as global leadership, global compensation, global talent management and global labour relations. Other books address special topics that arise in multinational enterprises, such as managing HR in cross-border alliances, managing global legal systems and the structure of the global HR function. There is also a book of global human resource management cases. Several other books in the series adopt a comparative approach to understanding human resource management. These books on comparative human resource management describe HRM topics found at the country level in selected countries. The comparative books utilize a common framework that makes it easier for the reader to systematically understand the rationale for the similarities and differences in findings across countries.

This book, the second edition of *Managing Human Resources in Asia-Pacific*, edited by Arup Varma and Pawan S. Budhwar, reflects the comparative human resource management perspective. As in the well-received first edition, the editors have assembled the very best authors to contribute chapters on 13 different countries in the Asia-Pacific region. In addition, the editors have provided an excellent introductory chapter that provides an overview of the book and description of the framework that is used in all the country chapters. In all the chapters the authors also utilize the most recent and relevant research and reflect the experiences of the specific country being described. The editors also contribute an excellent concluding chapter that offers an agenda for future research and policy associated with the HRM challenges in the Asia-Pacific.

The publisher and editor have played a very major role in making this series possible. Routledge has provided its global production, marketing and reputation to make this series feasible and affordable to academics and practitioners throughout the world. In addition, Routledge has provided its own highly qualified professionals to make this series a reality. In particular, we want to indicate our deep appreciation for the work of our series' editor, John Szilagyi. He has been very supportive of the Global HRM Series and has been invaluable in providing the needed support and encouragement to us and the many authors and editors involved in the series. He, along with Sara Werdon and the entire staff, has helped make the process of completing this series an enjoyable one. For everything they have done, we thank them all. Together we are all very excited about the Global HRM series and hope you find an opportunity to use this second edition of *Managing Human Resources in Asia-Pacific* – and all of the other books in the series!

Randall S. Schuler, Rutgers University and the
Lorange Institute of Business Zürich

Susan E. Jackson, Rutgers University and the
Lorange Institute of Business Zürich

Paul Sparrow, Manchester University Management School

Michael Poole, Cardiff University and Editor,
International Journal of Human Resource Management

July 2012

Managing Human Resources in Asia-Pacific: An Introduction

PAWAN S. BUDHWAR AND ARUP VARMA

The Asia-Pacific Context

The Asia-Pacific typically covers East Asia, Southeast Asia and Oceania. The region generally includes about 50 nations and islands belonging to the geo-political and economic organisations of ASEAN (the Association of Southeast Asian Nations), SAARC (the South Asian Association for Regional Coopera-tion), PIF (the Pacific Islands Forum) and others (for details see Wikipedia – 'Asia-Pacific', 2012). The region is home to the world's two most populous countries, the world's largest holders of foreign exchange reserves, two of the world's top three economies and three of the world's five largest militaries as well as being the recipient of the largest inward foreign direct investment (FDI).

When the first edition of this volume was published in 2004 (see Budhwar, 2004), many Asia-Pacific economies were recovering from the economic crisis of the late 1990s, which had suddenly halted their remarkable economic run. In a reversal of fortunes, when the majority of the developed world is under a serious economic recession most economies in the Asia-Pacific region are witnessing a sustained run of economic growth and providing the rest of the world the needed gross domestic product (GDP). At present, the Asia-Pacific region produces more goods and serv-ices than any other region of the world and this trend is expected to continue in the years to come. Moreover, out of the 25 most important emerging markets, 10 or more are regularly from the Asia-Pacific region (see *The Economist*, 2012).

Further, as per the latest United Nations' Conference on Trade and Development's (UNCTAD's) (2012) 'global investment trends monitor', the FDI flow to the Asia-Pacific region in 2011 increased by 11 percent over 2010. A break down by sub-region inflow of FDI shows that East Asia, Southeast Asia and South Asia received about US$209 billion, US$92 billion and US$43 billion, respectively. With a 16 percent increase, Southeast Asia continued to outperform East Asia in growth of FDI while South Asia saw its inflows rise by one-third after a slide in 2010. The good performance of Southeast Asia, which encompasses the ASEAN as a whole, was driven by sharp increases of FDI inflows in a number of countries, including Indonesia, Malaysia and Thailand (for details see UNCTAD, 2012). Apart from being an important destination for inward FDI, there has been a significant increase in the flow of outward FDI from a number of Asia-Pacific countries (in particular from India and China along with the established players like Japan and South Korea). This also coincides with the emergence of emerging-markets multinational corporations (MNCs), whose growth has picked up rapid pace over the last decade or so (especially from India and China). It is also predicted that most new members of the newly affluent nations would come from Asia-Pacific in this century (see Tan, 2002). Indeed, in order to sustain its impressive economic growth, the region faces a number of challenges in the form of talent management and professionalization of its management, organisational and governance systems. The efficiency of their traditional work value systems is also questionable in the present global business context (for example, Froese, 2011; Bae, Chen and Rowley, 2011).

Considering the governance systems prevalent in a majority of the Asia-Pacific economies, scholars (Puffer et al., 20012; Pattnaik et al., 2011; Young and Stanton, 2009) comment that these nations have a long way to go before they can be considered at par with their Western counterparts on management professionalism (clearly a statement that is less applicable to Japan, Australia and, to some extent, South Korea). Also, the comparative cost advantage available with emerging markets in the Asia-Pacific region continues to fade away on a regular basis (with the exception of China). For example, countries such as Singapore, South Korea and Taiwan have lost their cheap labour and property advantage to countries such as China, India, Indonesia, the Philippines and Thailand. Further, the sector-specific national advantage of specific countries (for example, manufacturing in China and software and information technology in India) is becoming a challenge to sustain. In such conditions a possible way forward is to further enhance their levels of innovation, research and development and further generate their own FDI. Such developments have serious implications for the human resource management (HRM) function in the region, especially when human resources (HRs) are known to play a significant role in the economic development of nations (see Debrah, McGovern and Budhwar, 2000).

This book highlights the dynamics of HRM systems in 13 Asia-Pacific countries – China (short for the People's Republic of China), Korea (short for South Korea), Japan, Hong Kong, Taiwan, India, Thailand, Vietnam, Malaysia, Singapore, Australia, Fiji (short for Fiji Islands) and New Zealand. The remainder of this chapter is structured as follows. The next section summarises the key issues reported in the literature related to the field of HRM in the region. We then present the framework adopted by contributors to write their country-specific chapters for this volume. Finally, we introduce the individual chapters.

Developments in Asia-Pacific HRM

As much as we would have liked, it is beyond the scope of this chapter to present a comprehensive review of relevant literature regarding the developments in the field of HRM in the Asia-Pacific region. Indeed, each country-specific chapter in this volume does this in an elaborate manner. Nevertheless, to set the stage for this volume, an overview of the types of topics being covered in the broad field of HRM is presented in this section. A thorough literature search highlights the absence of a systematic analysis, which can present a comprehensive picture regarding the dynamics of HRM in the Asia-Pacific region. Indeed, given the huge size of the region, the diversity among its nations, the lack of availability of reliable information and the real practical problem of covering most countries of the region in one book are some of the reasons for this lacuna. Still, over the past decade or so few books have been published on this theme (for example, Connell and Teo, 2011; Rowley and Benson, 2004; Budhwar, 2004; Bamber et al., 2000). Indeed, there are a number of country-specific books available for the region (see Cooke, 2012 for China; Budhwar and Bhatnagar, 2009 for India). Similarly, there are a number of special issues of leading journals that have been dedicated to HR-related research for specific countries in the Asia-Pacific region in particular and for Asian management in general. Further, a number of region-dedicated journals (for example, *Asia-Pacific Journal of Management*, *Asia-Pacific Journal of Human Resources*, *Asian and Business Management*, *Asia-Pacific Business Review* and *Management and Organization Review*) have been instrumental in disseminating research findings on HR-related investigations relevant to the region.

Apart from publications, a number of both academic and practitioner-oriented bodies have been playing a significant role in the creation of the much-needed platform to bring together researchers and practitioners in the field of HRM to share the latest developments in the field. Some of the prominent academic societies include ANZAM (Australia and New Zealand Academy of Management), AAOM (Asia Academy of Management) and IAM (Indian Academy of Management). On the practitioners front, forums like hrm Asia (www.hrmasia.com), Asia-Pacific HRM Congress (www.asiapacifichrmcongress.com) and Asia-Pacific Federation of Human Resource Management (www.apfhrm.com) and different HR leader series (for example, by Mercer – 2012 Asia-Pacific Platinum HR Leaders Series) are providing useful avenues for sharing best practices across the region.

In the first edition of this book, Budhwar (2004) presented a comprehensive review of HR-related available literature. His analysis revealed a good amount of literature existing on issues related to HRM in advanced countries of the region such as Singapore, Hong Kong, Taiwan and Korea. There was also a rapidly growing body of literature on different aspects of management in the Chinese context (also see Cooke, 2009). Budhwar's analysis also revealed issues related to the validity of a number of established ideal-typical management models in specific countries in the region, such as the three pillars of the Japanese employment system (that is, permanent jobs, seniority pay and enterprise union) and the management models of Singaporean, Chinese and Korean business groups. Further, there has been some research focusing on cultural values, which stressed the need to indigenise the management practices in particular of Asian organisations. There also has been an emerging theme of research examining the key HR issues faced by Western firms operating in the Asian context, which indicates that perhaps a certain level of standardisation of HRM systems is taking place around the globe. A further theme evolving has been that of the thesis of convergence-divergence of management practices in the Asia-Pacific context. Given the scarcity of comprehensive research, most of the above reported themes are based on only a handful of studies.

In a further comprehensive review of HRM literature in the region, Budhwar and Debrah (2009) report the existence of a variety of studies. These include a large number of country-specific studies and a few on emerging management models in the region, factors contributing to the changing nature of management and employment relations in Asia-Pacific based firms and business groups (like *chaebols* and *keiretsus*), HRM in the new industrial sectors (such as information technology and business process outsourcing), diversity management, HRM and organisational performance and convergence-divergence or crossvergence of HRM across national boundaries in the region (for details see Budhwar and Debrah, 2009).

Based on the above summary of the key themes on which research is available in the literature, a couple of conclusions can be drawn. First, there has been a massive surge in the number of management research studies being conducted in the region. Given the rapid economic developments in the region, there is an expected gap between theory and practice; nevertheless given the pace with which research is emerging for the region, this gap is being reduced. Second, it is clearly evident that the existing HRM research in the Asia-Pacific context (probably not applicable to Australia and China) is limited and, to some extent, lacks a systematic framework, which could help the reader draw a conclusive and comprehensive picture of HR in the Asia-Pacific region. As a result, the existing literature fails to provide a clear insight into the underlying processes regarding how HRM systems are organised and how such findings contribute to theory development. In the present global context, highlighting of region-/country-specific phenomena would help to generate theory for global-relevant issues. It could also contribute to validating region-specific constructs (for example, Chinese, Indian or Korean) and to a robust study of local and global issues. A possible way forward is to conduct a systematic analysis starting from a basic level and leading to an advanced level. This can help to provide a comprehensive analysis and a more reliable picture. This perhaps can be achieved by adopting a systematic framework, which can help to capture historical developments in the field and the existence of present HRM systems and aid in speculation on future developments. Such a framework is presented in the next section.

Framework Adopted to Develop Country-Specific Chapters

Building on the framework utilised to develop the country-specific chapters for the earlier edition of this book (see Budhwar, 2004) and in order to ensure that all the country-specific chapters in the volume are consistent in terms of their content, issues and themes we asked the contributors to structure their chapters along the following framework.

- Provide a historical development in HRM/Industrial Relations (IR)/Personnel Management (PM)/Personnel Administration in their country.
- Highlight the role, the importance of, and the level of business–HR partnership in most companies in the country.
- Highlight the key factors determining HRM practices and policies (such as laws, politics, national culture, competition, business environment, different institutions and the economy), with a review of most of the HR practices, such as pay, staffing, unions and training.
- Provide details of the key changes in the HR function since the publication of the first edition and the factors responsible.
- Discuss the key challenges presently facing HRM.
- Speculate on what is likely to happen to HR functions in the next five years.
- Provide a short case study of an actual company known for its HR practices. This could be developed based on the contributors' own consulting practice/research and, where necessary, they were free to develop this based on publications in the media.
- Give details of websites and current references for the latest information and developments in HRM that will provide more information to the reader over the years.

The adoption of such a coherent framework has helped to develop contributions that provide a comprehensive picture of HRM in the respective countries. In particular, it has helped to shed light on the past, present and future nature and structure of the HR function in the Asia-Pacific.

Plan of the Book

It is difficult to include all of the countries of the Asia-Pacific region in one volume. However, a conscious effort has been made to include a wide range of countries representing all the key parts of the Asia-Pacific – ASEAN, SAARC, PIF and others. It is hoped that such a selection of countries will present the reader with a rich flavour of the core aspects of HRM systems as well as presenting challenges and possible trends and patterns that are emerging for each country and discussion of how these are shaped by key determining factors. Highlighting the scenario of HRM in the Asia-Pacific region and key issues related to it, this volume contains fifteen chapters – chapters two to fourteen deal with country-specific content and the last chapter makes concluding remarks.

Many of the authors also contributed to the first edition of this book. All the contributors are either natives of the country for which they have authored the chapter or have worked and researched for long periods in the respective country. This helps to minimise the 'Western bias' in such projects and has enabled the authors to present a more realistic picture of HRM in the various countries. Each of the country-specific chapters follows a common pattern. This has been developed keeping in mind the broad objective of the book, that is, to highlight the dynamics of the HRM system in the respective countries. All the authors have made a conscious attempt to structure their country-specific contributions around the above-presented framework.

In Chapter two, Cooke assesses the developments in the Chinese HRM within the context of historical changes of key institutions (like legal, social, cultural and family businesses), especially since the mid-1980s, as part of the radical economic reforms that significantly influenced HRM policies and practices related to recruitment, training, performance and reward. She also examines the extent to which the HR function may be playing a strategic role in present-day Chinese organisations. Cooke's analysis brings out the major challenges faced by HRM in China regarding motivation-performance-reward, skill shortage and its associated problems of recruitment, retention and training and the absence of strategic HRM (SHRM).

Chapter three provides an in-depth analysis regarding the dynamics of HRM in South Korea. Rowley and Bae highlight how the key characteristics in Korean HRM revolve around practices based on 'regulation' (or 'seniority') versus more 'flexibility' in labour markets and remuneration (with greater focus on performance). Building on the 2004 edition of this chapter, the authors present a number of new trends in the Korean HRM. These include:

1 The performance-based HRM has been 'softened' or at least not intensified as companies recognise that the adoption of performance-based HRM can be a double-edged weapon.
2 Consequent to the adoption of cost-reduction strategies by many firms and the shift of status from contingent workers to regular workers, the job-based HRM system seems to have been diffused.
3 Workplace flexibility has been enhanced, such as the provision of flexitime, the relaxation of dress codes and various benefits for younger employees, which are related to enhancing employee creativity through the combination of 'play and work'.
4 In present-time Korea, work–family balance and global talent management have become critical issues.
5 Large corporations have become more actively involved in benchmarking activities.

In Chapter four, revisiting the changes taking place in advanced economies such as a strong move towards performance-based systems and the rise of flexible work, DeBroux analyses such developments in Japan. He discusses how the traditional Japanese HRM practices (for example, seniority-based pay and life-long employment) have been challenged during the last two decades. The evolving internal labour markets are being linked to performance-based practices. Such changes have serious consequences for recruitment, training, appraisal and reward policies and practices. He also analyses the serious issue of an ageing population in Japan, which calls for different career patterns for both elder and younger employees. DeBroux also highlights how the shift towards a shareholders' value-centered corporate governance is shaking the delicate balance between employees and investors in the traditional stakeholders' system in Japan.

Chapter five highlights employment relations in Hong Kong over the last thirty years. Chan and Man adopt a historical perspective in this chapter and review

Hong Kong's wider cultural, social and economic context since the 1980s and how it has affected HR practices. Highlighting the dominance of small enterprises in Hong Kong, the authors highlight how HR policies and practices have a direct causal relationship with business realities. The chapter traces the development of HRM in Hong Kong during the last thirty-two years in order to explicate what happens in workplace employee relations today. It also presents an account for the role of HRM in different business settings and a discussion on selected contingent factors that impinge on the development of key HR practices in the unique setting of Hong Kong.

In chapter six Chang adopts a historical perspective to present dynamics of the HRM system of Taiwan. Her presentation covers the background and development of HRM in Taiwan via different stages, the strategic role played by the HR function in Taiwanese firms, the key determinants of HRM policies and practices and the key changes and challenges facing HRM in Taiwan. She has supported her discussion with useful statistics and related analysis. Lastly, she presents on the future of the HRM function in Taiwanese firms.

Chapter seven is on HRM in India, where Saini and Budhwar present an overview of the socio-economic environment of India and its effect on Indian HRM. The authors highlight the roots of the HRM function in India and how it has evolved over the past several decades. The authors discuss the influence on the Indian HRM of national culture, national institutions supporting industrial relations, the legal framework, vocational, educational and training set-up and other factors. Highlighting the comprehensive list of both central and state level labour legislation, the authors share their concerns about the usefulness of the same in modern India. They propose the key areas in which changes are needed in Indian labour legislation. Later in the chapter, the discussion is focused on the possible direction for HRM in India from different perspectives (such as organisation, individual and national).

In chapter eight Siengthai presents the evolution of the HRM functions in Thailand. She contends how over the years the role of HRM has changed from a traditional payroll function to a business partner. While discussing these changes, the author highlights the influence of key factors such as the Thai national culture and the economic environment on the Thai HRM system. She also discusses how outsourcing and the adoption of new technologies is contributing towards HRM playing more of a partnership role. Further, Siengthai outlines the key changes in the HR function and the challenges facing HRM in Thailand.

Chapter nine provides an analysis of HRM systems and practices in Vietnam. Cox highlights the changing nature of HRM practices in Vietnamese enterprises and systematically analyses and compares the HRM practices of recruitment and selection of employees, performance management, compensation management, reward management, training and development and IR used in Vietnamese enterprises before and after the adoption of economic reforms in 1986 when the Communist government ended its previous approach of maintaining a closed and centrally planned economy and embraced a dramatic economic reform (*Doi Moi*). She also discusses the transformation of the HRM/IR system and contemplates key challenges facing further development of the system in Vietnam.

In chapter ten Malek, Varma and Budhwar discuss the evolving professional status of the HRM function in Malaysia. They highlight how the ministry of human
resources has been playing a significant role in the development of the national
HRM system, especially via close ties with the employers and trade unions and
by encouraging them to maintain conducive and harmonized industrial relations.
The authors also discuss the key determinants (for example, both Islamic and
Malaysian work-related values) on Malaysian employment policies and practices,
the key challenges facing HRM and the expected direction for the HRM function
in Malaysia.

Chapter eleven is about HRM in Singapore, where Templer, Wan and Khatri
highlight the affect of the economic development strategy and the national administrative system on Singaporean HRM policies and practices as well as various
cultural aspects. While doing so, they highlight the strategic role played by HRM
in Singaporean firms and also the challenges facing the HR function in Singapore
(for example, of talent retention, labour turnover, participation of both females
and older employees in the workforce and management of Singaporean expatriates). Next, the chapter presents the current state of HRM policies and practices
in both local and foreign firms operating in Singapore and finally the possible
direction for HRM in Singapore.

Clarke and Patrickson detail the scene of HRM in Australia in Chapter twelve.
They initially present an overview of the Australian HRM system in the context
of the changing economic and technological business environment and the role
played by the professional bodies like the Federal Institute of Personnel Management of Australia and the Australian Human Resource Institute towards the
development of the HR profession. Then they highlight the main factors influencing HRM in Australia and the impact of the same on specific HRM practices.
The authors then discuss the business–HR partnership and the key changes taking
place in the HRM function in Australia. Later, the chapter focuses on key challenges facing HRM and its future in Australia.

In Chapter thirteen, Naidu, Pathak and Chand analyse the scenario of HRM in the
Fiji islands. They start the chapter with a presentation on the historical development of personnel management, industrial relations, employment relations, HRM
and SHRM and the role of various institutions such as the state, trade unions,
employer association, non-government organisations (NGOs), donor agencies and
trade agreements on HRM in the islands. The authors further discuss the influence
of both the endogenous and exogenous environmental factors on HRM practices.
Later in the chapter, Naidu *et al.* discuss the key changes taking place in the HRM
functions, the key challenges facing HRM and the future of HRM in the Fiji islands.

Chapter fourteen presents the scenario in New Zealand. Hutchison and Donnelly
have conducted an in-depth analysis that has helped them to clearly highlight
how at a deeper level HRM in New Zealand has different aspects in comparison
to other Anglo-Saxon nations. Like other chapters, Hutchison and Donnelly also
provide an overview of HRM's historical development within New Zealand and
how the political, economic and cultural context of the country influences HRM
policies and practices. Their chapter also examines the current and future challenges facing HRM in New Zealand.

In the last chapter, Varma and Budhwar discuss the current HRM challenges in the Asia-Pacific region. It is believed that these issues will be the focus of future research and will help to further enhance our understanding of HRM in the Asia-Pacific.

References

Bae, J., Chen, S-J. and Rowley, C. (2011) 'From a paternalistic model towards what? HRM trends in Korea and Taiwan', *Personnel Review* 40(6): 700–22.

Bamber, G., Park, F., Lee, C., Ross, P. K. and Broadbent, K. (2000) *Employment Relations in the Asia-Pacific: Changing approaches.* London: Thompson Learning Press.

Budhwar, P. (2004) *Managing Human Resources in Asia-Pacific.* London: Routledge.

Budhwar, P. and Bhatnagar, J. (2009) *The Changing Face of People Management in India.* London: Routledge.

Budhwar, P. and Debrah, Y. (2009) 'Future research on human resource management systems in Asia', *Asia-Pacific Journal of Management* 26: 197–218.

Connell, J. and Teo, S. (2011) (eds) *Strategic HRM: Contemporary Issues in the Asia Pacific Region.* Prahan, Victoria, Australia: Tilde University Press.

Cooke, F. L. (2009) 'A decade of transformation of HRM in China: A review of literature and suggestions for future studies', *Asia-Pacific Journal of Human Resources*, 47(1): 6–40.

Cooke, F. L. (2012) *Human Resource Management in China: New Trends and Practices.* London: Routledge.

Debrah, Y. A., McGovern, I. and Budhwar, P. (2000) 'Complementarity or competition: The development of human resources in a growth triangle', *The International Journal of Human Resource Management* 11 (2): 314–35.

The Economist (2012) 'Emerging-market indicators', 11 May, pp. 82–84.

Froese, F. J. (forthcoming) 'Work values of the next generation of business leaders in Shanghai, Tokyo and Seoul', *Asia-Pacific Journal of Management*, doi: 10.1007/s10490-011-9271-7.

Pattnaik, C., Chang, J. J. and Shin, H. H. (2011) 'Business groups and corporate transparency in emerging markets: Empirical evidence from India', *Asia-Pacific Journal of Management*, published online, 4 November 2011 http://link.springer.com/article/10.1007%2Fs10490-011-9273-5#page-2.

Puffer, S. M., McCarthy, D. J., Jaeger, A. M. and Dunlap, D. (2012) 'The use of favors by emerging market managers: Facilitator or inhibitor of international expansion?', *Asia-Pacific Journal of Management*, published online on 16 May 2012, doi:10.1007/s10490-012-9299-3.

Rowley, C. and Benson, J. (2004) (eds) *The Management of Human Resources in the Asia-Pacific Region: Convergence revisited.* Portland: F. Cass.

Tan, T. T. (2002) 'Introduction to special issue of JBR on Asian business research', *Journal of Business Research* 55: 797–98.

UNCTAD (2012) 'Global investment trends monitor,' http://unctad.org/en/docs/webdiaeia2012d1_en.pdf, last accessed 24 January 2012.

Young, S. and Stanton, P. (2009) 'Governance and human resources,' *Asia-Pacific Journal of Human Resources* 47(2): 130–32.

Wikipedia (2012) Asia-Pacific, http://en.wikipedia.org/wiki/Asia-Pacific.

2

Human Resource Management in China

FANG LEE COOKE

Introduction

Despite a history of more than 5,000 years, the People's Republic of China (under the control of the Chinese Communist Party) has a history of just over 60 years. It is within this period that the current employment system and the current labour relations system were established, undergoing transformation since the mid-1980s as part of the radical economic reform. The assessment of the evolution of the personnel management/human resource management (HRM) practices of the country needs to be situated within this broader context of historical changes of key institutions.

In this chapter, we first review major changes in the HRM practices in China. We then examine key legislative, social, cultural and business factors influencing HRM policies and practices, such as recruitment, training, performance management and reward. We also evaluate the extent to which the HR function may have evolved from a personnel administration function to a more strategic role in line with what is prescribed in Western HRM literature. The chapter then contemplates key challenges facing HRM in China, notably the issues of motivation-performance-reward; skill shortage and its associated problems of recruitment, retention and training; and the absence of strategic HRM. The chapter finally explores the implications of all of these for the HRM function in the near future.

Historical Development of Personnel/Human Resource Management

The personnel management system in China was set up in the early 1950s after the founding of the Socialist China in 1949. For the first three decades until the opening up of the economy in 1978, the system was highly centralised under the state-planned economy regime. Personnel management during this period employees would be assessed (through tests) once a year on their competence to work (Cooke, 2005). Those who came last would be laid-off and would receive training to increase their competence while they were waiting for a post. These changes marked the end of state commitment to egalitarianism and the end of workers' dependence on the state (for example, Hassard *et al.*, 2007; Lee, 1999). They have also led to fundamental changes in the psychological and social contracts of the state sector workers.

In the next section, we examine the macro level factors that influence the HRM policies and practices adopted by firms in different ownership forms. We assess the role of the key institutional actors and their interactions in shaping the policies and practices. We also highlight the enduring role of societal culture in the configuration of HRM practices and how their affect may be contingent upon the demographic characteristics of the employees.

Key Factors and Actors Shaping HRM Policies and Practices

Following three decades of economic and social policy reform, the Chinese economy has been transformed from a state-planned economy to one that is market-driven, government-controlled and *guanxi* (relationship)-based (Si, Wei and Li, 2008). The creation of the external labour market and the conditions under which it was created and under which it operated has not only attracted millions of surplus rural labour to the urban area to seek employment but also enabled employers to take advantage of this readily available labour force by offering sub-quality jobs without penalty (see Table 2.1). After years of single-minded pursuit of economic growth at the expense of environmental protection and workers' well-being, the Chinese government is now turning its attention to improving workers' employment rights and levels of incomes in the hope of reversing the trend of widening inequity and the consequent rising level of social unrest.

Meanwhile, the one-child policy enforced by the government since the early 1980s and improved living standards in the rural areas have caused labour shortages in the Eastern developed areas, particularly in the export manufacturing zones. The increased level of awareness of their labour rights among the younger generation of Chinese workers has led to a string of self-organising and spontaneous industrial actions in foreign-funded plants across the country. These actions present a direct challenge to the global production sector and force employers to readjust their employment practices with respect to immediate concerns and to rethink their labour strategy for the longer term. More significantly, the series of high-profile strikes and protests in 2010 signals an important power shift towards labour and marks the beginning of the end of the era of cheap manufacturing in China. More broadly, the labour market has been transformed from a once rigid internal labour market with restricted labour mobility to a more fluid external labour market that favours those who possess desirable skills and educational qualifications, leading to immense challenges for many firms in terms of talent attraction and retention.

As summarised in Table 2.1 with simplification, there are significant differences (and some similarities) in the types of HRM policies and practices adopted by

Table 2.1 Major Similarities and Differences in HRM Practices and Employment Outcomes for Different Groups of Workers in China

Group of Workers	Differences in HRM Practices and Employment Outcomes	Similarities in HRM Practices and Employment Outcomes
Highly educated professionals (competent and experienced workers who are in short supply, hence strong bargaining power)	• Well-paid • Selective training provisions • Good career prospects • Partial social security coverage • Changing work values • Relatively strong individual bargaining power	• Performance-related pay • Employment insecurity • Gendered employment practices and outcomes • Employment outcomes mainly determined by their labour market positions in the absence of an effective collective negotiation mechanism or legal protection due to weak enforcement of laws • Work intensification, deteriorating work–life balance and well-being
Semi-skilled rural migrant workers (generally an over-supply despite skill shortages in localised areas in developed regions)	• Poorly paid • Few training opportunities • Few career prospects • Few social security provisions • Growing attempts of self-organising to enhance their terms and conditions	

Source: Adapted from Cooke (2012a: 203).

firms in managing workers at the two ends of the labour market spectrum. With competition intensifying, the polarisation of employment conditions and outcomes between these groups of workers is likely to continue, with widening gaps, despite efforts by the state to reduce social inequality.

The Role of the State

State intervention in shaping HRM policies and practices is universal to all countries, although the level and forms of intervention may differ across states and over time. State intervention often takes two forms: i.) direct intervention through HRM laws and regulations and ii.) soft or normative intervention through government-led initiatives and campaigns aimed to promote certain desirable HRM practices and managerial behaviour (for example, Martinez Lucio and Stuart 2004). The effectiveness of both forms of intervention varies but should never be over-estimated. This is particularly the case in the latter due to 'the lack of enforcement powers' of the state (Mellahi, 2007: 87).

In China, the change of government leadership to Premier Wen Jiabao and Chairman Hu Jintao in 2003 marked the beginning of the pursuit of an economic development policy that emphasises social justice, social harmony and environmental protection. This is a significant departure from an efficiency-driven economic development policy pursued by their predecessors typically influenced by the economic thinking of Deng Xiaoping – the architect of modern Chinese economic development. As part of the reform, visible changes can be seen in the role of the Chinese state in the employment sphere, for example, from a dominant employer to a regulator. Its intervention approach is also becoming more sophisticated, from the heavy dependence on administrative regulations towards a combination of legislation, standard setting, best practice sharing and the promotion of 'progressive' HRM practices and corporate social responsibility (CSR). In addition, the state has been mobilising other institutional actors in more subtle and strategic ways in order to promote, with a level of success, certain HRM practices and managerial behaviours.

There are two main objectives in the state intervention in employment relations and HRM practices in China. One is to facilitate enterprises to establish harmonious employment relations as part of an agenda to build a harmonious society (Li and Xiang, 2007; Warner and Zhu, 2010). The other is to combat the problem of severe skill shortage and raise the skills level of the workforce in order to enhance the competitiveness of the nation through innovation and high value-added production. This includes raising the level of management competence, raising professional standards and improving craft skills. In order to fulfil these objectives, a number of labour regulations and state-led human resource management and development initiatives have been launched. They are implemented via other institutional actors in coercive, directive, cooperative and voluntary manners (see Table 2.2).

Table 2.2 New Developments in HRM and the Role of Actors in China

HRM areas	New Labour Regulations and HR Techniques/ Initiatives	Sources of Influence and Dissemination
Recruitment and selection	• Assessment centre • Outsourcing of recruitment function	• Promoted by foreign multinational corporations (MNCs) and foreign HR consultancy firms, increasingly popular in large private firms
	• Overseas recruitment fairs	• Directed by central government policy; led by local government
	• Thousand Talents Plan to attract overseas Chinese scholars	• Directed by central government policy; implemented by top universities and research institutions
Skill training	• On-the-job training, coaching and mentoring	• Promoted by foreign MNCs and foreign HR consultancy firms,

		increasingly popular in large private firms
	• Skill contest, apprenticeship training and occupational qualification certification initiatives	• Government policy driven; initiatives mainly adopted by state-owned and privately owned firms; skill training and occupational qualification certification training also conducted outside enterprises and funded by individuals
	• Skill training for rural migrant workers	• Government policy driven; reluctant adoption of initiative by employers
Organisational development	• Learning organisation • *Chuangzheng* (创争) programme (2003) (see Cooke, 2012a: Chapter 3 for details)	• Central government led initiatives followed mainly by state-owned firms and some privately owned firms
Leadership / Management development	• Management development programmes	• Initially targeted at state-owned enterprise (SOE) managers and government officials/cadres
	• Master of Business Administration (MBA)/ Executive Master of Business Administration (EMBA) programmes	• Courses provided by business schools, sanctioned by the government, self-funded or funded by employers of all ownership forms
	• Short-term executive training programmes	• Extensive participation from Western business schools and training bodies/individuals
	• Corporate universities	• Foreign-funded MNCs and flagship Chinese firms
Performance management	• Performance appraisal techniques (for example, 360-degree appraisal)	• Promoted by foreign MNCs and foreign HR consultancy firms, increasingly popular in large private firms
Financial reward	• Market survey for benchmarking • Broadband payment system	• Promoted by foreign MNCs and foreign HR consultancy firms; emerging interest from private firms

Employee welfare	• Enterprise annual fund (企业年金) (superannuation fund)	• Policy regulation driven by the central government; emerging adoption by leading firms of different ownership forms
Employee well-being	• Work–life balance initiatives • Employee assistance programmes	• Promoted by foreign MNCs and foreign HR consultancy firms; being piloted in large private firms
Labour regulations	• Labour Contract Law (2008) • Labour Disputes Mediation and Arbitration Law (2008) • Employment Promotion Law (2008) • Social Security Law (2011)	• Enacted by the state, enforced by local government through labour inspectorates and the trade unions – local government has the power to adapt the law based on their local conditions, hence diluting the effect of favouring employers
Employees' representation	• Collective agreements • Labour standards • Training 'wage negotiators'	• Regulated by labour laws, enforced by local governments, reluctant adoption by MNCs and private firms • Promoted jointly by labour authority, trade union and employers' associations
HR competence	• HR professional qualification	• State-driven initiative, increasingly embraced by HR professionals

Source: Adapted from Cooke (2012a: 202).

Trade Unions

Trade unions are an important institutional actor in employment relations. Only one trade union is recognised by the Chinese government – All-China Federation of Trade Unions (ACFTU). The ACFTU is one of the eight 'mass organisations' (non-government organisations) in China that operate under the leadership of the Chinese Communist Party (see Warner, 2008; Cooke, 2012b for detailed discussion). Like many other trade unions in the socialist regimes, the primary function of the grassroots ACFTU organisations during the state-planned economy period was to facilitate the enhancement of productivity by participating in the democratic decision-making and organising skill developments of the workers. They also assumed the social actor role by engaging in the education and moral teaching of workers and by providing workplace welfare services in the state sector. They provided essentially the extended HR function in state-owned firms.

As China's economic transformation deepened from the mid-1980s, the function of the trade unions broadened to include their legal role in representing workers in the collective negotiation of contracts and terms and conditions, and in tripartite consultations and the delivery of welfare and other services. ACFTU grassroots organisations become an active labour market broker, providing training and employment services to displaced state sector workers as well as rural migrant workers. They are responding to, albeit belatedly and slowly, the changing nature of employment relations by adopting new initiatives and strategies to organise the workers, with particular reference to the rural migrant workers.

In conjunction with high-profile national campaigns backed by the state, two major strategies have been adopted by the trade unions to organise migrant workers. One is 'workplace organisation', that is, to gain recognition at the workplace and then unionise the workers with the support of the company. However, gaining employer recognition remains a difficult task given the persistent resistance of private firms. The other way of organising is 'distant organisation', that is to recruit migrant workers (those already in employment or who are seeking jobs) outside the workplace with services packages, such as free training and job referral, as inducement. This is usually carried out by operating in the labour market and in ways similar to what Kelly and Heery (1989: 198–9) classify as a 'distant expansion' recruitment strategy.

However, these organising techniques are essentially logistic innovations, whereas the key issue here is for the trade union to gain power and to be able to prevent rampant exploitation and mistreatment at the workplaces. Without recognition by the employer, union effectiveness is questionable as it is more difficult for the union to represent workers collectively outside the workplace. In addition, workers' dependence on the trade union and union impact are likely to be weakened where union organising attempts are duplicated and diluted by other functional bodies offering similar services in the labour market. While this service-oriented mode of organising has some tangible effects in increasing union memberships, rural migrant workers may be unionised but not necessarily organised in the strict sense.

Political, institutional and organisational constraints determine how far the ACFTU can make changes (Liu, Li and Kim, 2011) in view of its utmost responsibility to the Party-state in maintaining 'social harmony' by containing labour unrest. As Warner (2008) observed, the ACFTU plays multiple and at times conflicting roles, including being labour market actors, vehicles of anti-capitalist mobilisation and agents of social integration. The absence of legality of collective actions in the collective negotiation, collective consultation and collective agreement process (Feng, 2006) is perhaps the biggest constraint of the ACFTU in representing workers.

Not surprisingly, existing studies on the Chinese trade unions have mostly been critical of their institutionally incapacitated position and operational inefficacy (for example, Clarke, 2005; Hishida *et al.*, 2010; Taylor, Chang and Li, 2003). This inefficacy image of the trade union decays into a more grotesque one when grassroots union officials play an active role in preventing strike actions from the workers. For example, during the strikes at the Honda plant in Foshan in 2010, ten trade union officials tried to physically shut down the workers' picket line, although a thin apology from the local government was made afterwards (Watts, 2010). This suggests that peace keeping rather than defending workers' rights is the main priority of the trade unions' function.

In spite of the widely held view of the ineffectiveness of the grassroots unions, research findings show that the Chinese workers believe that it is necessary to have trade unions (for example, Cooke, 2011a; Nichols and Zhao, 2010). In other words, workers are supportive of the idea of unionism and the associated ideology of collectivism and representation to safeguard their rights and interests. They are not necessarily critical of the union officials/representatives as individuals. Rather, they are critical of the powerless position of the trade unions in fighting for their rights and interests. In workplaces where workers are satisfied with their work environment and pay and conditions and where union representatives play an active role in organising welfare services and social events, employees actually hold positive views of the trade unions and desire more services from them (Cooke, 2011a). It is reasonable to suggest that the social function of the trade unions remains beneficial to enhancing employee satisfaction and productivity. As this function does not present any challenge, employers are receptive to this role of the trade unions.

Employment Agencies

Despite being in existence for more than two decades (see Xu, 2009 for an overview), employment agencies represent a relatively new institutional actor in shaping HRM practices in China, although their role in the labour market is not always positive. An understanding of the role of employment agencies will shed light on the HRM policies and practices adopted by firms.

The majority of employment agencies and job centres have been set up by, or under the auspices of, the local governments since the mid-/late 1990s to provide services at the lower end of the labour market. In 2009, there were 37,123 employment agencies nation-wide. The number of employees working in the employment agencies increased from 84,440 in 2001 to 126,000 in 2009 (National Bureau of Statistics of China, 2002, 2010). This significant growth was a response to the large-scale downsizing in the state sector, the continuous inflow of rural migrant workers to urban areas to seek employment and the growing number of unemployed school leavers and college graduates (Li, Xu and Zhu, 2006). The employment agency industry is highly unregulated (Li, Xu and Zhu, 2006). They are governed mainly by administrative regulations issued at the local level and implemented with considerable discretion. Agency workers normally register with the employment agency for work. They only enter an employment relationship with the agency firm when they are sent to work in client firms (Li, Xu and Zhu, 2006).

It was anticipated (by the state) that the enactment of the Labour Contract Law in 2008 would see the reduction of those hired by employment agencies, promoting a more direct and stable employment relationship between the worker and the firm. The reality so far has been a stark contrast. To pre-empt the negative impact of the new law on employment cost, many employers dismissed their long-serving workers and rehired them under new temporary contracts. Others dismissed their workers and rehired them as agency workers through employment agencies. As a result, employment agencies have prospered and the number of workers registered with employment agencies continues to grow. Agency workers often receive lower wages and much less social security protection than employees of the user firms. And agency employment is becoming a major form of labour deployment, contrary to the objective of the Labour Contract Law.

HR Consultancy Firms and Outsourcing Providers

Not all employment agencies are controlled by the state or private firms; neither are employment agencies confined to the lower end of the labour market. The opening up of the labour market to foreign-owned HR businesses has led to the growth of foreign-owned recruitment/head-hunting agencies and HR consultancy firms in China. In 2002, the Chinese government issued the 'Regulation on Talent Market Management', which allows foreign-owned employment agency firms to enter the Chinese market and provide services, initially through the joint venture of Sino-foreign employment agencies (Zhou, 2002). The entrance of well-established foreign-owned HR operators facilitated the creation of an HR outsourcing/consulting market, albeit one that is still in its infancy. Together with multinational corporations in other industries, they play an important role in trend-setting and raising the HR standard and competence level of the country in a short period of time, given the low starting point of the profession. Western-originated HRM practices, such as assessment centres for recruitment and promotion, 360-degree appraisals and performance management systems, coaching and mentoring, work–life balance initiatives and HR outsourcing (see Table 2.2), are now becoming popular among Chinese firms. However, transferability remains the key challenge, as shown in the chapters that follow. The enactment of the Labour Contract Law and the Labour Disputes Mediation and Arbitration Law in 2008 also created opportunities for HR consultancy firms to provide administrative and legal services for firms that are keen to avoid operational hassles and that lack the legal knowledge required. In short, despite being in an embryonic form and, as private agencies with limited influence, HR consultancy firms and outsourcing providers can be seen as an emerging institutional actor in shaping HRM practices. As the HR consultancy and outsourcing industry becomes more developed, these firms are likely to help create some form of isomorphism in the development and implementation of HRM techniques in China.

The Role of Societal Culture

According to Westwood, Chan and Linstead (2004: 365), employment relations in western economies 'are characterized by a model of impersonal rational economic exchange', whereas 'Chinese employment relations remain more fully embedded in the wider socio-cultural system of which reciprocity is a vital and integral part'. For example, employee care in exchange of obedience to the authority is part of the paternalist reciprocal expectations. Studies of the organisational behaviour of Chinese employees and managers has revealed some interesting differences between them and their counterparts in other countries, indicating the influence of culture in moulding these behaviours. For example, in their comparative study of employees in Germany, Romania and China on the influence of cultural differences on employees' commitment and its impacts, Felfe, Yan and Six (2008: 230) observed that 'employees with a collectivistic orientation appreciate being part of a group and have a stronger striving to belong to a social entity'. This desire of social belonging fosters positive relationship-building behaviours in the organisation and 'leads to a stronger affective commitment' (Felfe, Yan and Six 2008: 230). Felfe, Yan and Six (2008: 230) also found 'a clear relationship between collectivism and normative commitment' and argued that 'persons who generally tend to accept norms, obey rules, and value loyalty to the group also experience a stronger duty and obligation to fulfil organizational requirements'. Similarly, Wang's (2008: 916) study that investigated 'the contribution of the emotional bond a Chinese worker has with his supervisor and with his co-workers in accounting for employees' organizational commitment in foreign-invested enterprises' highlighted the importance of 'personal relationships in shaping the linkage between employees and firms in China'.

Despite the prevalence of Chinese traditional culture, the cultural distance between Western societies and China is shrinking in part due to globalisation. Chinese employees' cultural values and personal goals are evolving as the economic and social reform of the country deepens. This is especially the case for the younger generation of the workers who were born and raised in the reform period.

The Influence of Demographics on HRM Outcome

Age and gender are important factors for career opportunities and labour market outcomes of individual workers. They also influence the perception of individual employees with respect to HRM practices in the organisation. For instance, Li, Liu and Wan's (2008) survey of 316 Chinese employees found that older workers, managers, better educated workers and male employees tend to hold higher work values than younger, less well educated, non-managerial and female workers. This finding has important implications for employers because many of them tend to discriminate against older workers during recruitment and in the selection for redundancy without realising the extra value they may get from the older workers. Li, Liu and Wan's (2008) study further revealed that neither generation of the workers feel satisfied because the younger employees recognise that they are often considered less experienced and the older employees are led to believe that they are of less value to the organisation. In a similar vein, Qiao, Khilji and Wang's (2009: 2,311) study of 1,176 workers in six manufacturing firms in two Chinese cities revealed that the perceived existence of high-performance work practices is correlated with organisational commitment. In particular, 'age, marital status, and education, but not gender, correlated significantly with organizational commitment'; and interestingly, 'male and unmarried Chinese employees were significantly more affected by the existence of HR practices than female and married employees' (Qiao, Khilji and Wang, 2009: 2,311).

By contrast, Peng *et al.*'s (2009) study of 582 employees in Beijing showed significant gender differences in organizational commitment with women displaying a lower level of commitment than their male counterparts. Women informants in this study clearly felt a level of discrimination. They were assigned to less challenging tasks and were 'engaging in a low level of leader–member exchange' (Peng *et al.*, 2009: 323). It is this perceived discrimination and lack of opportunities, rather than their marital status and family commitment, which contributed to female employees' lower level of organisational commitment relative to their male counterparts. It is clear that organisations that wish to enhance their competitiveness through effective HRM need to develop HRM practices that are sensitive to demographic differences in their workforce.

The Role of HRM and the HR Function

Given the significant changes in the labour market environment and challenges to talent management, are Chinese firms becoming more strategic in managing their human resources? Are we witnessing a level of convergence of HRM practices in Chinese firms towards the Western-originated HRM practices? Has the role of the HR function and HR personnel become more strategic and professional in recent years? We discuss these issues in this section.

Towards a Strategic Approach to HRM

Earlier studies of HRM in Chinese firms found that they tended to be less strategic than their Western counterparts in their approach to HRM (for example, Child, 1994). As the competition for talent intensified, Chinese firms are reported to have become more strategic in linking their HRM practices to organisational performance (for example, Wei and Lau, 2005; Wang, Bruning and Peng, 2007). They are now more market-oriented, with growing evidence of adaptation of Western HRM techniques (for example, Zhu and Dowling, 2002).

Studies by Wei and Lau (2005) and Wang, Bruning and Peng (2007) found that the differences in key HRM practices among firms of different ownership forms in China are diminishing, indicating a trend of convergence in the HRM practices adopted by foreign-invested and Chinese-owned firms. There is a continuing trend and increasing movement away from the traditional Chinese HRM practices to the Westernised HRM practices, and the gaps in the HR competence between Chinese-owned private firms and MNCs are closing. In addition, Wang, Bruning and Peng (2007: 699) found that 'while foreign-invested companies emphasize humanistic goals the most, it was private-owned enterprises that linked these goals most tightly with the high-performance HR practices'. This is in spite of the fact that they have adopted fewer high-performance HRM practices than the foreign-invested companies.

Evidence from a number of studies as cited above and elsewhere (for example, Warner, 2009) suggests that HRM practices in China are, in general, becoming more mature, systematic, relevant to organisational needs and a reflection of the labour market trends. These include, for example, the adoption of more sophisticated recruitment methods such as assessment centres and psychometric tests; the introduction of mentoring and coaching schemes; and the use of performance management systems and employee financial participation as a high-performance, but not necessarily a high-commitment, model of HRM (see Table 2.2). In addition, there is evidence that well-performing domestic private firms are adopting commitment-oriented HRM practices (for example, Ngo, Lau and Foley, 2008). The ability of the private firms to understand and align their HR strategy with the employees' expectation appears to be a crucial factor in managing talent effectively. This expectation is shaped by the need for personal growth. It is also informed by the deeply embedded traditional Chinese cultural values on the one hand and the emerging (modern) values of materialism and social elitism on the other. Social elitism is a Confucian value that had been suppressed during the first four decades of egalitarian socialism.

The Role of the HR Function

Despite growing evidence of the adoption of more strategic HRM practices, the role of the HR function in China remains far from being strategic and effective. For example, Cooke's (2012a) interviews with senior managers from 65 well-performing private firms in 2007–08 found that at least 16 firms did not have a formal set of HR policies in place. Eight managers reported that there was a formal set of HR policies but it was not effective. While a handful of managers believed that their firm had a strategic approach to HRM, few could articulate what that meant. A number of managers saw the absence of a comprehensive set of HR policies as a barrier to effective HRM in their firm. In addition, there was a broad consensus among those interviewed that line managers lacked people management skills. Insufficient understanding of the importance of HRM by line managers and the deficit of HR professional skills were commonly reported as the major stumbling block to talent management. Some managers also reported that the HR department had little power and was too much influenced by the business departments. There was a consensus that the HR department merely played a supporting role '*to execute the top management thinking*'. They became the scapegoat when HR plans failed. The remarks below summarise the perceived inadequate role of the HR departments:

> *The HR department has no voice and can't interfere by introducing HR initiatives because line managers have too much say and power, but no HR skills. They only focus on production needs. We need to train the line managers and let them know that the HR function is very important to retain talent.*
>
> (CEO of a hotel)

> *Before 2000, it was all called the personnel department. Now it is all called the HR department. Not many enterprises do their HR function well.*
>
> (Marketing Director of an electrical appliance manufacturing firm)

The lack of strategic importance and competence of the HR function has a direct impact on the resources allocated for HR activities. For example, a career development planning scheme was introduced in a wine-making company. According to the manager interviewed, each employee was given opportunities to have private conversations with their line manager every month to review their performance and to identify development needs. The effect was good but, unfortunately, the scheme ended after one year due to the lack of funds (Cooke, 2012a).

Key Challenges Facing HRM

HRM in China faces some major challenges. These include, for example, skill shortages and the related problems in talent management; the alignment of HRM practices with the demands and needs of the younger generation of employees whose work ethics and career aspirations have diverged from that of the older generation of workers; and the need to professionalise the HR function. In this section, we outline some of these challenges.

Skill Shortages and Talent Retention

The challenge to recruiting, developing and retaining managerial and professional talent in China has been widely noted (for example, Dickel and Watkins, 2008). Foreign MNCs and privately owned Chinese firms alike are facing difficulty in attracting and retaining managerial and professional talent due to the shortage of their supply at the national level. Talent shortage has become the bottleneck of business growth for many firms. Despite the fact that China is now producing about three million university graduates each year at home in addition to thousands of graduate returnees from abroad, the skill shortage problem is exacerbating. For example, a study of Chinese graduates returning from their overseas education revealed that half of them had no formal work experience – a major constraint for their employment opportunities. Only half of the companies were satisfied with the performance of their overseas returnee employees. Employers from industries that require China-specific knowledge, such as real estate, construction, consultancy, legal, finance and banking, and manufacturing were far less satisfied with their returnee employees than employers of other industries. In addition, foreign-invested companies were less satisfied (less than 30 per cent were satisfied) with their returnee employees compared with state-invested firms (more than 60 per cent were satisfied) (cited in Development and Management of Human Resources, 2008).

Acute skill shortage encourages both employers to poach talent and individuals to make demands with job quit threats. In order to attract and retain talent, many firms have reported that they have to offer job candidates job titles, salaries and responsibilities that are well beyond their current capability and level of experience (for example, Cooke 2012a). A study conducted by Manpower in China revealed that two-thirds of respondents made their job move for better career development opportunities. Only 15 per cent of respondents indicated that their main reason for leaving was the prospect of better pay and benefits (Arkless,

2007). However, other research studies revealed that pay is actually far more important in people's job choices and behaviours than we are led to believe and that financial reward is one of the most important factors in retention and motivation in China (for example, Chiu, Luk and Tang, 2002). Nevertheless, career development opportunities, training programmes, mentoring and a positive working environment remain crucial in attracting and retaining talent.

Training and Development

Paradoxically, to train or not to train to develop their key employees is a major issue that troubles employers. Many managers interviewed by the author expressed the dilemma of whether to invest in training their key staff or not. Many firms are cautious in spending money on training for fear of staff turnover. This has resulted in insufficient training provided to employees. For example, Yang and Li's (2008) study found that a significant proportion of university graduate employees in the Beijing area had never received any training from their employer due to the latter's concern about retention problems. Judging from job advertisements and the recruitment behaviour of firms, we can see that employers prefer to recruit those who are ready trained, with at least two or three years of work experience. For firms that have graduate training programmes in place, the quality of the trainees may be less than satisfactory. For example, a CEO of a large private firm interviewed by the author in 2008 believed that the one-child policy enacted in the 1980s by the Chinese government to control the population growth has produced a generation of young people (known as the 'post-80 generation') who are spoilt by their family, dependent, incompetent, inexperienced and unwilling to endure hardship but who are eager to have early success. Firms have to inflate job titles and pay well above the competence/experience level of the young employees for retention.

Performance Management and Rewards

Performance management and performance-based reward is perhaps one of the most challenging HRM functions reported by firms (see Cooke, 2012a for more discussion). Chinese employees in enterprises are becoming more receptive towards performance-oriented rewards and welcome career development opportunities through the implementation of a performance management system. However, the implementation of such a system in China is challenged by a number of factors that are generic or cultural-specific. In particular, Chinese cultural values seem to have a profound and enduring influence throughout the various stages of the performance management system. In general, the traditional performance appraisal system in China is reward-driven (that is, it focuses on retrospective performance) and tends to focus on the person's behaviour. By contrast, the performance appraisal system promoted in Western HRM literature takes a developmental approach (that is, prospective performance oriented) and focuses on the alignment between individual performance and organisational goals. The adoption of the Western approach in China is further hampered by the lack of strategic orientation of many Chinese firms and the deficiency of HR skills to design and implement an effective performance management system.

As noted earlier, pay remains an important factor in the Chinese labour market that is sensitive to skill and unemployment levels. Pay determination is perhaps the most crucial and challenging aspect of HRM that firms have to grapple with in attracting and retaining talent. Research evidence suggests that firms are primarily rewarding existing performance instead of investing in their employees for development and future productivity gains. This short-term orientation of the reward strategy is not conducive to human capital development for both the individuals and the firm in the long term. Research evidence suggests that many private firms are still non-strategic in their reward management and that their motivational mechanisms are simplistic, non-systematic and lack varieties and perceived fairness. There is insufficient consideration of what employees desire in order to match the reward practices with their expectations (for example, Ding, Akhtar and Ge, 2009). Nevertheless, there are clear signs (for example, Cooke, 2012a) that private firms are beginning to commission market surveys, via HR consultancy firms, to benchmark their wage levels. Moreover, benefits as an important component in employees' reward packages are used more strategically to elicit higher levels of performance and as a way to control labour cost more flexibly.

However, paternalism and egalitarianism remain two enduring values that influence the reward system. They reflect not just the traditional Chinese cultural values but also the socialist values. Employers are expected not only to take care of their employees but to also do so in a fair manner. As Confucius articulated in his Analects, 'he is not concerned lest his people should be poor, but only lest what they have should be ill-apportioned' (不患寡而患不均) (Waley, 1995 cited in Wu, 2009: 1,038). There is a strong perception that farmers and workers are underpaid and that 'senior government officials and executives in large state-owned companies are overpaid by a large amount' (Wu, 2009: 1,051). And much of the social unrest and discontent has been fuelled by this growing income disparity and distributive unfairness.

Professionalising the HR Function

The role of the HR function/department in the firm has a strong bearing on how strategic the firm views HRM as part of its strategic management. As noted above and reported elsewhere (for example, Zhu *et al.*, 2005), the HR capacity of firms in China remains relatively low. There is limited training and professional development for HR officers. Few of them possess HR qualifications and experience. Most come from the personnel administration background. As a result, HR personnel have little capacity or input in formulating HR strategies and policies, implementing HR initiatives and in aligning the HR outcomes with business performance. Instead, HR issues are often dealt with in a fire-fighting approach.

The absence of a well-developed nation-wide HR professional association in China to date also means that there is no central influence on the HR direction or coordination in the sharing of good HRM practices. By contrast, Western countries such as the United Kingdom, the United States and Australia have well-established HR professional associations that have become international bodies to provide effective forums for research and knowledge sharing among the organised HR professional and academic communities. At the national and organisational level, the low capability of HRM is undoubtedly a significant deficiency in the light of the rising number of Chinese-owned national and multinational firms and the important role of strategic HRM to organisational competitiveness.

Case Study: Managing Shopfloor Workers in a Private Manufacturing Plant

WheelCo is a large, family-owned company that specialises in designing and manufacturing vehicle wheels. WheelCo was initially set up as a small metal workshop by family members in the mid-1980s. Located at the outskirts of a major city in the eastern coastal area, the entrepreneurship of the owner managers has enabled the firm to grow rapidly into one of the largest and most successful privately owned firms in the local area. By 2009, WheelCo employed more than 4,000 employees, 80 per cent of whom were production workers.

In the manufacturing plant, production work is organised into workshops. Each workshop looks after one main stage of the production. Each worker is allocated to a specific position, performing a simple task repetitiously. There is little job rotation or mobility across workshops.

Workers are mostly young men in their early/mid-20s. Most of them have high school level education qualifications; a small proportion of them graduated from technical colleges. Local unemployment level is relatively high. Wage level of the production workers is decent compared to the market rate. In addition, the company provides a good range of welfare benefits to the workers, including subsidised meals, birthday cakes, uniforms, social events and entertainment programmes. Unlike many sweatshop plants that operate with a high level of overtime on the demand of either the firm or the workers, there is no overtime in WheelCo. The company believes that the production work is labour intensive and monotonous and that it is not cost-effective for workers to work overtime as their productivity will decline due to fatigue. Workers work six days and forty-eight hours per week. There is an employee code of conduct that specifies rules and procedures that employees need to observe.

The majority of the workers were recruited from the labour market or directly from the schools/colleges nearby. A small proportion of them were recruited as a result of nepotism – they are mainly relatives of the local government officials who requested WheelCo to provide jobs to the incumbents. There is little training provision to the production workers other than the induction training. Promotion opportunities are available to those who are deemed competent and well-behaved. In spite of deficiency in leadership skills, supervisors and junior managers receive limited in-house training due to production pressure.

According to the owner CEO, despite good employment packages and good treatment by the firm, sabotage behaviour is common in the factory. Another problem is staff turnover at about 20 per cent per year. Few production workers have stayed with the firm for more than four years. Those who stay for the first year are likely to stay longer. What do you think WheelCo should do to solve these problems?

Source: Compiled from fieldwork conducted by the author in 2009

Conclusions

This chapter has reviewed the development of the personnel/HRM function in China. It examined the role of the state and other key institutional actors in shaping the HRM environment and practices. We also highlighted a number of key characteristics of and challenges to people management during a period of economic and social transformation. There is clear evidence that HRM in China is becoming more strategic, although the capacity is still generally low. There are also signs of adaptation of Western HRM practices on the one hand, but Chinese cultural and social values appear to remain influential on the other.

Useful Websites

51job.com:
www.51job.com/bo/AboutUs_e.php

China Data Online: http://chinadataonline.org/member/yearbooksp/default. asp?StartYear=1981&EndYear=2010&ybcode=CHINAL

ChinaHR.com:
www.chinahr.com

Human Resource Association for Foreign and Chinese Enterprises:www.china-hrm.com/china-hrm-association.htm

Ministry of Human Resources and Social Security of China:
www.mohrss.gov.cn/index.html

Acknowledgements

This chapters draws heavily from Cooke (2012a).

References

Arkless, D. (2007) 'The China talent paradox', *China–Britain Business Review*, June: 14–15.

Child, J. (1994) *Management in China during the Age of Reform*. Cambridge: Cambridge University Press.

Chiu, R., Luk, W. and Tang, T. (2002) 'Retaining and motivating employees: Compensation preferences in Hong Kong and China', *Personnel Review* 31(4): 402–31.

Clarke, S. (2005) 'Post-socialist trade unions: China and Russia', *Industrial Relations Journal* 36(1): 2–18.

Cooke, F. L. (2005) *HRM, Work and Employment in China*. London: Routledge.

Cooke, F. L. (2011a) 'Gender organizing in China: A study of female workers' representation needs and their perceptions of union efficacy', *International Journal of Human Resource Management* 22(12): 2,558–2,574.

Cooke, F. L. (2011b) 'Unions in China in a period of marketization', in G. Gall, R. Hurd and A. Wilkinson (eds) *International Handbook on Labour Unions: Responses to neo-Liberalism*. Cheltenham: Edward Elgar, pp. 105–124.

Cooke, F. L. (2012a) *Human Resource Management in China: New Trends and Practices*. London: Routledge.

Development and Management of Human Resources (2008) 'Review', *Development and Management of Human Resources* 10: 4.

Dickel, T. and Watkins, C. (2008) 'To remain competitive in China's tight labour market, companies must prioritize talent management – and track compensation trends', *China Business Review*, July–August: 20–23.

Ding, D. Z., Akhtar, S. and Ge, G. L. (2009) 'Effects of inter-and intra-hierarchy wage dispersions on firm performance in Chinese enterprises', *International Journal of Human Resource Management* 20(11): 2,370–81.

Felfe, J., Yan, W. and Six, B. (2008) 'The impact of individual collectivism on commitment and its influence on organizational citizenship behaviour and turnover in three countries', *International Journal of Cross Cultural Management* 8(2): 211–37.

Feng, G. (2006) 'The "institutional weaknesses" of enterprise trade unions and their formative context', *Society* 26(3): 81–98 (in Chinese社会).

Hassard, J., Sheehan, J., Zhou, M. Terpstra-Tong, J. and Morris, J. (2007) *China's State Enterprise Reform: From Marx to the Market*. London: Routledge.

Hishida, M., Kojima, K., Ishii, T. and Qiao, J. (2010) *China's Trade Unions: How Autonomous Are They?* London and New York: Routledge.

Kelly, J. and Heery, E. (1989) 'Full-time officers and trade union recruitment', *British Journal of Industrial Relations* 27(2): 196–213.

Lee, C. K. (1999) 'From organized dependence to disorganized despotism: Changing labor relations in Chinese factories', *The China Quarterly* 157: 44–71.

Li, B. A. and Xiang, S. Q. (2007) 'Harmonious labour relations: An important foundation of building a harmonious society', *Labor Economy and Labor Relations* 6: 40–42 (in Chinese).

Li, W., Liu, X. and Wan, W. (2008) 'Demographic effects of work values and their management implications', *Journal of Business Ethics* 81(4): 875–85.

Li, X. J., Xu, Y. D. and Zhu, J. X. (2006) 'Employment relationship under the form of employment leasing', *Labor Economy and Labor Relations* 1: 5–8 (in Chinese).

Liu, M. Li, C. and Kim, S. (2011) 'The changing Chinese trade unions: A three level analysis', in P. Sheldon, S. Kim, Y. Li and M. Warner (eds), *China's Changing Workplace*. London: Routledge, pp. 277–300.

Martinez Lucio, M. and Stuart, M. (2004) 'Swimming against the tide: Social partnership, mutual gains and the revival of "tired" HRM', *International Journal of Human Resource Management* 15(2): 410–24.

Mellahi, K. (2007) 'The effect of regulations on HRM: Private sector firms in Saudi Arabia', *International Journal of Human Resource Management* 18(1): 85–99.

National Bureau of Statistics of China (2002) *China Labour Statistical Yearbook 2002*. Beijing: China Statistics Press.

National Bureau of Statistics of China (2010) *China Labour Statistical Yearbook 2010*. Beijing: China Statistics Press.

Ngo, H. Y., Lau, C. M. and Foley, S. (2008) 'Strategic human resource management, firm performance, and employee relations climate in China', *Human Resource Management* 47(1): 73–90.

Nichols, T. and Zhao, W. (2010) 'Disaffection with trade unions in China: Some evidence from SOEs in the auto industry', *Industrial Relations Journal* 41(1): 19–33.

Peng, K. Z., Ngo, H. Y., Shi, J. and Wong, C. H. (2009) 'Gender differences in the work commitment of Chinese workers: An investigation of two alternative explanations', *Journal of World Business* 44(3): 323–35.

Qiao, K., Khilji, S. and Wang, X. (2009) 'High-performance work systems, organizational commitment, and the role of demographic features in the People's Republic of China', *International Journal of Human Resource Management* 20(11): 2,311–30.

Si, S. X., Wei, F. and Li, Y. (2008) 'The effect of organizational psychological contract violation on managers' exit, voice, loyalty and neglect in the Chinese context', *The International Journal of Human Resource Management* 19(5): 932–44.

Taylor, B., Chang, K. and Li, Q. (2003) *Industrial Relations in China*. Cheltenham: Edward Elgar.

Wang, X., Bruning, N. and Peng, S. Q. (2007) 'Western high performance HR practices in China: A comparison among public-owned, private and foreign-invested enterprises', *International Journal of Human Resource Management* 18(4): 684–701.

Wang, Y. (2008) 'Emotional bonds with supervisor and co-workers: Relationship to organizational commitment in China's foreign-invested companies', *International Journal of Human Resource Management* 19(5): 916–31.

Warner, M. (1996) 'Human resources in the People's Republic of China: The "Three Systems" reforms', *Human Resource Management Journal* 6(2): 32–42.

Warner, M. (2008) 'Trade unions in China: In search of a new role in the "harmonious society"', in J. Benson and Y. Zhu (eds), *Trade Unions in Asia: An Economic and Sociological Analysis*. London: Routledge, pp. 140–56.

Warner, M. (ed.) (2009) *Human Resource Management 'with Chinese Characteristics'*. London: Routledge.

Warner, M., and Zhu, Y. (2010) 'Labour–management relations in the People's Republic of China: Seeking the "harmonious society"', *Asia Pacific Business Review,* 16(3): 285–98.

Watts, J. (2010) 'Chinese workers strike at Honda Lock parts supplier', guardian.co.uk, Friday 11 June 2010, www.guardian.co.uk/business/2010/jun/11/honda-china, accessed 28 August 2010.

Wei, L. and Lau, C. M. (2005) 'Market orientation, HRM importance and competency: Determinants of strategic HRM in Chinese firms', *International Journal of Human Resource Management* 16(10): 19,01–18.

Westwood, R., Chan, A. and Linstead, S. (2004) 'Theorizing Chinese employment relations comparatively: Exchange, reciprocity and the moral economy', *Asia Pacific Journal of Management*, 21(3): 365–89.

Wu, X., (2009) 'Income inequality and distributive justice: A comparative analysis of mainland China and Hong Kong', *The China Quarterly* 200: 1,033–52.

Xu, F. (2009) 'The emergence of temporary staffing agencies in China', *Comparative Labor Law and Policy Journal* 30(2): 431–62.

Yang, H. Q. and Li, J. (2008) 'An empirical study of the employment quality of university graduates', *Labor Economy and Labor Relations* 2: 87–90 (in Chinese).

Zhou, F. (2002) 'What does it mean when foreign investors enter the talent market?', *Development and Management of Human Resources* 2: 4–6 (in Chinese).

Zhu, C. and Dowling, P. (2002) 'Staffing practices in transition: Some empirical evidence from China', *International Journal of Human Resource Management* 13(4): 569–97.

Zhu, C., Cooper, B., De Cieri, H. and Dowling, P. (2005) 'A problematic transition to a strategic role: Human resource management in industrial enterprises in China', *International Journal of Human Resource Management* 16(4): 513–31.

3

Human Resources Management in South Korea

CHRIS ROWLEY AND JOHNGSEOK BAE

Introduction

This chapter is concerned with human resource management (HRM) in South Korea (hereafter just 'Korea'), the third largest economy in Asia and the 13th largest economy (in 2011) in the world (the 11th largest just before the 1997 Asian Financial Crisis). While at first sight it may be assumed to be a 'typical' Asian country in terms of its HRM, the reality is less clear-cut, with many particular practices. The key characteristics of Korean HRM revolve around practices based on 'regulation' (or 'seniority') versus more 'flexibility' in labour markets (with easier job shedding) and remuneration (with greater focus on performance). Paradoxically, some influences (such as globalisation) have generated a less homogenous HRM system in Korea today.

This chapter is an update of our earlier piece with the inclusion of some changes that have emerged. We add six points as new changes or trends in HRM. First, performance-based HRM has been 'softened' or at least not intensified. Companies began to recognise that the adoption of performance-based HRM was a double-edged weapon. Second, a job-based HRM system has been diffused, at least for certain job families (such as tellers in the banking industry). This change is related to cost-reduction strategies and the shift of status from contingent workers to regular workers. Third, workplace flexibility has been enhanced. Examples include flexitime. Other related developments include more relaxed dress codes and various benefits for younger employees, for example, the provision of break areas, tea rooms and music halls (for listening to music during break times), which are related to enhancing employee creativity through the combination of 'play' and work. Fourth, work–family balance has become a more critical issue. Many companies also provided various benefits for male staff (such as paternity leave). Fifth, global talent management has also become a more critical task. Large corporations have standardised job systems for cross-country mobility. Sixth, large corporations became more actively involved in benchmarking activities, at least until 2006. Fewer companies now have this kind of activity, which implies that the HRM systems of Korean firms are in their 'mature' stage, at least from the practice viewpoint. Since so many HRM practices have been benchmarked and adopted already, it is not an issue of the practice, but that of the functioning, of those practices.

This chapter is structured around a similar common framework and structure as others in this collection. First, the historical development of HRM is given. Second, partnership in HRM is presented. Third, the key factors determining HRM practices, such as politics, national culture, the economy, the business environment and institutions, are described, along with a review of HRM practices, such as staffing, pay, training and unions. Fourth, changes taking place within the HRM function recently and currently, and the reasons for them, are outlined. Fifth, some key challenges facing HRM are noted. Sixth, what is likely to happen to the HR function is explored. Seventh, some details of websites and current references for the latest information and developments in HRM are annotated.

Historical Development of HRM

The 'management of people' has a long and diverse history in Korea. This needs to be set within Korea's sometimes traumatic history. Here we delineate the more contemporary HRM system (see Kim and Bae, 2004, for earlier periods). HRM's evolution can be analysed within a three-dimensional framework. In this there are three critical historical incidents: the Great Labour Struggle in 1987, the Asian Financial Crisis of 1997 (Bae and Rowley, 2003; Kim and Bae, 2004), and the global financial crisis of 2007–08. This produces four stages – pre-1987, 1987–97, 1997–2007 and post-2007 – each with different HRM configurations. The HRM system can be conceptualised on two dimensions: (1) rewards and evaluation; (2) resourcing and flexibility. The first dimension indicates the basis of remuneration and appraisal, that is, seniority versus ability/performance; the second represents labour market choices, that is, internal labour markets and long-term attachment versus external labour markets and numerical flexibility. Simultaneously, we can also use Rousseau's (1995: 97–9) typology of psychological contracts: (1) 'relational', with high mutual (affective) commitment, high integration and identification, continuity and stability; (2) 'transitional', with ambiguity, uncertainty, high turnover and termination and instability; and (3) 'balanced', with high member commitment and integration, ongoing development, mutual support and dynamics.

The first stage, pre-1987, was a 'seniority-based relational' type HRM. 'Seniorit|yism' was pivotal for various HRM practices such as recruitment, evaluation, training, promotion, pay and termination. In addition, firms generally had long-term attachment to employees, who were rarely laid off. However, the first critical incident, the Great Labour Struggle, resulted in sudden wage increases, which partly reduced competitive advantage in this dimension. This led to the second stage.

The second stage, 1987–97, was an 'exploratory performance-based' type HRM. Firms started to specify performance terms more. The fulcrum of the HRM exhibited two major features in terms of its governance structure and the content of the personnel policy.

First, personnel policy and the practice of organisations were strictly under the control of the state through its regional and local labour departments. Centralisation, formalisation and standardisation of the personnel policies and practices were the primary tasks of the then Ministry of Labour and Social Security (responsible for manual workers) and the Ministry of Personnel (responsible for clerical, professional and managerial staff) – these two ministries were merged into the Ministry of Human Resources and Social Security in 2008. The state not only determined the number of people to be employed and the sources of recruitment but also unilaterally set the pay scales for different categories of workers. State intervention was also extended to the structure and responsibility of the personnel function at the organisational level. Managers in the latter largely assumed an administrative role to implement policies from the top under rigid policy guidelines (Child, 1994).

Second, for the majority of the urban workers, employment was imperative as an obligation to the country. A job was for life. Wages were typically low but heavily supplemented by a broad range of workplace benefits, including housing, pension, health, children's schooling, transportation to and from work and employment for spouses and school-leaving young people, as part of the responsibility of the 'nanny' employer (Warner, 1996, p. 33).

Major changes began in the early 1980s. The opening up of the economy and the ensuing rounds of downsizing in the state sector until the end of the 1990s led to the divergence of ownership forms and the significant shrinkage of the state sector in the share of total employment. For example, in 1978, the state sector employed nearly 80 per cent of the urban workers. By 2009, this had reduced to less than 21 per cent (National Bureau of Statistics of China, 2010).

The shift from state ownership towards private ownership and the rapid growth of foreign-invested firms in China have brought major changes to the patterns of personnel management and industrial relations at both the macro level and the micro level (see below). The socialist employment and welfare regime characterised by full-time employment and extensive welfare benefits as the rights for those employed in the urban sector was gradually replaced by a situation in which employment is no longer guaranteed and welfare is largely insurance-based.

Within the state sector, from the mid-1980s the managers of enterprises were given more autonomy to manage their businesses (Child, 1994). The 'three systems' reforms were implemented in most (state-owned) organisations in the mid-1990s, those being: fixed-term individual and collective labour contracts instead of jobs-for-life; new remuneration systems to reflect performance, position and skill/competence level; and new welfare schemes in which all employers and employees are required by law to make contributions to five separate funds: pension, industrial accident, maternity, unemployment and medical insurance (Warner, 1996). The new welfare system is intended to shift the huge financial burden from the state employer towards individual employees. In addition, a system called 'competing for the post' was introduced in the mid-1990s in which system began changing from seniority more towards performance. From the early 1990s firms started to adopt 'New HRM' (*sininsa*) systems to enhance fairness, rationalisation and efficiency (Bae, 1997: 93). Many firms revamped performance evaluation systems to make them actually function. However, adjustment on the resourcing and flexibility dimension was more rarely touched.

The third stage, 1997–2007, saw a 'flexibility-based transitional' type HRM developing. With the Asian Crisis large corporations launched massive restructuring efforts, for example, mergers and acquisitions, management buyouts, spin-offs, outsourcing, debt for equity swaps, downsizing and early retirement programmes. In these circumstances both public and private policies focused more on labour market flexibility. Bae (forthcoming) interpreted the changes of HRM during this period with the lens of self-fulfilling prophecy. On the other hand, the performance orientation adopted from the previous stage was consolidated. Hence, a more performance-based approach was internalised by organisational members (Bae and Rowley, 2001). At first, the HRM system after the Crisis was more like Rousseau's (1995) 'transitional' type. Top management and HRM professionals lost their sense of direction regarding the future of HRM. However, from the beginning of the 21st century firms started to become more like a 'balanced' type. This model of mutual investment and support has been adopted by large, progressive corporations, such as Samsung and LG. At the same time, firms began to utilise a dual strategy of 'balanced' type for core employees and 'transactional' type for contingent workers (Bae and Rowley, 2003).

The fourth stage, post-2007, can be characterised as 'reflective balanced or community' type HRM, with self-reflection on a decade of experiments of performance/flexibility-based HRM. After these experiments, many Korean companies realised that a market-like employment relationship was not really the answer. The performance/flexibility-based approach has been not that much intensified at least. For example, the Doosan Group use the term 'softened' (or 'warm') performance-based HRM (see case study in this chapter). Samsung also emphasised more the relational aspects in HRM again by changing to forms of profit sharing. Some firms thought that they may have gone too far. This may reflect the dialectical nature of organisational changes.

Partnership in HRM

Ideas of increased employee involvement and partnership have emerged at dual levels post the 1990s. Examples at the macro level include the neo-corporatist type Presidential Commission on Industrial Relations Reform (1996) and the tripartite Labour–Management–Government Committees (*nosajung wiwonhoe*) on Industrial Relations (1998) (Yang and Lim, 2000). At the micro level are examples such as LG Electronics, which emulated practices in plants in the United States (Saturn, Motorola) and Japan. LG Group used the concept of 'partnership' in its post-1998 employee relations reforms (see Park and Park, 2000). There is also a national Labour Management Council (LMC) system (Kwon and O'Donnell, 2001; Rowley and Yoo, 2008; Rowley and Bae, forthcoming).

Some indicators of employment relations, such as unemployment and real wage growth, worsened after the Asian Crisis, which the Tripartite Commission was formed to help to try to resolve. This was an unusual case given the hostile relationships among employee relations system actors and the government's policy direction towards a more market-based approach. Since 1998 several commissions have been initiated, summarised below:

- 15 January 1998: First Tripartite Commission (15 January–February 1998) with Han Kwang-ok as chairperson held its first session.
- 6 February 1998: Tripartite Commission held the 6th session and adopted the Social Compact to overcome the Crisis and agreed on 90 items, including consolidation of employment adjustment-related laws and legalisation of teachers' trade unions.
- 3 June 1998: Second Tripartite Commission (3 June 1998–31 August 1999) with Kim One-ki as chairperson held its first session.
- 24 February 1999: The Korean Confederation of Trade Unions (KCTU) withdrew from the Tripartite Commission.
- 1 September 1999: Third Tripartite Commission (1 September 1999–26 April 2007) was launched with Kim Ho-jin as chairperson and held its first plenary session.
- 27 April 2007: The Fourth Tripartite Commission launched (27 April 2007–present).

Although an assessment of the commissions is difficult, it can be summarised by the shorthand label of 'early effective, later malfunctioning' (Kim and Bae, 2004: 117–20). The Social Compact was path-breaking, the first autonomous tripartite agreement in Korean labour history. Although this helped the government enhance its capacity for crisis management and to tackle the Crisis, the Commission did not produce any significant agreements thereafter. Therefore, while the experiments with tripartite systems were meaningful, they did not turn out entirely successful.

There are also examples at the micro level. We present here the cases of LG Electronics (LGE) and Samsung SDI.[1] Both are in the electronics industry, have histories of severe labour disputes and are successful. During workplace innovations towards a high performance work organisation (HPWO), these *chaebol* took quite different routes and modes of HPWO. The 1997 Crisis pushed their management to make workplace innovations. Both management and employees developed more cooperative and participative employee relations. Management changed styles and attitudes from paternalistic and authoritarian towards more progressive and participative forms. Unions and employees were also effectively involved in the process of workplace innovation. Cooperation of the union leadership or employee representatives helped to establish a new work production system. While unionised LGE adopted a team production mode with a labour–management partnership, non-union Samsung SDI had a lean production mode emphasising Total Quality Management (TQM), Six Sigma and other management–initiated innovations. So, trade union status made a difference in the HPWO adoption process in terms of speed, method and persistence.

In the case of LGE, during 1990–94 labour–management cooperation remained at the affective and attitudinal level. However, at the next stage (post-1994), the partnership of labour and management changed towards a more structural and institutionalised level. In the high-tech electronics industry most competitors are non-union, such as Samsung Electronics in Korea and IBM, Motorola and HP in the United States. The initial adoption process was slow in LGE due to strong union resistance, whereas Samsung SDI more speedily adopted new approaches. While LGE used a more bottom-up approach, with the involvement of frontline employees, Samsung SDI chose a management-centred top-down approach. However, when an HPWO is established, we expect the team production mode to be more strongly institutionalised in the unionised setting, which may more likely prevent easy abandonment. Although LGE shows very active union participation in workplace (that is, lowest) and collective bargaining (that is, middle) levels, it is not practised in the strategic (that is, highest) level, such as product development, investment and restructuring. This may be a future agenda for labour. Samsung SDI operates an extensive system of open communications, information sharing and non-union employee representation. Although this has cultivated the attitudinal aspects of employee relations (that is, labour–management cooperation), its structural and institutional aspects (that is, employee participation through formal mechanisms), have not yet fully developed.

HRM Practices: Key Determinants and Review

This section has two main parts. First, there is an outline of key factors influencing HRM practices. Second, there is a review of those HRM practices.

Influences on HRM

Several key factors have influenced HRM. These include history and politics, national culture, the economy, the business environment, different institutions and globalisation.

Historical and Political Background

This North East Asian country now occupies almost 100,000 square kilometres of the Southern Korean peninsula (6,000 miles from the United Kingdom). Korea's very homogeneous ethnic population rapidly urbanised and grew, more than doubling since the 1960s, from 20.2 million (1966) to 48.8 million (2012). Of these, nearly 10 million (more than double that of the 1960s) are in the capital, Seoul, the dominant centre for political, social, business and academic interests.

Korea's nickname of 'the country of the morning calm' became increasingly obsolete with massive, speedy economic development. From the 1960s Korea was rapidly transformed from a poor, rural backwater with limited natural or energy resources, domestic markets and a legacy of colonial rule and war with dependence on US aid. Korea became one of the fastest growing economies in a rapidly expanding region. Gross domestic product (GDP) real annual growth rates of 9 per cent from the 1950s to the 1990s (with more than 11 per cent in the late 1980s) took GDP from US$1.4 billion (1953) to US$437.4 billion (1994) (Kim et al., 2000). Per capita GDP grew from US$87 (1962) to US$10,543 (1996) and gross national product (GNP) from US$3 billion (1965) to US$376.9 billion (1994). From the mid-1960s to the 1990s annual manufacturing output grew at nearly 20 per cent and exports over 25%, rising from US$320 million (1967) to US$136 billion (1997) (Kim and Rowley, 2001). Korea became a large manufacturer of a range of products from 'ships to chips', in both more traditional (steel, shipbuilding, cars) and newer (electrical, electronics) sectors. Employment grew and unemployment levels declined, to just 2 per cent by the mid-1990s.

How did the former 'Hermit Kingdom' reach this position? The 'Three Kingdoms' (39BC onwards) were united in the Shilla Dynasty (from 668), with the Koryo Dynasty (935 to 1392) followed by the Yi Dynasty, ended by Chosun's annexation by Japan in 1910. The colonisation experience, along with forced introduction of the Japanese language, names and labour, inculcated strong nationalist sentiments, a central psychological impetus for the later economic dynamism (Kim, 1994: 95). While colonised, Koreans were restricted to lower organisational positions and excluded from management. Other Japanese influences came via infrastructure developments, industrial policy imitation, application of technology and techniques of operations management and Korean *émigrés* (Morden and Bowles, 1998). Some later HRM indicated these influences, including lifetime employment and seniority pay, although with some distinctions. For instance, employee loyalty was chiefly to individuals – owners or chief executives (Song, 1997) – with little to organisations, in contrast to Japanese organisational commitment. While limited to regular, particular male employees in large firms, normative practice extended this model (Kim and Briscoe, 1997).

After 1945 came partition, with US military control until the South's independence government in 1948 followed by further widespread devastation with the Korean War from 1950–53. The large US military presence and continued tensions with the North remain. Furthermore, many Koreans studied the American management system, especially as the country was the destination of most overseas students. This affected managerial, business and academic outlooks, perspectives and comparisons. Korea also experienced 25 years of authoritarian and military rule until the late 1980s. Additionally, many business executives were ex-officers, while many male employees served in the military and had regular military training, while some companies maintained reserve army training units.

Cultural

The role of national culture, including Confucianism, retains a powerful, multifaceted and ingrained influence on Korean society in general and is embedded in HRM in particular (see Rowley and Bae, 2003; Rowley, 2013). This can be seen in summary in Table 3.1.

Table 3.1 Characteristics and Paradoxes of Culture and Management in Korea

Cultural Influences	Concepts	Meanings	Management Behaviours and Managerial Characteristics
	Inhwa	Harmony; solidarity	Company as family-type community
	Yongo	Connections: *Hyulyon*: by blood *Jiyon*: by geography *Hakyon*: by education	Recruitment via common ties; solidity within inner circles; kinship-based relationships with owners
Confucianism (family)	*Chung*	Loyalty; subordinate to superior	Paternalistic approach and taking care of employees and their families
	Un	Indebtedness to organisation/ members	Respect; tolerance; patience adhered to in business
	Uiri	Integrity to others in everyday life	Long-term relationships (for example, lifetime employment)
	Gocham	Senior in service; an 'old-timer'	Seniority-based rewards and promotions
Japan	*Kibun*	Good mood; satisfactory state of affairs	Maintain harmony; not hurting someone's *kibun*
	Sinparam	Exulted spirits	Management and making efforts by sentiment-based motivation rather than rational understanding
	Han	Resentment/ frustration felt over unjust or inequitable treatment	Confrontational and militant labour relations (for example, employment adjustment tensions)
Military	*Chujin*	Propulsion; drive; get through something	Can-do spirit; strong driving force; rapid accomplishment of plans/goals
	Palli	Quickly	Speed of action
	Sajeonhyupui	Informal consensus formation prior to making final decisions	Collaboration and participation of stakeholders in decision making

Source: Adapted from Rowley and Bae (2003).

Economic Environment

Korea's economic background, rapid development and the particular structure and organisation of capital and links to the state are all important to HRM's operating context. This developmental, state-sponsored, export-orientated and labour-intensive model of industrialisation (Rowley and Bae, 1998; Rowley et al., 2002) was reinforced by exhortations and motivations (often with cultural under-pinnings, as noted earlier). These included the need to escape the vicious circle of poverty, to compete with Japan, to repay debts and to elevate Korea's image and honour.

In late 1997 the contagion of the Asian Crisis hit Korea, with devastating effects on economic performance, employment (although both quickly recovered) and in turn HRM. This was partly because the post-Crisis International Monetary Fund (IMF) 'bailout' loan came with stipulations of labour market changes, for instance to end lifetime employment and to allow job agencies. Furthermore, the economy opened up to greater penetration from foreign direct investment (FDI), which in turn brought exposure to HRM practices to supplement the experiences of Korea's own multinational companies (MNCs) operating in other countries.

Key aspects of this economic performance and context can be seen in Tables 3.2 and 3.3. The different age and gender impacts are important to note. Basically, older and male workers remain more exposed to the vagaries and effects of unem-ployment, especially in a system with only a limited safety net and culturally influenced opprobrium. The situation post-1997 has been interesting. In terms of GDP there has been no real trend with large fluctuations following the massive near 11 per cent growth rate of 1999. For example, near 9 per cent in 2000, just over 7 per cent in 2002 and 6 per cent in 2010, but with lows of less than 3 per cent in 2003 and 2008 and a paltry 0.3 per cent in 2009 before bouncing back to more than 6 per cent in 2010 and falling back to more than 3 per cent in 2011. In terms of inflation, again wide fluctuations occurred, from nearly 6 per cent in 1998 to less than 1 per cent in 1999 and then 2 per cent to 3 per cent except for less than 2 per cent in 2006 and 2010 and just over 3 per cent in 2011. In terms of unemployment, this continued to decline from the 1998 peak of 7 per cent to 3 per cent to 5 per cent up to 2011.

Capital – The chaebol

These leading lights and drivers of the economy were family founded, owned and controlled large, diversified business groupings with a plethora of subsidiaries, as indicated in the label: an 'octopus with many tentacles'. They were held together by opaque cross share-holdings, subsidies and loan guarantees with inter-*chaebol* distrust and rivalry. Much of the large business sector was part of a *chaebol* network and they exerted widespread influence over other firms, management practices and society. The *chaebol* were underpinned by a variety of elements (Rowley and Bae, 1998; Rowley et al., 2002) and explained by a range of theories (Oh and Park, 2002). For some, the state–military links and interactions was the most important factor, producing politico-economic organisations substituting for trust, efficiency and the market. The state-owned banks (with resultant reliance

Table 3.2 Recent Trends in Korean Employment Patterns, Growth and Inflation

Year	Population ('000 persons)	Employment ('000 persons)	Participation (%)	Unemployment (%)	GDP Growth (%)	Inflation (%)
1990	42,869	18,085	60.0	2.4	9.3	8.4
1991	43,296	18,649	60.6	2.4	9.7	8.3
1992	43,748	19,009	60.9	2.5	5.8	6.2
1993	44,195	19,234	61.1	2.9	6.3	5.2
1994	44,642	19,848	61.7	2.5	8.8	5.1
1995	45,093	20,414	61.9	2.1	8.9	4.6
1996	45,525	20,853	62.0	2.0	7.2	5.1
1997	45,954	21,214	62.2	2.6	5.8	3.4
1998	46,287	19,938	60.7	7.0	-5.7	5.9
1999	46,617	20,291	60.5	6.6	10.7	0.3
2000	47,008	21,156	61.2	4.4	8.8	1.9
2001	47,357	21,572	61.4	4.0	4.0	3.6
2002	47,622	22,169	62.0	3.3	7.2	3.0
2003	47,859	22,139	61.5	3.6	2.8	3.1
2004	48,039	22,557	62.1	3.7	4.6	2.9
2005	48,138	22,856	62.0	3.7	4.0	2.3
2006	48,372	23,151	61.9	3.5	5.2	1.8
2007	48,598	23,433	61.8	3.2	5.1	2.4
2008	48,949	23,577	61.5	3.2	2.3	4.2
2009	49,182	23,506	—	3.6	0.3	3.6
2010	49,410	23,829	—	3.7	6.2	1.8
2011	49,779	24,244	—	3.4	3.6	3.2

Source: Korea National Statistical Office (http://ecos.bok.or.kr).

Table 3.3 Trends in Leaving by Age in Korea (%)

Age	15–20	21–24	25–29	30–39	40–49	50–60
1995	7.06	22.69	21.34	25.66	12.97	10.28
1997	5.63	21.62	23.57	25.22	12.10	11.85
1998	4.39	16.37	20.87	25.27	15.73	17.37

Source: Ministry of Labor (various).

for capital), promoted *chaebol* as a development strategy and intervened to maintain quiescent labour. These close connections were often damned as nepotism and 'crony capitalism'.

There were more than 60 *chaebol*, although a few dominated. At their zenith in the 1990s the top five (Hyundai, Daewoo, Samsung, LG and SK) accounted for almost one-tenth (9 per cent) of Korea's GDP, and the top 30 accounted for almost one-sixth (15 per cent), taking in 819 subsidiaries and affiliates. Some became major international companies in the world economy, engaged in acquisitions and investments overseas, dominated by the United States and China. A sketch of the top *chaebol* illustrates their typical development and structure.

Samsung is the oldest *chaebol*, with roots in the Cheil Sugar Manufacturing Company (1953) and Cheil Industries (1954), although it started as a trading company in 1938. It developed from a fruit and sundry goods exporter into flour milling and confectionery. Over the post-war decades it spread to sugar refining, textiles, paper, electronics, fertiliser, retailing, life insurance, hotels, construction, electronics, heavy industry, petrochemicals, shipbuilding, aerospace, bio-engineering and semiconductors. Sales of US$3 billion and staff of 45,000 (1980) ballooned to US$96 billion and 267,000 (1998) (Pucik and Lim, 2002). Samsung Electronics alone had 21 worldwide production bases, 53 sales operations in 46 countries, sales of US$16.6 billion and was one of the largest producers of dynamic random access memory semiconductors by the late 1990s. By 2002 Samsung still claimed global market leadership in 13 product categories, from deep-water drilling ships to microwaves, television tubes and microchips, and with a target to actually have 30 world beaters by 2005. In 2010 it still had 78 affiliates and assets of Won[2] 204,336 billion (www.kisvalue.com).

However, the Asian Crisis brought out into the open some of the inherent and underlying problems and strains that were beginning to be felt in the *chaebol* and in the Korean model more generally. There followed the collapse of some *chaebol*, scandals and bankruptcy and the reconfiguration of others, including even the takeover of some by Western MNCs. The more recent position can be seen in Tables 3.4 and 3.5 as well as later under the section on globalisation.

Labour

The critical management of labour has occurred in a variety of contexts, including military governments. Importantly, labour played an integral role against occupation and supporting democratisation. From the early 20th century low wages,

Table 3.4 Size and Businesses of the Largest *Chaebol* in Korea ('000 billion won) 2010

Name	Main Business	Assets
Samsung	Electronics, machinery and heavy industries, chemicals, construction	204.3
LG	Clothing, supermarkets and radio, television, electronics stores	90.2
SK	Refining, distributing and transporting petroleum products, production and sale of petrochemical products	94.4
Hyundai Motors	Manufacture and distribution of motor vehicles and parts	121.8
Hanjin	Construction, shipbuilding	33.4
Hyundai	Elevators, merchant marine, finance	11.2

Source: OECD in *Economist* (2003), www.kisvalue.com.

Table 3.5 Korean Large Business Groups ('000 billion won) (2010)

Name	Affiliate Number	Debt-Equity Ratios (%)	Assets
Korea Electric Power Corp	13	86.69	131.28
Samsung	71	52.03	204.34
LG	60	94.33	90.19
SK	84	113.10	94.35
Hyundai Motors	43	82.36	121.76
Korea Telecom	31	123.95	27.48
Korea Highway Corp	4	279.73	0.20
Hanjin	39	249.87	33.40
Korea Land Corp	4	3309.95	0.26
Hyundai	13	184.87	11.19
Gumho	45	284.30	24.45
Hyundai Heavy Industry	21	119.15	53.47
Hanwha	52	123.47	23.33
Koran Gas Corp	3	355.45	24.47
Doosan	25	175.31	26.63
Dongbu	32	208.58	12.20

Source: www.kisvalue.com.

hazardous conditions and anti-Japanese sentiments contributed to union formation (the following is from Kwon and O'Donnell, 2001; Rowley and Yoo, 2008;
Rowley and Bae, forthcoming). From the 1920s unions increased, reaching 488
and 67,220 members (1928). The 1930s witnessed a decline with harsh repression
and subordination to Japanese war production, and also internal organisational
splits. Union numbers fell to 207 and 28,211 members (1935). The post-war radical union movement (the *Chun Pyung*) was declared illegal by the American military government trying to restrict political and industrial activities to encourage

US type 'business unions'. The subsequent strikes and General Strike resulted in 25 deaths, 11,000 imprisoned and 25,000 dismissals. A more conservative, government-sponsored industry-based movement was decreed, signalling labour's incorporation by the state, conflict repression and an authoritarian corporatist approach. Thus, the government officially recognised the Federation of Korean Trade Unions (FKTU) and became increasingly interventionist, enacting a battery of laws regulating hours, holidays, pay and multiple and independent unions.

A diversity of approaches towards labour was also partly influenced by *chaebol* growth strategies (Kwon and O'Donnell, 2001). For instance, economic growth and focus on minimising labour costs resulted in the expansion and concentration of workforces in large-scale industrial estates with authoritarian and militaristic controls. The pressure and nature of the labour process was indicated in the volume of workplace accidents, some 4,570 (1987) compared to smaller numbers in larger workforces (although with sectoral impacts, of course), such as 513 in the United States and 658 in the United Kingdom (Kang and Wilkinson, 2000). Labour resistance was generated, the catalyst for conflict and re-emergence of independent unions. Employers responded by disrupting union activities, sponsoring company unions and replacing labour-intensive processes by automating, subcontracting or moving overseas. From the late 1980s companies also softened strict supervision and work intensification emphasis by widening access to paternalistic practices and welfare schemes (Kang and Wilkinson, 2000). Nevertheless, trade unionisation grew from 12.6 per cent (1970), peaking at 18.6 per cent (1989).

During the 1990s independent trade unions established their own national organisation, with federations of *chaebol*-based and regional associations. An alternative national federation, the KCTU (*minjunochong*), emerged in 1995. It organised the 1996 General Strike (Bae *et al.*, 1997), enhancing its legitimacy. However, the economic whirlwind of the Asian Crisis then hit. Trade union density fell back to 11.5 per cent (1998).

Further details on trade union developments in Korea covering the context and history of union development as well as membership, types and structures and also collective bargaining, wages and disputes are detailed in the literature (Rowley and Yoo, 2008; Rowley and Bae, forthcoming). Similarly, the developments in the labour markets in Korea are covered in terms of the size, employment, interactions with product and financial markets and technology, the political economy as well as types of labour markets (informal, primary and secondary) and institutions in the labour market and flexibility (Rowley, Yoo and Kim, 2011).

Globalisation

Large corporations, such as Samsung Electronics Company (SEC) and LGE now have more than half of their total employees overseas. In addition, the ratio of overseas sales is more than 85 per cent. Both companies established global HRM systems in the early 2000s. In the case of SEC, it forced standardisation of HRM practices in global subsidiaries in 2004 and started to more serious implementation in 2008. LGE prepared position-based job grades at the headquarters and global integration of job categories in 2005. In 2007 they recruited chief-level foreign executives (for example, chief marketing officer [CMO] and chief human-resource officer [CHO]). Then it implemented standardisation of performance evaluation systems in 2009 and compensation policy in 2010.

Furthermore, HRM globalisation in Korean companies shifted its focus from 'hardware' to 'software'. At first, companies focused on systems and practices, especially a performance-based HRM system. This hardware aspect includes performance-based compensation, position-based job grades, standardisation of performance evaluation and compensation policies (see also Yang and Rowley, 2008). The next issue was global top talent mobilisation including (re)allocation of global HRs, recruiting non-Korean executive members, decentralisation of HR directors in subsidiaries and leadership development of host country nationals. Finally, the focus of global HRM was internalisation. Some issues here include aligning different ways of doing things, vision and value sharing, and improvement of communication skills.

Review of HRM Practices

Second, a review of HRM practices is presented. First of all it is useful to compare the more traditional characteristics with newer ones in HRM and the varied influences on them, as in Table 3.6. We will then detail these categories that comprise much of HRM.

Employee Resourcing

Aspects of employee resourcing include recruitment, selection and contracts. The *chaebol*, traditionally seen as prestige employers, recruited graduates biannually with a preference for management trainees from prestigious universities. There have been some moves from such resourcing systems towards ongoing, atypical and insecure forms. For instance, flexibility was classified as 'low' numerically in pre-Crisis Korea (Bae et al., 1997). Since then flexibilities seemingly swiftly increased. The trend is indicated by a survey (of 300 firms) conducted in 1997 and 1998 (Choi and Lee, 1998). During the first period, virtually one-third (32.3 per cent) adjusted employment. By the second period this coverage almost doubled (to 60.3 per cent). For the first period, specific types of employment adjustment (firms made multiple responses) were: worker numbers (19.7 per cent), working hours (20 per cent) and functional flexibility (12.7 per cent). By the second period these types of employment adjustment massively increased: worker numbers more than doubled (43.7 per cent), while working hours (36.7 per cent) and functional flexibility (24.3 per cent) almost doubled. There was a more than doubling in both 'freezing or reducing recruitment', from 15 per cent to 38.7 per cent, and 'dismissal' from 7 per cent to 17.3 per cent, with rises in 'early retirement' from 5.7 per cent to 8 per cent. Thus, numerical flexibility increased. Indeed, it was argued that even by 1999 the number of temporary, contract and part-time workers comprised more than 50 per cent of the workforce (Kang and Wilkinson, 2000; Demaret, 2001). These employee resourcing areas can be seen in the growth and variety of types of non-permanent workers, as shown in Table 3.7.

Table 3.6 Influences on HRM in Korea: Traditional and New Compared

Influences ->	Traditional Characteristics	HRM Area	New Characteristics	<- Influences
Culture (traditional)	• Mass recruitment of new graduates • Job security (lifetime job) • Generalist-oriented	**Employee Resourcing**	• Recruitment on demand • Job mobility (lifetime career) • Development of professional	Culture (modern)
America Japan Military	• Seniority (age and tenure) • Pay equality • Evaluation for advancing in job/grade • No appraisal feedback • Single-rater appraisal	**Employee Rewards**	• Ability, performance (annual system) • Merit pay • Evaluation for pay increases • Appraisal feedback • 360° appraisal	Globalisation Asian Crisis State
State	• High induction • Company-specific • Functional flexibility context	**Employee Development**	• Overseas programs • Differentiated training • Numerical flexibility context	Management/Capital/ Investment (inward and outward)
Management/Capital Labour	• Authoritarian corporatism • Legal constraints • Less involvement • Less information sharing	**Employee Relations**	• Enterprise-based union and federations • More freedoms • Involvement of knowledge workers • Information sharing	Labour

Source: the authors.

Table 3.7 Trends in Employment Status in Korea (%)

	Regular workers	Temporary workers	Daily workers
1995	58.14	27.89	13.97
1996	56.81	29.60	13.59
1997	54.33	31.60	14.07
1998	53.14	32.87	13.99
1999	48.44	33.60	17.96
2000	47.87	34.49	17.64
2001	49.16	34.60	16.24
2002	48.39	34.45	17.16
2003	50.47	34.74	14.79
2004	51.19	34.12	14.69
2005	52.14	33.30	14.57
2006	52.76	33.07	14.17
2007	53.98	32.39	13.64
2008	55.57	31.34	13.09
2009	57.07	31.00	11.93
2010	59.43	29.86	10.71

Source: The Statistics Korea (KOSTAT) (www.kostat.go.kr).

In terms of more recent trends, we can see the following. For temporary workers, the percentage grew post-1995 to nearly 35 per cent but has since had steady, albeit small, declines to just less than 30 per cent by 2010. In terms of daily workers, there have been bigger changes and fluctuations, from just less than 14 per cent in 1995 to nearly 18 per cent in 1999 and about 14 per cent up to 2006 before declining to nearly 11 per cent by 2010. In terms of regular workers, the nearly 59 per cent level of 1995 declined continually to less than 50 per cent by 2002 but since increased constantly back again to nearly 60 per cent by 2010.

Another aspect of employee resourcing concerns the numbers of graduates and the attractiveness of small-and medium-sized enterprises (SMEs). The rate of increase in labour with university degrees exceeded demand. This over-supply started after the 1997 Asian Crisis when companies minimised new recruitment. It seems that there are simply not enough 'sought-after' *chaebol* jobs, as these provide only 10 per cent. While under 30 year old unemployment stands at 8.3 per cent and SMEs reported 250,000 unfilled vacancies in 2011, graduates are not attracted to SMEs due to lack of training and poor pay and welfare entitlements as well as the weak position of SMEs (Oliver and Buseong, 2012).

Some company cases also highlight employee resourcing practices. Samsung Electronics' 60,000 employees (1997) were massively reduced by about one-third to 40,000. LG Group in 1998 dismissed 14,000 (11.6 per cent of its total) employees (Kim, 2000). Daewoo Motor shed 3,500 jobs, despite violent protests and strikes. Some 30,000 employees at public companies like Korea Telecom, Korea Electric Power Company and Korea National Tourism Organisation were to be dismissed while another 30,000 (10 per cent) of local public servants were dismissed by the end of 1998 (Park and Park, 2000).

However, there were some limits to such employee resourcing practices. At first, neither government nor *chaebols* seemed overly keen to use the new legislation (*The Economist*, 1999). This inertia can be seen in the following cases where adjustment was constrained. Korea Telecom moved towards increased adjustment via changes in job categories, transfers and promotions (Kwun and Cho, 2002). Rather than dismissal, a Samsung subsidiary asked both men and women to take unpaid 'paternity leave' while Kia remained 'proud' of its 'no-lay-offs' agreement and Seoul District Court protected jobs by refusing to close Jinro (*The Economist*, 1999). One high-profile example concerned Hyundai Motor, whose initial plan to dismiss 4,830 of its 45,000 workers was diluted to 2,678 and then 1,538. The union went on strike in 1998, followed by illegal strikes and physical conflict until a negotiated compromise was reached. This provided for just 277 dismissals (with 167 of these from the canteen!), along with severance payment. As a result, while Hyundai's workforce fell to 35,000, this was mainly due to 7,226 voluntary retirements plus about 2,000 who will return after 18 months' unpaid leave (*The Economist*, 1999). Indeed, some collective dismissals, such as the 1,500 figure at Hyundia Motor, were regarded as 'illegal' and 'unreasonable' (Lee, 2000).

Employee Rewards

There has been some increasing importance attached to performance in employee rewards practices. Some of the reasons for this were: pay system rigidity making labour almost a quasi-fixed cost; weak individual-level motivational effects; and changing environmental factors (Kim and Park, 1997). However, there is actually more variety here than what an overly stark 'either-or' choice presents. Table 3.8 indicates this.

Data from the earlier survey (Choi and Lee, 1998) indicated that employee rewards flexibility almost quadrupled from about one-tenth (10.7 per cent) to

Table 3.8 Variations in Korean Pay Systems By Size And Sector (%)

System Options	Sector		All Firms
	Manufacturing (N = 210)	Non-manufacturing (N = 68)	
(1) Traditional Seniorityism	42.4	42.6	42.4
(2) Seniority-based with Performance Factor*	25.2	22.1	24.5
(3) Performance-based with Seniority Factor	29.0	29.4	29.1
(4) Ability/Performance-Based	3.4	5.9	4.0

Source: Adapted from Park and Ahn (1999).

Notes: * Originally labelled 'Ability-based system, but seniority-based operation'.

nearly four-fifths (38.7 per cent) from 1997 to 1998. Table 3.8 shows that about one-third (33 per cent) of firms had performance-based – (3) or (4) – systems. There seem to be common trends across sectors, although with some greater change in use of (4) in non-manufacturing *vis-à-vis* manufacturing. Slightly more variation by size of organisation would be expected given that size is a powerful variable in many HRM areas. Somewhat counter-intuitively, (1) was used by slightly more 'smaller' (although defined at a relatively high employment level here) firms, while more than twice the percentage (although still a small total percentage) compared to 'larger' ones used (4).

It has been noted that post-1997 pay for performance systems (*'Yunbongje'*) became more rapidly adopted (Yang and Rowley, 2008). For example, going from low coverage (just 1.6 per cent of firms) in 1996 to getting on for nearly one-quarter (23 per cent) by 2000 and nearly one-half (48.4 per cent) by 2005 (Ministry of Labor, various). Key features of *'Yunbongje'* include not only that differences in individual performance and contributions to organisational success are reflected in pay, but that many complex components (that is, base pay, various allowances and fixed bonuses) are merged and can be adopted in the form of merit pay (Yang and Rowley, 2008).

The example of annual pay, whereby salary is based on individual ability or performance, is another employee rewards practice. A survey (1999) of 4,303 business units (with more than 100 employees) found that 15.1 per cent had already adopted annual pay; 11.2 per cent were preparing for it; and 25 per cent were planning to adopt it (Korea Ministry of Labor, 1999). Thus, just over one-quarter (26.3 per cent) of firms had either introduced it, or were preparing to. Indeed, just over one-half (51.3 per cent) of firms were in some stage of changing pay systems. Again, there seemed to be common trends across organisational size.

Other evidence indicates employee rewards practices being used and considered. Some 13 per cent (more than double 1998's 6 per cent) of companies listed on the Korean Stock Exchange were giving share options, with some 18 per cent (more than quadruple 1998's 4 per cent) of 15,116 large companies sharing profits in January 2000, with another 23 per cent planning to do so by year end (Labor Ministry survey in *The Economist*, 2000).

Again, we give company examples of employee rewards. The operation of annual rewards systems can also be seen in specific cases. Instances among the *chaebols* are shown in Table 3.9. All used forms of annual pay systems. Samsung and Hyosung adopted a 'zero-sum' method, reducing salary for poorer performers while increasing pay by the same amount of reduced salary for better performers. Doosan, Daeang and SK used a 'plus-sum' method, increasing salaries of good performers without reducing those of poor performers. Finally, some firms accumulated performance evaluation results.

In Samsung remuneration had been composed of base pay (based on seniority), plus extra benefits (long service, and so on) until it introduced its 'New HR Policy' (1995) with its greater emphasis on performance. Now remuneration was composed of base pay (common pay, cost-of-living), plus merit pay (competence and performance used) (Pucik and Lim, 2002; Kim and Briscoe, 1997). The LG Group

Table 3.9 Comparison of Annual Pay Systems Among Korean *Chaebols*

	Doosan	Daesang	Hyosung	SK	Samsung
Adopted	1994	1995	1997	1998	1998
Target	Section chief + above	College graduates + above	College graduates + above	Deputy general managers + above	Section chief + above
Composition	– Basic annual – Performance	– Basic – Ability – Performance	– Seniority – Job-based – Ability – Performance	– Individual annual – Incentives	– Basic annual – Performance (individual + group)
Base-up	No	Yes	Yes	No	Yes
Plus-sum	Yes	Yes	No	Yes	No
Cumulative	Yes	Yes	No	Yes	No

Source: Adapted from Yang (1999: 232).

introduced (in 1998) practices to determine pay based on ability and performance (Kim, 2000). LG Chemical brought in a system of performance-related pay at its Yochon plant (*The Economist*, 1999). Korea Telecom made some moves towards more flexibility and performance in rewards (Kwun and Cho, 2002). Hyundai Electronics introduced (in 1999) share options. SEC used profit sharing. Originally its frame was to give profit sharing based on the performance of business unit up to 50 per cent of their annual salary. Since Samsung experienced that this pay scheme generated some sense of inequity among employees, they changed the scheme by having 20 per cent of profit sharing as a common rate that applied to all employees regardless of business performance in 2007; and the commonly applied rate was increased to 40 per cent in 2010. Hence, if they have sufficient resources, now the range of profit sharing to their annual salary is 20 per cent to 50 per cent.

The key lever in operationalising these employee rewards practices is performance appraisal (Yang and Rowley, 2008). Traditionally, it did not affect pay (or promotion). Given this new emphasis, however, Samsung's appraisal system was re-vamped and made more sophisticated in the search for greater objectivity and reliability. It was now composed of several elements, such as: supervisor's diary; 360-degree (supervisors, subordinates, customers, suppliers) appraisal; forced distribution; and two interviews (with the supervisor; 'Day of Subordinate Development'). The 'Evaluation of Capability Form' used was composed of interesting items, such as 'Human Virtues', for example, 'morality': willingness to sacrifice (*sic*) themselves to help colleagues (Kim and Briscoe, 1997).

Again, the extent of such employee rewards practices requires some consideration. Some practices are relatively limited in coverage and spread. For instance, data in Table 3.8 also indicated that seniority remained in large numbers, more than two-fifths of firms (nearly 43 per cent). Indeed, some form of seniority – (1) or (2) – accounted for the pay systems of over two-thirds (67 per cent) of firms. Likewise, data in Table 3.9 indicated that most firms applied practices only to certain groups, such as managers or the higher educated. Some, such as Samsung, Daesang and Hyosung, used 'base-up' methods, a uniform increase of basic pay regardless of performance or ability levels. Similarly, Hyundai's vaunted stock option policy covered just 7 per cent of the workforce while Samsung's profit sharing was restricted to 'researchers' (*The Economist*, 2000). At LG, although employee evaluation systems were in place, in most instances compensation did not reflect evaluation results as it remained 'largely determined by seniority' (Kim, 2000: 178).

Also, there are many problems with trying to link employee rewards and performance via appraisals with distal and proximal factors, along with intervening, judgement and distortion factors (see Yang and Rowley, 2008). These concern appraisals in general, when linked to rewards and in Asian contexts (see Rowley, 2003). For instance, well-known tendencies in human nature lead towards subjective aspects in appraisals. Furthermore, practitioner-type literature commonly recommends that appraisals should not be linked with remuneration. There are also concerns that appraisals cut against the 'professional ethos'. Finally, there are cultural biases to be aware of. For example, Korean managers are often unwilling to give too negative an evaluation, as *inhwa* emphasises the importance of harmony among individuals who are not equal in prestige, rank and power, while supervisors are required to care for the well-being of their subordinates and negative evaluations may undermine harmonious relations (Chen, 2000). Another Korean value, *koenchanayo* ('that's good enough'), also hampers appraisals as it encourages tolerance and appreciation of people's efforts and not being excessively harsh in assessing sincere efforts (Chen, 2000).

Employee Development

Korea's spectacular post-war economic growth and some *chaebols* have been influenced by a skilled and well-educated workforce with heavy investment in the development of HRs (Yoo and Rowley, forthcoming). It was argued that the success of companies such as Pohang Iron and Steel (the predecessor of POSCO) was due in part to its employee development and regular training (Morden and Bowles, 1998). Many espoused the Confucian emphasis on education with very strong commitment to it and also traditional respect and esteem attached to educational attainment. This is indicated by high levels of literacy, a high proportion of scientists and engineers per head of population and that 70 per cent of the workforce graduated from high school (Morden and Bowles, 1998).

Employee development can be classified (Kim and Bae, 2004) as: new recruits and existing employees; in-house and external; language proficiency, job ability, character building; and basic and advanced courses. Many *chaebols* put strong emphasis on training and have their own well-resourced and supported training centres. There is often many (three to six) months' in-house induction training with new employees staying at training centres or socialisation camps. Here they are inculcated in company history, culture, business philosophy, core values and vision, to develop 'all-purpose' general skills through which to enhance team spirit, a 'can-do' spirit, adaptability and problem-solving. They use *'sahoon'* (shared values explicitly articulated), a company song and a catchphrase to build-up feelings of belonging, loyalty and commitment (Kim and Briscoe, 1997; Kim and Bae, 2004). These centres also provide ongoing training and a variety of programmes. For instance, in 1995 Samsung spent US$260 million on training, Hyundai spent US$195 million and Daewoo and LG spent US$130 million each (Chung, Hak Chong and Ku Hyun, 1997).

Some companies use invited foreign engineers to work with them and transfer skills and some send their own trainees overseas (Kim and Bae, 2004). Managerial-level training focused more on moulding managers to the company's core values and philosophy rather than developing their job-related abilities and knowledge. Programmes placed more emphasis on building character and developing positive attitudes than on professional competence. One popular way to improve job-related skills was job rotation and multi-skilled training, but these were not applied systematically and varied between industries (Kim and Bae, 2004). Many large firms launched several programs to promote business–university partnerships. In addition, overseas training programmes to provide opportunities have been introduced and many companies give employees with requisite qualifications or appraisal results opportunities to study at foreign universities, for example, Samsung's 'Region Expert' program sends junior employees overseas for one year in order to obtain language skills and cultural familiarity (Kim and Bae, 2004).

In terms of more macro data, we can note the following on training and development (T&D). This is in terms of post-1980 trends in T&D 'intensity' measured by labour costs and total sales.

In more detail, this table shows that after the 1997 Asian Financial Crisis, the level of T&D intensity by total labour cost dropped and remained constant (see Figure 3.1). It also indicated that the post-1997 situation (see Figure 3.2) looks

Table 3.10 Level of T&D Intensity in Korea (Using Labour Cost and Total Sales): 1980–2010

Year	T&D intensity (1) (= investment/ total labour cost)	T&D intensity (2) (= investment/ total sales)*1000
1980	0.0111	0.4112
1981	0.0118	0.4364
1982	0.0129	0.4905
1983	0.0142	0.5184
1984	0.0154	0.5720
1985	0.0160	0.5541
1986	0.0165	0.5302
1987	0.0164	0.5579
1988	0.0206	0.7476
1989	0.0197	0.7335
1990	0.0226	0.9230
1991	0.0251	0.9248
1992	0.0286	1.0207
1993	0.0302	1.1089
1994	0.0277	1.0801
1995	0.0298	1.2149
1996	0.0278	1.1788
1997	0.0245	0.8996
1998	0.0167	0.5475
1999	0.0169	0.6630
2000	0.0181	0.7169
2001	0.0179	0.7392
2002	0.0175	0.8770
2003	0.0177	0.8183
2004	0.0170	0.8502
2005	0.0167	0.8354
2006	0.0168	0.8757
2007	0.0167	0.9364
2008	0.0157	0.7242
2009	0.0123	0.5856
2010	0.0158	0.7688

Source: www.kisvalue.com.

Notes: Calculation based on 243 firms with external audit by law and that have survived since 1980.

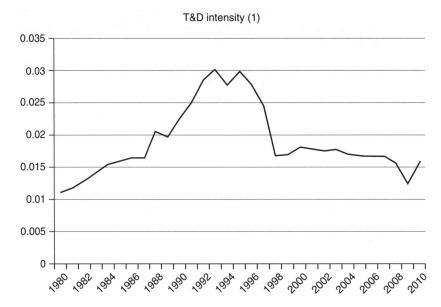

Figure 3.1 Training and Development (T&D) Intensity = T&D Investment/Total Labour Cost in Korea

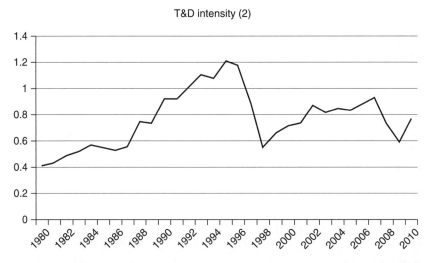

Figure 3.2 Training and Development (T&D) Intensity in Korea = (T&D Investment/ Total Sales)*1000

less clear for T&D intensity by total sales as the peak was during the mid-1990s and after the Asia Financial Crisis levels recovered, but not to the previous level. Further detail on workforce developments and skills can be seen in the literature (see Yoo and Rowley, forthcoming).

Employee Relations

By 1998 there were 1.40 million union members (12.6 per cent density) and increasing numbers of strikes, 129; rising to 1.53 million members (12 per cent) and 250 strikes by 2000 (Kim and Bae, 2004). Thus, unions can be highly militant. Furthermore, unions are strategically well located in ship and automobile manufacture as well as power, transportation and telecommunications. Conflicts had often been high-profile, large-scale and confrontational. For example, the 1992 week-long occupation of Hyundai Motor was ended by 15,000 riot police storming the factory (Kim, 2000).

From the late 1980s the institutions, framework and policies of employee relations all reconfigured under pressures from political liberalisation and civilian governments, joining the International Labor Organization (ILO) (1991) and the Organisation for Economic Co-operation and Development (OECD) (1996), trade union pressure and the Asian Crisis. Nevertheless, the frames of reference and perspectives for management remain strongly unitary. In contrast, this is less so for labour, with stronger pluralist, and even radical, perspectives evident. The position of the state is more ambiguous, especially given the background of the current president and some seeming shift from the initial pluralist stance, towards a more unitary one. This can be seen in the following examples.

There were strikes by power plants and major car makers in 2002, and a week-long truck driver strike in early 2003. This latter dispute crippled Pusan, the world's third largest port, which handles 80 per cent of Korea's ocean-going cargo, and which risked manufacturers, such as Samsung and LG Chem, grinding to a halt by choking their supply and distribution channels (Ward, 2003). The government made concessions to resolve this dispute, which included fuel subsidies, tax cuts and lower highway tools for trucks (Ward, 2003). It was also seen as part of the new President Roh Moo-hyun's policy of resolving labour disputes peacefully through dialogue. Similarly, the privatisation of the national railway network has been cancelled, while the sale of the state-owned Chohung Bank stalled, both amid fierce union opposition (Ward, 2003). These instances can be seen to support a more pluralist approach.

However, a more unitarist sentiment can also be detected. For instance, in 2002 there was imprisonment of unionists, refusal to recognise public sector unions and ending of the power workers' strike after several weeks of public threats and intimidation and surrounding their Myong-dong Cathedral camp with riot and secret police. In 2003 there were high-profile disputes by truck drivers and bankers and a four-day strike of railway workers was crushed by more than 1,000 arrests. Korea is still seen as repressive, flouting trade union rights and ILO Conventions 87 and 98 by restraining the rights to freedom of association, collective bargaining and strike action. Thus, in 2002 the president of the Korean Confederation of Trade Unions was imprisoned for two years for 'obstructing business' by simply coordinating a general strike (ICFTU, 2003).

In terms of union membership and density, as well as number of strikes, these can be seen in Table 3.11. Post-1997 the number of strikes rose to a peak of 462 in 2004 with rapid decline to just 65 by 2011. Membership grew to nearly 1.7 million by 2007 with a gentle decline, albeit still at a higher level than any years except 2007–08. Unlike trends in strikes and membership, union density has shown a consistent trend, and one going down gently from the post-1997 peak of 12 per cent to less than 10 per cent by 2010. Further details can be seen in the literature (see Rowley and Bae, forthcoming).

Changes Taking Place within the HR Function

Traditionally in the *chaebol* there were links between the HR department and the powerful chairperson's office, which made many important HR decisions. Thus the HR function was closely tied to the highest level of the *chaebol* (Kim and Briscoe, 1997). More recently, HR units have changed their roles from the traditional administrative aspects towards more strategic value-adding activities. This is shown and summarised in the Table 3.12. This is based on a survey that was done by the Korea Labor Institute in 1999 of HRM professionals both in academia and practice (for example, professors of HRM, researchers in research institutes affiliated to big corporations, senior HRM consultants and HR executives of the top forty companies in Korea). A total of 140 questionnaires were distributed and 107 were returned.

The first change is in HRM organisation. Traditionally Korean firms had the perception of 'anybody can assume HRM jobs', meaning that HR practitioners did not need any special competencies or qualifications. This reflects a 'lowest common denominator' syndrome: a small fraction of HRM activities created the large proportion of value-added, whereas most activities added little value

Table 3.11 Number of Strikes, Union Members and Density in Korea

Year	Number of Strikes	Union Members (1,000 persons)	Union Density(%)
1999	198	N/A	N/A
2000	250	1527	12.0
2001	235	1569	12.0
2002	322	1606	11.6
2003	320	1550	11.0
2004	462	1537	10.6
2005	287	1506	10.3
2006	138	1559	10.3
2007	115	1688	10.8
2008	108	1666	10.5
2009	121	1640	10.1
2010	86	1643	9.8
2011	65	N/A	N/A

Source: Ministry of Labor (various).

Table 3.12 Changing Perspectives on HRM in Korea (%)

Employee champion or advocate	29	Current	40	Strategic partner
	12	Future	68	
Reactive change agent for management	63	Current	17	Proactive change agent
	32	Future	57	
Internal-oriented for organisational issues	57	Current	17	External-oriented for social issues
	22	Future	48	
Focused on operational issues in organisation	68	Current	14	Focused on business goals and strategies
	16	Future	75	
Efficient management of HR	53	Current	23	Internal consultants for line managers
	38	Future	49	
Seniority-based HRM	70	Current	12	Ability/performance- for line managers
	2	Future	96	
Results-oriented HRM	51	Current	24	Process-oriented HRM
	26	Future	54	
Generalist orientation	62	Current	11	Specialist orientation
	6	Future	84	
Paternalism-based HRM	71	Current	9	Contract-based HRM
	3	Future	91	

Source: Adapted from Park and Yu (2001).

(Baron and Kreps, 1999). The shifts in this also occurred in several different ways. As aforementioned, the roles of HR professionals have changed to more strategic roles. To become business partners, HR managers started to align HRM configurations with business strategies and organisational goals. Some empirical evidence also confirms this (Bae and Lawler, 2000; Bae and Yu, 2003). In addition, firms also started to reorganise their HR units by differentiating them into several specialities and sections, that is, HR planning, recruitment, HR support team, and employee relations, and by adopting a separate shared service unit.

A second change in the HR function, related to the first, involves the efforts to enhance the competencies of HR professionals. Three different strategies are employed: (1) initiating various education programs for HR managers (see Kim and Bae, 2004); (2) transferring to HRM units people who have various experiences in organisations, such as planning, sales and research and development (R&D); and (3) recruiting HR professionals from outside who are trained in graduate-level programs or experienced in other organisations. All these strategies were unusual in the past.

Another change in the HR function is the outsourcing phenomenon (similar to that in some other countries such as the United Kingdm; see Rowley, 2003). Various HR activities may be outsourced. Areas highly prone to outsourcing were: education and training (by 85 per cent of respondents); outplacement (77 per cent); HR information systems (77 per cent); followed by job analysis (68 per cent); recruitment and selection (56 per cent); and then operation of salary and pay (53 per cent), as shown in Park and Yu (2001) using the same survey as that in Table 3.12.

Partly as a result of these trends, HR service firms have drastically increased (Rowley and Bae, 2003). These include outsourcing for general affairs and benefits, HR consulting, education and training, head-hunting, e-HRM and HR information system providers, outplacement, online recruiting, staffing service and HRM ASP (active server pages). The approximate gross sales for such businesses (in Won in 2002) are (Kim, 2002): HR consulting (one trillion); staffing service (one and half trillion); online recruiting (200 billion); head-hunting (100 billion); and HRM ASP (50 billion).

Fourth, the adoption of e-HRM is also an example of recent change in the HR function. By managing all employment-related data through such information systems, firms gained some benefits in terms of cost reduction and speed of operations. In particular, e-recruitment through which firms efficiently screen job candidates is actively utilised.

Fifth, there were active benchmarking activities until 2006. For example, a major electronics company spent a lot of money on benchmarking. They visited more than 50 major companies around the world such as GE, IBM, Sony, Philips and so on (Bae, forthcoming). Yet, benchmarking activities suddenly decreased. Perhaps this is because practices and systems have been well established by now with a more important matter being to make those practices function well.

Key Challenges Facing HRM

A range of key challenges are facing HRM. First, there are more macro ones stemming from the economy. These include the calls for greater transparency and openness in corporate governance issues, and the continued reorganisation of capital with *chaebol* restructuring, FDI and takeovers, and thus exposure to non-traditional HRM practices. HR practitioners can have a role in all of these.

There is also the challenge for HRM of an ageing workforce (Bae and Rowley, 2003). For example, in 1990 the economically active population aged 15 to 19 was 639,000; by 2010 it was down to 189,260, while over the same period those aged 40 to 54 increased from 5,616,000 to 8,879,213 (KOSIS, *Korean Statistical Information Service, http://kosis.kr/eng*). Of course, such trends are widespread, while the implications for Korea are stark given some of the traditional aspects of culture and society, not least its strong family basis and orientation, homogeneity and exclusiveness.

Second, there are challenges from the more micro HRM policy areas. This has several elements to it. One challenge is the so-called 'war for talent', that is, an attraction strategy to recruit top quality talent. Many Korean corporations actively pursued recruiting and retaining such talent. For this purpose, *chaebols* such as Samsung, LG, SK, Hyundai Motor, Hanwha, Doosan and Kumho, provide a fast-track system, a signing-on bonus, stock options and so on. This was not an issue earlier during the 'Seniority-Based Relational' HRM system. Since the 1997 Crisis, the mobility of people has increased within and across large corporations and venture firms. Corporations responded to labour market changes with multiple strategies (Kim and Bae, 2004). Firms divided employees into different groups, each with their own approach: 'Attraction Strategy' (that is, dashing into the war for talent) and 'Retention Strategy' (that is, taking measures to keep core employees) for core employees; 'Replacement Strategy' (that is, dismissing under-performing employees) and 'Outplacement Strategy' (that is, providing information and training for job switching) for poor performers; and a 'Transactional and Outsourcing Strategy' (that is, contract-based, short-term approach) towards atypical workers. All of these strategies had been unfamiliar to most Korean firms.

Third, another challenge is the work–family balance issue. Many firms have adopted family-friendly policies. For example, some companies keep every Wednesday as a family day; for this they turn all lights off at 6 p.m. Yuhan-Kimberly and POSCO are good examples of these efforts.

Fourth, Korean firms encountered the big challenge of enhancing creativity. Beyond catch-up or imitation strategy, Korean firms need to initiate new products and services. Samsung adopted 'Creation Management'. When Apple launched its iPhone, Samsung was absolutely devastated. Hence the new challenge for HRM is how to enhance individual initiatives and creativity for innovation.

Fifth, managing contingent workers is also a challenge for HRM. At first, these types of workers reduced company costs. Yet, managing these people is getting harder. There are several issues here, which include the shattering of the 'psychological contract', re-contracting, differentiated treatment (for example, lower pay and benefits) and disharmony with regular workers, and complicated and multiple configurations. These 'costs' have been seen in a range of countries, while additionally in Korea, some cultural aspects (see Table 3.1), that is, the strong perception of the equality norm and a strong union movement, makes management even more difficult. According to Korean labour law, firms that have employed contingent workers for two years need to change the status of these workers to regular workers or fire them. Many of these status-changed employees are related to job-based HRM. As mentioned earlier, job-based HRM has been somewhat diffused for cost reasons.

Finally, performance-based systems have also generated HRM challenges. In some aspects, firms gained higher productivity and performance after adoption. However, it also produced downsides too. Commonly, people only become involved in those activities that are evaluated by their organisation – the 'no evaluation, no act' syndrome or the dictum 'what gets measured gets done'. Therefore, organisational citizenship behaviours, which used to be more common in

Korean firms, are now more rarely observed. Another phenomenon is that people are more reluctant to cooperate with other teams or divisions. This has become even more critical since some profit-sharing programs were adopted. This is particularly problematic for electronics companies pursuing digital convergence, as this requires high levels of cooperation and coordination. Finally, people became more prone to focus on current and short-term goals, especially in R&D divisions or institutes. Researchers avert high-risk long-term projects, the critical foundation for future success.

We evaluated the institutionalisation of performance-based HRM as a half-success story in our earlier version. As mentioned previously, performance-based HRM has been challenged for the past few years. Many companies are currently trying to search for a more balanced employment relationship.

What is Likely to Happen to HR Functions?

With regards to HR units, we expect re-engineering of HRM processes and decentralisation. The shrinkage in headquarters' HR practitioners, and increases in business division HRM, will be accelerated. Decentralisation will be realised through the transfer of HRM-related activities to line managers. Again, some activities will be accomplished by outsourcing. However, the difficulties with the necessary control, coordination and consistency in HRM, with the importance of equity and fairness within and across businesses and people in such circumstances are clear (see Rowley, 2003).

As other functional areas (for example, planning, marketing and management information systems [MIS]) have experienced, the HRM function may encounter a challenge from top management regarding the value-added by the HRM unit. HR managers in many Korean firms are currently preparing for this challenge. Following Becker, Huselid and Ulrich (2001), many firms have recently developed HR performance indexes to link HRM activities and firm performance. HRM audit and review based on the HR scorecard approach will be more actively conducted. A focus on areas such as corporate governance, ethical business practices and top executive pay, as well as managing diversity, will further allow HR to add value.

Finally, as Korean firms continue to relocate production to other countries, such as China, South East Asia and further afield, global HRM is gaining significance. Several issues here include the globalisation–localisation choice, transfer of the 'best' people (for example, both expatriates and inpatriates) and HR practices, and global integration and coordination. Some companies, such as Samsung Electronics, employ inpatriates from host countries to work at the head office. Other companies, like LG Electronics, send executive-level management to regional head offices (for example, China) to establish and coordinate the whole of HRM in the region. The need for HRM to have a role in this area of cross-cultural management is clear.

Case Study: The HRM Case of Doosan Heavy Industries and Construction

(www.doosanheavy.com)

About the Company

Doosan Heavy Industries and Construction (hereafter Doosan HI&C) is an affiliated company of the Doosan group. The history of this firm goes back to 1962 when Hyundai Yanghaeng was founded. As part of the government's support of heavy industries (that is, its heavy industry promotion plan), Korea's first machinery industrial complex was established in Changwon. The name of the firm was changed to Korea Heavy Industries in 1980; and in 2001, it was privatised and renamed Doosan HI&C. Its products and services include power generation, water, castings and forgings, construction, material handling equipment, and green energy.

Doosan HI&C's vision is to become a 'global leader in power and water', which reveals the determination of the firm to be a global leader in the water and power plant industries. The areas that the company wants to upgrade include proprietary technology, price competitiveness, product quality, sales volume, profitability, HR development and corporate culture. Its management philosophy includes 'customers are our teachers', 'quality is our pride', 'innovation is our life' and 'people are the most important asset'. Here we focus on the company's emphasis on the importance of people.

HRM Policies and Practices

Recruitment, performance evaluation and pay system are briefly discussed. In the case of recruitment, the company takes a 2G strategy: Growth of business and Growth of people. The company pursues business growth through the growth of people. It has four values for the selection of the right people: passion of excellence; harmony; open mindset; and professionalism. The staffing processes are very selective. The first stage is the process of screening candidates by the documents including their career history. Grade Point Average (GPA) is not considered at all, but an essay is much regarded since it provides much information regarding candidates' values and their life story in depth. The second stage is an aptitude test using the DCAT (Doosan Competency Aptitude Test) for those who pass the first stage. Finally, the company has two interviews. The first interview is conducted by the business unit to test the competences of candidates through a structured interview and the DISE (Doosan Integrated Simulation Exercise) containing business case analysis and personal presentation. The second interview is conducted by top executives to test the values and passion of the candidates.

In the case of its evaluation and pay system, Doosan takes a strong performance-based system. Doosan was the first business group that adopted an annual pay system (a Korean-version merit pay system) in Korea. Doosan

HI&C classified employees into four groups based on performance evaluation: A (10 per cent), B (20 per cent), C (60 per cent), and D (10 per cent). Then they assign average employees to the C group. This scheme is utilised for pay increases and promotions. In the case of the pay system, the company has a dual approach: a seniority-based pay grade system for blue-collar workers and an annual-based merit pay system for white-collar (office) workers. Pay differentials based on performance are cumulatively applied, which make pay differentials wide.

In addition, Doosan also adopted a job-based approach for executive members. In the past, promotion just meant a change of job title and accordingly a pay increase. However, now it means the transfer to the other job having higher job worth (see Bae 2012).

HRM-Relevant Issues

For the past 15 years the company has laid off many employees three times. First, Korea Heavy Industries (the predecessor of Doosan HI&C) laid off 340 employees in 1998 as part of an effort to privatise it. This was a measure of restructuring of the firm as many Korean firms did at that time after the 1997 Asian Crisis. However, the compulsory redundancies became a 'signal' of company transformation given the facts that Korea Heavy Industries was a public corporation and had strong labour union organisation. Second, during the privatisation process, about 1,000 were laid off again in 2000 to reflect decreased demand and to enhance the efficiency of the business operation. Third, in 2003 Doosan HI&C had another round of redundancies with about 1,500 employees to have a quick turnaround. These series of redundancies made possible the corporation's new culture and ways of doing business.

Along with these redundancies, as mentioned above, Doosan HI&C adopted a performance-based pay system with strong incentive intensity. Pay differentials were wide and individual performance became much more important. These changes included an organisational culture characterised more by competition and individual performance orientation. However, the nature of the industry itself required the company to have long-term learning and knowledge accumulation, and effective collaboration and coordination. Hence there was some misfit between these two influences.

In 2007, when the plant business overseas was booming, two issues emerged. The first issue was a HR shortage since it had reduced their HR several times in order to gain efficiency. Especially, the company lacked frontline workers and lower-level managers. The second issue was HR outflow to other companies. Those who felt a sense of inequity under the strong performance-based HRM system left first. Many employees felt high pressure from pay differentials. Realising this problem, the company adopted a new direction for their HRM system towards 'warm performance orientation' by adopting such practices as team performance-based incentives and a common welfare system for everyone.

Useful Sources

There are a range of sources for the latest information and developments in HRM that can provide details to the reader over the years. These include the following.

Civil Service Commission: www.csc.go.kr
Korea Chamber of Commerce and Industry: www.kcci.kr
Korea Labor Institute: www.kli.kr
Ministry of Education & Human Resource Development: www.moe.go.kr
Ministry of Labor: www.molab.go.kr

Ministry of Science and Technology: www.most.go.kr
National Statistical Office: www.nsohp.nso.go.kr
Samsung Economic Research Institute: www.seri.org

There is also a range of journals in the area, especially:

Asia Pacific Business Review
Asia Pacific Journal of HRs
Asia Pacific Journal of Management
International Journal of HRM

Notes

1 The details of these cases are mainly from Kim and Bae (2004).
2 Won = KRW. 1 KRW = 0.000540924 GBP Sterling; 1 GBP Sterling = 1,849.16 KRW (21/5/12).

References

Bae, J. (1997) 'Beyond Seniority-based Systems: A Paradigm Shift in Korean HRM?', *Asia Pacific Business Review* 3(4): 82–110.

Bae, J. (2012) *Human Resource Management*, 2nd edn. Seoul: Hongmoonsa (in Korean: *jeok ja won non*).

Bae, J. (2012) 'Self-fulfilling processes at a global level: The evolution of HRM practices in Korea, 1987–2007', *Management Learning* 43(9): 579–607.

Bae, J., and Lawler, J. (2000) 'Organizational and HRM strategies in Korea: Impact on Firm Performance in an Emerging Economy', *Academy of Management Journal* 43(3): 502–17.

Bae, J. and Rowley, C. (2001) 'The Impact of Globalization on HRM: The Case of South Korea', *Journal of World Business* 36(4): 402–28.

Bae, J. and Rowley, C. (2003) 'Changes and Continuities in South Korean HRM', *Asia Pacific Business Review* 9(4): 76–105.

Bae, J. and Yu, G. (2003) 'HRM Configurations in Korean Venture Firms: Resource Availability, Institutional Force, and Strategic Choice Perspectives', Working Paper, Korea University.

Bae, Johngseok, Rowley, Chris, Lawler, John and Kim, D. H. (1997) 'Korean industrial Relations At The Crossroads: The Recent Labour Troubles', *Asia Pacific Business Review* 3(3): 148–60.

Baron, J. N. and Kreps, D. M. (1999) *Strategic Human Resources: Frameworks for General Managers*. New York: John Wiley & Sons.

Becker, B. E., Huselid, M. A. and Ulrich, D. (2001) *The HR Scorecard: Linking People, Strategy, and Performance*. Boston, MA: Harvard Business School Press.

Chen, M. (2000) 'Management in South Korea', in M. Warner (ed.) *Management in Asia Pacific*. London: Thomson, pp. 300–11.

Choi, K. and Lee, K. (1998) *Employment Adjustment in Korean Firms: Survey of 1998*. Seoul: Korea Labor Institute.

Chung, Kae H., Lee, Hak Chong and Jung, Ku Hyun (1997) *Korean Management: Global strategy and cultural transformation*. Berlin: de Gruyter.

Demaret, L. (2001) 'Korea: Two Speed Recovery', *Trade Union World* 21(1): 21–2.

Economist, The (1999) 'A survey of the Koreas', 10 June, pp. 1–16.

Economist, The (2000) 'Business in South Korea', 1 April, pp. 67–70.

Economist, The (2003) 'No Honeymoon for Roh', 7 June, p. 60.

ICFTU (2003) 'Trade Union Victory in South Korea', ICFTU Press Online, 4 March.

Kang, Y. and Wilkinson, R. (2000) 'Workplace industrial relations in Korea For the 21st century', in R. Wilkinson, J. Maltby and J. Lee (eds) *Responding to Change: Some Key Lessons for the Future of Korea*. Sheffield: University of Sheffield Management School, pp. 125–45.

Kim, K. D. (1994) 'Confucianism and Capitalist Development in East Asia', in L. Sklair (ed) *Capitalism and Development*. London: Routledge, pp. 87–106.

Kim, Y. (2000) 'Employment Relations at a Large South Korean Firm: The LG Group', in G. Bamber, F. Park, C. Lee, P. Ross and K. Broadbent (eds) *Employment Relations in the Asia-Pacific*. London: Thomson, pp. 175–93.

Kim, Y. (2002) 'Trends in HR Service Industry in Korea', *HR Professional*, 1 94–99 (in Korean: *Insa service sanupeui gyunghyang*).

Kim, D. and Bae, J. (2004) *Employment Relations and HRM in South Korea*. London: Ashgate.

Kim, D., and Park, S. (1997) 'Changing patterns of pay systems in Japan and Korea: From seniority to performance', *International Journal of Employment Studies* 5(2): 117–34.

Kim, J. and Rowley, C. (2001) 'Managerial problems in Korea: Evidence from the nationalized industries', *International Journal of Public Sector Management* 14(2): 129–48.

Kim, S. and Briscoe, D. (1997) 'Globalization and a New Human Resource Policy in Korea: Transformation to a Performance-Based HRM', *Employee Relations* 19(4): 298–308.

Korea Labor Institute (2012) 'The evaluation of employment relations of 2011 and the prospect of 2012', *Monthly Labor Review*, 1: 23–32.

Korea Ministry of Labor (1999) 'A Survey Report on Annual Pay Systems and Gain-Sharing Plans', Korea Ministry of Labor (in Korean: *Imgeumjedo siltaejosa*).

Korea National Statistical Office ( ) http://ecos.bok.or.kr.

Korean Statistical Information Service (KOSIS) ( ) http://kosis.kr/eng.

Kwon, Seung-Ho and O'Donnell, M. (2001) *The Chaebol and Labour in Korea: The development of Management Strategy in Hyundai*. London: Routledge.

Kwun, S. K. and Cho, N. (2002) 'Organizational Change and Inertia: Korea Telecom', in C. Rowley, T. W. Sohn and J. Bae (eds) *Managing Korean Businesses: Organization, Culture, Human Resources and Change*. London: Cass, pp. 111–36.

Lee, C. (2000) 'Challenges Facing Unions in South Korea', in G. Bamber, F. Park, C. Lee, P. Ross and K. Broadbent (eds) *Employment Relations in the Asia-Pacific*. London: Thomson, pp. 145–58.

Ministry of Labor (various) www.moel.go.kr

Morden, T. and Bowles, D. (1998) 'Management in South Korea: A Review', *Management Decision* 36(5): 316–330.

NICE Information Service ( ) www.kisvalue.com.

Oh, I. and Park, H. J. (2002) 'Shooting at a Moving Target: Four Theoretical Problems in Exploring the Dynamics of the Chaebol' in C. Rowley, T.W. Sohn and J. Bae (eds) *Managing Korean Businesses: Organization, Culture, Human Resources and Change*, London: Cass, pp. 44–69.

Oliver, C. and Buseong, K. (2012) 'SKorea's Graduates Struggle in job Market', *Financial Times*, 27 April, p. 5.

Park, J. and Ahn, H. (1999) *The Changes and Future Direction of Korean Employment Practices*. Seoul: The Korea Employers' Federation (in Korean: *Goyonggoanli byunhwawoa vision*).

Park, F. and Park, Y. (2000) 'Changing Approaches to Employee Relations in South Korea' in G. Bamber, F. Park, C. Lee, P. Ross and K. Broadbent (eds) *Employment Relations in the Asia-Pacific* London: Thomson, pp. 80–100.

Park, W. and Yu, G. (2001) 'Paradigm Shift and Changing Role of HRM in Korea: Analysis of the HRM Experts' Opinions and its Implication', *The Korean Personnel Administration Journal* 25(1): 347–369.

Pucik, V. and Lim, J.C. (2002) 'Transforming HRM in a Korean Chaebol: A Case Study of Samsung' in C. Rowley, T. W. Sohn and J. Bae (eds) *Managing Korean Businesses: Organization, Culture, Human Resources and Change*. London: Cass, pp. 137–60.

Rousseau, D. M. (1995) *Psychological Contracts in Organizations: Understanding written and Unwritten Agreements*. Thousand Oaks/London/New Delhi: Sage.

Rowley, C. (1998) (ed.) *HRM in the ASIA Pacific Region: Convergence Questioned*. London: Cass.

Rowley, C. (2003) *The Management of People: HRM in Context*. London: Spiro Press.

Rowley, C. (2013) 'The Changing Nature of Management and Culture in South Korea', in M. Warner (ed.) *Managing Across Diverse Cultures*. London: Routledge, pp. 122–50.

Rowley, C. and Bae, J. (1998) (eds) *Korean Businesses: Internal & External Industrialization*. London: Cass

Rowley, C. and Bae, J. (2003) 'Culture & Management in South Korea', in M. Warner (ed) *Culture & Management in Asia*. London: Curzon, pp. 187–209.

Rowley, C. and Bae, K. S. (forthcoming) 'The Waves of Anti-Unionism in South Korea', in G. Gall and T. Dundon (eds) *Global Anti-Unionism*. Palgrave Macmillan.

Rowley, C. and Benson, J. (2000) (eds) *Globalization and Labour in the Asia Pacific Region*. London: Cass.

Rowley, C. and Benson, J. (2002) 'Convergence and Divergence in Asian HRM', *California Management Review* 44(2): 90–109.

Rowley, C. and Benson, J. (2003) (eds) *HRM in the Asia Pacific Region: Convergence Revisited*. London: Cass.

Rowley, C. and Yoo, Kil Sang (2008) 'Trade Unions in South Korea', in J. Benson and Y. Zhu (eds) *Trade Unions in Asia*. London: Routledge, pp. 43–46.

Rowley, C., Sohn, T. W. and Bae, J. (eds) (2002) *Managing Korean Businesses: Organization, Culture, Human Resources & Change*. London: Cass.

Rowley, C., Yoo, K. S. and Kim, D. (2011) 'Labour markets in South Korea', in J. Benson and Y. Zhu (eds) *The Dynamics of Asian Labour Markets*. London: Routledge, pp. 61–82.

Song, B. N. (1997) *The Rise of the Korean Economy*. Oxford: Oxford University Press.

Ward, A. (2003) 'Government Deal Ends South Korean Truck Strike', *Financial Times*, 16 May, p. 10

Yang, B. (1999) 'The Annual Pay Systems in Korean Firms', Proceedings of the International Conference of Korea Association of Personnel Administration on the Change of HRM Paradigm and Annual Pay, November, Seoul, pp. 207–39.

Yang, S. H. and Lim, S. (2000) 'The role of government in industrial relations in South Korea', in R. Wilkinson, J. Maltby and J. J. Lee (eds) *Responses to Change*. Sheffield: SUMS.

Yang, H. and Rowley, C. (2008) 'Performance Management Systems in South Korea' in A. Varma, P. Budhwar and A. DeNisi (eds) *Performance Management Systems Around the Globe*. London: Routledge, pp. 316–40.

Yoo, K. S. and Rowley, C. (forthcoming) 'Workforce Development in South Korea', in J. Benson, H. Gospel and Y. Zhu (eds) *Workforce Development and Skill Formation in Asia*. London: Routledge.

4

Human Resource Management in Japan

PHILIPPE DEBROUX

Introduction

Recent decades have seen important changes in the HRM practices of advanced economies. A fundamental change has been the rise in performance-related appraisal and compensation systems. Another significant development has been the adoption under different names of the concept of a flexible firm (Atkinson, 1985) that has led to the rise of atypical (for example, part-time, temporary or dispatched) employment patterns. The widespread emergence of those trends in the main economies suggests that some form of convergence in employment practices is at work.

This chapter analyzes these developments in the specific case of Japan. Considered as trend-setting and inspirational examples in the 1970s and 1980s Japanese human resource management (HRM) architecture, policies and practices, that is, the ideas of what should be considered as legitimate, effective and efficient, have been challenged during the last two decades.

Changing values, work and lifestyles impose changes in the very concept of "company" in the minds of the employees. The internal labor market linked to a seniority-based pay system is put in question with important consequences on the recruitment, training, appraisal and reward policies and practices. Characterized by their high level of workforce homogeneity Japanese companies must manage a more diversified labor force, including an increasingly large number of women and foreigners. An ageing population calls for different career patterns for both elder and younger employees. The emergence of product modularization in an open technology era threatens the integrated product system and requires a transformation in the philosophy and practices of knowledge management. The shift toward a shareholders' value-centered corporate governance shakes the delicate balance between employees and investors in the traditional stakeholders' system.

Historical Development in Human Resource Development

Stable Corporate Governance and Industrial Relations

After World War II corporate governance in large companies was character-ized by stable shareholding and criteria of performance privileging a long-term, growth-oriented strategy. This facilitated the adoption of a HRM system that offered long-term guarantees for the permanent employees and seniority-based pay. In the early post-war period, industrial relations were marred by disputes. It changed with the emergence of in-house unions that have been pillars of the employment system up until now. They played a key role in the diffusion of information between labor and management, and they were instrumental in the acceptance of new technologies.

Dynamics of the Internal Labor Market

New graduates were recruited with a long-term perspective, and most manag-ers up to the top of the hierarchy were rising up from their ranks. As a result, work and training patterns could be adopted by which labor could also take on a productive function by working together with management with a long-term focus. Cross-fertilization of interconnected networks favored the creation and flow of knowledge embedded in each employee's mind. The planning and imple-mentation of operations were not strictly hierarchically structured, and rotation was frequently practiced for both white- and blue-collar workers. Workers were expected to cope with needed changes or problems and it required constantly upgraded problem-solving capabilities (Fujimoto, 2007).

Japanese companies never assumed that longer tenure necessarily implies higher productivity. For that reason the training needs were constantly monitored and appraised during the entire career in order to get a close fit between the employ-ees' individual needs and the needs of the organization (Salmon, 2003). The rationale has always been that the investment in skills would not be sunk even if workers switched to a different type of job (Koike, 1994). In the line of what Becker (1964) argued, higher productivity was believed to correlate to company-specific skills. Since the mid-1960s, On-the Job Training (OJT) and Off-the Job Training (OFF-JT) have been available and methods of job enlargement and enrichment have been widely applied, especially at the shop-floor level.

Broad-based Performance Evaluation and Reward

The motivation of employees required an incentive mode that allows individuals to commit fully to the teamwork process without fear of losing compensation. The basic wage developed as a mix of person-related and job-related elements. To that was added age and merit-based elements. The person-related payment was determined by position in the hierarchy and was based upon seniority and past merit. In the skill-grading system that became dominant in the 1970s, merit is taken into account in pay and promotion but with an indirect relationship between compensation and job allocation (Aoki, 1988). The job-related elements were determined by a job evaluation system. But since the job descriptions were vague and since assignments were broadly defined, jobs have tended to be evaluated on the basis of employees' skills and experiences in a broad sense. Continuous evaluations assessed potential ability, based on adaptability to technical changes as well as soft skills such as loyalty and teamwork ability.

Overall the wages differential has remained small up until now but the speed of promotion and, thus, the level of remuneration, always varied. Up until the last decade a large number of average performers could expect to be promoted to middle management while outstanding employees could aim to fill positions where they could enjoy a much higher wage and improved fringe benefits, such as golf membership, during the later stage of their career. Conversely, under-performing employees could be confined to activities that would not lead to a promising career, or could be relegated to minor subsidiaries or related companies. Therefore, the seniority wages was considered as an incentive mechanism closely linked to the internal labor system (Lazear, 1979).

Japanese-style Flexicurity: Balance of Power, Culture and Rationality

Welfare corporatism and the absence of a large external labor market made permanent employees dependent on their employers. They faced pressure to act in accordance with management wishes, lest they would lose their status and fall into the category of the unprotected peripheral workforce. Companies were always legally authorized to unilaterally change the working conditions, including the place and type of work (Araki, 2002). Lifetime employment was never based on any explicit contractual promise and neither was it a fiduciary duty on the part of the company. But an employment relationship was deemed to be continuous. The legal doctrine and court precedent since the 1950s concludes that an employer would only be found to have just cause for termination if all less drastic alternatives had been ruled out (Araki, 2002). Therefore, management was in command, although there was to some extent an effective balance of power with the state intervention.

HRM policies and practices were rationalized according to ethical and cultural principles insisting on social harmony and collective efforts (Sugimoto, 2010). Bargaining power favored management but it could be argued that Japanese companies nevertheless became organizations where trust that induced genuinely loyal sentiments could develop (Matanle, 2003). In such a context lifetime employment grew into much more than just an agreement between the parties where separate interests were based on individualistic utilitarian assumptions. It became a social norm enjoying large societal legitimacy.

Long-term employment and the ideals of welfare corporatism were always shared beyond the circle of the large companies. But stress was put on market rationality to justify the creation of dual labor markets. High pay and cooperative long-term work arrangements with permanent employees always went along with the use of buffer-type contingent labor having much less access to fringe benefits and working for lower wages without job guarantees, as well as a wide wage gap between large and small companies. Institutional structures, patriarchal gender norms and stereotypes limited women's position in the labor market. Like the non-regular workers, they were considered as a buffer, ancillary type of workforce, kept at the lower end of the job market, and considered as not worthy of much investment in training up until the end of the 1980s (Sugimoto, 2010).

Key Factors Determining HRM Practices and Policies

Macroeconomic and Business Changes

The decline in stocks and land prices, weak internal demand, and excess capacity led to stagnation in the 1990s and a shaky economic growth pattern since then. A more shareholders' driven corporate governance concurs to a continuous decline of the share of profit going to labor since the 1990s (Sueki, 2009). The focus on core competences and divestment of activities has made redundant many employees. Product modularization has favored outsourcing and rendered many workers' skills and experience obsolete.

In order to answer to short-term product development and changes in demand companies cannot rely only on company-specific skills. It requires both the presence of specialized people on short notice and a higher numerical and financial flexibility pushing for utilization of atypical workers.

Shift Toward Performance-driven HRM

From the 1980s the performance element in appraisal and reward increased but the link between age/tenure and merit was not cut. It largely remained unchanged under the skill-based classifications, based on the assumption of employees "being capable of doing" because of supposedly mastered skills. This led to the introduction of performance-related pay (PRP) and appraisal systems in the 1990s (*seikashugi*) that put a focus on work-related skills with performance appraisal linked to demonstrations of their mastering.

The person-related pay element determined by rank and based on seniority and past merit is fast disappearing. Age and tenure-based pay and promotion components have by now been removed or drastically reduced in many companies. Annual pay rises are not a given anymore at all stages of the career. Managers promoted through seniority but without having subordinates and not having real responsibilities are becoming a thing of the past (Salmon, 2003). The job-related wage element of the pay of managerial and non-managerial personnel reflects more strictly defined job classes or roles. Companies are not adopting a purely occupation-based pay system (*shokumukyu*) and the tendency is rather more to shift away from this approach. The ability-/skill-based element of pay (*shokunokyu*) still counts but it is incorporated into individual competency frameworks. The job component consists of a fixed amount and a further one where roles and competency frameworks linked to performance are increasingly important (MHLW, 2010).

Some companies propose to their new employees the option of renouncing their retirement lump sum in exchange for a higher salary. The objectives are to increase work mobility and to respond to the desire of both parties to develop more contingent work relationships. At the same time, the performance element in the determination of the retirement lump sum has significantly increased for managers (Meyer-Ohle, 2009). Unions have always considered the bonus as part of regular pay but it is comparatively easier to negotiate its variation than in the case of salary. A minority of listed companies have removed it altogether for managerial personnel. In most cases, one part of the bonus is still paid twice a year as a certain multiple of base pay but the remaining part is based on individual performance leading to larger differences than before.

Remaining Importance of the Labor Market Logic

Internal equity is of utmost importance in a system based on the internal labor market. Wage differentials increased in the last 15 years but they remain limited by international standards even for managers (MHLW, 2009b). External benchmarking is increasingly important because there is now a sizeable external labor market for managerial jobs. But companies are reluctant to rely too much on the external labor market to determine pay, lest it proves to disrupt their long-term-oriented HRM policy. To control labor cost and create incentives they prefer to introduce a pay component linked to companies' performance connected to the evolution of the markets for raw materials, semi-finished products and the financial markets (Nakata and Miyazaki, 2011). Stock options are increasingly used for managers and non-managers but they are not significant incentive tools so far in most companies.

Toward a New Legal Basis of Flexicurity

Since the 1980s the power of companies has been broadened to deal more flexibly with working conditions and the category of workers themselves. At the same time, policy makers have tried to keep the balance with job stability and social fairness. Since 2003 the judicial doctrine against unjust dismissal is incorporated into the Labor Standards Law (Wolff, 2010). Some laws have reinforced the workers' rights in line with changing social values. The Whistleblower Protection Law (2004) prohibits the dismissal of whistleblowers in the public interest. The law responds to the need for a greater opening of companies to society. Likewise, the new amendment of 2006 to the Equal Employment Opportunity Law (EEOL) 1986 strengthens the rights of women at work, including dismissals attributable to direct and indirect discrimination (Nakakubo, 2007).

Conversely, the Company Law Reform Bill (2006) allows more flexibility to develop differentiated HR policies at departments and smaller units' levels and reinforces the pressure from the financial markets. The Law for Dispatch Workers enacted in 1985 increased the opportunity to offer and utilize short-term employment contracts. The scope was enlarged in 2003 to all types of jobs, including in manufacturing (Hisano, 2007). The Labor Standards Law contains since 1998 an amendment introducing a discretionary work scheme defining work time by reference to the tasks that are completed rather than the hours worked. It allows companies to control their overtime budgets while responding to the needs for accommodating diverse life- and working-styles and allows them to satisfy the demand for short-term and specific expertise. Since 2003 the legal maximum limit for an employment contract is three years instead of one. It provides the opportunity to make strategic, medium-term recruitment of skilled workers while partly externalizing the costs of training (Wolff, 2010).

At the same time companies also gradually curtail the allowances and services that are associated with traditional welfare corporatism.

Keeping and Creating Competitive Advantages in a Globalized World

Since the 1990s Japanese companies have tried to keep research and development (R&D) and production value-added in Japan while investing abroad. It is argued that to create products with unique features long-term relationships with internal and external partners and cultivation of broad integrative skills and problem-solving abilities have to remain at the center of HRM strategy (Itami, 2011). On the one hand, it calls for keeping the internal labor market logic. On the other hand, responses to short-term product development and to the need for access to world knowledge, as well as needing to master intangible assets such as branding and intellectual property rights, requires a more diverse workforce.

Companies continue to mostly recruit new graduates and to devote important resources to the selection process and subsequent training. At the same time, since the 1990s they have applied the concept of "employment portfolio" combining long- and short-term employment (Nikkeiren, 1995). High performance working systems (HPWSs) based on concepts of employability, engagement, empowerment and individual performance, are adopted for the core employees. It goes with the utilization of specialists for specific tasks and projects, and atypical workers for the routine and standardized jobs. Specialists can be recruited from the outside and can be managed flexibly thanks to the discretionary work scheme. But since the 1990s companies also started to nurture a pool of professional managers with technical and/or management backgrounds (Salmon, 2003). They are given the opportunity to progress in the hierarchy while specializing, and are rewarded accordingly.

Changes in Knowledge Management

The traditional concept of knowledge management where knowledge is built through intensive personal interactions among members (Nonaka and Takeuchi, 1995) is put in question. The high level of institutionalization of personal relationships is a strength but also a weakness because of the difficulties in integrating outsiders. Moreover, it may be simultaneously jeopardized by the growing external mobility of the managerial and technical personnel and by the lower inter-department mobility that reduces personal contacts. This problem is compounded by the fear of losing the embedded knowledge of the older generation that will retire in a few years' time (Hentschel and Haghirian, 2011). All those factors are conducive to the shift toward more codified knowledge, as in documents and databases, which would be more easily accessible to outsiders in Japan and abroad.

Evolution of Corporate Culture: Toward a Clash of Values

The sustained ability to compete on the basis of quality and responsiveness to customers' specialized needs was often associated to a value system engrained in Japanese culture. The principles of loyalty, commitment, discipline and a strong work ethic that are inculcated during the induction period in a company are parts of this tradition. For instance, the "five S" principles applied in the workplace (*seiri, seiton, seiso, seiketsu, shitsuke*) are said to be embodied in the moral fabric of Japanese society, whose values are claimed to be influenced by Confucianism, Buddhism and Shintoism (Hirschmeyer and Yui, 2006).

Based on this mindset, the employment patterns have provided social anchors as well as ideals to be strived for by everybody. The societal legitimacy of the concept of company as a "community of fate" has been internalized for a long time. As a consequence, large companies are still widely expected to continue to recruit a large number of new graduates every year and to provide long-term job guarantee and career opportunities. Responsibility toward permanent employees continues to be thought to extend beyond the mere respect of contracts. Top managers are expected to make personal financial sacrifices in case of downturn. Lay-off may be unavoidable at times but it is still considered as a managerial failure and should remain a measure of last resort, not something that can be done for economic convenience.

This mindset increasingly clashes with the spirit of the reforms of the corporate governance and HRM systems during the last two decades where emphasis is put on shareholders' value, individual performance and equality of opportunity rather than on outcome. Conversely, concern about social exclusion and perceived growing inequality has been expressed since the last decade. It is thought that letting differences in income grow too much may lead to a point at which the sense of community is endangered, be it at the levels of the country, the neighborhood or the company (Sugimoto, 2010). Those two contradictory trends put management into a double bind. Companies have to motivate ambitious managers who are eager to be rewarded according to their merits but growing feelings of insecurity must also be taken into consideration in the HRM reforms.

Relative Decline of the Union Pillar

The last decade has seen the decline of the unionization rate, dropping below 18 per cent in 2009 (MHLW, 2010a). Individualization of contracts and diversification of status limits the effects of collective bargaining. Workers with skills in demand do not need the unions' protection. They are more concerned by their career and employability. Unions have been unable to gain wage increases and their contribution to improvement of employment conditions has been small.

Their strategy during the yearly "Spring Offensive" has shifted toward security of employment since then. However, it is becoming difficult to do so with senior workers with obsolete skills (Nitta, 2009). A shift toward occupation-based unions should be a normal development in view of the growing specialization and higher work mobility. However, so far the development is still limited by the slow rise of external labor markets for many jobs (DeBroux, 2003). It is important for the unions to enroll the non-permanent workers (MHLW, 2010). Although unionization level is still low their potential of growth is not negligible in a period of fluidity of work patterns and status where all workers share concern on access to skills, pay, and pension.

It is to be pointed out, however, that no trend toward an anti-union "unitarism" has emerged. In most large companies they remain an important partner. It had always been said that Japan had a kind of corporatism without labor (Shinoda, 1997). Unions now intend to play a more important role in long-term policy in the tripartite system with employers and government representatives in order to redesign the workplace environment (Nitta, 2009).

Key Challenges facing HRM

Adoption of Diversity Management

Large companies diversify the ports of entry to broaden talent mix but still tend to recruit in the same institutions. Management remains mostly composed from Japanese graduates from a limited number of Japanese universities. Japanese companies cannot remain competitive without attracting qualified people from outside Japan. But optimizing the talent of non-Japanese human resources is still difficult, including those in foreign subsidiaries (Brannen, 2011). Moreover, except for a small number of high-potential employees they often do not yet offer a working environment permitting average women to pursue a career while creating a family. Work–life balance schemes are adopted but the male breadwinner family model is not significantly put into question. It continues to reinforce the lifetime career pattern of male employment and to perpetuate the under-utilization of female talents.

Necessary Reconsideration of Career Patterns

Despite the trend toward specialization too many workers still have generalist-type career patterns. Fewer promotion opportunities are offered, and companies struggle to respond to the career and reward expectations. The removal of the seniority elements renders irrelevant the reward system according to which the higher salary (that could be below their individual productivity) that employees receive in the second part of their career compensates the lower salary (lower than their individual productivity) that they receive during the first part of the career (Lazear, 1979). As a result, in absence of a large external labor market companies run the risk of ending up with employees feeling trapped. This may explain why the level of engagement is lower than that in US companies

(*Gallup Business Journal*, 2013) that offer less job stability. Trapped workers may not only be less productive but they can impede the recruitment of better employees with a higher level of engagement.

New Basis for Management Legitimacy

Japanese employees were always likely to look on their managers as people who had (starting from school) performed better in a meritocratic system (Sugimoto, 2010). So far, employees have accepted their positions in a hierarchy that they acknowledge to be legitimate. As a result they have always willingly acted in accordance with prescribed roles rather than having engaged in a struggle to alter the distribution of power and rewards. This legitimacy is now put into question with management coming from different origins, companies casually terminating relationships and employees accordingly thinking about their individual careers and employability in priority. It could end up with conflicts and a breakdown of cooperation if managers take for granted the legitimacy of the hierarchical social order. Different career and reward expectations require new practices and instruments backed up by different sets of values to reach the right level of engagement and trust that companies expect.

Coping with an Ageing Society

Following Lazear's (1979) assumption, if the retirement age is set correctly the wage sum for the whole career is equal to the marginal product. Companies were able to keep the rationale of their pay policy despite retirement age moving up from 55 to 60 during the last 30 years. But the planned lift of the entitlement age for public pension to 65 years old makes it more challenging. It is all the more true because the flexibility companies' now enjoy to select the elder workers whose skills fit with companies' needs is bound to disappear with the new regulations (Conrad, 2009). From April 2013, employers will be obliged to keep all workers until they reach 61 years of age. The retirement age will gradually increase and, by the end of March 2025, companies will have to keep their workers until they reach 64 years of age (MHLW, 2013).

The cost implications are important but it also creates a moral dilemma. Early retirement is costly and transfers are more difficult because of the loosening of relationships between companies. It pushes for an acceleration of changes in the appraisal and pay system. Because it includes the possibility of a significant wage reduction even retrenchment senior workers consider such policies to be a breach of the psychological contract. It obliges companies to devise training programs in order to make some of the workers more employable and to utilize more extensively and much earlier outplacement services.

Integration of the Atypical Workers

There is an increased vagueness in the horizontal division of labor and in the emergence of sub-categorization of employees. The non-permanent employees cannot be necessarily considered anymore as buffer-type human power.

Companies need skilled, "core" non-permanent employees for a growing array of tasks. However, although they are expected to acquire the same skills and demonstrate the same level of teamwork as permanent employees the gap in remuneration and fringe benefits is wide. Besides the issue of social fairness, it could lead to a moral hazard in teamwork and cause deterioration in organizational efficiency.

Clash of Work Values in a Westernized HRM System

In the HPWS engagement is expected from core employees and not purely utilitarian personal calculation. But the objective is not to reproduce the community of fate. High engagement does not exclude mobility. Linked to employability it is a crucial element of HR cross-fertilization. However, this way of thinking fits with the mindset of a culture where public and private concerns are neatly separated. It may create mistrust and feelings of betrayal in Japan where professional relationships are expected to extend beyond functional purposes. Likewise, self-development and autonomy have always been promoted in Japanese companies but it is in well-defined hierarchically organized frameworks and with subtle social control influencing behavior and attitudes. Teamwork dynamics with empowerment in flat hierarchical structures presuppose a pro-active management of conflicts and an acceptance of diversity of opinion. But "impatience with rule" and high discretion in work organization is still difficult to conciliate with the traditional deep respect for hierarchy and a mindset where humility and self-restraint are considered as virtues.

Role and Importance of Business–HR Partnership

The HR manager is almost never a member of the board of directors but the HR department always played a strategic and integrative role. The HR department is in charge of recruitment and selection and is a key partner in devising strategic HR planning and in designing various HR processes and programs. So, it is directly involved in inter-department transfers of personnel and, through monitoring the rotation system, it always actively participated in career development. Up until the end of the 1990s skill development was done basically under the HR department's aegis. However, while powerful, the corporate HR department was always in close contact with line managers. The line managers were in charge of intra-department moves, of recruitment of non-permanent workers, and moreover, in the selection of expatriates. The HRM corporate department plays only a small role in this respect and in the overall management of foreign operations.

Key Changes in the HR Function

A Response to Career Individualization

The HR function is under pressure to bring financially measurable results. Alignment with investors' interests makes companies reluctant to invest in HR development if return in the short term is uncertain. Moreover, self-development training is bound to become more important in the years to come with the emphasis on employees' self-reliance in career development. Conversely, the needs for assisting systems will increase concurrently. As a result, corporate HR departments move from a management of employees' promotions toward management of individual careers. Companies proceed to an earlier selection of the fast track group. The HR department role is to increase the capability and capacity of the elite members. It has to devise and monitor employability schemes and participate in career design. The role of the HR department will thus be to enhance both the value of the employees and the value of the organization. This is important in order to respond to individual career needs but also to select and nurture future leaders. So, involvement in executive training and coaching is bound to grow furthermore in importance.

Needs for More Sophisticated Service-Related Expertise

The evolution toward profit centers that are line- and department-based reinforces the role of line managers in providing career support, coaching and mentoring but also their role in recruiting permanent and non-permanent employees. But corporate HR plays a growing role as provider of internal customer service. Implementing HR practices (from recruitment to integration) reflecting the larger diversity of human capital in terms of status, career patterns and training needs requires specialized expertise. Corporate HR can provide a career evaluation and consulting service for one specific unit, as well as consequently designing custom-made training programs. HR departments are now being installed with information equipment that facilitates interactive learning under a more codified knowledge management system. At the same time the corporate HR integrative role is also growing with the need of binding together company structures that are submitted to increasingly strong centrifugal forces (MHLW, 2009a).

Changes in the Following Five Years

Responses to the Diversification of Career Patterns

The decentralization of HRM along with cash-flow-based and profit performance at the line and department levels pushes for more recruitment flexibility according to specific needs. Overall permanent employment is unlikely to rise and systematization of the management of the hybrid permanent and non-permanent employees is a priority. Already there are more employees recruited under conditions of no transfer away from their living area, performing only certain types of work, or with shorter and more flexible working hours while having the status of permanent employees (MHLW, 2010). Nowadays, such policies concern mainly female employees but they attract the interest of an increasing number of male employees. As a result, a broadening and deepening of the concept of life–work balance can be expected in the years to come.

It is advocated that the treatment of some segments of non-permanent workers should also move toward a kind of role/competency-based system in order to facilitate their integration into the organization. Some of them should even be incorporated into the permanent group if they have appropriate potential to adapt in a long-term perspective (Nakata and Miyazaki, 2011).

Adaptation of Performance-Based Systems to the Japanese Context

PRP systems directly linked to outcome are credited for boosting performance and creating new dynamics. But in focusing on quantitative outcome and neglecting the fact that they depend most often on uncontrollable factors by individuals they are also accused of being inflexible and of destroying trust. They encourage employees to eschew extra tasks and challenging goals in order to protect their own arena of job responsibilities and circumvent the risks of a bad evaluation. Moreover, in discouraging altruistic behaviors they impose narrow concepts of organizational learning and knowledge creation (Takahashi, 2004).

Companies are likely to shift to holistic systems that are considered to be more consistent with Japanese HRM traditions of performance and fairness. Performance appraisal is increasingly based not only on the results of performance attained but also on the process of demonstrating abilities that contributed to the performance (Nakamura, 2006).

It is pointed out that adoption of a knowledge management system completely based on low-context communication could be detrimental to the organizations (Hentschel and Haghirian, 2011). Maintaining the constant formal and informal exchange of knowledge inside the entire organization is necessary in order to retain the meaning of the communication. In what the Japanese call *genbashugi* (field presence) the middle managers are in constant personal touch with their subordinates. They play a key role in nurturing the talent of the younger generations and encouraging knowledge creation. This could be lost if they were just becoming transmission links between the field and top management under narrowly defined management by objectives (MBO) schemes.

The Need for Cross-Cultural Skills

The task to come is to extend the knowledge management philosophy outside of Japan. It requires the mastering of cross-cultural communications in view of the persisting cleavage of corporate values and beliefs. Therefore, they have to develop suitable cross-culture training programs and design international HR recruitment and career development policy and practices suitable to non-Japanese people (Brannen, 2011). But they also have to train their Japanese managers so that they can optimize their global relational capital capabilities and select their dispatched personnel abroad in taking account of that factor.

Talent Management

More explicit career fast tracks have already been created that single out certain employees for elite development as soon as they are recruited. It can be expected that many companies introduce remuneration and promotion systems that increase the opportunities for younger employees to enter into positions of responsibility.

Core employees can expect long-term employment security but with greater uncertainty concerning remuneration and advancement. The trend toward professionalization is likely to accelerate in the line of what NEC (Meyer-Ohle, 2009) and Nissan (Gupta and Muthukumar, 2011) are doing. Some employees will be given the opportunity to nurture higher specialized capabilities and their treatment will be furthermore upgraded in the organization.

With employability and empowerment higher mobility of managerial and technical resources can be expected. It remains to be seen how companies will utilize HRM as competitive advantage to attract and retain the best employees. Recruitment policy used to be based on name value but it becomes difficult for companies to stick to relatively uniform employment practices. They need to devise new, attractive working conditions and career opportunities in order to position themselves as employers of choice.

Case Study: Nissan Motor Company

The Nissan Motor Company HRM reforms focus on many points that have been at the center of the transformation process in other companies during the last two decades. The case highlights the merits and drawbacks and the difficulties in implementing reforms. At the beginning of the 1990s recruitment and selection policy was very traditional. A high percentage of Nissan's managers and especially engineers were coming from a very limited number of Japanese universities (Pelata, 2003). In response to production over-capacity Nissan started at that time to decrease the headcount of permanent employees. It limited the recruitment of new employees and started early retirement strategies. To control the production costs it adopted a policy similar to that of their rivals, that is, it utilized a growing number of contract employees on site.

While smoothing the wage curve of senior employees, Nissan also took stopgap measures such as temporary work stoppage on some of the sites and negotiated with the union the renouncement to the yearly across-the-board "base-up" pay increase. In a longer-term perspective the company introduced the basis of a more merit-based system that offers faster promotion to the best performers and creates larger wage differentials according to performance. So, when Nissan concluded an alliance with Renault in March 1999, the foundations had been laid to adopt HRM reforms more rapidly and on a larger scale.

In the line of practices adopted by other companies such as Sony, the number of board members was reduced from 37 to 10 and external directors were nominated. Seniority would not be anymore the sole criteria for membership. To rejuvenate the board, new directors were selected relatively lower in the managerial pecking order (Gupta and Muthukumar, 2011). The company did not proceed through straight lay-off but conducted a large-scale early retirement program. About 15 per cent of the total worldwide workforce was asked to retire, to accept a part-time status or to be transferred to a subsidiary. Because of the low recruitment during the 1990s, employees' average workforce age had significantly risen in Japan, with labor cost growing accordingly (Pelata, 2003).

Senior employees were strongly opposed to measures that they considered to be a breach of the psychological contract. They fought against them through the union but it ended up with the departure (sometimes forced through unfavorable transfers) of most of them in a relatively short time. This resulted in a drastic decline of total labor cost permitting a rapid improvement of the key financial ratio, an objective considered to be essential for making the reforms credible in the minds of the key stakeholders (Gupta and Muthukumar, 2011).

The new leadership instilled a culture of extremely transparent, open, precise and factual communications. The organization was divided into profit-management units with clear and ambitious objectives. Very precise financial performance control instruments were adopted in the different units and departments in order to cultivate a culture of quantitative target-based commitment (Hauter, 2001). It went along with a differentiated HRM policy in terms of wages, bonuses and fringe benefits based on the respective contribution of each unit to the company performance. Labor costs were not to be considered as fixed costs anymore but rather as variable costs. The goal was to create a self-reliant managerial model, with a strongly performance-oriented pay system including the overseas divisions that rewarded outstanding performers significantly higher than the average ones (Pelata, 2003). However, employees were requested at the same time in order to communicate across functions, borders and hierarchical lines. Mechanisms using multimedia devices were put in place to reinforce personal and direct contacts at all levels all over the world and evaluation criteria included teamwork contribution (Donnelly and Donnelly, 2005).

Policies were put in place in order to provide women with more career opportunities. It had to go along with the recognition that the issue of work–life balance is not a "woman issue". So, Nissan started attempts to change the traditional culture of overtime in encouraging employees to adopt a more balanced working life. It was acknowledged that Nissan was not suffering from a shortage of internal talents but from the rigidity and bureaucratization of its culture. So, younger managers relatively low in the hierarchy were selected for leading important projects (Pelata, 2003). Another new practice was the recruitment of specialists at mid-career. Nissan started to scout for marketing, finance and engineering talents in Japan and abroad and gave them important responsibilities in the organization from the start (Hauter, 2001).

In the line of the need for differentiation in recruiting policy Nissan began to offer to a selected group of new graduates a better monetary reward from the start and the opportunity to make a career without any seniority-based impediment. It went along with an internal "self-career" system with employees being offered the opportunity to apply to jobs offers all over the company. This was linked to the adoption of a pro-active succession planning policy giving high priority to the training of the future elite (Gupta and Muthukumar, 2011).

Assessment of the results of the reforms is mixed. Symbolic of the slow pace of change in those respects in the immense majority of Japanese companies, there are still few female managers and the recruitment channels, especially of the engineering staff, have not significantly enlarged in Japan.

Conversely, the reforms are widely recognized to have not only permitted the turnaround of the company but to have created a more open and dynamic culture. Nissan is now arguably one of the most innovative and profitable carmakers in Japan, putting on the market a larger range of more attractive models. The international strategy is becoming increasingly more ambitious.

Conclusion

Japanese companies' HRM approaches are increasingly consistent with flexible, high-performance work systems (HPWS). A more strategic role for HRM managers and HRM departments is emerging. Growing professionalization and career diversification are important steps toward a departure from the internal labor market logic. Isomorphism is fading away. Even in the same industry companies adopt differentiated HRM practices. Different kinds of occupational rules and human resource practices are adopted that are based on new forms of labor contract, recruitment practices or career formation patterns that are increasingly of disruptive types. It can be argued that the companies are liable in the longer term to put into question the traditional social contracts and labor stratifications.

However, so far, the changes toward Japanese-style "flexicurity" have proceeded in a typically orderly manner. Most companies continue to stick to the traditional corporate governance model with boards composed from managers promoted from the inside. The tenets of the stakeholder model remain in place, albeit with more emphasis on Return on Equity (ROE) and Return on Investment (ROI). Therefore, it may be too early to tell that the specificity of the Japanese HRM and employment institutions and practices is over, despite their transformations. Considering the entrenchment of the HRM practices within Japanese society (Matanle, 2003), and their interdependence with other managerial practices, notably related to the production process and knowledge management, market-oriented reforms have to be conciliated with organization-driven systems.

The pragmatic approach of Japanese companies concerning PRP systems and other quantitative appraisal methods is typical of their concern for keeping the management system stable. They do not want to replace the secured worker with the unsecured, frightened one. They want to nurture a talented elite group of professional managers who have a high level of engagement but they do not want mercenaries.

Nevertheless, it is true that contradictions and dysfunctions appear not only in the organization but also at the societal level. The basis of welfare corporatism is now largely obsolete. The schemes are costly and they absorb important resources but they do not fit with the needs of the new generations. Still they have not yet found how to replace them with appropriate incentives.

Business structures, institutional frameworks and a number of socio-cultural attributes remain important constraints. As a result some human resources are still neglected or not utilized optimally, notably foreigners and women but also Japanese people with a different mindset. The vicious circle impeding the full integration of women in the HR system is particularly disastrous for companies and society.

Likewise, the internal labor market has proved not only to be less efficient than before but also to have external, maligned societal effects. Not only does it create legions of trapped employees with low engagement but it is also instrumental in creating "lost generations" of people who, because they have not been recruited as permanent workers just after graduation, are denied access to training in the first stage of their professional life and are likely to have difficulties in finding jobs in good conditions for the rest of their lives. The problem is compounded by the absence in Japan of vocational schools of the kind found in Germany. However, the legitimacy of the internal labor market is such and it still fits so well with the integrated production model that Japanese companies want to preserve as a basis of sustainable competitive advantages that it can only be reformed very gradually.

This last point is symptomatic of the elusive character and the unpredictability of the process and outcome of the reforms. Japanese companies are looking for practices and policies that ideally combine effectiveness, efficiency and fairness. It cannot be denied that there is a dynamics at work but reforms reveal to be a zig-zagging, lengthy and difficult process.

Useful Websites

The Japan Institute for Labour Policy and Training: www.jil.go.jp

Japan Management Association: www.jma.or.jp

Japanese Trade Union Confederation (JTUC—Rengo): www.jtuc-rengo

Nihon Keidanren: www.keidanren.or.jp

Works Institute: www.works-i.com

References

Aoki, M. (1988) *Information, Incentives, and Bargaining in the Japanese Economy*. Cambridge: Cambridge University Press.

Araki, T. (2002) *Labor and Employment Law in Japan*. Tokyo: The Japan Institute of Labor.

Atkinson, J. (1985) *Flexibility, Uncertainty and Manpower Management*, IMS Report No. 89. Brighton: Institute of Manpower Studies.

Becker, G. S. (1964) *Human Capital*. New York: Columbia University Press.

Brannen, M. Y. (2011) "Global talent opportunities and learning for the future: Pressing concerns and opportunities for growth for Japanese multinationals", in R. Bebenroth and T. Kania (eds), *Challenges of Human Resources in Japan*, pp. 124–130. Abingdon: Routledge.

Conrad, H. (2009) "From seniority to performance principle: The evolution of pay practices in Japanese firms since the 1990s", Oxford University Press, downloaded from ssjj.oxford-journals.org, 22 January 2011.

DeBroux, P. (2003) *Human Resource Management in Japan: changes and uncertainties*. Aldershot: Ashgate Publishers.

Donnelly, T and Donnelly, T. (2005) "Renault-Nissan: A marriage of necessity", *European Business Review* 15(5): 428–40.

Dore, R. (1973) *British Factory–Japanese Factory*. London: Allen and Unwin.

Fujimoto, T. (2007) *Competing to Be Really, Really Good*. Tokyo: International House of Japan.

Gallup Business Journal (2013) Grim News for Japan's Managers, business.journal.gallup.com/content/17242/Grim-News-Japan's-Managers.aspx, accessed 5 February 2013.

Gupta, R. and Muthukumar, R. (2011) *"HR Restructuring at Nissan"*. Donthanapally: IBS Center for Management Research.

Hauter, F. (2001) "Carlos Ghosn: En situation de crise, la transparence s'impose '", *Le Figaro Magazine*, 2 July, pp. 28–29.

Hentschel, B. and Haghirian, P. (2010) "Nonaka revisited: Can Japanese companies sustain their knowledge management processes in the 21st century?", in P. Haghirian (ed.) *Innovation and Change in Japanese Management*. Basingstoke: Palgrave Macmillan, pp. 199–220.

Herbes, C. (2010) "Restructuring of Japanese enterprises – Programs for a special institutional environment", in P. Haghirian (ed.) *Innovation and Change in Japanese Management*. Basingstoke: Palgrave Macmillan, pp. 15–38.

Hirano, M. (2011) "Diversification of employment categories in Japanese firms and its functionality", in R. Bebenroth and T. Kanai (eds) *Challenges of Human Resources in Japan*, pp. 188–209. Abingdon: Routledge.

Hirschmeyer, J. and T. Yui. (2006) *Development of Japanese Business*. London: Routledge.

Hisano, K. (2007) "Employment in transition: Changes in Japan since the 1980s", in J. Burgess and J. Connell (eds) *Globalisation and Work in Asia*, pp. 275–293. London: Chandos Publishing.

Sueki, N. (2009) *21 seiki nihon no chinginzo wo egaku*. Tokyo: Nihon Seisansei Honbu [*Description of the Wage Structure in 21st Century Japan*].

Ishida, M. and Sato, A. (2011) "The evolution of Japan's Human-Resource Management", in H. Miyoshi and Y. Nakata (eds) *Have Japanese Firms Changed?*, pp. 70–87. Basingstoke: Palgrave Macmillan.

Itami H (2011) "Restoring Japanese-style management rudder". JapanEchoWeb, No. 5, February–March 2011, www.japanechoweb.jp/jew0518, accessed 28 March 2011.

Koike, K. (1994) *Human Resource Development*. Tokyo: The Japan Institute of Labour.

Lazear, E. (1979) "Why is there mandatory retirement?", *The Journal of Political Economy* 81(6): 1,261–84.

Matanle, P. (2003) *Japanese Capitalism and Modernity in a Global Era: Re-fabricating lifetime employment relations*. London & New York: Routledge-Curzon.

Meyer-Ohle, H. (2009) *Japanese Workplaces in Transition*. Basingstoke: Palgrave Macmillan.

Ministry of Health, Labour and Welfare (MHLW) (2009a) *Basic Survey on Labour Unions*. Tokyo.

Ministry of Health, Labour and Welfare (MHLW) (2009b) *Basic Survey on Wage Structure*. Tokyo.

Ministry of Health, Labour and Welfare (MHLW) (2010) *White Paper on the Labour Economy*. Tokyo.

Ministry of Health, Labour and Welfare (MHLW) (2013) *Amendment to the Old People's Employment Security Act*, www.mhlw.go.jp/english/orgnew-info/2012.html, accessed February 5, 2013.

Morishima, M. (1995) "Embedding HRM in a social contract", *British Journal of Industrial Relations* 33 (4): 617–40.

Nakakubo, H. (2007) "Phase III of the Japanese Equal Employment Opportunity Act", *Japan Labor Review* 4(3): Summer: 9–17.

Nakamura, K. (2006) *Seika Shugi no Jijitsu*. Tokyo: Toyo Keizai Shinposha [*The Reality of Performance-based Management*].

Nakata, Y. and Miyazaki, S. (2011) "Have Japanese engineers changed?" in H. Miyoshi and Y. Nakata (eds) *Have Japanese Firms Changed?*, pp. 88–108. Basingstoke: Palgrave Macmillan.

Nikkeiren (1995) *The Current Labor Economy in Japan*. Tokyo: Japan Federation of Employers' Associations.

Nitta, M. (2009) *Nihonteki Koyo System*. Tokyo: Nakanishiya Shuppan.

Nonaka, I. and Takeuchi, H. (1995) *The Knowledge-creating Company: How Japanese companies create the dynamics of innovation*. New York: Oxford University Press.

Pelata, P. (2003) "Nissan: le nouveau et le renouveau", *Seminaire Ressources technologiques et Innovation*, www.ecole.org, accessed 23 March 2012.

Salmon, J. (2003) "HRM in Japan", in P. S. Budhwar (ed.) *Managing Human Resources in Asia-Pacific*. London: Routledge.

Shinoda, T. (1997) "Rengo and policy participation: Japanese-style neocorporatism?", in M. Sako and H. Sato (eds) *Japanese Labour and Management in Transition: Diversity, flexibility and participation*. London: Routledge, pp. 187–224.

Sugimoto, Y. (2010) *An Introduction to Japanese Society*. Cambridge: Cambridge University Press.

Takahashi, N. (2004) *Kyomo no Seikashugi* (Misconceptions of performance-based pay system). Tokyo: Nikkei Business Publications, Inc.

Wolff, L. (2010) "Lifelong employment, labor law and the lost decade: The end of a job for life in Japan", in P. Haghirian (ed.) *Innovation and Change in Japanese Management*. Basingstoke: Palgrave Macmillan, pp. 77–9.

5 Human Resource Management in Hong Kong

ANDREW CHAN AND DEREK MAN

Introduction

To understand the current challenges and future prospects of HRM in Hong Kong, we take a historical perspective in this chapter and review Hong Kong's wider cultural, social and economic context since the 1980s. We recount the unfolding of HR practices as the city evolved from an enclave economy to a metropolitan business and financial centre. According to recent statements by officials, the vision of Hong Kong is to re-position itself as the world's most service-oriented, knowledge-based economy that capitalises on its strength in value-added producer services to complement the growth of the Chinese economy.

We agree with Budhwar, Schuler and Sparrow (2009) that HRM practices are largely driven by external factors – in Hong Kong, the most important factors are economic conditions, company size and the owner's background and culture. In spite of much discussion over the aims of HRM in academic literature, we consider for the purpose of this chapter that HRM in Hong Kong comprises a set of practices followed by employers in order to maintain relationships with employees.

Preferences and shifts in company policies, regarding human power and succession planning, recruitment, training, performance evaluation and compensation management are predominantly determined by whether the owner's business is prospering, struggling or merely surviving. In a free economy like Hong Kong, where more than 90 per cent of employers are small enterprises, HR policies and practices have a direct causal relationship with business realities. It makes sense, therefore, to maintain an optimum relationship with employees through versatile HR practices.

This chapter sketches a profile of the key features influencing the development of HRM in Hong Kong. For employers in Hong Kong, HRM refers to management practices used for regulating relationships with employees in sizable organisations, including Chinese family-owned business conglomerates, the Hong Kong civil service, quasi-governmental organisations and subsidiaries of foreign companies in Hong Kong. This chapter is organised into four parts. We first trace the development of HRM in Hong Kong during the last thirty-two years in order to explicate what happens in workplace employee relations today. We then account for the role of HRM in different business settings. This is followed by a discussion of selected contingent factors that impinge on the development of some key HR practices in the unique setting of Hong Kong. Lastly, we review the prospects and challenges facing HRM in Hong Kong today.

The Development of HRM in Hong Kong

Early Service-Base (1980s)

During the 1980s, growth of manufacturing in Hong Kong slowed as small-scale manufacturing companies faced protectionism from advanced economies and shortage of affordable land and factory space within the city. To maintain their cost advantage, these companies started relocating their labour-intensive production facilities to China where land and labour were inexpensive and abundant. Their logistics and support functions, however, were kept in Hong Kong. Thus small companies with a dozen employees in Hong Kong are able to comfortably oversee the running of a factory with several production lines and hundreds of workers in China. At the same time, Hong Kong gradually built itself up as a trade support centre. It became a hub for traders and business people looking for financial services such as seed money from merchant banks and help from investment banks for raising capital by initial public offerings (IPOs). Taking advantage of China's open door policy, many companies engaged in re-export activities to and from China in the early eighties, and Hong Kong regained its role as a very active *entrepôt*.

The Sino–British Joint Declaration that announced the reversion of sovereignty over Hong Kong to China thirteen years later was signed in 1984. After that Hong Kong's social, economic and cultural integration with China gathered momentum, which created uncertainty among the people and led to high emigration, causing a brain-drain of managerial and professional personnel to countries like Australia, Canada, New Zealand and Singapore, especially in the ten years between 1984 and 1994. This resulted in a widespread surge in real wages and increased costs in the service sector from 1986 onwards (Chen, 2000).

The completely different patterns of development in service and manufacturing sectors posed two HRM issues. First, as manufacturing companies split their operations between Hong Kong and South China, they needed a specific set of HRM practices to optimise employee relationships as they had to deal fairly in the midst of intricate issues of workplace diversity, pay differentials and differences between legal systems in the two places. Second, the thriving service sector demanded more skilled human resources than the residual labour-intensive manufacturing sector, and this created a scarcity of labour. A falling birth rate in Hong Kong, outward emigration by the middle class and tightened border controls on illegal entrants from China added to the problem (Chen, 2000; Chiu and Levin, 1993).

The Hong Kong government at that time used various measures to address the critical issue of labour scarcity. These included the setting up of a quasi-govern-mental body, the Vocational Training Council, in 1982. The council was respon-sible for identifying human power and training needs and providing training in industrial, technical and management skills to the Hong Kong workforce. This was followed by expansion of tertiary education opportunities for secondary school graduates, with a target of placing 18 per cent of the eligible age group in degree or sub-degree programs. The government also launched successive labour importation schemes throughout the early 1990s for the purpose of addressing labour shortages in specific industries (Ng and Wright, 2002).

At the company level, more effective channels of recruitment were explored. Newspaper advertisements was the most often used recruitment method. Interest-ingly, Chinese newspapers were generally used for lower level employment while local English newspapers were used for senior level employment. This segrega-tion has continued into the 2000s. Employment agencies became more popular, and executive search firms came to be used for top level vacancies, at least by larger companies, which also started to invest more in training and development in order to retain employees and reduce turnover. Relatively more structured suc-cession planning and promotion from entry-level positions became slightly better accepted practices among private enterprises.

Kirkbride and Tang (1989) provided a general review of HRM practices in Hong Kong based on a survey conducted in 1988 of 361 companies. They concluded that HRM policies in Hong Kong were not very sophisticated compared with developed countries. In-house training focused narrowly on technical and voca-tional abilities while management skills received scant attention. Although formal appraisal systems were common, they were often accompanied by employee collusion and inadequate appraisal training. In terms of time spent on HR issues, respondents in that survey reported spending most of their time on recruitment, followed by employee relations, human power planning, pay administration, training and appraisal. The importance of recruitment again reflected the scarcity of labour in the society at the time.

Full Service-Base (1990s)

The 1990s saw Hong Kong successfully positioning itself as an international commercial, business and financial centre. The de-industrialisation of Hong Kong was followed by a re-commercialisation process that saw growth in financial, banking and business sub-sectors throughout this decade. According to govern-ment economists, more than 80 per cent of Hong Kong's gross domestic product (GDP) comes from commercial and service-oriented activities, one of the highest percentages in the world. On the other hand, during this decade, manufacturing shrank below 10 per cent of GDP (Chen, 2000). Enright, Scott and Leung (1999) argued that Hong Kong focused on developing value-added producer services that supported production of goods and services by others, as opposed to consumption services. As producer services were subject to increasing returns to scale and attracted further services to cluster together, it became logical for more multinational corporations (MNCs) to choose Hong Kong as their regional headquarters. During the 1990s, more than 2,000 MNCs had regional offices or headquarters in Hong Kong, including more than 200 Fortune 500 companies.

Another feature of Hong Kong's service sector is its external orientation, as a service hub for China and Asia. Repercussions of the 4 June 1989 crackdown on student demonstrators in Beijing haunted HR managers well into the 1990s in the run-up to reversion to China of sovereignty over Hong Kong. During this period, there still was considerable labour shortage in many sectors, and it was intensified by substantial outward migration of professionals and other workers. It was at this time that companies of all sizes began to provide more internal training and more promotion opportunities.

On a macro level, the government set up the Employee Retraining Board in 1992 to deal with the imbalance between demand and availability of workers for industrial and service jobs. As the business situation became more complex with globalisation, rapid environmental changes and increased competition, a closer partnership between HRM and firm strategy became more accepted, and this paved the way for HR managers to play a more strategic role in their organisations.

In 1995, the government established the Equal Opportunities Commission with the aim of protecting individuals against prejudices in terms of age, gender, religion, family status and physical or mental handicaps. Anti-discrimination ordinances on gender (1996), disability (1996) and family status (1997) were passed. These have implications for employers in areas of recruitment (such as newspaper job advertisements) and the provision of access to facilities and benefits in the workplace. This has kept Hong Kong's labour regulations in line with international norms in terms of workplace amenities and employment standards.

HR practices have become more sophisticated to meet the needs of the increasingly services dominated economy. For instance, Ng (1997) noted that increased training and internal promotion were being provided to junior staff. Snape *et al.* (1998) found the use of performance appraisal to be more widespread in Hong Kong than in Britain, but that the process tended to be more directive and less participative in Hong Kong. McCormick (2001) rightly pointed out the need to use more term-based appraisals to suit the local collectivist and group culture.

However, a survey of more than 1,000 medium and large companies in 1991 showed that only 33 per cent employed full-time HRM personnel. Of these, 3.9 per cent were appointed at a strategic job level (HKVTC, 1992). Two subsequent large scale surveys in 1995 (see Tang, Lai and Kirkbride, 1995; Cheung, 1998) conducted by the Hong Kong Institute of HRM showed the limited influence of HR in Hong Kong companies on strategic issues such as human power planning, changes in work culture of the organisation and the introduction of new technologies. These two surveys showed that while HRM was becoming more important, it still played a limited role in a strategic sense. This perception has since changed, as we shall see later.

Restructuring Phase and a Time of Turbulence (2000s)

In 1997, Hong Kong reintegrated with China as a Special Administrative Region, retaining its laws and institutions. The Asian Financial Crisis of 1997 struck a huge blow to Hong Kong's externally oriented service-based economy. The post-1997 crisis environment in Asia was one of rapid globalisation. Traditional inter-firm relations were reshuffled, and the industrial environment became highly competitive (Kidd, Li and Richter, 2001). Other complex issues also emerged. Labour importation schemes were introduced to bring more skilled labour into Hong Kong to address the brain-drain before the hand-over. Seeing that the political environment was stable after the hand-over, emigrants started returning to Hong Kong. Unfortunately, the financial crisis and a depressed property market created a very unfavorable situation for employment. The outbreak of Severe Acute Respiratory Syndrome (SARS) in 2003 further aggravated the problem. The seasonally adjusted unemployment rate increased from 7.2 per cent in the fourth quarter of 2002 to 8.7 per cent in May–July 2003. HRM faced tremendous challenges during this phase.

Companies in Hong Kong painfully adjusted to this new business environment with revised HR measures (Cheung *et al.*, 2000; Fosh *et al.*, 1999). They became more cautious in recruitment and moved towards performance-based compensation. Companies also needed to address new HR issues. The Mandatory Provident Fund (MPF) scheme was introduced in 2000. Under this scheme, both employers and employees are required to contribute to employees' retirement benefits. It was a belated government response to the call for provision of basic employee benefits for the general labour force. Similar schemes have been set up much earlier in other Asian countries such as Malaysia (in 1951) and Singapore (in 1955). However, the MPF in Hong Kong has retained features of high risk and a privatised nature (Ng and Wright, 2002). At the same time, its introduction in the midst of an economic downturn drew criticism that it represented an extra burden on the cost of running a business. Due to a tougher business environment with increased competition and operational costs, organisation downsizing, employee retrenchment and labour disputes became more common phenomena. Chu and Siu (2001) reported how some small companies in Hong Kong faced the crisis by first cutting staff development funds and wages, using layoffs only as the last resort, in order to try to prevent employee morale from declining. On the other hand, industrial conflicts in large companies were still notable. The more prominent ones were the pilot pay dispute at Cathay Pacific Airlines in 1999 followed by labour disputes, pay cuts and redundancies at Pacific Century CyberWorks Ltd in 2002.

Being majority Chinese, who are mostly industrious, versatile and resilient, the people of Hong Kong are well known for their ability to survive even under great economic turbulence. With the passing of SARS in 2003 came a time of economic recovery. However, organisations, having survived the down time with a reduced labour force and the cutting of numerous jobs, were now more reluctant to go back to the previous mode and scale of operations. They were much more cautious in hiring and tried to have fewer people doing more. This put greater emphasis on selecting the right employees and expanding their job scopes through training and development. The bottom-line has become the key issue and HRM is viewed as more of a strategic tool to enhance company performance. The concept of strategic HRM has become much more prevalent, especially in large and multinational corporations. More companies adopted strategic HRM than traditional HRM. Training was often provided to employees to address changes in products, new technology and organisational re-engineering. Results-oriented performance appraisal with targets to meet was more widely used at all levels of staff. There was also more outsourcing of HR functions, particularly in training, development and recruitment. This amply reflected the vibrant environment and the adaptation of HRM to be tied to the bottom-line.

Riding the Next Wave (Beyond 2012)

Now Hong Kong's economy relies primarily on services, comprising the four pillar industries identified by the Chief Executive in his policy address in 2007: finance, logistics, tourism, and information services (Tsang, 2007). Given the nature of these industries and their inter-dependence with the rest of the world, Hong Kong was by no means immune to the big waves created by the financial tsunami in 2008. The downgrading of US fiduciary instruments by Standards and Poor in 2011 further shocked the whole business world. Although nobody can predict for certain when and in what form the next big wave will strike, it must be accepted that the times are turbulent and that ripples and changes are here to stay. It is also predicted that new challenges in HRM will continue to emerge. The foreseeable challenges are, among many, changes that are brought about by increased globalisation and corporate transparency, continual legislative intervention and government policy involvement in employee welfare, changing demographics, an ageing population and the diversity of the workforce. All these changes will have significant and long-lasting implications for HRM in Hong Kong.

Continuing globalisation is generating more opportunities but also, at the same time, more competition and vulnerability. Hiring the right people and retaining talent are challenges given the mobility of the workforce. Job descriptions have to be much more flexible and dynamic. Employees have to constantly expand and upgrade their skill sets in order to deal with the latest developments in both knowledge and technology. Recruitment, training and development, remuneration and benefits all have to be strategically linked in order to attract and retain the right talent. Outsourcing and efficient utilisation of resources, particularly human capital management, has to be high on the priority list. A strong correlation has been found between human capital and economic development (Hart and Tian, 2009). Not only does HRM have to decide what functions are to be outsourced, but it also has to manage the expectations from the outsourced functions. It should, however, be cautioned that aspects of HRM like talent management and employee relations should not be outsourced.

Evidence of legislation, that is, government policy initiatives, affecting HRM has been very apparent and this trend is likely to continue. Launching of the

Qualifications Framework (QF) in Hong Kong in 2008 stresses the importance of life-long learning. Organisations and professional bodies are taking the issue of training and development much more seriously. Licence and membership renewal for some professions is now contingent upon practitioners undergoing continued professional development (CPD) courses for a minimum number of hours per year. Such requirements have prompted HR managers to put in more thoughts into training and development programs that they may have to go through for accreditation by designated authorities. In the same year, the racial discrimination ordinance was promulgated to protect ethnic minorities, particularly the South Asians in Hong Kong. The minimum wage law in Hong Kong was introduced in May 2011. Controversies on operational issues like whether employees are entitled to be paid for lunch and rest time continue to be debated. On the one hand, increased operational cost is definitely an issue. On the other hand, organisations are also worried about their reputations as responsible and ethical employers. Another government initiative in the pipeline is the proposal for a privatised medical system. It is likely that medical benefits traditionally paid by employers will be shared by employees. The benefits program may be re-structured to operate on a cost-sharing basis. The percentage of compulsory contribution or the cap in the MPF scheme may also be amended to better protect employees' retirement benefits. As a consequence, the cost of operations may go further up for employers.

We are also moving towards times of unusual demographics. On the one hand, the working population is ageing. On the other, the arrival of the new generation – Generation Y, Millennials, Netizens or whatever we call them – into the workplace has resulted in interesting dynamics and management issues. This is not to say that there never was in the history a generation gap and confrontations between different generations at the workplace, but the reality is that the gap or transition has never been so huge and multifaceted as it is now. Technological changes have brought about drastic differences in mentality, value systems and behaviours of the baby-boomers and Generation Y (Erickson, 2009; Hewlett, Sherbin and Sumberg, 2009). Communication, for one, is no longer relying on traditional means of face-to-face encounters. Instantaneous and electronic means of communication have revolutionised the way that recruitment and appraisals are done. More timely and spontaneous feedback has to be given. HRM work has to be undertaken by immediate supervisors and line managers also, implying the need for more training to be offered by the HR department. In addition, more generous career development opportunities have to be offered in order to retain the highly mobile and impatient youngsters.

We are indeed at a time and stage when we are facing unprecedented changes and challenges. While the role of HRM is to help a business succeed through its people, HR professionals must be able to ride the waves and survive the turbulence in order to carry out their missions and deliver results. They must possess the correct combinations of competencies in order to be recognised and taken seriously. According to a global Human Resources Competency Study (HRCS) conducted by Brockbank and Ulrich (2003), six competencies that deal with both people and business (namely, credible activist, culture and change steward, talent manager/ organisational designer, strategy architect, operational executor and business ally) are required. The essence is that HR managers must go deeper into the business and be a real part of it. They must be able to understand the key drivers of the business, in addition to considering views of the employees. Its role in different business settings is, therefore, a fundamental concept not to be overlooked.

The Role of HRM in Different Business Settings

Next we examine the HRM function and the unique sets of issues that HRM has faced in different business settings in Hong Kong. We characterise these changes by looking at a spectrum of relative degrees of HRM partnership that underpinned HR policies and practices – from strategic partnership on one end to pragmatic administration at the other. This relative continuum of HRM involvement in business strategy is attributable to the size and ownership of firms. We outline the contours of HRM partnership found in two types of firms in Hong Kong: small and medium enterprises, and multinational corporations.

Small and Medium Enterprises

As in other Asian economies, a dual labour market exists in Hong Kong (Ng and Wright, 2002), made up of a primary sector and a secondary sector. Large private firms, the civil service and the quangos constitute the primary sector while small and medium enterprises (SMEs) constitute the secondary sector. SMEs (with fewer than 100 employees in manufacturing and fewer than 50 employees in non-manufacturing enterprises) make up the majority of businesses in Hong Kong. In March 2011 there were about 299,000 SMEs in Hong Kong. They accounted for more than 98 per cent of the total business units and provided job opportunities to more than 1.2 million persons, about 48 per cent of total employment (excluding civil service). Most of the SMEs were in import/export and wholesale trade, followed by the retail industry. They accounted for more than 50 per cent of SMEs in Hong Kong and represented about one half of SME employment (HKISD, 2011).

Compared with the primary sector, HRM practices in the secondary sector are ad hoc, much less structured and less formalised. Because of the small size, these firms have lean regimens that are able to manage only the sheer essentials of what may be called the core HRM functions. According to Cheung (2001), most SMEs provide limited on-the-job training to their employees as these employees can move around easily in Hong Kong's free labour market. To retain employees, firms generally resort to a high pay strategy. This decision partly leads to a high-cost structure in these firms, and it greatly reduces their competitiveness in times of economic adversity.

To summarise, HRM plays only a minimal role in the overall management of SMEs. HRM is mainly non-strategic and administration focused and has low influence on a firm's operations as far as small companies in Hong Kong are concerned.

Multinational Corporations

In June 2010, 1,285 companies had their regional headquarters in Hong Kong (Hong Kong Census and Statistics Department, 2010). The majority of them came from the United States, Japan and the United Kingdom. China has moved upward in the list recently. The major lines of business were wholesale and retail trade, and business services.

In HRM, MNCs need to deal with expatriation, repatriation, adjustment and adaptation of home-based practices to blend with local norms and the particular laws and regulations of the host nation. As MNCs are relatively more experienced in managing HR globally, the role of their HRM functions is more strategically oriented compared with other companies in Hong Kong. Most often cited in literature are MNCs' well-managed management training programs and their structured, performance-based reward systems (Dowling, Welch and Schuler, 1999).

Research has consistently pointed to the differences between HRM practices followed by foreign firms and local firms operating in Hong Kong (Tsui and Lai, 2009). For instance, Shaw *et al.* (1993) found that British and American firms were more likely than local firms to use formal performance appraisal and technically sound methods of job evaluation. Ng and Chiu (1997) found that British and American firms were more likely to adopt women-friendly HR practices. Ngo *et al.* (1998) extended the comparison to Japanese firms and found that they were more likely to adopt seniority-based compensation than local Hong Kong firms but had no differences in provision of training and development, or in retention-oriented compensation. Fields, Chan and Akhtar (2000) found that foreign firms tended to spend more effort on securing and retaining managers. Contrary to the above, McGraw (2001), however, found relatively minor differences between the HR practices of local and foreign firms and supported a global convergence of HR practices.

Contingent Factors Shaping HRM

At the beginning of this chapter, we referred to Budhwar, Schuler and Sparrow (2009) who suggested a way forward to research international HRM practices. There, the factors that affect HRM practices in any country or culture are categorised into national factors, organisational strategies and policies, and other contingent variables. As we trace the historical development of HRM in Hong Kong, three such contingent variables stand out as influential in shaping the present state of HRM practices: legal and institutional factors, the China factor and globalisation.

Legal and Institutional Factors

The free market principles underlying the economy, coupled with the weak bargaining power of labour unions and the Chinese culture of paternalism engendered what Ng and Wright (2002) talked of as institutional permissiveness in the workplace. Institutional permissiveness refers to loose and informal regulatory institutions in the labour market that help maintain harmonious industrial relations. This is reflected in the relatively weak legal regulations. The Hong Kong government has so far regulated the labour market and employment mainly through the Employment Ordinance of Hong Kong. Although we see an increasing trend of government involvement, intervention is still on the mild side, compared with most Western countries. Introduction of the MPF scheme and the minimum wage law seem to be the strictest regulations introduced thus far.

According to government statistics, there were 824 registered trade unions in Hong Kong in 2010. Of these, only 107 unions had declared a membership of more than 1,000 (Registry of Trade Unions, Hong Kong Labour Department, 2011). The role of trade unions in Hong Kong has remained weak. Snape and Chan (1999) offer three reasons for this: the small size of establishments in manufacturing and private sector service organisations, cultural resistance of workers towards joining unions and openly challenging their employers, and employers' hostility towards unions.

Surveys have shown that the role of unions in pay negotiations in the private sector has been limited (Cheung, 1998, 2001; Tang, Lai and Kirkbride, 1995). Instead of work-related issues, unions engage mostly in activities outside of the workplace, such as organising recreational and social activities, and providing educational and health services to members. However, collective bargaining has become more common after the Asian Financial Crisis. Several high-profile strikes were reported in large private companies, such as the cases of Cathay Pacific and PCCW Ltd mentioned earlier. Ng (1997) suggested that this may signal a change in the way that conflicts between firms and employees are handled, as a more Western-style adversarial approach is adopted. The consequence of institutional permissiveness in HRM is that managers can adopt a set of highly versatile and relatively flexible HR practices based on individual employment contracts (Cheung et al., 2000; Ng and Wright, 2002).

The China Factor

The economic and political development of Hong Kong is closely linked to China. This factor affects HRM development through labour supply and opportunities for businesses of all types. Two waves of immigration from China have provided the needed labour in Hong Kong at crucial moments (Chen, 2000). The first wave of immigrants came to Hong Kong in the early 1950s, when the Communist Party came to power. The huge influx of refugees brought capital and entrepreneurial skills. This generation of immigrants formed the source of labour throughout Hong Kong's industrialisation in the following decade. The second wave of immigration during the 1970s, consisting of illegal immigrants, provided a large pool of cheap labour to Hong Kong at the time of its rapid industrialisation.

The China factor has also been influential in attracting MNCs to Hong Kong. In order to tap into the huge China market for their products, MNCs have often opted to set up their headquarters in Hong Kong in order to test the waters. These MNCs brought with them new HRM skills and procedures. Local companies benefit from their presence by imitating these HR practices. Indeed, some researchers suggest that MNCs may have been the major impetus towards increasing personnel sophistication (Budhwar, Schuler and Sparrow, 2009).

Globalisation

The effect of globalisation on Hong Kong may be much stronger than elsewhere because of its externally oriented and open economy. To enhance its legitimacy as a global business partner, Hong Kong has adopted international industrial regulations and set up human rights watchdogs such as the Equal Opportunities Commission. This commission has mainly adopted a non-coercive approach, focusing on conciliation and public education rather than invoking its statutory power to issue enforcement notices against non-compliance (Ng and Wright, 2002).

Globalisation has opened Hong Kong to external market forces, and its influence in directing HRM development in Hong Kong was particularly crucial in the 1980s and 1990s. In the early 1980s, Hong Kong's manufacturing firms moved their operations first into Southern China and then to Southeast Asia. At that time, this development solved the labour scarcity problem. In hindsight, we suggest that this may have slowed down the development of HRM in Hong Kong, especially in terms of training and skills development. In the 1990s, facing a fast changing global market, firms had to be adaptive, fast to change and efficient. Globalisation resulted in China becoming the global production site, supporting Hong Kong's service role. In our view, China's entry into the World Trade Organization in 2001 has clearly provided an impetus for any firm to use more developed HR practices and will accelerate the need for high-quality employees in the foreseeable future.

Future Prospects of HRM in Hong Kong

The last part presents a point–counterpoint discussion about the future of Hong Kong and the implications for the future of HRM. Economic swings dictate HRM activities in corporations, big or small. Familiar tactics like salary cuts, redundancies, lay-offs, early retirement schemes, downsizing and corporate restructuring prevail. Insolvencies are not uncommon and, therefore, HR practitioners have been busy looking at ways to rationalise human power, minimise expenses and freeze hiring in order to sustain a low-cost operating environment.

Many HR practitioners are dealing with downsizing programs, budget cuts, salary cuts and early-retirement schemes. They are fine-tuning appraisal and performance management and putting very few resources into training and development. However, there are exceptions. Some employers hire aggressively, for example, in financial services, insurance, transport and logistics, information systems and property development. Broadly speaking, medium- and long-term HR planning should consider the declining birth rate and a greying population. Measures such as labour re-training, continuing education, importation of skilled labour, experts and professionals and the luring of investment emigrants are becoming standard steps.

Closer Economic Ties with China

Hong Kong has almost fully transformed into a truly metropolitan service economy and the HR scene in Hong Kong companies presents the corresponding new challenges. While Hong Kong retains the distinctive 'one country, two systems' for 50 years to 2047, Hong Kong will continue to offer businesses incentives like a low tax base, a liberal environment for movement of capital and freedom of exchange of information. As in other metropolitan economies, high value-added activities will continue to replace low value-added activities. Hong Kong's strength is that it has established itself as a regional centre and one of the most service-oriented economies in the world, with producer services that support Hong Kong's offshore production operations. In 2011, Hong Kong's services sector accounted for more than 90 per cent of its GDP. The physical process of production of manufactures will play a less prominent role in Hong Kong's GDP.

These trends constitute important signals to HR practitioners and their senior policy makers and strategists. Given that de-industrialisation of Hong Kong has materialised, Hong Kong must continue to focus on value-added producer services and related activities. Similar changes have been experienced in cities like New York and Tokyo. The outward relocation of manufacturing activities does not represent a 'decline' of this sector as far as Hong Kong capitalists are concerned. Hong Kong is a metropolitan business centre that provides value-added services and Hong Kong-based service providers, and offices of multinationals should be geared up to reap the first-mover advantage. Opportunities to compete for providing financial, business and professional services to China are highly likely to be available to Hong Kong-based companies. Markets there tend to be fragmented by China's restrictions on foreign firms. As the regulatory environment changes and service sectors open up further, Hong Kong firms and their HR functions are advised to concentrate on even higher value services and attract, hire and retain employees in the fields of banking, finance, accounting, consulting and other similar activities.

A Knowledge Workforce for a Knowledge Economy

Given the importance of knowledge-intensive and the highest value-added activities in businesses, HRM priorities should be to allocate even more resources for supporting these activities. To help businesses meet their needs, university education should focus on training personnel for logistics management, process engineering, information systems, finance and management. We suggest to HR practitioners that the skills that will be in greatest demand are those involved in managing organisations, coordinating across borders, generating and processing information and communicating with international partners. For Hong Kong firms and their HR managers, the strategic focus should be on identifying long-term human resources' needs. If they are to compete in the knowledge- and information-dominated economy, they had better become highly efficient in information processing. They must begin by knowing what staff they need, with what skills, how they can find and retrain them as needed, and how they can motivate them to work more effectively and raise their awareness of the need for life-long learning of skills for future roles. In-house career counselling and advice about training needs and opportunities will be very much needed.

Case Study: MTR's Executive Continuous Learning Program: The HR Trend for Developing a Knowledge-Based Workforce

(Source: Hong Kong Institute of Human Resource Management, 2011)

Being one of the major transportation providers in Hong Kong, the MTR Corporation (MTRC) employs about 14,000 employees and operates nine main commuter lines, providing services to an average of four million passengers every weekday. Facing various business challenges and economic uncertainties, including a changing and competitive environment, rising expectations in terms of corporate responsibility, and a fast-growing global economy, the MTRC is actively engaging its HR division in some pro-active strategies.

After the merger with the Kowloon–Canton Railway Corporation in 2007, the MTRC saw a pressing need for staff development and continuous improvement in order for the company to grow and move forward. In particular, a need was identified for the leaders to refine their skills and understand the community concerns from a broader perspective. In partnership with line management, the Management Training and Development Department of MTRC's Human Resource and Administration (HR&A) Division has developed a demand-driven program – the Executive Continuous Learning Programme (ECLP) for its executives and senior managers. At the same time, the HR&A Division is fulfilling the mission of bringing to all staff a sense of pride through nurturing a continuous learning and improvement culture. Specifically, the ECLP is built around a competency model with four foci:

• Professional and Commercial Focus
• Leadership and Management Focus
• Personal Qualities Focus
• People Focus

By engaging in the ECLP, managers are able to:

• learn and keep abreast of the latest best practices and economic developments
• further equip themselves with personal competencies and functional skills
• gain broader perspectives through being exposed to contemporary practices in other organisations.

In order to provide flexibility in both place and time, different learning approaches, including workshops, seminars and self-learning through a web-based learning platform, are blended together. To create and enhance a culture of continuous learning, a positive top-down push has also been provided to spread the program across the organisation. Divisional champions at executive managers' level have been appointed to be role models as well as for co-hosting workshops and seminars.

It can be said that the MTRC is just one of many organisations in Hong Kong now setting the HRM trend for developing a knowledge-based workforce.

In our view, the past and future of HRM policies and practices in Hong Kong are predominantly subject to external contingent factors (for example, economic conditions and business sentiment). From colony to Special Administrative Region, from window to China to the metropolitan driver of hinterland cities, Hong Kong's macro-environment mandates that it sustains its role as a business and financial nerve-centre and a hub for services providers.

At a practical level HR managers need to look more carefully at the wide pool of talents, experts and professionals resident in South China and Taiwan and among ethnic Chinese and other nationals overseas who are familiar with China. This skilled workforce is what Hong Kong seriously lacks now. As stated in the many policy addresses of the chief executive of HKSAR over the years, the priority is to make it attractive for mainland Chinese specialists, skilled workers, experts and other professionals worldwide to come with their families to work in Hong Kong. This emphasises establishing even closer ties and integration with the Pearl River Delta hinterland. The re-positioning of HR-related policies for many companies has been in full swing as it is clear that the most recent 2011 version of *Closer Economic Partnership Agreement* (CEPA), augmented eight times since 2003, will continue to allow zero tariffs on exports from Hong Kong to mainland China. Service firms in Hong Kong in areas such as legal services, accountancy, banking, advertising, transport and logistics, and management consulting will enjoy the benefits of 'no trade barriers' and hence be able to set up their businesses. With these openings in late 2011, HRM's future in Hong Kong continues to acquire new definitions with their accompanying implications.

For Hong Kong to attract and retain the required human power, HRM blueprints for companies here will need to assert that skilled and professional people will make up the most critical portion of Hong Kong's knowledge workforce. Immigrants will continue to be welcomed because, in the long term, a continually renewing and thriving population is needed to overcome problems caused by the low birth rate and the greying of Hong Kong citizens. Incentives to lure 'investment immigrants', whether ethnic Chinese or not, are offered under the current immigration policy. The time has come for HR managers in Hong Kong to revisit expatriation and kindred international HR management issues, which were hot topics in the 1990s. This time their internal customers may well be local Hong Kong Chinese moving across the border to work in the mainland, as well as indigenous Chinese coming to work in Hong Kong from all parts of China and the rest of the world.

Useful Websites (as of January 2012)

Government Departments

Hong Kong Government	*www.gov.hk*
Labour Department	*www.info.gov.hk/labour*

Government Information Services
Department

www.info.gov.hk/isd/index.htm

Hong Kong Trade Development Council

www.tdc.org.hk

Employees Retraining Board

www.erb.org

Vocational Training Council

www.vtc.edu.hk

Non-government Organisations

Hong Kong Management Association

www.hkma.org.hk

Hong Kong Institute of Human Resource
Management

www.hkihrm.org

References

Brockbank, W. and Ulrich, D. (2003) *Competencies for the New HR*. Arlington, VA: Society of Human Resource Management.

Budhwar, P. S., Schuler, R. and Sparrow, P. (eds) (2009) *International Human Resource Management in Developing Countries*. London: Sage.

Chen, E. K. Y. (2000) 'The economic setting', in D. G. Lethbridge and S. H. Ng (eds), *The Business Environment in Hong Kong*. Hong Kong: Oxford University Press, pp. 3– 46.

Cheung, G., Ho, E. Y. Y., Ng, S. K. and Poon, C. Y. W. (2000) 'Business restructuring in Hong Kong', in D. G. Lethbridge and S. H. Ng (eds), *The Business Environment in Hong Kong*. Hong Kong: Oxford University Press, pp. 154–84.

Cheung, S. (1998) *Human Resource Management Practices in Hong Kong Survey Report 1998*. Hong Kong: Hong Kong Institute of Human Resource Management.

Cheung, S. (2001) *2001 Human Resource Management Strategies and Practices in Hong Kong*. Hong Kong: Hong Kong Institute of Human Resource Management.

Chiu, S., and Levin, D. A. (1993) 'From a labour-surplus to a labour-scarce economy: Challenges to Human Resource Management in Hong Kong', *International Journal of Human Resource Management* 4(1): 159–89.

Chu, P. and Siu, W. S. (2001) 'Coping with the Asian economic crisis: The rightsizing strategies of small- and medium-sized enterprises', *International Journal of Human Resource Management* 12(5): 845–58.

Dowling, Peter, Festing, Marion and Engle, Allen D. (2009) *International Human Resource Management: Managing People in a Multinational Context*, 5th edn. Mason, OH: South Western.

Enright, M., Scott, E. and Leung, E. (1999) *Hong Kong's Competitiveness beyond the Asian Crisis*. Hong Kong: HKTDC Research Department.

Erickson, T. (2009) 'Gen Y in the workplace', *Harvard Business Review* 87(2): 43–46.

Fields, D., Chan, A. and Akhtar, S. (2000) 'Organizational context and human resource management strategy: A structural equation analysis of Hong Kong firms', *International Journal of Human Resource Management* 11(2): 264–77.

Fosh, P., Chan, A. W., Chow, W. W. S., Snape, E. and Westwood, R. (1999) *Hong Kong Management and Labour: Change and continuity*. London: Routledge.

Hart, D. and Tian, F. (2009) *Human Resources: Hong Kong's challenges and opportunities*. George Mason University School of Public Policy Research Paper No. 2010–19.

Hewlett, S. A., Sherbin, L. and Sumberg, K. (2009). 'How Gen Y and boomers will reshape your agenda', *Harvard Business Review* 87(7/8): 71–78.

Hong Kong Census and Statistics Department (2010) *Report on 2010 Annual Survey of Regional Offices Representing Overseas Companies in Hong Kong.* Hong Kong: Census and Statistics Department.

Hong Kong Information Service Department (HKISD) (2011) *Hong Kong: The facts.* Hong Kong: HKISD.

Hong Kong Institute of Human Resource Management (2011) 'MTR's executive continuous learning program', *Human Resources* June: 25–29.

Hong Kong Labour Department, Registry of Trade Unions (2012) *Annual Statistical Report of Trade Unions in Hong Kong*, August 2011.

Hong Kong Vocational Training Council (HKVTC) (1992) *1991 Survey Report on Manpower and Training Needs of Human Resources Management Personnel.* Hong Kong: Vocational Training Council.

Kidd, J., Li, X. and Richter, F. (2001) 'Affirmation of the central role of human resource management in Asia', in J. B. Kidd, X. Li and F. J. Richter (eds), *Advances in Human Resources Management in Asia.* New York: Palgrave, pp. 1–24.

Kirkbride, P., and Tang, S. F. K. (1989) 'Personnel management in Hong Kong', *Asia Pacific Human Resource Management* 27(2): 43–57.

Legge, K. (1995) *Human Resource Management: Rhetorics and realities.* Basingstoke: Macmillan.

McCormick, I. (2001) 'Performance appraisals in Asia', *HR Focus* 4: 20–21.

McGraw, P. (2001) 'Human Resource Management in Hong Kong: Convergence or divergence', in S. Gray, S. McGaughey, and W. Purcell (eds), *Asia Pacific Issues in International Business.* Cheltenham: Edward Elgar, pp. 235–52.

Ng, C. W. and Chiu, W. (1997) 'Women-friendly HRM good for QWL? The case of Hong Kong based companies', *International Journal of Human Resource Management* 8(5): 644–59.

Ng, S. H. (1997) 'Reversion to China: Implications for labour in Hong Kong', *International Journal of Human Resource Management*, 8(5): 660–76.

Ng, S. H. and Ip, O. (1999) 'Manpower', in L. C. H. Chow and Y. K. Fan (eds) *The Other Hong Kong Report 1998.* Hong Kong: Chinese University of Hong Kong Press.

Ng, S. H. and Wright, R. (2002) 'Hong Kong', in M. Zanko (ed.) *Handbook of Human Resource Management Policies and Practices in Asia-Pacific Economies.* Cheltenham: Edward Elgar, pp. 167–259.

Ngo, H. Y., Turban, S., Lau, C. M., and Lui, S. (1998) 'Human Resource practices and firm performance of multinational corporations: Influences of country origin', *International Journal of Human Resource Management* 9(4): 632–52.

Shaw, J. B., Tang, F. Y. T., Fisher, C. D. and Kirkbride, P. S. (1993) 'Organizational and environmental factors related to HRM practices in Hong Kong: A Cross cultural expanded replication', *International Journal of Human Resource Management* 4(4): 785–815.

Snape, E. and Chan, A. (1999) 'Hong Kong trade unions: In search of a role.' in P. Fosh, A. W. Chan, W. W. S. Chow, E. Snape and R. Westwood (eds) *Hong Kong Management and Labour: Change and Continuity.* London: Routledge, pp. 255–70.

Snape, E., Thompson, S., Yan, F. K. C. and Redman, T. (1998) 'Performance appraisal and culture: Practice and attitudes in Hong Kong and Great Britain', *International Journal of Human Resource Management* 9(5): 841–61.

Tang, S., Lai, E. and Kirkbride, P. S. (1995) *Human Resource Management Practices in Hong Kong: Survey report 1995.* Hong Kong: Hong Kong Institute of Human Resource Management.

Tsang, D. (2007). 'New direction for Hong Kong', *2007–2008 Policy Address*, 10 October 2007.

Tsui, A. and Lai, K. T. (2009) 'Future prospects for HRM in Hong Kong', in A. Tsui and K. T. Lai (eds), *Professional Practices of HRM in Hong Kong.* Hong Kong: Hong Kong University Press, pp. 281–91.

6 Human Resource Management Practices in Taiwan

WAN-JING APRIL CHANG

In this chapter the human resource management practices in Taiwan will be introduced by nine sections, which are the background and development of HRM, the development stages of HRM, the strategic role of HRM, the key factors determining HRM practices, a review of HR practices, key changes in the HR function, key challenges facing HRM, what is likely to happen to HR functions in the next five years, and a case study of HTC, a worldwide known smartphone and tablet company in Taiwan.

Background and Development of HRM

Socio-economic Background of Taiwan

The island of Taiwan is located in the Pacific Ocean about 160 kilometers off the south-eastern coast of China, with Japan in the north and the Philippines in the south. In 2010 the population was approximately 23.162 million and the area was approximately 36,129 square kilometers, the combination of which made Taiwan one of the most densely populated areas in the world (640 persons/ km^2). Lacking natural resources, Taiwan has relied heavily on human resources for economic development. As a result of sustained economic growth over the past few decades, the per capita gross national product (GNP) of Taiwan has risen from US$97 per year in 1950 to US$19,155 in 2010, an almost 200-fold increase (Council for Economic Planning and Development, 2011).

In the mid-1980s, the global economic boom greatly accelerated Taiwan's economic growth, which registered annual percentage growth rates in the double digits. Taiwan's export trade spurred on the vigorous development of the island's manufacturing industry, which accounted for 39.4 percent of gross domestic product (GDP) in 1986, the highest recorded percentage up to that point. From 1987 onward, export expansion slackened while domestic demand strengthened. The dampening of exports reversed industrial growth, resulting in an appreciable reduction in its share of GDP. The rapid expansion of domestic demand led to the rapid development of the service sector, whose relative importance in the economy rose tremendously (Huang, 2004) (see Figure 6.1).

The employment structure also showed the same shift (see Figure 6.2). Agricultural employment declined from 18.8 percent in 1981 to 5.2 percent in 2010. Industrial employment reached a peak of 42.8 percent in 1987, but by 2010 it had dropped to 35.9 percent. Service employment has grown at a relatively stable pace over the years. It has been the largest share of total employment since 1988, increasing to 58.8 percent in 2010.

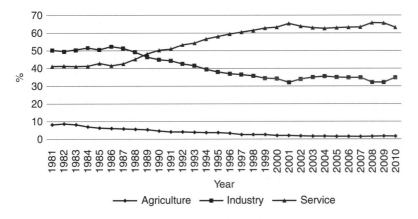

Figure 6.1 Gross Domestic Product (GDP) of Taiwan by Industry Structure (1981–2010)
Source: Council of Labor Affairs, Executive Yuan, *Monthly Bulletin of Labor Statistics*, various years

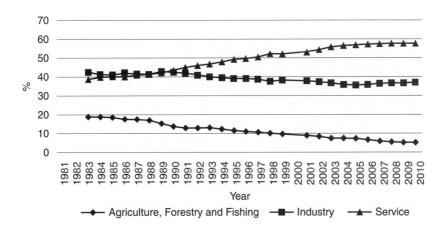

Figure 6.2 Employed by Industry Structure in Taiwan (1981–2010)
Source: Council of Labor Affairs, Executive Yuan, *Yearly Bulletin of Labor Statistics*, various years

Taiwan's civilian population of age 15 and over has risen from 10.8 million in 1978 to 19 million in 2010. During that same stretch of time, the labor force increased from 6 million to 11 million. At its peak, the labor participation rate (LPR) accounted for 60.93 percent of the civilian population (aged 15 and over) in 1987, and then decreased gradually to 58.1 percent in 2010 (Council of Labor Affairs, 2010). Taiwan's unemployment rate by the late 1960s had fallen to below 2 percent, and Taiwan enjoyed a low unemployment rate for a long time (Directorate General of Budget, Accounting and Statistics, 2011). Although Taiwan's economy was affected by the Asian Financial Crisis in 1998, its economic growth rate was 4.8 percent, higher than the growth rates of each of the other three Asian tigers (Hong Kong, South Korea and Singapore) (Directorate General of Budget, Accounting and Statistics, 2011; IMF, 2011; HIS Inc, 2012). In 2000, the unemployment rate dramatically increased to 2.99 percent and reached 5.2 percent in 2010. The main reasons for these statistical spikes included the influences of several unexpected important events, such as 1999's 921 earthquake, 2000's dotcom bubble, 2001's 9/11 terrorist attacks, the Toraji and Nari Typhoons and 2008's global financial crisis. However, in 2010, Taiwan's economic growth rate reached 10.9 percent, the highest in the past 20 years (Council of Labor Affairs, 2010). Compared to 2009, an additional 2.1 percent of the population joined the labor force in 2010. Unemployed persons and the unemployment rate decreased from 639,000 people and 5.9 percent of the population to 577,000 people and 5.2 percent of the population (see Figure 6.3).

On average in Taiwan, the total monthly working hours of individual laborers throughout all industries decreased from 215.1 hours/month in 1980 to 181.2 hours/month in 2010; and on average in Taiwan, the total monthly earnings

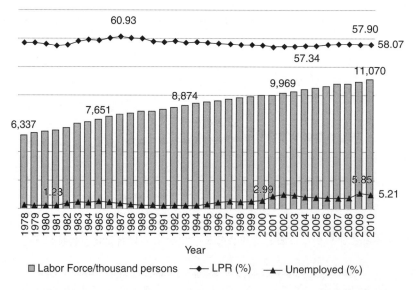

Figure 6.3 Labor Force, Labor Participation Rate and Unemployment Rate in Taiwan (1978–2010)

Source: Council of Labor Affairs, Executive Yuan, *Yearly Bulletin of Labor Statistics*, various years

of individual laborers (1) in the manufacturing sector increased from US$262 in 1980 to US$1,383.1 in 2010 and (2) in the services sector increased from US$331.7 in 1980 to US$1,490.7 in 2010 (see Table 6.1). The fast growth of labor costs has contributed to the decline of Taiwan's manufacturing sector, especially in Taiwan's labor-intensive companies, many of which have transferred plants to Mainland China or southeast Asian countries. Taiwan is currently transforming itself from a labor-intensive industrialized economy to a capital- and technology-intensive industrialized economy.

Without plentiful natural resources, one of the factors that contributed to the success of Taiwan is commonly considered to be the development of human resources. Therefore, Taiwan's HRM development stages will be introduced in the following section.

Development Stages of HRM

Taiwan's HRM development has proceeded through four stages. Stage I took place before the mid-1960s. In that period, HRM was a part of administration. Its major responsibilities were hiring, attendance and leave, payroll and employee welfare, and performance appraisal (Yao, 1999). According to Negandhi (1973), Taiwanese firms never stated or documented human power policies, never established independent personnel departments, seldom engaged in job evaluations, established no clear criteria for selection and promotion, based most promotions

Table 6.1 Working Hours and Monthly Earnings in Taiwan (1980–2010)

Year	Average Monthly Working Hours			Average Monthly Earning (USD)	
	Regular	Overtime	Total	Manufacturing	Service
1980	202.7	12.4	215.1	262.0	331.7
1985	194.2	9.6	203.8	413.3	512.4
1990	187.5	9.5	197.0	717.7	872.5
1995	184.6	9.7	194.3	1,059.3	1,223.0
2000	180.2	9.9	190.1	1,268.8	1,441.5
2001	171.8	8.6	180.4	1,252.4	1,461.3
2002	172.5	8.9	181.4	1,253.2	1,438.1
2003	172.1	9.2	181.3	1,289.5	1,439.6
2004	173.5	10.0	183.5	1,325.6	1,447.5
2005	172.4	9.5	181.9	1,364.8	1,444.1
2006	171.8	9.1	180.9	1,382.2	1,446.3
2007	171.4	9.1	180.5	1,407.5	1,479.6
2008	171.5	8.2	179.7	1,405.5	1,481.9
2009	170.4	6.3	176.7	1,276.6	1,431.8
2010	172.3	8.9	181.2	1,383.1	1,490.7

Source: Council of Labor Affairs, Executive Yuan, Republic of China, *Monthly Bulletin of Labor Statistics*, various years.

on age and experience, focused their training programs only on operatives, and relied on financial rewards as the main incentives for promoting worker productivity. Therefore, he concluded that the people-management practices in local Taiwanese firms could not effectively harness the available high-level human power.

The second stage began in the mid-1960s and extended into the late 1970s. In that time, some US multinationals (for example, IBM, RCA and TI) and Japanese multinationals (for example, Matsushita and Mitsubishi) established operations in Taiwan while transplanting their home-country personnel-management practices. During the 1970s in Taiwan, there emerged some informal organizations that, devoted to personnel management, would meet regularly to exchange related information (Farh, 1995). Also during this same period, Taiwanese HRM tended to be operational and reactive: Its major responsibilities were hiring and retention, providing competitive packages and basic training programs, and maintaining harmonious employee–industry relations.

The third stage lasted approximately from 1980 to 2000. In this period, the HRM departments in Taiwanese firms began to play a stronger functional role, particularly in new areas such as personnel planning and control, management training, career development, and counseling for line managers. Human resources started to be viewed as a professional field. Active during this stage were two notable professional HRM organizations (Chinese Human Resource Management Associations and the Human Resource Development Association of the Republic of China (ROC)). Both of them organized and sponsored a number of seminars, workshops and training programs to promote modern HRM practices. In addition, the establishment of two academic institutions—the National Sun Yat-sen University and the National Central University—contributed extensively to HRM insofar as both of them offered master and PhD programs in the field (Huang, 2004).

The fourth stage started in approximately 2000 and is ongoing. Taiwan joined the World Trade Organization (WTO) in 2002. To successfully survive in the twists and turns of competitive business environments, organizations have to adjust their strategies accordingly. During this stage, some HR departments became involved in the formulation of business strategies. The role of HRM transformed from administrative to strategic by providing value-added practices and by establishing mechanisms and contexts to facilitate organization change and development. The 2002 Human Resource Survey for Twelve Nations in Asia, conducted by the Towers Watson Company, showed that in more than half of 65 listed companies, HR had inked policies and practices reflective of core organizational values, established an evaluation system of HR effectiveness and invested in the development of HR professionals. Also, 40 percent of the sample companies had engaged in long-term human power planning (Byars and Rue, 2010).

The Importance and Strategic Role of HRM

According to Huang's study (1998), HR managers in the late 1990s declared that HR departments' most important contributions to organizations were training and development, followed by compensation and benefits, and then by HR planning.

As the importance of HR topics increased, HR planning, training and development, and performance appraisal acquired the greatest emphasis.

Beaumont (1993: 16–17) defined 'strategic' as the type of HRM that makes human factors an integral part of broad-based, long-term planning for implementing an organization's objectives. Strategic human-resource management (SHRM) implies a managerial orientation ensuring that human resources are employed in a manner conducive to the achievement of organizational goals and missions (Gomez-Mejia, Balking and Hardy, 1995).

Several Taiwan-based empirical studies have supported the assertion that SHRM can enhance firm performance. For example, Chi and Chang (2006) found that the HR role of strategic partners can be positively associated with firm performance, while the role of administrative experts can be negatively associated with organizational performance. Lee, Lee, and Wu (2010) argued that integrating HRM practices with business strategies can be positively associated with firm performance. The research results of Hsu and Leat (2000) also show that HRM policies can be integrated with corporate strategy and that HRM should be involved in decision making at a broad level.

The results of the 2008 Cranet Taiwan Survey show that, in Taiwan, 85.8 percent of organizations had an HR department and that 69.6 percent of those organizations that lacked an HR department tended to rely chiefly on administrative directors' handling of HR practices. In addition, 67.1 percent of the people responsible for HR practices had a seat on the board of directors or in an equivalent committee. They were involved in different stages of the strategy-formation process: 50.9 percent were participants from the outset, 20.5 percent were participants through subsequent consultation, 21.8 percent were participants upon implementation of a particular project, and only 6.8 percent helped form strategy even though the organization had not consulted them.

Another critical requirement of SHRM is the full involvement of line departments in HRM functions and activities. SHRM emphasizes close coordination between such internal HRM functions as recruiting, selection, training, development, performance appraisal, and compensation. At the same time, HRM must be integrated with functions external to HRM departments such as marketing, finance, production, and research and development (Anthony et. al., 1996).

The results of Hsu and Leat (2000) show that some HRM decisions have been shared between line management and HR specialists and that line managers have had a particularly influential role in decisions regarding recruitment and selection, training and development, and workforce expansion and reduction. The results of the 2008 Cranet Survey show that in Taiwan major policy decisions on recruitment and selection (42.4 percent), training and development (45.1 percent), pay and benefits (39.4 percent) and industrial relations (30.9 percent) have been made primarily by HR departments in consultation with line managers, whereas major policy decisions on workforce expansion and reduction have been made primarily by line managers in consultation with HR departments (42.5 percent). That is, both line management and HR departments have primary responsibility for major HR policy decisions.

Key Factors Determining HRM Practices

HR practices are greatly influenced by external environments. Economy, demography, culture, education, and politics and governmental policies generally are primary factors.

Economy

Taiwan's economy experienced several critical transformations, starting out as chiefly an agricultural economy (before 1960), then coming to rely on labor-intensive industries (1960–80) before expanding heavily into technology and service industries (1980–90) and most recently capital-intensive and knowledge-intensive industries (1990–present).

In addition to the difficulties stemming from a rapidly evolving economy, Taiwanese companies have faced a sometimes brutally competitive business environment. In order to obtain a further comparative advantage, many companies relocated their operations to low-wage countries, especially to mainland China and Southeast Asia (Zhu and Warner, 2001). Global competition is also reflected in the formation of regional economic arrangements such as the Association of Southeast Asian Nations (ASEAN), the North American Free Trade Agreement (NAFTA) and the European Economic Community (EEC) and in the establishment of global economic arrangements such as the General Agreement on Tariffs and Trade (GATT) and the World Trade Organization (WTO). Therefore, the need for knowledge and skill acquisition and upgrades, as well as diversification and internationalization, has become crucial to HRM.

Demography

The population growth rate during the 1950s and 1960s was very high. However, as a result of the success of family-planning programs, the rate decreased dramatically to less than 2 percent in the 1970s and kept decreasing to around 1 percent in the 1980s. In 1998 it stood at 0.86 percent (Huang, 2004). It is expected that the older labor forces will increase as a percentage of the population and that young labor forces will decrease as a percentage of the population (see Figure 6.4). In the near future, a large number of employees will retire, and the subsequent benefits, retirement and succession issues will influence HR practices greatly. To reduce the negative impact of population structure change, companies would adopt outsourcing (41.5 percent), investment on autonomy (32.0 percent) and introducing foreign workers (29.5 percent) (Yan, 2006).

Culture

Confucianism is the most clearly identified traditional culture in Taiwan. Harmony, *guanxi* and paternalistic leadership are the major features of Taiwan's Confucian business culture.

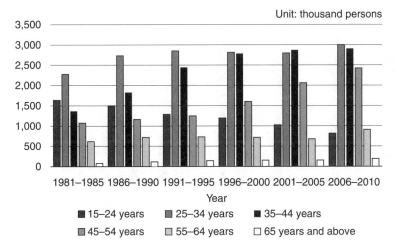

Figure 6.4 Employed Person by Age in Taiwan (1981–2010)
Source: Council of Labor Affairs, Executive Yuan, *Yearly Bulletin of Labor Statistics*, various years

Harmony is one of the basic tenets of Confucian philosophy. It reflects an aspiration toward a conflict-free, group-based system of social relations. In order to maintain harmony and to save face in the workplace, managers generally handle with great delicacy any policy calling for the implementation of full performance appraisals or of highly individualized pay. *Guanxi* (relationship) is a distinctly East Asian feature that also existed in Taiwanese business operations. For example, the use of personal connections or networks is a popular method for recruitment and selection (Stone, 2009). In addition, Confucianism emphasizes hierarchy and status: Employees are expected to respect their supervisors; at the same time, managers are expected to be role models for subordinates by establishing sound rules for subordinates, fairly meting out rewards and punishments, and generally looking after the welfare of employees and their families, all of which reflects paternalistic leadership (Cheng, 1995). However, the influence of traditional culture seems to be declining owing to globalization, company size and type, and senior managers' education and experience (Huang, 2004).

Education

In 1970, Taiwan implemented nine-year compulsory education, and twelve-year compulsory education is to be implemented in 2014. In the past decades, the Taiwanese people's average level of education has increased significantly; in particular, the number of employees whose education level went beyond a senior high school degree has grown during this period (see Figure 6.5).

The prevalence of higher-education attainment has improved the quality of the labor force, which has facilitated industry transformation. For organizations, higher levels of human capital mean better added-value knowledge and skills

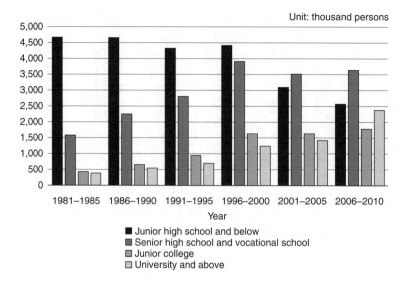

Figure 6.5 Employed Person by Education Attainment in Taiwan (1981–2010)
Source: Council of Labor Affairs, Executive Yuan, *Yearly Bulletin of Labor Statistics*, various years

and better problem-solving capabilities, which enhance employee productivities. For example, the rapid expansion of college trained workers in production work suggests that increasing numbers of these workers are no longer working on assembly lines but instead are becoming highly skilled workers and technicians engaged in roles where independent judgment and problem-solving abilities are necessary (Lee, 2002). However, higher educational levels also result in employees' higher expectations regarding job content, career development and rewards. Thus, the need for comprehensive HR practices increases as well.

Politics and Governmental Policies

Legislative environments are coercive for organizations and yet are critical for HR functions. For example, in order to cope with the increase in production costs, many companies employ foreign workers with the permission of the government (up to 30 percent of their total employees) (Zhu, Chen and Warner, 2000). Labor laws generally cover the conditions of employment, labor relations, anti-discrimination matters and employment safety, which—in Taiwan—are the province of the Council of Labor Affairs in the Executive Yuan. The following are several major Taiwanese labor laws.

The Labor Standard Law (1985) is the most important base for HR policies, covering the areas of labor contracts, wages, working hours, leave-taking, retirement, compensation for occupational accidents and other terms and conditions of employment. The New Collective Employment Laws, including the Labor Union Law, the Collective Agreement Law and the Settlement of Labor Disputes Law were passed in 2010. They regulate the establishment, membership, officers, meetings, operational funds, supervision and protection of labor unions. Other important labor laws include the Employee Service Law (1992), the Gender Equality in Employment Act (2002), the People with Disabilities Rights Protection Act (2007), the Labor Insurance Act (1958), the Employment Insurance Act (2002) and the Labor Safety and Health Act (1974).

A Review of HR Practices

Staffing

This section describes Taiwanese companies' staffing approaches, which include recruitment and selection methods, employee reduction and formal programs for enhancing labor participation and flexible job arrangements.

The results of the 2008 Cranet Taiwan Survey show that organizations have adopted different approaches to recruiting employees according to the *type* of employee being sought. At the time of the recent survey, the common methods preferred by company managers were internal recruitment (80.5 percent), commercial websites matching job positions with job-seekers (74.3 percent), recruitment agencies (48.7 percent) and company websites (44.3 percent). Job-seeking professionals tended to prefer commercial websites matching job positions with job-seekers (91.1 percent), company websites (61.3 percent) and internal recruitment (52.9 percent). For clerical job-seekers, commercial websites matching job positions with job-seekers (89.8 percent), company websites (58.4 percent), and internal recruitment (51.8 percent) were the most prominent methods used. Manual laborers in search of work were most likely to rely on commercial websites matching job positions with job-seekers (50.7 percent), job centers (45.3 percent) and speculative applications (38.2 percent). It is obvious that, nowadays, websites and internal recruitment have been the most common methods whereas use of advertising, word of mouth and educational institutions for employee recruitment has been relatively rare.

As to selection, although various kinds of methods have been developed, organizations have preferred to adopt traditional methods, such as one-on-one interviews and application forms oriented toward select knowledge and skills. For managers as of 2008, organizations used chiefly one-on-one interviews (85.4 percent), application forms (49.6 percent) and psychometric tests (42.0 percent). For professionals, one-on-one interviews (89.7 percent), ability tests (49.6 percent) and technical tests (42.0 percent) dominated. The preferences of clerical job-seekers were for one-on-one interviews (86.7 percent), application forms (55.3 percent) and ability tests (55.3 percent), and the preferences of manual workers seeking employment were for one-on-one interviews (46.9 percent) and application forms (37.2 percent). Overall these days, interview panels, references, assessment centers and graphology have played relatively small roles in selection processes.

In addition, organizations have decreased their number of employees in several ways. The 2008 survey shows that 71.2 percent of organizations used recruitment freezes; more than 50 percent used redeployment, non-renewal of fixed-term contracts and voluntary redundancies; and more than 20 percent used early retirement, compulsory redundancies, and outsourcing.

Organizations have provided recruitment, training and career programs for enhancing labor participation, especially for people with disabilities (50.0 percent, 25.7 percent and 8.4 percent respectively), women (33.2 percent, 27.9 percent and 18.6 percent respectively), and workers under the age of 25 (35.0 percent, 35.0 percent and 15.6 percent respectively). The same types of programs have also served ethnic minorities, older workers, women returning to the workforce after an absence and low-skill laborers.

More and more flexible job arrangements have emerged in the past several years. Atypical employment (such as temporary work and part-time work) has increased gradually. The most common forms of job flexibility—as of 2008—were overtime (92.9 percent), fixed-term contracts (72.6 percent), shift work (69.1 percent), weekend work (65.2 percent), temporary or casual work (56.4 percent), flexible hours (53.8 percent), and part-time work (36.6 percent). Other arrangements that have gained prominence include shared work, annual hourly contracts, tele-work, compressed work weeks and home-based work.

Training and Development

Taiwanese organizations have, in recent years, implemented training, career-development, and performance-appraisal programs, described as follows.

According to the 2008 Cranet Survey, organizations were spending an average of 3.63 percent of their annual payroll on training. Organizations were devoting an average of 7.2, 8.5, 5.9, and 5.6 days per year to training for managerial, professional, clerical and manual work respectively. Of all the organizations surveyed, 60 percent were systematically evaluating the effectiveness of training. The methods that organizations employed for evaluating training effectiveness included reaction evaluations immediately after training (73.6 percent), goal realization (71.4 percent), informal feedback from line managers (67.6 percent), informal feedback from employees (63.7 percent) and total number of training days (62.1 percent). Of less prominence were methods involving job-performance evaluations either months after or immediately after training, and evaluations of return on investment (ROI).

For career development, the methods that organizations generally used (according to the 2008 survey) were special projects (96.8 percent), project-oriented team work (90.5 percent), cross-organization or cross-discipline tasks (87.3 percent), planned job rotation (83.6 percent), experience schemes (74.9 percent) and secondments to other organizations (72.6 percent). More than 50 percent of firms adopted mentoring, coaching, e-learning, succession plans, networking, formal career plans and high-flier schemes.

Of the surveyed organizations, 91.0 percent had a formal appraisal system for managerial employees, 92.7 percent had one for professional employees, 93.2 percent had one for clerical employees and 76.7 percent had one for manual employees. Immediate supervisor, supervisors' supervisor and employee were ranked as the first three contributors—in order of importance—to performance management, regardless of position; subordinates, peers and customers also were part of raters sometimes. Organizations used appraisal data when making pay decisions (92.8 percent), training and development decisions (79.6 percent), workforce planning (67.0 percent) and career moves (51.6 percent).

Compensation and Benefits

Recent trends in Taiwanese organizations' implementation of pay levels, incentive programs and benefits packages are described as follows. In general, pay levels are determined by a variety of factors, such as the external labor market, internal equity and employees' seniority and performance. According to the 2008 Cranet Survey, three organizational entities—an organizational division, an individual within an organization and establishment/site—determined pay levels of managers, professionals, clerical workers and manual workers.

Incentive programs that managers were most likely to use when dealing with employees were bonuses based on individualized goals (73.5 percent), profit sharing (69.8 percent) and employee share schemes (64.0 percent). For professionals, the most popular incentive programs were bonuses based on individualized goals (75.7 percent), profit sharing (61.5 percent) and performance-based pay (56.2 percent). For clerical workers, the most popular incentive programs were bonuses based on individualized goals (69.5 percent), profit sharing (60.6 percent), performance-based pay (47.8 percent) and bonuses based on team goals (44.2 percent). For manual workers, the most popular incentive programs were bonuses based on individualized goals (46.6 percent), profit sharing (37.6 percent), performance-based pay (34.5 percent) and bonuses based on team goals (32.3 percent). Stock options and flexible benefits appeared to be less important. It is clear to see that bonuses based on individualized goals and profit sharing were the most commonly used incentive programs in businesses, regardless of which level employees hold.

Employees at organizations ranked types of benefits in the following order: maternity leave (91.6 percent), career-break schemes (90.2 percent), paternity leave (88.4 percent), training breaks (72.4 percent), parental leave (71.1 percent), pension schemes (63.1 percent) and private health-care schemes (32.4 percent). Workplace child care (8.9 percent) and childcare allowances (6.7 percent) were of considerably less importance.

Employee Relations and Communications

Trade unions did not play a significant role in the relationships between organizations and employees. Organizations communicated to employees by verbal means (96.8 percent), written missives (93.5 percent), electronic formats (89.4 percent), team briefings (73.3 percent) and representative staff bodies (50.7 percent). Employees communicated to organizations through immediate supervisors (98.6 percent), senior managers (86.9 percent), electronic formats (80.5 percent), attitude surveys (80.1 percent), regular workforce meetings (75.1 percent), work councils (74.0 percent), suggestion schemes (73.3 percent), team briefings (58.8 percent) and trade-union representatives (29.0 percent)

Only 21.5 percent of employees were members of a trade union. The results show that 64.1 percent of companies considered trade-union activity to have no influence on their organizations, and 77.2 percent stated that the influence of trade unions had remained the same during the past three years.

Key Changes in the HR Function

Taiwanese companies face intense global competition. They must have the ability to respond rapidly and effectively to unexpected but influential "black swan" events, such as the 2008 financial crisis. The McKinsey Quarterly (2007) identified the three most important factors affecting business operations: competition for talent, global and regional economic activities, and business connection with technology. For businesses, human resources factors are no less important than changes in an economic environment or the creation of highly competitive business performance.

Overall, the HR orientation of Taiwanese companies has gradually shifted from administration to strategy. In the past, companies focused mostly on the sub-functions of HR, operational activities and policy implementation, but in recent years companies have focused more on overall business management, strategic activities and decision-making participation (Wu *et al.*, 2011).

Technology has also facilitated the transformation of HR's role. First, human-resource information systems' (HRISs') digitalized administrative tasks, including payroll, attendance and insurance. Employees could maintain and update information on their own and therefore improved the effectiveness of the HR personnel. Second, HR portals could facilitate the sharing of personal information among employees and their supervisors for different purposes. Moreover, some companies have adopted outsourcing for activities such as training and recruiting, so HR professionals have more time for strategic and other value-added activities.

What follows is a series of descriptions regarding specific changes in the sub-functions of HR, staffing, employee development, compensation and employee relations.

Staffing

In the midst of globalization, Taiwanese companies have started to attract international talent, and the need to manage diverse employee populations has grown. For example, Taiwanese businesses that move to China must meet the requirements of related employment contracts and the five-year income plan (that is the average annual growth of income being no less than 15 percent) (Huang, Ci and Cheng, 2010). Also, China-based Taiwanese businesses must have the ability to manage local talent and a large number of employees (Chung and Wang, 2010).

Not only has the scale of operations grown for such businesses, but also most of them cannot directly replicate in China their previous successful Taiwanese experiences.

Another change involves e-recruiting, which is defined as using the Internet to disseminate recruitment ads and to attract job applicants. Many companies adopt this approach because of cost advantages over non-Internet recruitment strategies. HR-recruiting sites include corporate career websites, commercial websites, talent databases and various professional websites (Wu *et al.*, 2011). The first two types of resources are the most commonly used in Taiwanese businesses (Sun *et al.*, 2008).

In addition, owing to businesses' need for human power flexibility and the imbalance between the supply of labor and the demand for skilled labor, more and more companies have extensively hired atypical employees (for example, dispatched employees, temporary workers) and have adopted flexible work schedules (for example, employee-tailored work weeks) (Noe *et al.*, 2008).

Employee Development

The training systems of large and small companies develop in different directions. For large companies, their rapid expansion strains their efforts to find sufficient and adequate talent coming from the current education system and from company-based training mechanisms. Therefore, some large companies establish their own business universities (Ding, 2011). On the other hand, small and medium-size enterprises (SMEs) lack resources for large-scale talent development, and in response, the Council of Labor Affairs has promoted the Taiwan Train Quali System (TTQS), similar to International Organization for Standardization (ISO) certification, to help SMEs enhance their training quality and effectiveness (Council of Labor Affairs, 2010).

New training methods such as experiential learning and e-learning are available to many companies. The process of experiential learning takes a step-by-step approach to observation, reflection, summary and application. The purpose of experiential learning is to link games and work through personal involvement rather than through listening and watching in classrooms (Yan, 2011). Another factor influencing people's learning is technology, such as web-based training (WBT) (Chung, Tsen and Yeh, 2008). Companies convey training content to their workers via the Internet, and employees choose and proceed through courses at their own pace. This method not only overcomes time and space constraints in physical classrooms but also creates learner-centered learning environments.

In traditional East Asian culture, the preservation of both inter-personal harmony and individual dignity has been a critical factor in governing performance-appraisal outcomes, which thus have been, at least until recently, unreliable as accurate reflections of employees' real contributions. In recent years, however, due to intense competition, Taiwanese companies have started to recognize the importance of performance management. More and more companies have used the results for development purposes and have linked the results of performance appraisal and compensation to the goal of motivating employees.

Compensation and Employee Relations

Rewarding employees with bonus stocks at par-value has been a prominent characteristic of the Taiwanese high-tech industry but has come under heavy criticism for their possible threat to stockholders' equity. After 2008, the employee bonus shares are recognized as company expenses and the receiving individuals are taxed by fair market value. This change has encouraged high-tech companies to use cash instead of bonus stocks for talent attraction and retention.

Many companies view incentive programs as important rewards. Take Hon Hai as an example: They have used organizational, departmental and individual performance as the basis for bonuses, such as performance bonuses, year-end bonuses, year-end banquet lotteries and bonuses for research and development (R&D) projects (Hon Hai Precision Ind. Co., Ltd, 2010).

In recent years, increases in vocational pressures coinciding with younger generations' growing valuation of extra-vocational time have led Taiwanese to pursue higher-quality work experiences and better work–family balance. Benefits—in addition to salary and incentives—have become an important means by which companies can meet employees' needs and can, thereby, achieve talent retention. Companies have developed a variety of benefit programs. Take TSMC's Employee Assistance Program (EAP) as an example: They provide their workers with employee services, health centers and an employee-welfare committee. Employee services include a food court, a laundry service, dormitory security, transportation, an activity center, art galleries, bookstores, a coffee bar, a lounge and convenience stores; the health center provides outpatient services, health examinations, health seminars, health camps, nursing rooms and legal, relationship, and family counseling; the employees' welfare committee provides a variety of clubs and associations, internal publications, emergency assistance, film and art activities, family days, children's summer camps, coupons and kindergartens (Taiwin Semiconductor Manufacturing Company (TSMC, 2012).

Key Challenges Facing HRM

Ageing Population

In recent years, Taiwan has been experiencing the trends of high divorce rates, low crude marriage rates, late marriages and late childbearing; within this context, Taiwan's fertility levels have been steadily decreasing, and the average age of the population has been increasing (from 34 years old in 2001 to 43 years old in 2011). The changes in the Taiwanese population's age structure have not only influenced the supply of young workers but also influenced the size of consumer markets while hampering the development of businesses. Also, the increased number of older workers has led to a spike in the demand for related HR practices, such as life-long learning, opportunities for atypical employment and medical-care systems (San, 2011).

Low Labor Participation Rate

The LPR of Taiwan in 2009 was 57.9 percent, which is lower than that figure in most other developed economies, such as South Korea, Singapore, Japan, the United States, Canada, Germany and the United Kingdom. The female LPR of Taiwan was 49.6 percent in 2009, with more room for development than was available to male workers (San, 2011). Also, young Taiwanese have been entering the labor market later than traditionally because of longer educations and different work values. In addition, family–work conflict has created a situation where the percentage of Taiwanese women who are over 45 years old and returning to work after an absence is lower than the corresponding percentages in South Korea, Japan and the United States (San, 2011).

The Gap between School Education and Business Needs

The number of the college and above graduates increased rapidly in past decades (Figure 6.5); however, 28.4 percent of the unemployed are college graduates. Also, there has been a mismatch between the disciplines of higher-education institutions and the specialized demands of businesses—a mismatch that has been quite difficult to adjust to in the short term (San, 2011), such as the lack of technical manpower in traditional manufacturing. A related point concerns the upgrades that most Taiwanese vocational education institutions have undergone in recent years and that have blurred the distinctions between the general education system and the vocational education system, leading to a lack of skill-based workers (G. He, 2011). Also of interest is the fact that most research and development (R&D) talent potentially available to the Taiwanese business/industrial community has been shifting to other sectors of the economy. A case in point: 87.3 percent of Taiwanese PhD graduates chose to take on work at academic and research institutions in 2009 (San, 2011).

Weaknesses in Human Capital Investment for SMEs

The Taiwanese government's expenditures on vocational training accounted for 0.02 percent of GDP in 2006, which is similar to the corresponding statistics for Japan and the United Kingdom. However, Japanese businesses have a legal obligation to provide their own workers with vocational training, and companies in the United Kingdom also train their own employees. In Taiwan, more than 98 percent of companies are SMEs and have less than 200 employees. Without either legal requirements for minimum expenditures or adequate resources, the companies' investment in human capital is less than their counterparts in other economies (San, 2011). Plus the gap between school and business, as discussed above, has strengthened the importance of public training institutions in this area of concern.

Shortage of Professionals and Talent Recruitment

OEM (Original Equipment Manufacturing) was once the major strategy of Taiwanese manufacturing companies (Ceng, 2010); however, Taiwan is facing economic transformation and needs different types of labor. For example, the manufacturing industry needs software developers (Lin, 2011), semiconductor engineers, integrated-circuit design experts and green (energy-related) professionals (Ding and Gu, 2010); the service industry requires catering, logistics (Wang and Wang, 2011), and financial professionals (S. He, 2011); and the upgraded agriculture industry needs bio-tech and transportation professionals.

The results of the 2008 Cranet Survey in Taiwan show that succession planning and talent management have been the first two challenges besetting HR systems. The Talent Shortage Survey (Manpower, 2007) showed that the main reason for the turnover of middle-managers has been a lack of career-development programs. The vast majority of businesses in Taiwan are owned by single families; that is, the businesses exhibit no rigorous separation between ownership and management and, consequently, few businesses implement succession planning for high-level managers. In addition, the failure rate of foreign-company managers working for local firms is about 60 percent owing to irresolvable differences between their management philosophies (Li, 2011). Talent management is another issue. Lacking competitive compensation packages and the international working environment make attracting foreign talents more difficult. Moreover, Taiwanese expatriates generally lack satisfactory adaptability, regional-management, and sales capabilities (Gao, 2010).

Shortage of Entry-Level Laborers and Taiwan's Foreign-Worker Policy

The development of technology has led to the polarization of the labor force: on the one end is professional talent and on the other is unskilled, entry-level labor. So that Taiwanese businesses have access to insufficient human power, the government and the private sector have adopted several approaches to the issue of labor supply (San, 2011). The Taiwanese government agreed to permit the entry of foreign workers into the island's labor-supply pool beginning in 1992, and mandated that the basic-monthly-pay for workers would increase from NTD17,880 to NTD18,780 in 2012. Businesses have improved the safety of workplace conditions, as well as job security, fair labor practices and employee benefits. Also, businesses have adopted business process reengineering, outsourcing and automation in order to reduce the need for human labor. Although the labor-shortage problem has slackened, the situation remains unstable.

The Inflexibility of Atypical Employment

Taiwan is ranked 13th out of 139 economic bodies in the International Institute for Management Development (IMD) 2010 Global Competitiveness Report and 45th out of 183 economic bodies in the 2010 Doing Business Report. However, in terms of employment-flexibility indexes, Taiwan is ranked 153rd in the former publication and 114th in the latter (San, 2011). That is, the inflexibility of atypical labor contracts and atypical labor systems hampers not only the recruitment of foreign talent, but also the competitiveness of Taiwanese businesses.

The provisions for contracts in Taiwan's Labor Standards Law are more restrictive than the terms in other developed countries' corresponding laws. However, as Taiwan's industries have evolved and Taiwan's labor force has diversified, atypical employment there has become a notable trend. It is important for the Taiwanese government to review related policies and to provide a more friendly and flexible environment for workers and businesses (San, 2011).

Future of HRM in Taiwan

According to the 2011 *Asian Competitiveness Annual Report* announced by Beijing University of International Business and Economics Publishing Co., Ltd, Taiwan is ranked second, after South Korea, among 35 Asian economic bodies. The report states that the strength of Taiwan rests on the island-economy's education and innovation systems.

To attract and develop talent for maintaining and even enhancing business-competitiveness advantages on the basis of current strengths is critical for Taiwanese businesses, especially in the turbulent economic environment that started in 2008. Of use at this point in the chapter would be a discussion, which follows, about the related trends of global talent development, work–life balance, new workforce dimensions and new technology.

Global Talent Development

Gunz and Peiperl (2007) surmised that from 2000 to 2040, as globalization progresses, the talented labors that companies seek will divide into three phases: expatriates, local talents and global citizen. In the third phase, global talent will search for job opportunities on the basis of personal experiences and career plans.

It has been predicted that the GDP of the Asia-Pacific region will account for approximately 45 percent of global GDP in 2015 (S. Li, 2010). Owing to emerging markets' demand for specifically skilled labor, international companies—especially those based in China—have doubled their talent-recruitment efforts, often targeting Taiwan. The strengths of Taiwanese workers are their understanding of Chinese culture and business, their bilingual skills and their notable integration and innovation capabilities. The most popular areas in which Taiwanese workers exhibit notable skills are semiconductor engineering, LCD (Liquid Crystal Display) engineering and Integrated Circuit (IC) design. More and more Taiwanese professionals are willing to work in China because of the country's rapid economic development.

Taiwanese companies are good at developing effective business models in order to take advantage of niche markets. However, they started to face different challenges when they went beyond Taiwan to engage in more large-scale operations in China where scalability of operation skills and business models is important (Li, 2011). Given that they speak the same language and have the same root of culture as Chinese mainlanders, the task of recruiting a large labor force and the follow-up training and development still pose a formidable challenge. The well-publicized multiple suicide incidents in Foxconn's China factories in recent years reflected the need for more understanding on the subjects of stress management for employees in a high-pressure working environment, the enterprise–employee relationship in a fast-changing society, compensation augmentation at a very high pace, training of special skills for a large number of workers, and so forth.

The agreement between China and Taiwan to allow for direct cross-strait flights greatly strengthened the convenience of allocating skilled labor from one state to the other. The major types of workers that Chinese businesses need are entry-level workers, middle-level managers, and professionals. Regarding the growth of China's internal markets, entry-level workers are for the rapid growth of the service industry, middle-level managers are for Taiwan experiences, and professionals are for sales and marketing, design, and the financial industry (You, 2010).

Balance Between Work and Life

According to the 2011 Neilsen Survey, the percentage of Taiwanese ranking work–life balance as the most pressing issue they face increased by 31 percent from the last such survey (The Nielsen Company, 2012). In Taiwan, per capita annual income was about US$20,000; however, Taiwanese workers generally put in more hours over the course of a year than do Chinese, whose per capita income was less than US$4,000. The employee productivity of Taiwan has increased more than that of China, South Korea, Hong Kong and Singapore in the past five years because of the long work hours and the stagnant wages and salaries in Taiwan (Chen, 2011). Taiwanese work hours added up to 2,074 hours per year in 2009, which is higher than the 1,911 hours per year in the United States. These figures imply that Taiwanese workers are under heavy stress. The common disorders stemming from work-related stress are psychosomatic disorders and generalized anxiety disorders. From 1998 to 2009, psychosomatic disorders underwent a fourfold increase in Taiwan. Generalized anxiety disorders afflicted 31.7 percent of Taiwan's population of age 20 and over (Lin and Sie, 2011).

The highest risk segment of this population is female, young and working for flexible pay; also at high risk are those who work significantly long hours and get over-involved in their work, and those who lack job security. A total of 80 percent of female workers needed to take care of elders or children at home and, in general, female workers' salary was only 80 percent of their male counterparts' salary (He, Huang and Lu, 2010). The suicide events that happened in Foxconn during the years of 2010 and 2011, given that they all happened in China, also reflected the stress that this new generation of workers faces. Work-related strains for individuals, organizations' emphasis on maximum efficiency and income and wealth disparities are all major contributors of stress for workers (Jiang and Huang, 2010).

More and more Taiwanese companies have started to increase the flexibility of employees' schedules and have established and strengthened employee assistance programs (EAPs) and other types of programs aiming to help employees balance vocational responsibilities with life outside work. In addition, the Taiwanese government amended the Occupational Safety and Health Act in 2011, requiring employers to devote more resources to the physical and psychological health of employees. Companies with more than 50 employees must provide health-related services to employees. Also, employers are responsible for occupational injury if they cannot prove that they had provided appropriate protection such as protective clothing or equipment.

New Dimensions of the Workforce

The increase in older, female and atypical employees is a global trend. The high percentages of populations that are middle-aged or older have led to pressing financial problems. Potential solutions include increasing the birth rate, employing more immigrants and extending the retirement age of employees (Wu, 2010). These are some of the measures that promise to increase the supply of labor and counter the negative stereotypes about older and immigrant workers. In response to the need, the Taiwan Labor Standards Law, passed in 2008, extended the mandatory retirement age from 60 to 65.

The Council of Labor Affairs' statistics showed that, among females, the labor-participation rate would peak for those aged from 25 to 29 and would subsequently decrease, mainly because women who were above that age would likely have extra responsibilities with respect to taking care of their newly formed families. Of women who exit the workforce after giving birth, the percentage who return to the workforce is far lower in Taiwan than in Europe, Japan and other regions. Taiwan's Council of Labor Affairs also showed that in the United States, Canada, France, Germany, and other developed countries, women aged from 35 to 54 can maintain a high labor-participation rate of about 60 percent to 70 percent: For Taiwan, the rate of reemployment is only about 40 percent (Council of Labor Affairs, 2010).

A Women Employment Survey conducted by 104 Job Bank (2011), Taiwan's largest online job site showed that, in Taiwan, 56 percent of female workers decided to return to the workplace within two years of taking family leave; however, companies generally considered that women could not simultaneously perform salaried work and care for their families (41 percent), while more women needed flexible working hours that were not provided by most companies (40 percent). In short, the stereotypes attached to mothers and the lack of time flexibility are two major obstacles that women face when returning to work after a family leave. While the LPR rate for Taiwan-based males has exhibited a downward trend, the rate for females has moved in the opposite direction. To improve their own business performance, businesses could make good use of their advantages, such as their sense of responsibility and their resistance to stress.

Atypical employment is another trend. In the past decade many businesses have sought greater flexibility for hiring employees, and dispatched employees or employees under contract are becoming more popular. Based on Huang's study (2011), the number of employees in Taiwan's industrial and service sectors in February 2010 increased by approximately 93,000 people compared to the number in the same month in the previous year. Of which, 18,000 were dispatched employees. Other forms of atypical employment such as temporary workers and short-term contractors have also gained in popularity. The first priority for some older and female workers seeking jobs is a flexible work schedule, which enables them to hold down a steady job without sacrificing their life outside the workplace.

New Technologies

New technologies such as the Internet affect business operations tremendously. In particular, notable features of Web 2.0—participation, sharing and interaction among users—influence HR practices in several ways. The core concept of "mass collaboration" of Web 2.0 is widely accepted. Underlying Web 2.0's architecture is participation. The most well-known tools that serve this purpose are blogs, wikis, social networking sites (SNSs; for example, Facebook, Twitter and Plurk) and video-sharing sites (for example, YouTube and TED).

Web 2.0's applicability to HR practices varies from recruitment and training to development and efficiency enhancement. Companies can use SNS to recruit employees and to check references. Moreover, companies can construct meaningful short videos that serve as teaching-material, thereby saving time and money. Worthy of note here is a study by Lytras, Castillo-Merino and Serradell-Lopez (2010). Using a sample of 2,029 SMEs, the researchers demonstrated that the efficiency of firms exhibited a significant improvement when the firms combined information and communication technologies (ICTs) with employee-assessment systems and other HR practices. These new tools are especially helpful in improving worker autonomy, flexibility of worker schedules and decentralization of decision-making processes within the firms.

Of the seven Web 2.0 principles that O'Reilly (2005) proposed, two of them —the "web as platform" principle and the "harnessing collective intelligence" principle—have important implications for innovation management. McAfee (2006) argued that email, intranet and portal are not the best tools for knowledge management, but Web 2.0 provides solutions. First, wikis can record knowledge in a work-in-progress form whose revision function promotes fast idea exchange. Second, effective usage of "tags" changes approaches to knowledge classification. Traditional taxonomies would set a first-level category, under which existed a second-level category; however, the bottom-up feature of tags reflects the actual cognition map of workers and also constitutes invisible links connecting workers to one another. Third, Rich Site Summary (RSS) enables workers to access dynamics knowledge for further knowledge accumulation. Fourth, workers can increase their weak-ties through their original strong-ties via SNS, which provides more opportunities to exchange heterogeneous ideas and to engage in innovation.

Case Study: Case Study: Beating out Apple and Samsung, HTC earns the "2011 Device Manufacturer of the Year" award

(The text of this case is summarized from the *2010 HTC Annual Report*.)

Background Information

HTC was founded in Taiwan in May 1997. It sustained expansion in overall business operations and HTC's brand development crowned HTC's experiences. They shipped 24.67 million smartphones in 2010, the first time in their history where shipments surpassed the 20 million mark; that is, the firm more than doubled their 2009 shipment record, giving HTC a year-on-year growth rate much higher than the sector average. Net profits after taxes for the year reached NTD39.5 billion, to set a new all-time record. By the close of 2010, global recognition of the HTC brand had risen to 50 percent.

HTC today holds the attention of many global businesses and many exponents of technology media. *Bloomberg Businessweek*, *Fast Company* and MIT's *Technology Review* put HTC on their respective lists of the world's 50 most innovative companies in 2010 (Einhorn and Amdt, 2010). That same year, *T3 magazine* proclaimed HTC its "tech Brand of the year" (Mayne, 2011). Also that year, *Newsweek* named HTC one of the top ten innovative companies. At the 2011 Mobile World Congress, HTC overcame competition from Apple and Samsung to earn the "Device Manufacturer of the Year" award. In October 2011, Interbrand Company announced HTC as the 98th global brand, estimating their brand value to be about US$3.605 billion, having increased 163 percent over the previous year.

Human Resources

Employees represent one of HTC's most valuable assets. The company has in recent years actively recruited outstanding talent into its ranks, particularly in the areas of product design, user interface, brand promotion and sales and marketing. While bringing on professionals from Europe and the Americas, they have also invested significant resources into making the work environment at HTC diverse, challenging and encouraging. As of the close of March 2011, HTC employed 12,943 staff worldwide, and 22.9 percent of all HTC managerial positions were held by 218 non-Taiwanese managers. Non-Taiwanese managerial and technical staff filled 13.5 percent of HTC managerial and technical positions. Women have held 16.2 percent of HTC's 951 managerial positions since the company's inception. HTC has consistently devoted considerable resources to in-house R&D capabilities. Today, R&D professionals account for almost 30 percent of HTC's headcount, and annual R&D investments regularly represent 4 to 6 percent of total revenues.

At HTC, the Division of Talent Management handles corporate HR development and administration, promotes HTC corporate culture and employee benefit programs, and conducts organizational and HR planning to support corporate development.

Staffing

Hiring and retaining exceptional employees is a key objective of HTC's HR strategy. They are an equal opportunity employer and recognize the practical benefits that employee diversity brings to HTC corporate culture and to the reinforcement and extension of innovation. HTC hires all new employees through open selection procedures, with candidates offered positions based on merit. HTC works through cooperative programs with universities, internship programs and summer work programs to provide work opportunities to a large number of students each year. They participate actively in job fairs and recruitment events in Taiwan and abroad as part of their ongoing, organized effort to tap the best talent available.

For employee retention, HTC offers incentives to employees possessing special skills in order to keep them with the company and to ensure that they benefit from their employer-oriented efforts. Long-service awards are presented at a company-wide ceremony that recognizes employees with five- and ten-year-long service records. In order to enhance employees' professional experience and career planning, HTC facilitates employee transfers within the company.

Employee Development

HTC operates a workplace environment highly conducive to learning and professional growth. By encouraging employees to improve themselves and to maintain and enhance their professional skills, HTC helps sustain its competitive advantage while keeping a promise to help employees grow as individuals. Supplementing their extensive in-house technical training curriculum, HTC offered its employees in 2010 specially designed management and personal development curricula (including language training and new-staff orientation) to help employees diversify their skill sets, explore new potentials and deepen expertise. HTC has also launched a dedicated e-learning and mobile learning platform able to deliver a diverse range of learning tools within a highly accommodating learning environment. HTC further has offered its employees in-service training scholarships, effectively subsidizing off-site training to encourage growth and permit the pursuit of personal fulfillment (see Table 6.2).

Compensation and Benefits

HTC employees earn market-competitive salaries that take into consideration academic background, work experience, seniority and current professional responsibilities. On the basis of HTC's current-year business performance, the president proposes—and the board of directors approves—the amount of funds to be set aside for the annual employee-performance bonuses. The firm also allocates employee profit-sharing bonuses to employees each year on the basis of motions that derive from the board of directors and that are adopted by resolution at annual shareholders' meetings.

Table 6.2 Staff Training Hours Expenditures in Taiwan During 2010

Category		Total Training Hours	Expenditure (NT$)
Technical		66,590	958,227
Management		18,171	5,355,261
Personal Development	Orientation Training (for New Staff)	9,854	680
	Effectiveness Enhancement	55,412	5,323,335
TOTAL		150,027	11,637,503

Source: *2010 HTC Annual Report.*

The Labor Pension Act (the "Act"), which provides for a new defined contribution plan, took effect on July 1, 2005. Employees can choose to remain subject to the defined benefit pension mechanism under the Labor Standards Law (the "Law") or can choose to be subject instead to the Act. The Act mandates that the rate of a company's required monthly contributions to an employee's individual pension accounts shall be at least 6 percent of the employee's monthly wages salaries, and that these contributions shall be identified as pension expenses in the employee's income statement.

Employee Relations and Communications

HTC's work environment is geared to challenge, stimulate and fulfill employees. The company maintains various outreach initiatives designed to motivate employees, enhance employee benefits and facilitate greater dialogue between the company and its workforce.

HTC is committed to fostering an atmosphere of trust in its labor relations and assigns great importance to internal communications. HTC further offers employees various channels through which to submit opinions, suggestions and complaints, which may be delivered via a telephone hotline, an email address or physical mail—all of which are made known through HTC's regular employee opinion surveys.

Future Challenges

HTC is now an important player in global telecommunications, and anticipates continued growth in the smartphone sector. HTC is responding to intense competition, and in this regard the company's future efforts will continue to focus on tailoring innovative products ever more closely to users' daily lives and on winning over increasing numbers of consumers.

In order to achieve long-term sustainability and competitiveness, HTC in 2010 acquired the software-customization house Abaxia. HTC made this acquisition specifically to broaden and deepen its capabilities in software development, integrated cloud computing and the development of varied connected services. HTC also announced a great recruitment plan in the first half of 2011: The company's goal is to hire more than 1,000 R&D employees, equal to 30 percent of the current research team.

It is a big challenge for a fast-growing international company to effectively manage its employee talent, especially so large a number of R&D personnel, foreign workers and high-level managers. To balance discipline and innovation at the same time is the other challenge for any team to pursuit high performance. HTC, with its past record of achieved excellence, carries the promise of a bright future for all smartphone consumers.

Useful Websites

104 Assessment Expert: www.104assessment.com.tw/service.jsp

104 Job Bank: www.104.com.tw

1111 Job Bank: www.1111.com.tw

Adecco: www.adecco.com.tw/index.asp

Asia-Learning: www.asia-learning.com

Bureau of Employment and Vocational Training: www.evta.gov.tw

Bureau of Labor Insurance: www.bli.gov.tw

Career Consulting: www.career.com.tw

China Human Resources Development Academic Society: www.hrda.tidi.tw

Chinese Human Resource Management Association: www.chrma.net/eng/index.php

Chinese Management Association: www.management.org.tw

Chinese Personnel Executive Association: www.hr.org.tw

China Productivity Center: www.cpc.org.tw

Council of Labor Affairs: www.cla.gov.tw

e-job Bank: www.ejob.gov.tw

Kung-Hwa Management Foundation: www.mars.org.tw

Manpower Group: www.manpower.com.tw

Taiwan Academy of Management: www.taom.org.tw

Taiwan TrainQuali System: http://ttqs.evta.gov.tw/Default.aspx

Yes123 Job Bank: www.yes123.com.tw/admin/index.asp

References

Anthony M. S., Clarkson, R. B., Hughes, C. L., Morgan, T. M. and Burke, G. L. (1996) 'Soybean is flavones improve cardiovascular risk factors without affecting the reproductive system of peripubertal rhesus monkeys', *The Journal of Nutrition* 126: 43–50.

Beaumont, P. B. (*1993*) *Human Resource Management: Key concepts and skills.* London: Sage.

Beijing University of International Business and Economics Publishing Co., Ltd (2011, May) *The Research Institute of Boao Forum for Asia: Asian Competitiveness Annual Rreport 2011.* http://english.boaoforum.org/u/cms/www2/201109/07135115oewz.pdf, accessed February 1, 2013.

Byars, L. L. and Rue, L. W. (2010) *Human Resource Management.* KY: Muze Inc.

Ceng, R. (2010) 'Goodbye, 5 Electronic Companies', *Business Weekly, 1191:* 114–22 (in Chinese).

Chen, Y. (2011) "'Jin' Indisputable Force", *CommonWealth* 464: 98–104 (in Chinese).

Cheng, B. (1995) 'Chaxu geju (concentric relational configuration) and Chinese organizational behavior', *Indigenous Psychological Research in Chinese Societies* 3: 142–219 (in Chinese).

Chi, N. and Chang, H. (2006) 'Exploring the Relationships Between Human Resource Manager Roles, HR Performance Indicators and Organizational Performance', *Journal of Human Resource Management 6*(3): 71–93 (in Chinese).

Chung, M., Tsen, H. and Yeh, F. (2008) 'The Study of the Effectiveness of Web-Based Training', *Taiwan Business Performance Journal 2*(1): 119–40 (in Chinese).

Chung, Y. and Wang, W. (2010) 'The Limit of Blood-and-Iron', *Business Weekly* 1176: 114–24 (in Chinese).

Council for Economic Planning and Development (2011) *Taiwan Statistical Data Book 2011.* Taiwan: Council for Economic Planning and Development, www.cepd.gov.tw/m1.aspx?sNo=0015742, accessed February 1, 2013.

Council of Labor Affairs. (2009, May 27). Yearly Bulletin. Taiwan: Council of Labor Affairs. www.cla.gov.tw/cgi-bin/siteMaker/SM_theme?page=49c056e1, February 1, 2013.

Ding, S. and Gu, S. (2010). 'Three Emerging Areas of Shortage', *CommonWealth* 451: 56–60 (in Chinese).

Ding, Y. (2011) 'Domestic enterprises, "corporate universities"', *Management Magazine* 444: 38–39 (in Chinese).

Directorate General of Budget, Accounting and Statistics (2013, January) *Monthly Bulletin Of Statistics.* Taiwan: Executive Yuan, http://eng.dgbas.gov.tw/lp.asp?CtNode=1998&CtUnit=1053&BaseDSD=35&mp=2, accessed February 1, 2013.

Einhorn, B and Amdt, M. (2010, April 15) *The 50 Most Innovative Companies.* www.businessweek.com/magazine/content/10_17/b4175034779697.htm, accessed February, 1, 2013.

The Epoch USA, Inc (2011, May 18). 'Taiwanese Women Who Turnover After Marriage 9 to 5 Intend to Return to the Workplace', http://tw.epochtimes.com/b5/11/3/8/n3190862p.htm (in Chinese), accessed February 1, 2013.

Farh, J. (1995). 'Human Resource Management in Taiwan, Republic of China', in L. F. Moore and P. D. Jennings (eds), *Human Resource Management on the Pacific Rim: Institutions, Practices and Attitudes.* Berlin, New York: de Gruyter, pp. 265–94.

Gao, F. (2010). 'Two Wings for the Talent', *Management Magazine* 427: 102–03 (in Chinese).

Gomez-Mejia, L. R., Balking, D. B. and Cardy, R. (1995) *Managing Human resources.* New York: Prentice-Hall International, Inc.

Gunz, H., and Peiperl, M. (2007) *Handbook of Career Studies.* Thousand Oaks, CA: Sage.

He, G. (2011). 'Three Times Competitive—I was Highly Paid', *CommonWealth* 473:102–04 (in Chinese).

He, G., Huang, Y., and Lu, J. (2010) 'Affairs of State? Family? A Woman Thing?', *Common-Wealth* 451: 82–87 (in Chinese).

He, S. (2011) 'What Kinds of People Would the Boss Want?', *Business Weekly* 1,217: 116–17 (in Chinese).

Hon Hai Precision Ind. Co., Ltd. (2010) *Welfare*. Taiwan: Hon Hai Precision Ind. Co., Ltd, www.honhai-hr.com.tw/welfare.htm (in Chinese).

Hsu, Y. and Leat, M. (2000) 'A Study of HRM and Recruitment and Selection Policies and Practices in Taiwan', *International Journal of Human Resource Management* 11(2): 413–35.

HTC (2011, April 17) *2010 HTC Annual Report*. Taiwan: HTC. www.corpasia.net/tai-wan/2498/annual/2010/CH/2010%20HTC%20Annual%20Report%20(C)_FkajQyaI-qnNf_C4rBALHNJEiL_FfQr7JnnHEkj_uMunDAc3kJCR.pdf (in Chinese), accessed February 1, 2013.

Huang, T. (1998) 'The strategic level of human resource management and organizational performance: Empirical investigation', *Asia Pacific Journal of Human Resources* 36(2): 59–72 (in Chinese).

Huang, T. (2004). *Human Resource Management*, 7th edn, eds L. L. Byars and L. W. Rue. Taipei: McGraw Hill (in Chinese).

Huang, T. (2011). *Human Resource Management*, 10th edn, eds L. L. Byars and L. W.Rue. Taipei: McGraw Hill (in Chinese).

Huang, T., Ci, D. and Cheng, S. (2010) *Human Resource Management: Theory and practice*, 3rd edn.Taipei, Taiwan: OpenTech (in Chinese).

IHS Inc. (2012). *IHS Global Insight: Country and Industry Forecasting*. Colorado: IHS Inc, www.ihs.com/products/global-insight/country-analysis, accessed February 1, 2013.

International Monetary Fund (IMF) (2011) *IMF elibrary-data*. Washington, DC: International Monetary Fund, http://elibrary-data.imf.org.

Jiang, Y., and Huang, J. (2010) 'High-voltage failure, the dilemma of a new generation of man-agement', *CommonWealth* 448: 36–39 (in Chinese).

Lee, F., Lee, T. and Wu, W. (2010) 'The relationship between human resource management practices, business strategy and firm performance: evidence from steel industry in Tai-wan', *The International Journal of Human Resource Management* 21(9): 1,351–72.

Lee, J. S. (2002) *Human Resource Development and Taiwan's Move towards a Knowledge-Based Economy*. Taiwan: The Pacific Economic Cooperation Council.

Li, S. (2010) 'Taiwan staged to grab people's congresses combat', *Management Magazine* 434: 68–71 (in Chinese).

Li, Y. (2011) 'Organizational transformation—the boss to do, or to introduce the CEO of?', *Business Week* 1,236: 36–40 (in Chinese).

Lin, S. (2011) 'Technology industry to get people—cottage[s] provide[d]? to lure them away to dig to [in?] China', *Business Weekly* 1,227: 58–62 (in Chinese).

Lin, S. and Sie, M. (2011) 'Health Killer—Psychosomatic Disorders', *CommonWealth* 473: 128–37 (in Chinese).

Lytras, M. D., Castillo-Merino, D. and Serradell-Lopez, E. (2010) 'New Human Resources Practices, Technology and Their Impact on SMEs' Efficiency', *Information Systems Man-agement* 27(3): 267–73.

McAfee, A. (2006). Enterprise 2.0 – the dawn of emergent collaboration, *MIT Sloan Manage-ment Review 47*(3): 21–28.

McKinsey Quarterly, The (2007, November) *The Organizational Challenges of Global Trends: A McKinsey global survey*. London: McKinsey & Company, http://download.mckinsey quarterly.com/organizational_challenges.pdf., accessed February 1, 2013.

Manpower (2007, April 9) *2007 Talent Shortage Survey Results*. Wisconsin, United States: Manpower Inc, www.manpower.com.tw/pdf/talent_shortage_2007_en.pdf, accessed February 1, 2013.

Mayne, M. (2011, September 8). *HTC Scoops Top Gongs at T3 Gadget Awards 2010*. www. t3.com/news/htc-scoops-top-gongs-at-t3-gadget-awards-2010, February, 1, 2013.

Negandhi, A. R. (1973) *Management and Economic Development: The Case of Taiwan*. The Hague: Martinus Nijhoff.

Noe, R. A., Hollenbeck, J. R., Gerhart, B. and Wright, P. M. (2008) *Fundamentals of human resource management*, 3rd edn. New York: McGraw-Hill Irwin.

O'Reilly, T. (2005, September 30). *What is Web 2.0*. California: O'Reilly Media, Inc, www. oreillynet.com/pub/a/oreilly/tim/news/2005/09/30/what-is-web-20.html, accessed February 1, 2013.

San, G. (2011) 'Retrospect and Prospect of Taiwan's human resources planning,' *Yan Kao Shuang Yue Kan* 35(2): 71–93 (in Chinese).

Stone, R. J. (2009). *Managing Human Resources: An Asian Perspective*, 1st edn. Milton: John Wiley & Sons.

Sun, S., Lou, Y., Chao, P. and Wu, C. (2008) 'A study on the factors influencing the users' intention in human recruiting sites,' *Journal of Human Resource Management* 8(3): 1–23 (in Chinese).

The Neilsen Company (2012, February 27) 'Consumer confidence, concerns and spending intentions, http://nl.nielsen.com/site/documents/NielsenGlobalConsumerConfidenceQ12012.pdf, accessed February 1, 2013.

TSMC (2012) *Employee and People Care*. Taiwan: Taiwan Semiconductor Manufacturing Company, www.tsmc.com/english/csr/employee_and_people_care.htm, accessed February 1, 2013.

Wang, Y. and Wang, S. (2011) 'Recruiting! 58% increase in the Job vacancy', *Global Views Monthly 299*: 200–06 (in Chinese).

Wu, Y. (2010) 'Seventy-year-old retired is not too late', *CommonWealth* 458: 181 (in Chinese).

Wu, B., Wun, J., Liao, W., Huang, J., Han, J. and Huang, L. (2011) *Human Resource Management: Basis and Application*, 1st edn. Taipei, Taiwan: Hwa Tai Publishing (in Chinese).

Yan, C. (2011) 'Experiential learning method like the real thing', *Management Magazine* 446: 84–87 (in Chinese).

Yan, J. (2006). *The Reuse of the order Retired Professional Human Resource: The orientation of enterprise requirements*, unpublished master's thesis, National Chengchi University, Taiwan (in Chinese).

Yao, D. (1999). 'Human resource management challenges in Chinese Taipei', *Human Resource Management Symposium on SMEs Proceedings* 2: 30–31.

You, Z. (2010) 'New Cross-Strait Their Jobs Report,' *Business Weekly* 1,156: 88–94 (in Chinese).

Zhu, Y., Chen, I. and Warner, M. (2000) 'HRM in Taiwan: An empirical case study', *Human Resource Management Journal* 10(4): 32–44.

Zhu, Y. and Warner, M. (2001) 'Taiwanese business strategies vis a vis the Asian financial crisis', *Asia Pacific Business Review* 7(3): 139–56.

7 Human Resource Management in India

DEBI S. SAINI AND PAWAN S. BUDHWAR

This chapter presents an overview of the current scenario of human resource management (HRM) in India, the national institutions that support the HRM framework, the challenges that the HR profession and companies in India face, and a short case reflecting the type of HR issues that usually arise in India. To provide the required context, next relevant demographic details of the Indian economy and society are presented.

India is a republic in South Asia and the largest democracy in the world. It has the second highest population in the world (after China), which as per the 2011 census reached 1.21 billion people living in 640 districts of 28 states and seven union territories (Budhwar and Varma, 2011a). The literacy rate for seven years and above for the country stands at 74 percent; the corresponding figures separated for males and females are 82.12 percent and 65.46 percent respectively. The density of population (per sq. km) is 382 and the sex ratio (females per 1,000 males) is 940.

India attained independence from the British on 15 August 1947 and is governed by a constitution that came into force on 26 January 1950. The country has 179 languages and 544 dialects (Saini, 2011). The constitution recognises twenty-two languages, 'Hindi' and English being the two official languages. India has one of the largest English-speaking populations in the Asia-Pacific region (Budhwar, 2003), which is a major advantage in the globalised world.

The National Commission for Enterprises in the Unorganized Sector (NCEUS) has estimated that total employment in the country in 2004–05 was 457.5 million. Of these, 394.9 million were in the informal/unorganised sector, and 62.6 million were in the formal/organised sector (Government of India, 2009). In 2011, the total workforce in the country was believed to be about 500 million. As per the data available, in 2004–5, the percentage of those employed in wage employment was about 15 percent. About 60 percent of the workforce is engaged in agriculture with the remaining engaged in the non-agriculture sector. The second National Commission on Labour (NCL) estimated that only 5 percent of the workforce in the age group of 20–24 years had acquired some kind of a formal vocational training (Government of India, 2002). This percentage in the case of most developed countries ranges from 60 to 80 percent.

India is rich in both natural and human resources, even as it faces tremendous challenges in its efforts to enhance economic growth and development. It is estimated that about 160 million people (comprising of about 31.40 million households) are in the middle class, which is becoming larger with the liberalisation of the Indian economy. This class is also viewed in the developed countries as an important market for exporting their goods from a long-term point of view. The country has multiplied its foreign direct investment (FDI) several times since adopting the New Economic Policy (NEP) in 1991, but it is still far behind China and a few other countries. It is estimated that there are now more than 20,000 multinational firms operating in India and that this number is increasing rapidly (Budhwar and Varma, 2011a). The country started liberalising its economy in July 1991 when its foreign exchange reserves reached a dangerously low level; the new model has saved the country from any worry on that count. In December 2011 these reserves stood at $296 billion. The new model also led to an exponential rise in its annual GDP growth, which in the past decade has ranged from 6 to more than 9 percent. This along with other changes in the economic environment has made India an FDI destination for global firms. India is now projected to become the world's third-largest economy in dollar terms (behind China and the United States) within the next 20 years or so as per the global investment banking and securities firm Goldman Sachs; others like Citibank Financial have still better projections for the country.

As global firms seek success in their Indian operations, and as Indian firms reach a higher degree of professionalism in the global context, they have to make critical decisions related to HRM models as strategic choices. This will necessitate the appreciation of the factors, which influence HRM policies and practices in the Indian context, and the challenges that the HR function faces. These factors, among others, include the availability of requisite skills and competencies, required mindsets, desired values and customs, a facilitative legal framework and institutions and a cultural environment for promoting excellence (Budhwar and Varma, 2011b). These factors are the products of a country's socio-economic and political realities. A comprehensive understanding of such realities and insights helps a fuller comprehension of the HRM model of a country (Budhwar and Sparrow, 2002a). Next, we summarise the historical developments in Indian HRM.

Historical Developments in HRM

One of the first companies to have adopted formal concern for labour in India is the Tata Iron and Steel Manufacturing Company Ltd (now known as Tata Steel). The emergence of the personnel function in India is attributed to the appointment for the first time of labour welfare officers by this company in 1920; others followed suit much later. Interestingly, provisions similar to those provided by Cadbury in Britain were provided by the Tata group in India around this time (see Budhwar and Khatri, 2001). One of the earliest pieces of labour legislation in the country emerged in the form of the Trade Unions Act of 1926, which gave formal recognition to the workers' right to form unions. The Royal Commission of Labour 1931 recommended the appointment of labour welfare officers, and the Factories Act of 1948 made that mandatory in all factories employing 500 or more workers. Around the time when India got independence in 1947 and immediately after that a number of pieces of labour and industrial legislation were enacted that led to managing the labour legislation as an important area of activity for personnel managers. The Industrial Disputes Act 1947 (IDA) formed one of the most important areas of labour legislation, which envisages a concilia-tion–adjudication–arbitration model of industrial disputes settlement. It provides for compulsory adjudication of industrial disputes – both rights and interest. Although a compulsory adjudication system was a World War II legal instru-ment used by the British to contain industrial conflict during the war time, it was formalised by the British Indian government by incorporating this concept in the IDA, in April 1947. Despite much debate and despite controversies in post-inde-pendence India, the system still survives even in resolution of interest disputes and there are no signs of its replacement by a less-regulated collective bargaining framework of the Western type.

After independence, in the 1950s, two professional bodies related to the person-nel function emerged. The Indian Institute of Personnel Management (IIPM), a counterpart of the Institute of Personnel Management (IPM) in the United Kingdom was formed at Calcutta and the National Institute of Labour Manage-ment (NILM) at Bombay. Since the 1960s onwards, massive case law on labour legislation emerged that added considerable legal complexity to the personnel management function. In the 1960s, the personnel function also began to expand beyond the welfare aspect with three areas of labour welfare, industrial relations and personnel administration developing as the constituent roles for the emerging profession. In the 1970s, the thrust of personnel function shifted towards greater organisational 'efficiency', and by the 1980s it began to use and focus on terms such as organizational development (OD) and human resource development (HRD). The two professional bodies that is, IIPM and NILM, merged in 1980 to form the National Institute of Personnel Management (NIPM) at Bombay (Bud-hwar and Varma, 2011b).

In the 1990s and later, HRD became the main focus of the personnel function apart from the existing focus on industrial relations (IRs), especially in larger companies. But this was seen mainly as a tool for improving business perform-ance. The vigorous efforts by some academics helped in popularising the concept of HRD among both academics and practitioners. Programmes of HRD and organisational development at the individual enterprise level in public as well as private sectors are being adopted. The formation of 'The National HRD Network' in 1985 was a landmark in the history of HR evolution in the country. In Febru-ary 2012 it had a membership of 12,500, which included HR and other managers as well as academics. It is the largest forum for debating HR interventions in the country, which has definitely helped in sharpening the abilities of HR profes-sionals and in the benchmarking of the best HR practices by different firms. On the above date, there were 30 regional chapters of the HRD Network in different parts of India. Even as this forum has been named HRD Network for historical reasons, for all purposes its activities include all areas of HRM including industrial relations. The 1990s also witnessed the elevation in the status of personnel managers to the board level, although only in professionally managed organisations (Budhwar and Sparrow, 1997). Subsequently, there has also been a massive upsurge in re-labelling the title of personnel managers to HRD managers or HR managers, and re-labelling the personnel department as the HRD department or HR department. Simultaneously, due to globalisation as well as the adoption of new technology considerable downsizing took place in the last decade of the 20th century. This gave rise to the need for the measurement of HR performance. The concept of an HRD scorecard is being used and now several metrics are being used as devices to measure the effectiveness of people-development activities.

As is well known, the concept of HRM as a strategic approach to employment management (or HR philosophy as it is referred to by many Indian academics and managers) developed in the Western countries during the 1980s and the 1990s both in its hard (instrumentalist) and soft (empowerment) dimensions (Legge, 1995). Empowerment was viewed as 'the elixir of the 1990s' and the key focus area of new HR thinking in the Western organisations. Its Indian counterpart was the HRD discourse that lasted nearly two decades. The HRM debate as such, which seems to have concluded especially in the United Kingdom, almost never started in India, although trade unions remained very critical of globalisation policies as they have been hard hit by it. This is symptomatic of the state of HR as an academic discipline, which had not developed on a large scale. The IR academics, on the other hand, remained busy arguing for the promotion of genuine collective bargaining that was believed to be hindered by the compulsory adjudication system. But the new thinking in the HR domain did travel through the MNCs' route. As far as HR teaching was concerned, this necessitated the introduction of new courses and an updating of the existing ones by the concerned faculties. Most business schools and university departments (except the top ones), however, are still in the process of devising innovative courses in this area, knowledge of which is necessary for realising the goal of professional excellence in people management; in reality the basic HRM course for general MBA students is still functional HRM including training and development (or old personnel management with minor adjustment). Courses in strategic HRM are taught in the top business schools even as HR managers in many private sector professionally managed organisations in the country are using the modern methods and interventions of HRM (see Budhwar and Sparrow, 1997; Cooke and Saini, 2010a).

The fast-growing Indian economy has created a pressure on the Indian HRM function to become more creative and innovative. The HRM profession promises to commit itself to improving the efficiency and engagement of the human resource, getting better results and improving industrial relations. This highlights, among others, the role of training and development and team or group HRM activities. Due to such changes the use of terms like 'talent management', 'employer branding', 'competency mapping', 'performance management', 'leadership development' and 'the alignment of the HR strategy with business goals' are now being talked about or are seriously implemented, especially in leading private sector organisations and MNCs operating in India as well as being taught by leading business schools in the country. Indeed, the rapidly changing business context of India is forcing such development. In order to better understand the impact of such forces, next we examine the influence of major national factors in Indian HRM.

National Culture and HRM

The long rule of the British in India promoted feudalism, inequality and hierarchy among both the urban and non-urban populations. The caste system in the country too has also played a contributory role in promoting hierarchy and inequality. The family-owned business houses made full use of the inculcation of these societal values in practising a kind of neo-feudalism in industry. This is reflected in the organisational structures and social relations that reflect hierarchy, status consciousness, power distance and low individualism. These values have helped strengthen hierarchical superior–subordinate relationships, which acts as a kind of a mechanism of social control on the employee. Studies have shown that Indian managers attribute high priority to the importance of cultural assumptions that guide their employees' perceptions and organisational thinking (Budhwar and Sparrow, 2002b). It is also revealed that the common Indian values, norms of behaviour and customs exercise considerable influence on their HRM policies and practices (Budhwar and Varma, 2011a). The Indian social and cultural environment puts primacy on strong family ties that dilute individualism, resulting in greater dependence on others. This highlights the importance of interpersonal relations in people management in India, more than the importance given to it in other societies. The core bases of the management system in social and family relationships can then be attributed to various factors including a strong caste system, an agrarian-based society, a high incidence of illiteracy, a high level of poverty and an indifference of the state system to the needs of the individual (Budhwar and Sparrow, 1997).

Kanungo and Mendonca (1994) have shown significant cultural differences between India and Western countries on the basis of Hofstede's (1991) four initial cultural dimensions of power distance, uncertainty avoidance, individualism, and masculinity. India stands relatively high on uncertainty avoidance and power distance and relatively low on individualism and masculinity dimensions. Relatively high uncertainty avoidance implies an unwillingness to take risks and accept organisational change. The relatively low individualism implies that family and group attainments take precedence over work outcomes. The relatively high power distance implies that managers and subordinates accept their relative positions in the organisational hierarchy and operate from these fixed positions. Obedience is facilitated by the supposedly superior authority of the position holder and not on any rational basis. This is simply by virtue of the authority inherent in that status. The relatively low masculinity implies that employees' orientation is towards personalised relationships rather than towards performance (Kanungo and Mendonca, 1994: 450). On the fifth dimension of long-term versus short-term orientation, traditionally, India is known as a long-term oriented nation (see Tripathi, 1990). However, results of a recent research (see Budhwar et al., 2006) suggest that due to the severe pressure created by the liberalization of economic policies and the presence of foreign operators in Indian organisations, the question of immediate survival has become more important. This explains a recent shift of emphasis towards short-termism but, more importantly, an emphasis on developing rationalised, formal and structured HRM systems (see Budhwar and Varma, 2011b).

From the above discussion, it can be deduced that the Indian societal culture has made a lasting impact on most management functions such as staffing, communication, leadership, motivation and control. Staffing for top managerial positions among Indian organisations (especially in the private sector) is generally restricted by familial, communal and political considerations. Authority in Indian organisations is likely to remain one-sided, with subordinates leaning heavily on their superiors for advice and directions. Motivational tools in the Indian organisations are more likely to be social, inter-personal and even spiritual.

National Institutions Supporting the HRM Framework

The IR Framework

The hallmark of the Indian IR is a massive state presence in it through the Industrial Disputes Act, 1947 (IDA). This Act empowers the 'appropriate Government', in its discretion, to refer to an industrial dispute for adjudication either on failure of conciliation or even without any resort to conciliation. Apart from the IDA, two other laws form part of the IR law in the country, that is, the Trade Unions Act 1926 (TUA) and the Industrial Employment (Standing Orders) Act 1946 (IESOA). The TUA confers on workers freedom of association and provides to unions immunity against civil and criminal liability for conspiracy in taking industrial action. The IESOA seeks to ensure standardisation of the terms of employment and their certification by a government officer, who is obliged to satisfy himself that they are just and fair. These sets of laws were intended to facilitate the realisation of the individual and collective rights of the workers.

Promoting industrial growth with social justice has projectedly guided the IR policy of the Indian government. Towards this end, apart from providing a facilitative legal framework, the central government has effectively used a consultative tripartite conference institution for promoting industrial peace. This is called the Indian Labour Conference (ILC) and it brings together representatives of employers, labour and government to its meetings that have been held annually since 1940. One of the most notable non-legislative initiatives in IR came from the government in 1958 as a result of the deliberations at this forum in the form of the Code of Discipline and the Joint Management Councils. These instruments were to be used as a formal basis for recognition of unions and the facilitation of collective bargaining. However, the impact of these bodies was merely transitory (Johri, 1998: 49) and they have now almost petered off with the passage of time. Legal means and interventions continued to dominate the IR scene in the country, although lately, collective interest disputes rarely come before the adjudication machinery due to considerable fear in the working class of the rising managerial prerogatives in the neo-liberal world. Labour is now more prone to accepting the unilateral decisions of the employers regarding pay and benefits, especially in the private sector.

But by conferring the working-class rights and the individual labour rights, these laws, along with others, did succeed in creating a working-class consciousness in the country. They led to a situation of clash between workers' aspiration and employers' willingness to grant benefits. Being a labour surplus economy, the country's labour market realities helped the employers to obtain cheap labour and violate minimum labour employment standards by colluding with the labour bureaucracy. But the IDA model – that could not be replaced or even diluted despite considerably long debate on its fate – substantially diluted collective labour rights by ensuring massive state presence in IR to control labour power. It resulted in the juridification of IR (Saini, 1997, 1999). Its influence has been so strong that labour arbitration as a method of industrial disputes' resolution in the country is almost dead. Employers manage IR, among others, by diluting the efficacy of IR laws through consultation as well as adoption of extra-legal means. Variegated unfair labour practices (ULPs) are committed by them in the process, and even by workers/unions. Over the years the pressure of unions, opposition parties, other pressure groups and union federations have succeeded in influencing the state agencies to enact a large number of labour laws. One finds the situation paradoxical and perplexing. On paper, even industries that have become sick beyond hope are required to comply with these laws, including payment of minimum wage and minimum bonus. In reality the system works such that employers have learned to get away with these legal requirements. However, MNCs and other conscientious employers want an IR framework with simpler laws that do not require them to indulge in manoeuvring and shenanigans. By and large, the IR law framework in larger organisations adversely affects the cause of forging workplace cooperation so as to meet the challenges of HRM in responding to the changed needs of industry in the era of globalisation.

Unions

Being a democracy, India has at least a seemingly union-friendly legal framework of IR. The compulsory adjudication system of the IDA has kept the unions weak (Saini, 1999). The first two decades after the independence witnessed rapid unionisation of the organised sector in the country (both private and public). But unionisation in India started declining after the famous Bombay Textile Strike, which lasted more than a year and was not officially withdrawn until recently (Venkata Ratnam, 2001). This has brought a sea change in the concept of collective bargaining, which is less and less on an industry basis and more on a unit basis.

Membership of unions that are submitting returns is still low; as per the latest estimates it is barely 4 percent of the total workforce. The total trade union membership as per the latest estimates is about 20 million in an aggregate workforce of about 500 million in 2011. This is despite the fact that in the 1970s and 1980s the judiciary delivered several judgments in the area of industrial relations and other labour laws that reflected its attitude of extreme sympathy with the working people and less to the basic principles of industrial organisation. However, in the present economic environment some aspects of the existing legal framework are required to change its strong pro-labour stance. Lately, some of the recent labour judgments reflect the belief that the judiciary is more sympathetic with the employers and realise the need for efficiency, discipline and productivity in the new environment. Presently, there is reduced workers' resistance to employers' change initiatives, despite patches of working-class success in resisting the individualisation of IR through HRM. Interestingly, in contrast to national firms, the impact of unions on the HRM policies and practices of MNCs operating in India is negligible (see Budhwar, 2012), although there are many cases of union success including through grave violence in the two cases discussed by Saini (2006, 2012). However, the workers' stance is slowly changing and becoming more cooperative towards their employers.

It has to be admitted that the liberalisation of the Indian economy has put tremendous pressure both on the employees and employers. As a nation, India is lagging far behind in productivity standards and production of quality goods (see Budhwar and Varma, 2011a). These realities have begun influencing the mindsets of unions and union leaders, who now seem to be meekly giving in to the legitimacy of the globalisation agenda, as they are aware of these burning problems. In such circumstances, the possible consequence of the adoption of appropriate HRM policies is likely to be salutary. They will lead to minimum wastage of human and financial resources at the micro level. Their adoption will also give due importance to professional activities as per market exigencies. But, values of 'association', 'industrial justice' and 'workers' dignity' will face crisis; 'minimum standards of employment' are also getting clouded due to the unofficial support of the state to cost-cutting preferences of employers that are hidden in the globalisation agenda. But being a democracy, the country cannot openly adopt policies that disapprove of these IR values.

Diluting 'workplace pluralism' as a value by superimposing HRM on it may work successfully if a significant chunk of the workforce is 'gold-collared'. The merger of HRM and IR agenda can possibly work effectively in such a situation. If that can happen, one can also forecast greater possibility of the use of HRM as a broad model of workplace justice. Some of the best examples in this regard are most software companies in the country, which have used empowerment HRM as a model of workplace justice, which automatically keeps the law and adversarialism away (see Budhwar et al., 2009). The viability of the use of soft HRM as the principal philosophy in managing human resources increases in the case of such companies that employ knowledge workers. However, without question this will be too much of an asking from firms that do not have knowledge workers. Nevertheless, to a great extent this is successfully practised in many MNCs operating in India, irrespective of having knowledge or non-knowledge based employees (see Bjorkman and Budhwar, 2007; Budhwar, 2012). It needs a macro level of overhauling of the Indian HRM system, which has made quite some progress so far. Still, India has to go a long way in this direction (also see Budhwar and Varma, 2011b).

Going by the way the Indian government has reacted to the situation, the continuance of its sympathy to the cause of social justice in the organised sector appears only remote. This is despite the fact that there has been no labour law reform at all in the post-liberalisation era. This may appear surprising to the champions of globalisation. But principally, governments' unwillingness to effect labour reforms in the past decade or so is largely explained by their fragility at the central level; they have not shown the courage to antagonise the trade unions openly by undertaking these reforms. Interesting as it may appear, most employers have been able to manage the show despite the archaic laws. However, there is always a limit to everything, including the regulatory laws for workplace functioning. An amendment has been recently made to the IDA in 2010, but it has not touched at all the controversial parts of the labour legislation that the Congress government had promised in 1991 while announcing the new economic policy.

At the executive level, state governments' attitudes have changed considerably. Many of them have announced far-reaching changes in their labour policies, which henceforth appeared sacred cow in favour of the workers. Now they tacitly support hire and fire policies; forbidding of *bandhs* (closures), as happened in the case of Kerala (a state in South India); and easing of requirements for labour inspection, for example in the state of Rajasthan. The West Bengal state government (which was until recently headed by a Marxist party) during its regime cancelled the registration of hundreds of unions for non-submission of returns to the Registrar of Trade Unions, which is contrary to its earlier position. The incidence of granting permission for closure and retrenchment (as required under the IDA) in the state of Tamil Nadu has gone up, thus reflecting the new thinking among the states.

The above developments in Indian IR augur fairly well for developing HRM, for it is difficult to sustain it in situations of zero-sum IR. This is especially important when India's HR systems and processes have to be attuned to facilitating efficiency and productivity, and eventually the export-promotion model of development. But the government's support can be said to be forthcoming indirectly, that is, by remaining oblivious to the legal intent. The question is whether this is enough for the country's needs to attract higher levels of FDI. MNCs and other professional establishments need more tangible ways of state support including having the changed legal framework itself. Intriguingly, it should be appreciated that one way of tackling the problem of flexibility at the micro level is the effective adoption of HRM thinking. It has been used in many organisations including leading ones like Reliance and Tata Steel. The latter had about 80,000 workers when it realised the state of crisis due to overstaffing. Today it has managed to reduce itself to about 35,000 employees through well thought-out and sagacious employee relations policy. But most other organisations are unable to do this, especially in the public sector, for example, Air India, which is continuously incurring massive losses. The need for reforms in IR law so as to be facilitative to the globalisation policies then remains paramount.

The Labour Law Framework

India has about 50 major pieces of central labour legislation and about 150 pieces of state labour legislation. All of these can be grouped into five major categories, that is, laws relating to working conditions; laws relating to wages and monetary benefits; laws relating to industrial relations; laws relating to social security; and miscellaneous labour laws. Some of these laws were already in existence at the time of independence; more were added to give way to the philosophy of a welfare state adopted by the Indian state and enshrined in the Constitution. But the size of the organised sector workers who are protected by these laws has always been small and never exceeded 10 per cent of the total workforce in the country. Presently, it is estimated to be around 7 percent including the informal workforce in this sector. Some of the most salient pieces of Indian labour legislation can be listed as follows.

- Apprentices Act, 1961
- Beedi & Cigar Workers (Conditions of Employment) Act, 1966
- Bonded Labour System (Abolition) Act, 1976
- Building and Other Construction Workers (Regulation of Employment Service) Act, 1996
- Child Labour (Prohibition and Regulation) Act, 1986
- Cine-Workers and Cinema Theatre Workers (Regulation of Employment) Act, 1981
- Contract Labour (Regulation and Abolition) Act, 1970
- Dangerous Machines (Regulation) Act, 1983
- Dock Workers (Regulation of Employment) Act, 1948
- Dock Workers (Safety, Health and Welfare) Act, 1986
- Emigration Act, 1983
- Employees' Compensation Act, 1923
- Employees' Provident Fund and Miscellaneous Provisions Act, 1952
- Employees' State Insurance Act, 1948
- Employers' Liability Act, 1938
- Employment Exchanges (Compulsory Notification of Vacancies) Act, 1959
- Equal Remuneration Act, 1976
- Factories Act, 1948
- Industrial Disputes Act, 1947
- Industrial Employment (Standing Orders) Act, 1946
- Inter-State Migrant Workmen (Regulation of Employment and Conditions of Service) Act, 1979
- Labour Laws (Exemption from Furnishing Returns and Maintaining Registers by Certain Establishments) Act, 1988
- Maternity Benefit Act, 1961
- Mines Act, 1952
- Minimum Wages Act, 1948
- Motor Transport Workers Act, 1961
- National Commission for Safai Karamcharis Act, 1993
- Payment of Bonus Act, 1965
- Payment of Gratuity Act, 1972
- Payment of Wages Act, 1936
- Plantations Labour Act, 1951
- Public Liability Insurance Act, 1991
- Sales Promotion Employees (Conditions of Service) Act, 1976

- Trade Union Act, 1926
- Weekly Holidays Act, 1948

Supporters of globalisation have often argued that Indian labour is over-pro-tected, and many pieces of labour legislation have lost their relevance in the glo-balising India. They have also felt a dire need for carrying out labour law reforms so as to meet the flexibility needs of the changing global economy. A critical look at the labour law framework reveals the following points.

- Among others, problems are faced when an employer wants to close their oper-ations or lay-off or retrench workers in a factory, plantation or mine employing 100 or more workers. This requires requisite permission from the government, which is sometimes difficult to obtain. It is a reality that a lot of arbitrariness is often exercised in handling the permission issues. Sometimes, decisions are taken by government officials on extraneous considerations. Many organisa-tions that are perennially sick are denied the permission. Globalisation phi-losophy is difficult to sustain if firms do not have the requisite flexibility in the formal labour market. The presence of chaotic competition caused by the new realities is bound to compel employers to search avenues of flexibility so as to try to excel. Therefore, a review of the existing structure of retrenchment and closure law is long overdue.
- Also, it is believed that the Indian organised sector provides too much job security to workers without relating it to performance, accountability and productivity. Consequently, these laws have a debilitating effect on labour mobility, which is an essential pre-requisite of efficient working of firms in a competitive environment. On the contrary, countries like China are able to re-structure their labour market much more rationally as per the needs of globalisation.
- Another area that requires the government's attention is section 9-A of the IDA. This section envisages an employer providing 21 days' notice to a union/workmen in case he or she wants to make any change in workers' service conditions. When this is so done workers raise an industrial dispute about the change, and many times employers miss some critical opportunities to make their competitive position better. This tends to become the biggest stumbling block in managing change.
- The multiplicity of labour laws in India is a big hurdle for employers. This has made the system very complex for ordinary managers as well as workers. Many of the problems in this regard relate to the applicability of these laws; the defi-nitions of various terms like 'worker'/'employee', 'appropriate government' and 'wages'; the different administrative structure for enforcement of these laws; the creation of special dispute resolution bodies; and so on. This leads to an excessive role for lawyers, which should be avoided so as to promote a greater degree of voluntarism in IR. There is a need for the simplification of Indian labour laws, which is something that would be beneficial to workers as well as employers.
- A plethora of case law has been delivered by the judiciary to clarify labour law complexities. Many of these decisions are not quite easy to comprehend, which adds to the existing confusion of the employers. This has made the grasping of

labour laws a very complex affair. In fact, labour law complexity often tends to convert union leaders into full-time pleaders, who have set up labour law practice as a vocation; even though they should be seen to be busy resolving workers' grievances or organising workers for collective strength and collective bargaining.

Interestingly, there are some silver linings for the employers so far as their competitive position *viz a viz* workers is concerned. The recent signals from the judiciary in the labour field are encouraging from the employers' point of view. Some of these recent labour judgments reflect the belief that the judiciary is more sympathetic with the employers' problems in the era of globalisation and realises their susceptibilities in the new environment. The number of strikes resorted to by workers is declining and employers have successfully used lockouts to face the union power. The higher number of dismissal decisions of employers is being upheld by the higher judiciary so as to make stronger the employers' position in industrial relations.

Shifting Agenda in the 21st Century: Possible Directions for HRM in India

In the present competitive business environment the Indian HR function faces a large number of challenges. Many of these were discussed above. To survive and flourish in the new dispensation, drastic changes are required at the national, organisational and individual levels. Some of these seem to be taking place, although possibly not with the required rigour and not quite in the right direction. One serious problem while making such judgment and analysis is the availability of reliable empirical research evidence. On the basis of the available information and our own experiences, the following observations can be made.

The National Level

The above section highlighted some of the main national factors that significantly influence HRM in India (for details in this regard also see Budhwar and Sparrow, 1998, 2002b). Early indications suggest that the nature and accordingly the impact of most of the national factors (especially different institutions such as trade unions, the legal framework and the dynamic business environment) on Indian HRM is going to change. The legislations have to be amended so as to suit the present economic environment and help both workers and employers in the 'real' sense. The stance of unions is further expected to become more co-operative. The dynamic business environment is further going to dictate the nature and type of HRM systems suitable for the country. With the rapid developments in the software and IT enabled services (ITeS) sector and an increased emphasis on business process outsourcing (BPO), one can expect the emergence of sector-specific HRM patterns (see Budhwar et al., 2006).

The Organisational Level

A Strategic Approach to HRM

The existing research evidence (see Budhwar and Sparrow, 1997, 2002b) regarding the strategic nature of HRM in Indian national firms suggests that there is a low representation of the personnel function at board level, and few organisations have devised formal corporate strategies. Of these, a handful seem to consult the personnel function at the outset (comparing to a norm of about 50 per cent in European organisations), many involve personnel in early consultation while developing corporate strategy and many also involve personnel during the implementation of their corporate strategy. Of course, the status of the personnel function in India has improved in the last two decades or so. The number of personnel specialists moving to the position of CEO has increased over the last few years. On the other hand, it seems that Indian firms are witnessing a significant devolvement of responsibility of HRM to line managers. One can notice this in the areas of pay determination, recruitment, training, industrial relations, health and safety, and expansion/reduction decisions. Moreover, Indian firms have been showing an increased emphasis on training and development of HR (see Budhwar and Varma, 2011b). However, if a strategy of devolvement is not associated with a closer integration of HRM into the business planning processes, it may create a situation of chaos in organisations as they attempt to cope with the HRM implications of liberalisation. Hence, the way forward is the adoption of a more strategic approach to HRM.

Structured and Rationalised Internal Labour Markets (ILMs)

The existing literature suggests the existence of unique ILMs in Indian organisations, one based on social relations, political affiliations; political contacts, caste, religion and economic power (see Budhwar and Khatri, 2001). However, considering the present dynamic business environment, Indian organisations need to pursue more rationalised HRM practices and build still stronger ILMs (which should emphasise solely on performance and should be less influenced by the mentioned social, economic, religious and political factors). There are some indications regarding such developments (in the form of increased emphasis on training and development, preference for talent in the recruitment and performance-based compensation), however, these tend to be more in the MNCs or the professionally run sectors such as the BPO, ITeS, pharmaceuticals. Globalisation dynamics require that there is a need to speed-up the merit- and performance-based decision making in all sectors (also see Budhwar and Varma, 2011b).

Open to Change, Sharing and Learning

In the present competitive business environment radical changes are taking place, and it is difficult to keep a track of many such changes. The new economic environment, although it presents a number of threats to local firms, also offers many opportunities to learn, collaborate and change to suit the new context. To make the best use of the existing conditions, Indian firms need to be flexible and to demonstrate readiness to change. Regular interaction with competitors and relevant stakeholders is becoming a necessity in the modern networked organisations. In this regard, a lot can be learned from HR managers working in MNCs operating in India who are open and flexible in their approach to managing human resources. For example, a research investigation with 65 top HR managers in as many foreign firms operating in India (see Bjorkman and Budhwar, 2007) reports that local firms are more rigid to change, are less transparent in their operations, provide less learning opportunities and operate on traditional ILMs. However, the HR managers also perceive that the scenario is rapidly changing and such a gap between the working of MNCs and local firms is going to decrease in future. This should be one of the main items on the agenda for Indian firms. The liberalisation of economic policies, globalisation realities and the operating practices of foreign firms will all put pressure on Indian firms for a more professional performance. The increasing number of Indian students graduating from the developed countries and going back to India will also contribute a great deal towards resorting to a greater degree of professionalism by visionary Indian firms.

Crossvergence of HRM

With the coming-in of a very large number of MNCs to India one can expect an active mixing-up of different management systems (such as the Japanese or the American way of doing things). In such conditions, there will be a greater possibility of standardisation of managerial roles across different firms. This is an outcome of the globalisation exigencies or some kind of *'crossvergence'*, that is, a blending of work cultures (due to the active interface of diverse groups). Hence, one can expect cultural convergence and cultural overlap among different types of firms operating in the country. Already, Japanese and many American firms operating in India are able to adopt their respective HR practices in their operations with minor modifications (see Budhwar, 2012).

The Individual Level

Many Indian educational institutions (such as the Indian Institute of Management and the Indian Institute of Technology) are known to be producing world-class graduates. Considering the rapidly changing business environment and the emergence of a large number of MNCs in the country, a paradigm shift in the mindsets of individuals can be witnessed. The HRM policies of the foreign companies have exercised considerable power in influencing the traditional scenario of preference for secured jobs. For example, the professional customer handling by the Citibank has been positively influencing the public sector banks in the country that have to now operate in a competitive environment. The Indian managers view these practices as benchmarks. Further, most foreign firms and an increasing number of local firms emphasise the need to attract talent. They are increasingly adopting formal, structured and rational approaches to attract, acquire and retain talent (Budhwar et al., 2009). This has significantly influenced behaviour at both the individual and organisational levels. The opportunities provided by the new sectors such as software, call centres and IT on the one hand and the MNCs on the other have encouraged females to come and join the mainstream workforce. Such developments are expected to continue and will eventually help transform the adoption of HRM practices in the country.

Key HRM Challenges

The HR environment in the country has been changing rapidly over the years. New HR challenges are emerging due to the new contextual factors. These challenges are discussed below.

Even though the size of the Indian workforce is huge, there is an acute skill shortage in the fast-growing economy. Until recently, there was no all India authority to oversee skill development and to certify skill attainments. Only very recently, the National Skill Development Corporation (NSDC) has come into being as a public private partnership (PPP) initiative. The scarcity of skills is noticeable at all levels. MNCs are finding the existing skill levels of graduates highly inadequate. Ironically, this is despite the fact that India is believed to have the largest number of English-speaking people. A recent survey of employers in 20 sectors such as IT, power and infrastructure in India reported that 64 per cent of the employers were not satisfied with the skill sets of fresh engineering graduates, even as most employers were happy with the English communication skills of the new graduates (*The Economic Times*, 2011). The skill gaps were found to be the largest within higher order thinking skills and smallest among the lowest order thinking skills. Further, a McKinsey report in 2005 observed that only 25 per cent of Indian engineering graduates are employable in MNCs. The primary reason for the inadequacy of skills is consequent of an insufficient number of educational and skill development institutions as well as the quality of the faculty in the existing institutions. It is estimated that India needs to create 1,500 new universities to add to the existing 380 universities and 11,200 colleges so as to meet the educational needs of the growing populations (Budhwar and Varma, 2011b). For several companies in highly competitive sectors, the talent crunch constitutes a 'make-or-break' HR issue, which makes the value of good HR management readily apparent to top executives (Grossman, 2006). Thus in several companies a much higher respect of HR is gaining ground. Another factor that compounds the skill shortage is the large percentage of women who are hired but who do not join or who leave early, which is a significant problem when one considers that women in many sectors make up a significant percent of the workforce in urban areas.

So far as vocational education and training in India is concerned, it divided into two sub-systems. At the central (federal) level, while the vocational education is under the control of the Ministry of HRD, vocational training is basically regulated by the Ministry of Labour. Partly the former ministry also exercises some control even in matters of training. Further, some 35 ministries of the central government are involved in providing and supporting some kind of training in their respective areas of operations (Saini, 2003). Vocational education is provided at the senior secondary stage in schools. This is over and above engineering, management and other technical education that takes place under the overall supervision of the University Grants Commission (UGC) and the All India Council of Technical Education (AICTE), both of which are central statutory bodies. State governments also exercise control in matters of accreditation of education at the engineering diploma level. Among the specialised vocational training institutions, more than 4,000 industrial training institutes (ITIs) are being run at present; out of these 1,654 are run by the government and 2,620 are run privately. Altogether, they have a training capacity of 625,000 students. Apart from these, the Apprentices Act 1961 has been applied to some notified industries. The Act obliges the employers covered under the Act to engage apprentices in certain predetermined trades as well as those holding degrees and diplomas as per the specified ratio. This scheme is, however, working much below the projected capacity for lack of proper enforcement. Various government ministries and non-governmental organisations (NGOs) are running vocational training schemes for the informal sector. Apart from these, companies in the public and private sectors are also involved in providing skills training and their upgradation.

It has been found that private training-provider institutions have been able to grow with a good degree of effectiveness and have some remarkable stories of success. But the government-run industrial training institutes (ITIs) are functioning under several constraints and this should be kept in view while planning for effective training strategies. The following factors have been considered as crucial in the efficaciousness of a training implementation framework: autonomy (operational, financial), quality of skills delivery, the dedication of staff, a holistic approach, a focus on specific target groups and skills, freedom of admission and staff policy, effective management, adequate fees, employability of skills, marketability of products, capacity building of providers, networking, needs' assessment, local resource base and scientific support in training and technology design (Adams and Krishnan, 2003).

Further in view of the scenario of skill shortages, another crucial issue for Indian HRM is recruitment and selection. The criticality of recruitment arises from the fact that the attrition rate in many industries is very high – as high as 150 per cent, especially in many BPOs. This is largely due to talent shortages, which open more opportunities to candidates with the requisite competencies. Recruitment also becomes crucial due to the growing needs of industry in many sectors; many HR managers claim that 80 per cent of their time goes on recruitment (Grossman, 2006). Since Indian organisations have to keep in view the recruitment and engagement practices of the MNCs, they need to work on devising appropriate recruitment tests and devices. For recruiting the managerial category employees companies have to go to the institutes of excellence like the IIMs (Indian Institute of Management), IITs (Indian Institute of Technology) and other institutes known for pursuit of excellence. These institutes invite companies for recruitment on the basis of the employer brand of the recruiter concerned. So, companies with a lower recruitment brand are always seen to be struggling to get the best possible candidates, as they are already placed with companies having better employment brands. Thus, HR departments have to consistently work on getting the best possible opportunities to recruit from top institutions and then have to make policies to retain them. Most leading companies are providing in-house HRD facilities so as to meet their talent needs, which also help as retention tools. Companies especially in the private sector are using employee involvement devices to enhance the engagement of their employees (Cooke and Saini, 2010a). Use of employee involvement and empowerment devices is becoming common place with most software companies; but others have also begun using them. Companies like Tata Steel and Maruti-Suzuki are well known for their suggestion schemes, which prove useful techniques for employee engagement and retention. But given the fact that India is primarily a high-power distance country, it is not very easy to use empowerment devices in the Indian context. Overall, the employee engagement scores have been found to be as low as just 7 per cent. The reasons for this have been found to be 'indifferent managers, low wages, caste discrimination, hierarchical relations, rule-centricity, and misuse of managerial power' (Budhwar and Varma, 2011b: 321).

Quite like the way generation Y is throwing challenges to HR managers globally, the Indian situation is no different. It has a serious challenge of meeting the reasonable expectations of this section of the Indian workforce. HR managers need to understand the precise factors that are relevant for recruiting and motivating them. They do not get attracted to economic considerations alone. Factors like interesting work, job design, flexibility, challenging work, opportunities for development and work–life balance are some of the important factors that they look for in any organisation. They also desire to be subjected to a lesser degree of control. Since globalisation is promoting values of individualisation as opposed to collectivisation, HR will need to evolve more relevant motivation and engagement devices for the idiosyncratic younger generation.

The issue of leadership development too has been further exacerbated by the talent crunch. With a rising number of Indian MNCs and the increase in success and profitability of other Indian companies, HR will be on its toes to work on succession planning and leadership development. With the amazing expansion plans of these companies sagacious leadership becomes ever more difficult. Unlike Japanese MNCs that mostly rely on their own nationals to work in their facilities in India, most others rely on Indian nationals and less on expatriates.

HR also needs to assume a greater presence in its strategic role and move away from the transactional HR. Presently, it is so in isolated cases only, especially software companies. They need to learn to align their work and processes with business goals and strategies. The alignment is more a rhetoric than reality. Business schools also have a responsibility of popularising this aspect of their role in training the MBAs in HR. The discipline is growing but at a lesser pace. The greater use of metrics in measuring the efficacy of human capital deployment will also be an important part of the HR's role.

Last but not least, employee relations have been re-surfacing as an important issue in many industries and industrial belts. Many cases of grave violence were noticed in cases such as Honda Motorcycles and Scooters India Pvt Ltd, Glaziano (an Italian MNC), Maruti-Suzuki (a Japanese MNC that witnessed four strikes by its young Manesar workers over a union registration issue) and many other Indian companies. Glaziano witnessed the murdering of their Indian CEO in 2008 by the workers. Another case of murder of the company president was recently witnessed in Regency Ceramic in January 2012. In 2009, workers of Pricol killed its vice-president over an industrial dispute. There have been recent cases in Gurgaon where contract workers burnt public and private vehicles out of disgust when their colleague was assaulted by the contractor for not obeying his orders. These incidents reflect the rising unrest among workers due to their declining labour power. It also underscores that industrial relations (IR) issues can not be believed to be wiped out by pursuit of neo-liberal policies by the state where it throws the working class to the pure exigencies of the market. Conflict can not remain suppressed for a long time. It does manifest itself sometime in very violent manners. Given that IR as a discipline is weakening considerably and fewer HR students are willing to take an interest in it, HR managers will have a grave responsibility of innovating ways to handle these issues. Interestingly, even as contract labour is not legally a responsibility of the principal employer, lately it is raising its voice in a way that the latter cannot ignore it as an issue for the contractor to handle. In many cases of recent IR disruptions contract labour issues came to the surface, production came to a halt and some serious socio-legal issues concerning them had to be tackled by many companies. With the rising incidence of contract labour employment in the country, this is likely to be one of the key challenges for HR.

Case Study: Maruti-Suzuki India Ltd

Maruti-Suzuki India Limited (MSIL), which is a subsidiary of Suzuki Motor Corporation of Japan, is India's largest passenger car manufacturing company. It offers 14 brands with 150 variants of cars to its Indian and foreign customers. The company has its older plant in Gurgaon (Haryana state) on which the first car rolled out in December 1983. Presently, there are three plants in Gurgaon employing about 8,000 workers in total. The company set up another production facility in Manesar (Haryana) in 2010 that has two plants. These two plants employ 3,500 workers including trainees, contract workers and apprentices. The Manesar plants produce its premium brands like A-Star, Swift and SX4. Manesar plant workers are younger, mostly unmarried, with an average age of 25, whereas most of its Gurgaon plant workers are above 40 years.

HR Systems in MSIL, Gurgaon

MSIL had adopted Japanese management practices. Its workers had formed a union, that is, Maruti Udyog Employees' Union (MEUA); but there was a major battle between the union and the management in September 2000 when the company had to declare a lock-out. MEUA lost that battle, and got severe drubbing at the hands of the management. Of the 92 union activists who were dismissed, 46 were not taken back at all as per the settlement that ended the deadlock; and a new weak union with the name Maruti Udyog Kamgaar Union (MUKU) came into being.

The management took lessons from that IR breakdown, and initiated the new HR systems and policies to promote work–life balance, passion for the work and company loyalty. The new HR activities included the recruitment system now aimed at focusing on workers' commitment and organisational loyalty, and induction too became more comprehensive. A human resource initiative development committee was formed that consisted of employees from various levels, to evaluate all policies impacting employees before their final implementation. Senior management mentored new employees. The new Family Connect Scheme is aimed at familiarising the spouses of the executives with the organisation and the workplace. The family day involved celebration with the families of all employees including those of the workers. Other measures included a suggestions scheme, quality circles, a 360-degree performance evaluation, and a reward and recognition scheme. Welfare measures, among others, included: crèches, a gym, higher study leaves, women day celebration and more liberal maternity leaves.

Maruti workers still enjoy a social prestige. The annual salary of a worker with about 10 years of service is about Rs. 450,000 (US$8,400) and for those with about five years of service it is about Rs. 300,000 (US$5,500). In contrast, the minimum monthly wage of a skilled worker in Haryana in March 2012 is roughly Rs. 6,000 (US$100) per month. MSIL also had the same HR systems in the Manesar plants, but since these workers had lesser service length, they got lesser total compensation and were not happy overall.

IR Breakdown at Manesar

The company confronted a major problem in relation to Manesar workers as they wanted to have a separate union and not be a part of MUKU, but the management was against it. The real reason for this was that MUKU was seen by Manesar workers as a company union, and thus as weak. The management's resistance to this initiative by workers led to serious IR disruptions during June to October 2011. The company witnessed four strikes in this period. During the IR breakdown in Manesar, many cases of disciplinary action took place against workers. The Indian IR system so works that management and the state are often in some kind of understanding. Consequently, the government-controlled registrar of unions often delay or refuse union registration on extraneous considerations; that happened in this case as well. Some of the other reasons for the Manesar workers' agitation were difficult work schedules. During the day workers have just two breaks of only 7.5 minutes each and one lunch break of 30 minutes; they are granted permission on only one occasion to go to the toilet. In comparison, the Honda (HMSI) in the same region provided two breaks of 10 minutes each, and Mahindra Motors in Maharashtra provided two breaks of 15 minutes each. Interestingly, the break times are the same at the Gurgaon plant and in Japan. But the experienced Gurgaon workers have got used to it. It was also found that the pro-active HR policies were practised in the Manesar plant only in name. The plant was producing 20 per cent more than its capacity, which put added strain on all employees.

The Settlement and After

Eventually, like the 2000 Gurgaon plant workers' situation, the centre of attention in this case as well shifted from union registration to negotiating for having the dismissed workers reinstated. The fourth strike ended on 19 October 2011 through a tripartite settlement that included the concili-ation machinery. The company suffered a loss of sale of vehicles produc-tion worth Rs. 20 billion (US$18,564,900). As per the settlement, the company took back most of the dismissed/suspended employees except for 12 key union activists who were to face enquiry proceedings. But the media reported that each of these 12 workers was made to retire from the company by way of a settlement, with an underhand deal of Rs. 1.6 mil-lion (US$297,000) per head as the price for the separation, as they feared that the enquiry would hold them guilty of misconduct and then they would be dismissed with no such compensation. But this act of theirs made the common worker quite angry and disgusted. The management admittedly learned leadership lessons from the Manesar plant strike.

Interestingly, the Manesar workers succeeded in registering their separate union: the Maruti Suzuki Workers' Union (MSWU) on 29 February 2012. The workers celebrated this event on 1 March by closing the plant for about two to three hours, understandably with the tacit permission of the management.

MSIL was thinking of the appropriate strategic HR interventions to build sustainable cooperation with Manesar workers, and how the Gurgaon HR policy be made actually operational for Manesar workers as well. It recently put employee engagement responsibility on the line managers concerned. Some Manesar managers were made to leave and some were demoted for the developments in employee relations. The company was cautious of the fact that the Gurgaon workers were much younger.

Discussion Questions

1 Explain the factors that led the MSIL to make changes in the HR policy after the strike of 2000, including cross-cultural issues, if any.
2 Why has the employee relations policy at the Manesar plant failed, and what should the company do now?

Source: Saini (2012).

Conclusion

This chapter has focused on the present state of HRM in India that has emerged through its historical evolution, the institutional framework that supports the existing HR paradigm in the country, the challenges that Indian HR presently faces, and the future imperatives that HR managers have to attend to. It has highlighted that there is a remarkable progress in the professionalisation of HRM in the country in the organised sector. Attempts towards greater professionalism can be attributed partly to the progressive policies brought along and pursued by the MNCs and the professionally managed Indian organisations including some of the public sector enterprises. The attitude towards business practice in general is changing, and people are realising how far they need to change so as to cope with the change needs. Among others, the key problems that have adversely influenced the management of human resources in India include the problems of skill and competency development, the rigidity caused by the labour law framework, scarcity of talent to assume leadership roles, the hierarchy-driven mindsets of employers, low employee engagement in general, HR professionals who can play the strategic partner's role, a dynamic government's indecisiveness in matters of privatisation and dis-investment, and fragility of political coalitions that adversely affects the government's willingness to take bold decisions.

Another important factor affecting the HRM policies at the macro level is the deceleration in the employment growth in the organised sector and the massive under-employment in a labour surplus economy. This increases the power of employers, and enables them to shape their HR strategies towards cost reduction and other instrumentalist devices. Thus a greater reliance is put on employment of peripheral rather than core employees. With the weakening of the employee power, the HRM practices vis-à-vis this section of employees are bound to reflect the hardest possible devices including resort to denial of minimum standards of employment and commission of unfair labour practices (ULPs) in their IR policies. In the time to come India will have to respond to the need to mainstream the millions of socially, economically and educationally deprived Indians who are unprotected by law and/or are underemployed or are self-employed. This today is also an issue of intense debate among business and academic communities. The Mahatma Gandhi Rural Employment Guarantee Scheme (MNREGA) launched by the Indian government is a salutary step in restoring some semblance of dignity to them. It will be a challenge to all concerned as to how HR policies are devised for this large section of informal sector workers so as to mitigate social unrest among them.

At the same time several MNCs are leading and practising some of the most modern HR interventions to seek competitive advantage. In such settings, it is noticeable that the role of HRM managers is getting transformed from that of adopting the legal compliance approach to that of culture building, communication, change management, performance management and measuring effectiveness of HR systems and interventions. Within the organised sector, however, the HRM practices are quite varied depending upon variegated factors. The majority of management schools, however, are still struggling with getting qualified faculty so as to adequately respond to the challenges of the new environment in terms of evolving appropriate courses, even as the professionals have responded well to the challenges by using some of the most modern interventions – more so in the software industry. A shift is noticeable in the attitude of the government. It is less concerned with social justice dispensation, and has demonstrated a far greater degree of willingness to ensure the success of the globalisation model of development. Interestingly, this has been possible to quite an extent despite the rigid labour law framework, for it is the governmental power that activates that framework. A rapidly growing industry of HR professionals has emerged, which is increasingly becoming sensitive to the needs of aligning HRM with business needs and strategies. Apart from the performance of the traditional HR functions, new transformational themes are being identified, even though not to the extent they are in vogue in the developed world (Cooke and Saini, 2010a, 2010b; Varkky, Pradnya and Gautum, 2001). These, among others, include concepts like 'People Capability Maturity Model', work–life balance, diversity management, talent management, innovative welfare measures and benefits, employee involvement devices and strategic leadership.

Some of the key challenges before the Indian state include streamlining the working of the unorganised sector and providing a workable model of competency and skill development at the national level. This is corroborated by the setting up in May 2008 of the NSDC. And the hitherto adversarial model of employee justice dispensation promoted by the present legal framework is getting weakened due to the change in the attitude of the social partners; but at the same time several instances of workers' wild responses to industrial conflict are visible in the recent past, which certainly establish that the possibility of disruptions in employee relations is far from over. Many companies are putting primacy on the pro-active management of employee relations, beside their other strategic HRM priorities. If the HRM function grows fast, then it can help in diluting or even altering the hurdles created by the existing cultural realities to facilitating professional excellence. MNCs are expected to further contribute towards a still faster dawn in India of the era of strategic HRM as a way of organisational life.

Useful Websites

Indian Society For Training & Development: www.istdtrg.org

The National HRD Network: www.nationalhrd.org

National Skill Development Corporation: www.nsdcindia.org

Strategic Human Resources Management India: www.shrmindia.org

References

Adams, S. and Krishnan, P. (2003) 'Documentation of the consultative workshop on the project SCEC' under the programme: Restructuring and Strengthening the National Vocational Training System (NVTS). Proceeding of a two-day workshop organized by GTZ

(Germany) and DGET, Ministry of Labour, Government of India, India International Centre, New Delhi, 16–17 January.

Bjorkman, I. and Budhwar, P. (2007) 'When in Rome . . .?: Human Resource management and the performance of foreign firms operating in India', *Employee Relations* 29(6): 595–610.

Budhwar, P. (2001) 'Human resource management in India', in P. Budhwar and D. A. Yaw A. (eds), *Human Resource Management in Developing Countries.* London: Routledge, pp. 75–90.

Budhwar, P. (2003) 'Culture and management in India', in M. Warner (ed.), *Culture and Management in Asia.* London: Routledge, pp. 66–81.

Budhwar, P. (2012) 'Management of human resources in foreign firms operating in India: The role of HR in country-specific headquarters', International Journal of Human Resource Management 23(12): 2514–31.

Budhwar, P. and Khatri, N. (2001) 'Comparative human resource management in Britain and India: An empirical study', *International Journal of Human Resource Management* 13(5): 800–26.

Budhwar, P. and Sparrow, P. (1997), 'Evaluating levels of strategic integration and development of Human Resource Management in India', *The International Journal of Human Resource Management* 8: 476–94.

Budhwar, P. and Sparrow, P. (1998) 'National factors determining Indian and British HRM practices: An empirical study', *Management International Review* 38 (special issue 2): 105–21.

Budhwar, P. and Sparrow, P. (2002a) 'An integrative framework for determining cross-national human resource management practices', *Human Resource Management Review* 12(3): 377– 403.

Budhwar, P. and Sparrow, P. (2002b) 'Strategic HRM through the cultural looking glass: Mapping cognitions of British and Indian HRM managers', *Organization Studies* 23(4): 599–638.

Budhwar, L., Reeves, D. and Farrell, P. (2000) 'Life goals as a function of social class and child rearing practices: A study of India', *International Journal of Inter-cultural Relations* 24: 227–45.

Budhwar, P. and Varma, A. (2011a) (eds) *Doing Business in India.* London: Routledge.

Budhwar, P. and Varma, A. (2011b) 'Emerging HR management trends in India and the way forward', *Organization Dynamics* 40(4): 317–25.

Budhwar, P., Varma, A., Malhotra, N. and Mukherjee, A. (2009) 'Insights into the Indian call centre industry: Can internal marketing help tackle high employee turnover?', *Journal of Services Marketing* 23(5): 351–62.

Budhwar, P., Varma, A., Singh, V. and Dhar, R. (2006) 'HRM systems of Indian call centres: An exploratory study', *The International Journal of Human Resource Management* 17(5): 881–97.

Cooke, Fang and Saini, Debi (2010a) 'Diversity management in India: A study of organizations in different ownership forms and industrial sectors', *Human Resource Management* 49(3): 377–400.

Cooke, Fang and Saini, Debi (2010b) '(How) does the HR strategy support an innovation-oriented business strategy? An investigation of institutional context and organizational practices in Indian firm', *Human Resource Management* 49(3): 477–500.

The Economic Times (2011) 'Skill shortages present hurdle to India's growth: World Bank,' *Economic Times*, 5 June.

Government of India (2002) *Report of the National Commission on Labour* (Second), Ministry Labour, New Delhi.

Government of India (2009) *Report on Conditions of Work and Promotion of Livelihoods in the Unorganized Sector*, National Commission for Enterprises in the Unorganized Sector (NCEUS), New Delhi.

Grossman, R. (2006) 'HR's rising star in India', *HR Magazine* 59(9): 46–52.

Hofstede, G. (1991) *Cultures' Consequences: Software of the mind*. London: McGraw-Hill Book Company.

Johri, C. K. (1998) 'INDIA', in R. Blanpain (ed.), *International Encyclopaedia of Laws: Labour law and industrial relations*. Deventer, The Netherlands: Kluwer Law International, pp. 1–305.

Kanungo, R. N. and Mendonca, M. (1994) 'Culture and performance improvement', *Productivity* 35(3): 447–53.

Legge, K. (1995) *Human Resource Management: Rhetorics and realities*. London: Macmillan Press.

Saini, Debi (1997) 'Labour court administration in India', in ILO (ed.), *Labour Adjudication in India*. New Delhi: International Labour Organization—South Asian Advisory Team, pp. 1–48.

Saini, Debi (1999) 'Labour legislation and social justice', *Economic and Political Weekly* (Special issue on Review of Labour) xxxiv(39): L-32–L-40.

Saini, Debi (2003) 'Alleviating poverty through skills development: Lessons for law-making in developing countries', Paper presented at Workshop on Law and Poverty V, organized by CROP programme of the International Social Science Council and the Social Science Academy of Nigeria at Abuja (Nigeria) 24–26 November.

Saini, Debi (2006) 'Declining labour power and challenges before trade unions: Some lessons from a case study on private sector unionism', *Indian Journal of Labour Economics* 49(4): 911–24.

Saini, Debi. (2011) *Social Security Law in India*. The Hague: Kluwer Law International.

Saini, Debi (2012) *Case: Human Resource management dynamics in an automobile MNC in India*. Gurgaon: Management Development Institute.

Saini, Debi S. and Sami A. Khan (eds) (2000) *Human Resource Management: Perspectives for the new era*. New Delhi: Response Books – A division of Sage publishers.

Tripathi, R. C. (1990) 'Interplay of values in the functioning of Indian organizations', *International Journal of Psychology* 25: 715–34.

Varkky, B., Pradnya, P. and Gautam, B. (2001) *Human Resource Management: Changing roles, changing goals*. New Delhi: Excel Books.

Venkata Ratnam, C. S. (2001) *Globalization and Labour–Management Relations: Dynamics of change*. New Delhi: Response – Sage Publications.

8 Human Resource Management in Thailand

SUNUNTA SIENGTHAI

Human resource management practices in Thailand have gone through a gradual pace of learning and development. Until about the 1980s, most companies still had a so-called "traditional" personnel management (PM), which is perceived as the payroll function. Since the 1990s, the business landscape started to change. With the availability of information and communications technology (ICTs), modern human resource management practices have been more adopted in business firms. Outsourcing practices have also been widely adopted by firms to reduce their cost of operations and have led to changes in HRM business. Such practices require more partnership of HRM with other business functions. In this chapter, we will first briefly describe the historical development of HRM in Thailand. Then, we discuss the role and importance of the HR business partnership with other business functions. We review some HR practices in firms and identify some key factors that determine such HRM practices. Following this, some key changes in the HR function and key challenges facing HRM in Thailand will be outlined. Finally, a short case study is provided and details of relevant websites are given.

Development of the HRM Concept in Thailand: A Historical Perspective

The influences of military-dominated regimes, the cultural values, the centrality of Buddhism to the Thai culture and the practices of "middle-path" in Thailand (Siengthai, 1993; Lawler and Siengthai, 1997) led to a unique pattern of HRM and development practices for more than 60 years since the country first embarked on its economic development. The cultural values that emphasize power distance are reflected in much of the hierarchy between employer and employees or between supervisor and subordinates. Such value is more significantly observed in the public sector organizations in Thailand.

There are four main sectors in Thailand that exhibit distinctive characteristics in management practices and philosophy. These are the public sector, the public-enterprise sectors, the private business indigenous sector and the foreign direct investment (FDI) sector (Lawler and Siengthai, 1997; Lawler, Siengthai and Atmiyananda, 1997). The public enterprise sector is categorized as a separate sector since it has experienced significant changes in recent years in its management system. In fact, it has adopted many modern concepts of management as well as more advanced technology to improve its performance. The use of human resources in these sectors changes over time along with more available advanced technology and quality of human capital, which is enhanced by the public education system and its compulsory education requirements. At the early stage of economic development, due to the government-led economic growth, the public and state-owned enterprise sectors played a significant role in employment generation especially for the abundant supply of cheap unskilled and semi-skilled labor (Siengthai and Bechter, 2004). They have also become more or less an outlet for the capable high government ranking officials or politicians from the dominant parties who were appointed as administrators and members of the state-owned enterprise board of advisors. This practice by the governments in the past had made the public-enterprise organizations vulnerable to slow growth and internal fragmentation and political-related conflicts among key group employees. Although the number of public enterprises has been reduced mainly through government privatization policies, the concept of public management as opposed to traditional public administration has not been realized. However, together with the regionalization and globalization movements, organizational change and development has become the main focus of these public enterprises, especially after the financial crisis that forced the Thai government to effectively implement the privatization program in spite of the strong resistance from these state-owned enterprise labor unions.

In the early stage of industrialization in Thailand, the manufacturing activities were mainly labor-intensive types and their workforces were largely unorganized. The economic development was monitored through the national five-year socioeconomic development plan that was started in 1961. Most of the industrial activities, apart from the agricultural activities that are the mainstream of Thailand's economy, were mainly involved with basic infrastructure building in the country. Not until foreign direct investment started to flow into the country did modern management become the more common practice.

In Thailand, during the industrialization movement period (about the 1960s to the 1970s) and then during the significant political changes from a military-dominant to a democratic system in 1975, the threat by the unions was very significant. During 1973–75, there were many workers' strikes; unionization was their strategy to demand change in their terms and conditions of employment (Siengthai and Bechter, 2004). The impact of the unions using industrial weapons such as strikes led to the necessity for a firm to have a formal personnel manager as well as a personnel department within the organization. The labor movement in Thailand was very strong in the public enterprise sector. Many public enterprise unions have been very well established under the Public Enterprise Labor Relations Act 1991. However, in 1990, this act was demolished. Hence, all the public enterprise unions became regulated under the general Labor Relations Act 1975, just like any other labor unions in the private sector. In 1990, the Social Security Act was passed. But it took some years for the administration of the Social

Security Act to cover all types of employment insurance, such as sickness, accidents out of the workplace, being handicapped due to accidents in the workplace, old age (retirement) insurance and maternity leave and unemployment insurance.

By the time that the Labor Relations Act 1975 was issued, there were already many professionals practicing HRM. The role of these professionals and the personnel department highlighted their contribution in reducing work stoppages in the workplace and to making sure that the companies complied with labor law. Their contributions during the 1980s included keeping track of the payroll. After the financial crisis, many public enterprises came under the privatization scheme, which required organizational restructuring. So the unions' role in the organizations has become somewhat weak. On the contrary, the role of the human resource management practices becomes more significant in facilitating such organizational changes.

Progression in HRM initiatives accelerated after the 1997 collapse of Asian financial markets. Since then large Thai organizations and particularly some small- and medium-sized financial institutions have considerably developed their HR systems (Siengthai and Bechter, 2004; Siengthai, Dechawatanapaisal and Wailerdsak, 2009). In mid-1997, when Thailand was impacted by the financial crisis, many companies had to restructure and downsize. Consequently, layoffs were experienced by many firms that had been financially involved in international markets either through exporting their products, investing overseas or even making loans from international sources through the Bangkok International Banking Facilities office. Financial insecurity and soaring inflation from the financial crisis reinvigorated the reform initiatives (of earlier periods) in many family businesses (Suehiro and Wailerdsak, 2004; Pinprayong and Siengthai, 2011). In particular, the establishments in the financial and banking sectors, owned by many of the Chinese descents' families, had to relinquish their control in such businesses. Many were compelled to engage professional managers and/or entertain foreign direct investment or equity so that their businesses could be restructured, streamlined and recapitalized. More professional management concepts and frameworks were implemented. For instance, after the financial crisis, when many of these family-owned enterprises entered the securities market and became public companies, business practices were adjusted to improve transparency and to achieve greater efficiency. In this "era of change," greater professionalism of HRM is expected to support marketization of various public enterprises, worker participation, welfare benefits and better job security. Some business organizations have changed the nomenclature of their human resource department to that of the "resourcing department." Thus, the traditional concepts of personnel management and HRM have been adjusted to a broader perspective. Such action is in line with the concept of the resource-based view of an organization that advocates that an entity will gain a greater competitive advantage through the development and sustainability of its renewable and inimitable human resources.

HRM as a Business Partner

In this section we will discuss the changes in the role and functions of HRM and its transformation into the HRM business partnership. The ways in which enterprises are managed to achieve organizational goals are affected by the globalization process. The latter brings many rapid changes into the competitive environment, especially changes that have been brought about by the advancement in the new information and communications technology environment. These rapid economic changes have led to the notion of the HR system as a strategic asset (Amit and Shoemaker, 1993). This ideal is delineated by Becker, Huselid and Ulrich (2001) who asserted that the development of HRM practices can be represented by four evolutionary processes. These processes are identified as (1) the personnel perspective, (2) the compensation perspective, (3) the alignment perspective, and (4) the high-performance perspective. Interestingly, these authors claim that the compensation perspective is revealed in firms that use bonuses, incentive pay and meaningful distinctions in pay to reward high and low performers. Meanwhile, the high-performance perspective is experienced when senior executives of firms view HR as a system embedded within the larger system of the firm's strategy implementation. This is when HRM becomes a full-fledged business partner to other functional areas of firm business. The notion evolves from a concentration on employee welfare to one of managing people for the best possible productivity of the employee. In Thailand we can say that due to the earlier strong labor movement in the public enterprise sector, the pressure from the globalization process, the fiercer competition in the market and rapid changes that are taking place in the business sectors, the HRM division of these organizations have become more active as a partner for change implementation. They have to become more strategic in their orientation and align their business plans to the strategic direction of firms. However, this change in HRM orientation is taking place more evidently in larger firms and particularly those playing in the global markets.

Key Factors Determining HRM Practices

There are many factors that determine HRM practices in any country. In this section we will describe and discuss some of the key factors that are found to have influences on HRM practices in Thailand. These include external factors such as economic and socio-political development, and internal factors such as management development, ownership, cultural values—both national and corporate values, technological innovation availability, organizational restructuring and development of an industrial relations system.

Economic and Socio-political Developments in Thailand

The economic and social development in Thailand became the formal mission of each government since 1961 when the first National Economic Development Plan was formulated. However, the HRs or social development concern did not come into consideration until the Third Plan (1973–78) when the notion was incorporated into the national planning and was recognized as the National Economic and Social Development Plan. The Thai economy experienced the peak and trough of its economic development from late 1980 to 2010. It made a sharp turn with a rapid growth during 1986–97. Then, the Asian Financial Crisis led to the collapse of the economy. After some years, Thailand could achieve a fast resilience of the economic growth. Table 8.1 shows that during 2000–10, the population growth of Thailand seems to be growing at a decreasing rate. But the labor force has been increasing steadily, that is, from 33.22 million in 2000 to 38.04 million in 2010. Notable is the drastic low level of unemployment after 2004. It was almost a full-employment situation in Thailand. Wage levels are reflected in the minimum wages in each region of Thailand, which are also rising reflecting the higher ability of the employer to pay. In addition, there has been fewer strikes and lockouts in recent years. Private consumption is increasing gradually, which should induce more investment for production and services. In general, the external debt of the country is reducing. Trade balance is positive, which suggests that Thailand was exporting more than importing goods and services. Gross domestic product (GDP) dropped sharply in 2008 but then increased significantly again in 2010. However, the country experienced some setbacks due to the "Hamburger crisis" when global trade collapsed following Lehman's failure in September 2008. This collapse has profound consequences for Thailand where exports account for over 60 percent of GDP. The country then experienced the political turmoil in 2010. In spite of all these profound shocks, the Thai economy seems to perform sufficiently well and stood the severe tests (IMF, 2010).

The government has been one of the key drivers for the economic growth in the country. They are the player, the rule-maker and the referee in the socio-economic development process particularly in terms of employment practices, fair labor standards and the labor movement. In Thailand, the labor movement has been very strong in the public enterprise sector, reflected in the high level of membership (Siengthai *et al.*, 2010). About two-thirds of union members work for public enterprises, with a union density rate of about 60 percent. However, with the government policy to deregulate and privatize by 2006, agreed in the Association of Southeast Asian Nations (ASEAN) forum, the union has become low profile and inactive in some cases. On the other hand, the HRM divisions of these organizations have become more active as a partner for change management. To a large extent, the change has somewhat reduced the strengths of the labor union movement as the human resource management practices become more like those of the private business sector, which in general life-time employment or the seniority system as practiced in the public sector is no longer observed. In the same year, however, the Social Security Act was passed but without the unemployment insurance, which only became effective much later. Thus, the influence of the government, as a socio-political factor in HRM and IR practices, has also been significant in its legal initiatives.

Management Development and the HRM/IR Interface

With the establishment of industrial estates in many provinces in the country to promote foreign investment, the demand for managerial skills has increased. This has led to the transfer of management knowledge among member firms in the MNC networks as well as among firms within certain industrial estates. The personnel management function played a significant role in reducing the interruption

Table 8.1 Thailand's Economy at a Glance

Indicator/Year	2000	2002	2004	2006	2008	2010p
Population (mil., ave.)	61.88	62.96	61.97	62.83	63.39	63.88
Labor force (mil.)	33.22	34.25	36.26	36.43	37.70	38.64
Employed (in 000s)	33,001	34,262.6	35,711.6	35.69	37.02	38.04
Unemployed (in 000s)	812.6	616.3	548.9	0.55	0.52	0.40
GDP at 1988 price	3005.4	3,224.6	3,688.1	4,054.5	4,364.8	4,596.1
(%)	4.6	5.3	6.3	5.1	2.5	7.8
GDP at current price (baht, bil.)	4,916.5	5,433.3	6,489.4	7,844.9	9,080.4	10,104.8
(%)	6	6	9.7	10.6	6.5	11.8
Gross National Product (GNP) per capita (baht)	77,551	84,246	96,053.7	114,803.5	131,717.8	143,655.1
Trade balance (US$, bil.)	5.5	3.4	11.1	13.6	17.3	31.76
Balance of payment (US$, bil.)	−1.6	4.2	5.7	12.7	24.6	31.3
Private Consumption Index [1]	95.20	102.70	115.94	122.36	131.72	132.38
Total external debt (US$, mil.) [2]	79,715	59,456	701.5	561.6	426.2	388.4
Balance of payment on current acc. (% in GDP)	7.5	5.5	1.7	1.1	0.7	4.6
Inflation (core cpi, 2007 = 100) [3]	93.20	94.70	95.30	99.00	102.30	103.57
Minimum wages [4]	n.a.	n.a	181	184	191	203
International reserves (USD bil.)	32.7	38.9	42.1	52.1	111.0	172.1

Source: Bank of Thailand.

p = preliminary

[1] PCI series are rebased according to the Ministry of Commerce (MOC) import prices index and hence data from 2000 onwards are disseminated.
[2] Exclude Bank of Thailand and Financial Institutions Development Fund's Debt.
[3] Exclude raw food and energy items from the consumer price index basket.
[4] For Bangkok Metropolis area.

in the manufacturing process of the firms in question. Personnel managers, particularly the experienced ones, were highly sought after and hence the knowledge and know-how transfer among firms. Various management development programs became more available and widespread, especially those offered by higher education institutes. The fact that managerial employees are developed leads to low level of conflicts between labor and management. So did the possibilities of effective union avoidance strategies.

Ownership and its Impact on HRM Practices

It was not until foreign direct investment started to flow into the country in about the mid-1970s that modern, or professional, management became commonly practiced. This transition of traditional to modern management was reflected by the fact that foreign, or joint venture, firms recruited managers with formal training in HRM and those who were previously expatriates sent from the headquarters to operate their HR businesses. Notably, the introduction of professional HRM practices was underpinned by managers who were educated in the foreign countries, particularly in the home countries of the multinational enterprises (MNEs), or the joint venture companies (Siengthai and Bechter 2004). Different nationality or ownership of firms may then have significant impact on HRM practices and organizational performance. In Thailand, during the first wave of foreign direct investment, the competition for skilled human resources tended to be among the four main nationalities: American, European, Japanese and Thai. The latter naturally tended to be the least attractive for the job-seekers since they are least competitive in the job market with respect to pay and fringe benefits, except for very large Thai domestic firms such as Siam Cement Company, Siam Commercial Bank, Krungthai Bank and public-enterprises such as the Telecoms Authority of Thailand (TOT) and the Communications Authority of Thailand (CAT). In fact, in the 2000s, after the Asian Financial Crisis, many of the Thai large public firms also have been transformed to some extent. Many of them had entered into some joint-ventures with foreign firms. So, it is basically those small and medium firms that still retain their being Thai wholly-owned. Through this process of organizational transformation under the globalization process, it can be expected that the HRM practices become more diffused and modernized.

Cultural Influences on HRM Practices

The central notion of Buddhism, the national religion, to the Thai culture, the practices of "middle path," which means no encouragement of extremism, has contributed to the unique HRM and industrial relations framework of Thailand (Siengthai, 1993).

Some of the Thai cultural norms that are now well recognized among expatriates include the following: *krengjai* (being considerate); *bunkhun* (reciprocity of goodness; exchange of favors; *jai yen yen* (take-it-easy); *mai pen rai* (never mind); *sanuk* (fun); and *nam-jai* (being thoughtful, generous and kind combined) (Siengthai and Vadhanasindhu, 1991). Certainly, these norms are social values emphasizing harmonious social relations and consideration for others (Kamoche,

2000). They tend to reinforce the hierarchical structure (patron–client system) in the society as well as in the workplace. Currently, most of the entrepreneurial firms are started up by the second or third generation of founders. With the new ICTs environment, they now adopt more of the modern HRM practices. Yet, we cannot expect that the HRM practices will be more pro-active or systematic when compared to the former generation or those of the more developed and large-sized family enterprises where professional staffs are more prevalent. As most of them are small, constraints of available resources are still experienced by these new generation entrepreneurs. In Thailand, in the Buddhist context, the development of human resource management is embedded in family values reflected in compassion and kindness. One of the many principles of management taught in Buddhism is known as "*Brahmvihaara* 4." This principle advances a notion that those who are the leaders of others, either in the household or in the workplace, should practice four central tenets. These are (1) *Met-taa* (compassion), (2) *Garunaa* (kindness), (3) *Mudhitaa* (Sharing the joy of success of others), and (4) *Ubekkhaa* (Let go and accept that it is up to the other person's karma when one cannot be of any further help to others even when you have already tried very hard to be so) (Siengthai and Bechter 2004). Undoubtedly, they also are dealing with more knowledgeable workers or employees (Kamoche, 2000). Thus, this affects much of their styles of leadership and people management. More specifically, HR initiatives include a more realistic commitment to training and career development, providing meaningful feedback on a timely basis, formalizing practices that currently rely too heavily on subjective criteria and balancing the need to "control" with the need to "develop."

Technological Innovation Availability

With the availability of the information and communication technologies, firms can now be more responsive to their customers through these technologies, which enhance better communication between the producers of goods and services and their customers. New job roles such as call center operators are created and in some cases outsourced. These lead to some changes in how firms manage and measure their employee performance. In the HRM function, electronic-HRM (e-HRM) also has been introduced in various large companies in Thailand, such as Thai Airways Public Co. Ltd, TRUE, Michelin, and Hong Kong Shanghai Bank Co. Ltd. E-HRM has become more important for organizations as it enhances the efficiency in HR practices. In some other cases, outsourcing of some HR functions is adopted. The primary reason for outsourcing is to reduce capital expenditure over a business process. But HR-outsourcing does not suit the organization that functions under many changing and flexible conditions. However, the trends of HR-outsourcing will increase because the service providers in the market are increasingly providing better quality at a reasonably lower price, which results in a reduced workload for HR staff.

Organizational Restructuring

There have been changes in the structure of many organizations in the recent past. Large organizations in the service sectors, such as banks and particularly some small- and medium-sized banks, had earlier developed their HR systems in a similar way to the government bureaucratic system (Lawler and Siengthai, 1997). Today, many large organizations have restructured and implemented the business process re-engineering to cope with the fierce competition that comes with the ICTs (Pinprayong and Siengthai, 2011). These changes have been implemented to improve the efficiency and reduce the costs of operation. Organizations have attempted to become flatter. Hence the notions of empowerment and broad banding in compensation management have also been observed in recent years. (The broad banding in compensation management has resulted from the fact that many business organizations such as banks have downsized or restructured and many job position classifications were merged into a broad band of jobs that require similar skills, knowledge and abilities.) The changes in organizational structure also lead to the need for multi-skilled employees to avoid workforce redundancy.

Development of the IR System

Before 1975, workers' associations had already been established. However, trade unions have only been legalized since 1975, and strikes have only been made legal since 1981. The trade union movement has been weak, both in coverage and in workplace industrial relations. Most unions are recognized at the enterprise level (Siengthai, 1999). Union membership has not been growing extensively and rapidly; in fact, it has been declining due to the globalization process and outsourcing practices. In 2011, there have been demands from the unions to the government to make the subcontracting work illegal, as it does not provide job security for workers.

In short, key factors that determine HRM practices in Thailand include economic and socio-political factors, development of the IR system, ownership, management development, technological development, organizational restructuring and cultural values. In other words, the changes in HRM practices in Thailand have been more driven by external factors rather than representing pro-active development internally.

Key Changes in the HR Function

Based on the changes in the factors discussed above, changes in the HR function can be observed in many aspects. Many leading firms are now forced to become leaner and to bring more technology and its software to applications in their business operations. Business sustainability has become one of the main goals. Firms now are moving towards an electronic-HRM system or towards outsourcing some of their HRM processes. The practices of shared services have become more common among large firms.

While e-HRM helps the company to develop the business process, it needs high investment in system development and it also reduces the personal touch between employees and the HR team. Many problems that organizations experienced with the systems are due to inadequate investment in ongoing training for involved personnel, including those implementing and testing changes, as well as a lack of corporate policy protecting the integrity of the data in the systems and its use. Softwares are often seen as being rigid and difficult to adapt to the specific work-flow and business process of some companies.

Key Challenges Facing HRM

Many challenges are brought about to the HRM function by the globalization process. At the regional level, the ASEAN integration initiatives are taking place and expected to be effective in 2015. We would expect the integration in product, labor and financial markets. Thus, many changes in the external environment cre-ated both challenges and opportunities for firms in general and for firms' HRM in particular. In terms of labor markets development, Thailand is experiencing more advanced economic development. Thus it is expected that there will be more labor migration with respect to both the unskilled and the skilled and professional workers within the region. How firms can capture opportunities while the labor law still presents limitations with respect to work permits and non-discrimina-tion employment practices is still a great challenge. It needs to be considered how diversity can be enhanced when most of the Thai workforce is not fluent in English and when the foreign workers may not be able to communicate in Thai. Differences in religious practices will need to be taken into account and mutually respected in order to allow diversity. The HRM function must be more pro-active and needs to take initiatives in this new role as a business partner. Among these challenges are still the deregulation policy or privatization scheme by the govern-ment, the restructuring or downsizing policies of firms, the advantage of the new ICTs and firm policies to exploit it, the shift from low-wage to high-wage and high-skilled labor as well as the need for management development to cope with these changes, the need to link between the HRM and the financial performance of the companies, organizational innovation and productivity improvement, the empowerment of employees, project-based contracts, the management or work-force redundancy, the bipartite labor-management relations, and so on.

The current government, led by the first female prime minister, has put forward that the minimum wages will be increased up to 300 baht/day. This suggests the higher purchasing level and ability to pay on the part of the employer. The full imple-mentation of this wage policy will, however, take some time since the small- and medium-sized enterprises will need time to adjust their pay system. It is expected that such policy will encourage firms to introduce higher labor-saving technology and to invest more on training for their existing employees. This implies that the HR division of the firm will need to plan for HRD activities to further improve the competencies of its employees to cope with technological changes.

Together with the fierce competitive environment, it is observed that in recent years there have been serious attempts by firms to retain their talents. At the same time, it is foreseen that organizations will have to keep on shredding the redundant workforce that has resulted from bringing in more labor-saving technology such as IT and from the automation of certain service functions in the organization. Thus, it is expected that employees of the older generation who are less equipped with technological skills will likely be dismissed through early retirement programs or will be laid off. This is because even though the introduction of such technology will create the need for some certain skilled labor, the workforce needed would not be equivalent to the earlier period of economic development. The other implication of this is the increase in overhead costs as higher-skilled employees will imply higher wages and salaries, hence, the need for organizational restructuring to become flatter and for large corporations to continue to enhance customer responsiveness. For those now moving into more high-tech-led operations, the new competitive landscape will necessitate that they resort to more of the individualized terms and conditions of employment for higher-skilled and scarce employees.

Based on the discussion above, it can be said that the HRM functions that are very important to facilitate changes in the organizations in conditions of fierce competition are performance appraisal and training and development. Firms need to improve their performance management system if they want to sustain their business.

Future of HRM in Thailand

It is likely that the HR functions of firms in Thailand will become more focused on performance management. As firms will pay more attention to the business plan and strategies, they will formalize their human resource management practices. The practices of strategic human resource management are expected to be in place for larger firms. More objective performance management will be implemented. With the rapid change in global markets, firms that are engaged in production and export activities will tend to resort to outsourcing activities and transform parts of their human resource management to e-HRM. At the same time, because of the climate change that has become a more serious concern of the community, firms are expected to demonstrate more of their corporate social responsibility especially with respect to environmental and labor management. To survive and sustain their business, firms will need to continuously green their people to be more conscious of the environmental concern. Thus, this movement of greening the HRM process also would eventually transform the conventional HRM into e-HRM for many of its business processes to fit with the business strategies.

In the public sector, currently, the life-time employment system that entitles the former "civil servants" has been changed to a "public sector employee" system. Therefore, those who were recruited to the public sector are not entitled nowadays to many of the benefits that the former generation "civil servants" enjoy. The ironic situation is that although the salary of the public sector employees is higher than that of the "civil servants," it is lower than those who work in the private sector proper. In fact, the transformation of the traditional public sector system into its current form was meant to allow many public sector organizations to be able to recruit and select their own employees based on their own organizational needs and revenues without having to go through the House of Senate and public hearing processes. In reality, this transformation has not yet brought about the expected full benefits. There are no public sector unions to protect the rights and benefits of the public sector employees. No collective bargaining rights are stipulated by existing labor law. Thus, if there is no change in labor law, this situation would call for a very strong and effective leadership to assure the effective performance of the public sector organizations.

Similarly, significant changes are expected for the public-enterprise sector since the government has been deregulating. Their operating environment became fiercer since new investors: foreign and domestic alike come into the scenario. To sustain their business, the public-enterprise organizations must improve their efficiency and effectiveness. However, coupled with the political intervention, it seems to be very difficult for them to improve in terms of creativity, innovation and productivity since their employees are observed to be losing their morale. Again, this suggests that these public sector organizations need a very strong and effective leadership to breakthrough the organizational politics.

Case Study: PTT Exploration and Production Public Company Ltd

PTT Exploration and Production Public Company Limited or PTTEP is a national petroleum exploration and production company established since 1985, with Petroleum Authority of Thailand (PTT) Public Co. Ltd as a major shareholder. It is a top-10 publicly listed company in the Stock Exchange of Thailand, which operates more than 40 projects around the world and has a workforce of more than 3,000. PTTEP human resources can be classified into two main categories: the technical staffs (core competencies) such as engineers and geologists; and non-technical staffs, such as administrators and accountants. About 50 percent of the employees in the PTTEP are in generation X whose age group ranges from 30 to 44 years. More than 30 percent are in generation Y, that is, those aged less than 30. The minorities are those over 45 years of age or the baby boomer generation. It is predicted that in the year 2020, almost 100 percent of all engineers (the core competencies) will be those in generations X and Y. With the disappearance of the baby boomer, the experience and knowledge will also be vanished along with them. To overcome this issue, the top management and the HR department are focusing on developing a succession plan.

PTTEP Human Resource Management Practices

In recent years, PTTEP's HR has become a partner with various other departments and treated them as their customers. Each department looks at HR as their business partner, a recruitment agency, assisting in finding the best candidates for vacant positions. With HR line partners, each serving different departments, the recruitment becomes faster and more effective since the HR can focus on the department that they are serving. Its recruitment system can be separated into two channels, namely, PTTEP's own HR department and PTTEP's subsidiary, called PTTEP Services Company.

Since PTTEP is an oil- and gas-related company, the human resources essential for the company business are engineers, geologists and geophysicists. Therefore, the PTTEP HR department is responsible for recruiting core competency human power while the PTTEP Services Company is established as a recruitment agency to recruit supporting and administrative positions such as administrators, secretaries, expat staffs or technical staffs for short-term projects. PTTEP and PTTEP Services have adopted several methods of recruitment. These include referrals, a company website, a recruitment agency, campus recruitment, conferences and exhibitions.

Training and Development

Training and development are given high priority in PTTEP since the company values their employees as one of the valuable assets of the company. PTTEP pays high attention to safety, so basic training such as fire fighting and first aids are mandatory for all employees. Many other training programs, concerned with both soft and technical skills, which may be in-house or may be outsourced, are also encouraged. Employees are required to fill out their training needs every year when conducting performance appraisals. Their supervisors are also responsible for suggesting the training courses they believe their subordinates could benefit from. PTTEP invests a great deal in training. Overseas courses and conferences are nonetheless encouraged.

PTTEP has developed an "Accelerated Development Program" or "ADP" for newly recruited young engineers. This is a six to seven months' on-the-job training program. The engineers are assigned to work for different assets (such as Arthit or Bongkot project site assets) and are relocated once they finish their terms. This program is designed to expose young engineers to different engineering disciplines. As a result, they gain a wider first-hand knowledge and experience in a short period of time. With each assignment completion, the engineers are evaluated by the project site manager. At the end of the ADP, engineers, HR staffs and related managers sit together to assess the engineers' performances in order to identify the most suitable placement. This program also leads to better job satisfaction and a high retention rate, since engineers have had experience in various disciplines and different teams so they are able to make decisions based on their best interest. From the managers' point of view, they are able to match engineers with the jobs according to their performance. In terms of development, PTTEP provides both domestic and overseas scholarship for its own employees. In order to reserve and share the employees' knowledge within the company, PTTEP has formed a Knowledge Management (KM) team, which is divided into sub-teams according to job family. There are also teams set up to capture knowledge from the world's oil and gas conferences. Knowledge-sharing sessions are also organized regularly.

Employees' career path at PTTEP is taken into high consideration. Rotations of staffs usually occur once every two years. Job rotation and overseas assignments are means of exposing employees to various job disciplines and broadening their experiences. For technical staffs there are two main paths. One is to acquire knowledge and experience from a variety of technical disciplines or broad branding; their skills will be broad but generalized. They will be provided opportunities to expand their knowledge to management skills and will be moved towards management directions. The other is to acquire specific knowledge and experience to become technical expert in that area.

Performance Evaluation

Employee performance appraisal is conducted on an annual basis. At the beginning of the year, employees are required to complete their own Performance Development Appraisal (PDA) form according to their agreed key performance indicators (KPIs) with the supervisors. At the year end, staffs are required to evaluate themselves and supervisors are to evaluate their subordinates. The score is used to determine salary, bonus and promotion as well as a further competency development plan.

Compensation and Benefits

PTTEP is one of the companies known to provide outstanding compensation for its employees, which results in a high retention rate. The salary rate ranks top 10 in the country. PTTEP benchmark the remuneration packages with other oil and gas companies in Thailand and constantly survey the job market to ensure that the packages are equivalent to the rival companies. Basic benefits include health insurance, life insurance, provident funds, bonuses, loans and an employee stock ownership plan (ESOP). Other higher level benefits include cars with drivers for manager level up and subsidized education fees for the children of employees. For those assigned to work overseas, the remuneration packages are based on the cost of living in the countries to which they are assigned. The overseas package also includes housing, cars and three return tickets to Thailand annually. PTTEP has a welfare committee established to promote a good relationship between employer and employee for the benefits of both parties.

Conclusion

This chapter has provided the historical development of HRM, IR and personnel management in Thailand. It discusses the changes in the role and the significance of HRM from a payroll function to a business partner in the business operations in the country that is still struggling to achieve a sustainable economic development. The empirical evidence suggests that, currently, although the role of HRM practices has become more highlighted as contributing to achieve a competitive advantage of the firms, the top management perception of this function as a business partner is still not very positive, as most of the survey respondents suggest. Following this, the key factors influencing the HRM practices in Thailand are identified. The author then offers her observations of the challenges ahead to be faced by HRM and also provides the readers with some websites where information on HRM practices and development in Thailand may be accessed for future reference.

Epilogue

At the time that the chapter was prepared in October 2011 Thailand was experiencing an overwhelming natural disaster due to floods. Over half of the country's land areas were inundated and a large number of firms had to shut down and let the floods take over after fighting without success. This irregular phenomenon no doubt would have some impact on the current human resources management practices in Thailand. It was expected that more than 300,000 employees would be without jobs for at least six months as the positions vacant in other areas where business firms operate would not be able to absorb the entire affected workforce immediately.

This was a tragic phenomenon. Just a few days before that some of the major labor unions in electronics and electrical equipment had organized a meeting with another 120 labor unions. They had come to the conclusion that they would submit a demand to the government for the following: 1) the minimum wage increase to 300 baht must be in effect in January 2012 and applicable to all provinces in Thailand to ensure justice; 2) all the contract employment that had its nature being insecure must be abolished; 3) the government must control the inflation rate.

It is our view that we may expect in the future more of the uncontrollable consequences of climate change such as global warming and natural disasters in spite of all the human-made efforts. Thus, in the short term, the role of human resource management in Thailand based on the Buddhist-related values will be paying attention to the welfare of employees (reflecting the compassion of the management) while trying to improve the firm performance management to increase the productivity of employees (reflecting competency-based performance). In the long term, human resource management practices must be able to increase the job satisfaction and productivity of employees for the sustainable competitiveness of firms.

Useful Websites

Bank of Thailand (BOT): www.bot.or.th

Federation of Thai Industries (FDI): www.fdi.or.th

Hongkong Shanghai Bank (HSBC): www.hsbc.co.th

Ministry of Labour Protection and Social Welfare: www.mol.or.th

National Statistical Office of Thailand (NSO): www.nso.or.th

Personnel Management Association of Thailand (PMAT): www.pmat.or.th

Siam Cement Co. Ltd. (SCG): www.scg.co.th

http://hrm.siamhrm.com/ (in Thai)

www.themanager.org/Knowledgebase/HR/SHRM.htm

www.pttep.com/en/aboutPttep.aspx?changelang=1 (accessed 31 October 2011)

Thailand Management Association of Thailand (TMA): www.tma.or.th
(all accessed 31 October 2011)

References

Amit, R. and Shoemaker, P. (1993) "Strategic Assets and Organizational Test," *Strategic Management Journal* 4(1): 33–46.

Becker, B, Huselid, M. A. and Ulrich, D. (2001) *HR Scorecard: Linking People, Strategy and Performance*. Boston, MA: Harvard Business School Press.

International Monetary Fund (IMF) (2010) *Thailand: Staff Report for the 2010 Article IV Consultation*, 3 September 2010.

Kamoche, K. (2000) "From Boom to Bust: The Challenges of Managing People in Thailand," *International Journal of Human Resource Management* 11(2): 452–68.

Lawler, J. J. and Siengthai, S. (1997) "Human Resource Management Strategy in Thailand: A Case Study of the Banking Industry," *Research and Practices in Human Resource Management* 5(1): 73–88.

Lawler, J. J., Siengthai, S. and Atmiyananda, V. (1997) "Human Resource Management in Thailand: Eroding Traditions," in C. Rowley (ed.), *Human Resource Management in the Asia Pacific Region*. pp. 170–96. London: Frank Cass.

Pinprayong, B. and Siengthai, S. (2011) "Strategies of Business Sustainability in the Banking Industry of Thailand: A Case of the Siam Commercial Bank," *World Journal of Social Sciences* 1(3): 82–99.

Siengthai, Sununta (1993) 'Tripartism and Industrialization of Thailand', research paper prepared for the ILO, December.

Siengthai, Sununta (1999) 'Industrial Relations and Recession in Thailand', research report prepared for the ILO.

Siengthai, S. and Vadhanasindhu, P. (1991) "Management in the Buddhist society," in J. Putti (ed.), *Management: Asian Context*, pp. 222–238. Singapore: McGraw-Hill.

Siengthai, S. and Bechter, C. (2001) "Strategic Human Resource Management and Firm Innovation," *Research and Practice in Human Resource Management* 9(1): 35–57.

Siengthai, S. and Bechter, C. (2004) "Human Resource Management in Thailand," in P. Budhwar (ed.), *HRM in Southeast Asia and the Pacific Rim*, pp. 141–172. UK: Routledge.

Siengthai, S. and Bechter, C. (2005) "Human Resource Management in Thailand: A Strategic Transition for Firm Competitiveness," *Research and Practice in Human Resource Management* 13(1): 18–29.

Siengthai, S., Dechawatanapaisal, D. and Wailerdsak, N. (2009) "The Future Trends of HRM in Thailand," in T. Andrews and S. Siengthai (eds), *The Changing Face of Management in Thailand*, pp. 113–145. United Kingdom: Routledge.

Siengthai, S., Lawler, J. J., Rowley, C. and Suzuki, H. (2010) *The Multi-Dimensions of Industrial Relations in the Asian Knowledge-Based Economies: An Enterprise-based Case Book*. Oxford: Chandos Publishers.

Suehiro, A. and Wailerdsak, N. W. (2004) "Family Business in Thailand: Its Management, Governance and Future" *ASEAN Economic Bulletin* 21(1): 81–93.

9 Human Resource Management in Vietnam

ANNE COX

Introduction

Shaped like an elongated S, the Socialist Republic of Vietnam stretches the length of the Indochinese Peninsula and covers a surface area of 329,560 square kilometres. The history of this small country can be described as nothing less than heroic and is marked by a nearly continuous fight for independence and autonomy against some of the biggest economies in the world, such as China, Japan, France and the United States of America.

In 1975, after ending the war with the United States, Vietnam committed to the development of a hard-line socialist economic system, which shortly resulted in economic failure. More than a decade later, in 1986, the Communist government ended its previous approach of maintaining a closed and centrally planned economy and embraced a dramatic economic reform (*Doi Moi*). The reform's focus was on five main areas: (1) the market economy was accepted; (2) an 'open door policy' in foreign economic relations was adopted; (3) private ownership was allowed in all activities; (4) the industrialisation model that gave top priority to heavy industry at the expense of agriculture and light industry was dismantled and reversed; (5) state-owned enterprises (SOEs) were downsized and re-structured (Tran, 1997). A series of laws were enacted to implement the new direction of the economy. The new economic system was firmly established when the National Assembly adopted a new Constitution in 1992. These larger developments have produced a transformation in human resources management (HRM) and in industrial relations (IR) in Vietnam.

The broad aim of this chapter is to describe the changing HRM practices in Vietnamese enterprises and to develop an explanation of why their HRM practices have developed along this path. More specifically, the chapter seeks to systematically identify and compare the following HRM practices used in Vietnamese enterprises before and after *Doi Moi*: recruitment and selection of employees, performance management, compensation and reward management, training and

development, and IR. The chapter then discusses the transformation of the HRM/
IR system and contemplates key challenges facing further development of the
system in Vietnam.

Historical Development in HRM

Under the socialist economic system, the state sector is the backbone of the economy. Adopting the Soviet Union economic model, the Vietnamese government
believed that a focused development of the state sector was the quickest way to
achieve industrialisation and develop the economy. As a result of this development strategy, as early as 1960, 100 per cent of industrial establishments, 99.4
per cent of commercial establishments and 99 per cent of transportation facilities,
which once belonged to foreign and Vietnamese capitalists, were nationalised and
transformed into SOEs (Vu, 2002). SOEs were under the direct control and management of line ministries of the central and/or local government. They operated
as production units only, leaving the management side of it to the government.

Several studies have suggested that during this period HRM practices in Vietnam
were the product of the ideological, political and economic factors prevailing
in that period, which followed the Soviet model (see, for example, Nguyen and
Tran, 1997). HRM was centrally and tightly controlled by the state and characterised by a lifetime employment system, state-administered reward systems and
labour immobility. The HRM system under the centrally planned system can be
summarised as follows.

Recruitment and Selection

There was no concept of an external labour market as employees were assigned to
enterprises by the government, except for a small proportion of the labour force
who chose to enter the private sector. The government guaranteed permanent
employment and lifetime welfare coverage in SOEs. The recruitment, allocation
to firms and dismissal of employees were all subject to the official approval of
state personnel departments. Geographical mobility was tightly controlled by a
system of residence permits, which allowed persons to legally reside and work in
one area only. Transferring to another job or locality also involved dealing with
civil authorities who controlled residence registration, housing and food supply
allocation. The complex system of keeping employees' personnel files and registering them with various government bodies, in addition to facilitating administrative planning, also served the purpose of social and political control (also see,
for example, O'Connor, 1996).

Performance Management

Performance management, during this period, was a lengthy and highly hierarchical process, involving staff at all levels of a company. Any performance appraisal
decision had to be made with the agreement and supervision of the Communist

Party representative, the board of directors, the trade union representative, the Youth Union representative and sometimes the Women's Associations representative. Performance criteria were vague and included factors such as political attitude, work attitude, work performance, technical skills, cooperation and personal (harmonious) relationships with colleagues (especially with managers). Two non-performance related criteria, namely political attitude and work attitude, were commonly used for evaluation of employees' performance. In this way, performance appraisals were subject to vagueness and were open to individual interpretation (see, for example, Vo, 2009).

Rewards

SOE managers had virtually no discretion over workers' wages. Wages were calculated according to a government pay scale, based on educational level, grade and length of service. Salary and rank of employees were determined by the length of their service and by political attitudes and beared no relationship to the economic performance of the firm or even the individual's performance. Salaries were paid as roughly 60 per cent in food coupons and subsidised commodities, and 40 per cent in cash (Che, 1995). The gap between the grades was small in order to achieve 'egalitarianism'.

Training and Development

Bounded by bureaucratic rules and procedures, and secured by the lifetime employment system, SOE employees were not motivated to learn and develop new skills and knowledge. Training offered to workers was mainly on-the-job as required by the production lines that they were assigned to. Training programs were conducted for workers at a company-wide level with the main aim of enhancing productivity and improving organisational health and safety. Short courses to strengthen employees' political beliefs were widely available and employees were required to attend if they wished to be promoted. As SOEs were considered merely as production units, SOEs managers were not trained in business management as the skills were deemed unnecessary.

Industrial Relations

At the workplace level, employees were managed by four pillars of power: the Communist Party representative, management, the trade union representative, and the representative of the Youth Union. The Party official carried the most power. The unions' role was to act as a transmission belt between the Party and the masses (Fahey, 1995). Their major roles included activities such as acting on behalf of the enterprises in distributing goods to workers, organising social activities, allocating workers' housing and looking after other material needs. They mobilised workers to fulfil and over-fulfil production quotas set by the command economy. They also provided the human touch for bureaucratic institutions by serving as counsellors for employees' work-related and personal family problems.

In terms of economic performance, despite a large amount of investment that the government poured into this sector and its rapid expansion, the state sector performed very poorly. This was also the situation of the whole economy. In 1980, Vietnam's growth domestic product (GDP) growth rate was negative 1.6 per cent (Statistical Office of Ho Chi Minh City, 1995). By the mid-1980s, the Vietnamese economy was only barely sustained thanks to significant assistance from the Eastern bloc. At the Sixth National Congress of the Communist Party in December 1986, the Vietnamese government introduced an intensive economic reform, known as *Doi Moi*, with the objective of re-directing the economic system from being centrally planned to being market oriented. This was the major turning point in the economic development of the country. This economic reform had an enormous impact on the structure of the Vietnamese economy and consequently on the working conditions of employees.

With these rapid changes, along with the expansion and diversification of the system, the traditional labour legislation proved increasingly inadequate. Recognising the necessity of adjusting to the changing labour situation, the Vietnamese government started passing many new laws addressing labour issues. Decision 25-CP, which was enacted in 1981 by the government, was probably one of the most important pieces of legislation that influenced the development of the HRM system in contemporary Vietnam. It provided guidelines and measures to increase the initiatives and financial autonomy of SOEs in business operations (Nguyen and Tran, 1997). After this milestone legislative piece, the Vietnamese government gradually introduced a series of guidelines, policies, laws and so forth for reforming the structure and management of SOEs. Most significantly, the new Trade Union Law was introduced in 1990, the Trade Union Constitution in 1993 and the Labour Law in 1994. These legislations have provided a common legal framework for new labour-management relations in both the public and the private sector and marked the beginning of the transformation of HRM and IR systems in Vietnam.

These new laws and regulations focused on some of the most important aspects of SOE management, such as formulation of plans, the purchase and sale of assets, profit-based accounting systems, reduced budgetary support, investment of an enterprise's own resources, acquisition and leasing of assets and greater managerial flexibility in hiring and firing of employees, setting of wages, salaries and benefits and so on (Nguyen and Tran, 1997; McCarty, 1993). As far as labour recruitment was concerned, the lifetime employment system was gradually replaced by a 'labour contract' system. SOEs now have the freedom to hire employees or request governmental labour offices to recruit for them according to criteria set by the enterprises (Le, 1997; Nguyen and Tran, 1997). SOEs could now design their own reward systems in line with their own operating situation and on the principle of remunerating in accordance to performance. They could choose to pay and promote their workers in conformity with the government's policy on salaries and wages. The government had only imposed a floor income but not an income ceiling (Le, 1997; Nguyen and Tran, 1997). Wage differentials within the state sector between skilled and unskilled workers had been significantly increased (O'Connor, 1996). With the growth of the private sector and foreign-invested enterprises, the demand for educated workers grew and with it education-related wage differentials. In an effort to retain more highly trained personnel, the government adjusted its official wage schedule, thereby encouraging a rise of the relative pay of educated workers in SOEs. The labour mobility restriction had been relaxed. These were early signals of a trend towards a more flexible and mobile labour market.

The Level of Business-HR Partnership

Before *Doi Moi*, SOEs were directly controlled and managed by the government. Both managers and employees paid little attention to production targets, knowing that operating profits were pre-determined in the plan, and losses were made up from the government budget expenditure (Vu, 2002). HR departments were called personnel or administration departments and were policy implementers rather than strategic decision makers. In fact, their roles and responsibilities focused more on administrative activities than on organisational management.

Although significant changes have occurred since *Doi Moi*, overall, HRM in Vietnam is still in an embryonic form. HRM is not considered a major contributor to the success of businesses, nor integrated into business strategies. Research indicates that the majority of SOEs have simply changed their personnel function to 'HR' without any change in its administrative focus or the adoption of a strategic role (see, for example, Vo, 2009). As a legacy of the centrally planned economic system, there is a very weak link between organisational objectives and HR objectives. HR managers do not work closely with the board of directors and/or line managers to achieve shared organisational objectives, such as designing and implementing HR systems and processes that support strategic business objectives. The common profile of a HR professional in an SOE is that of a person who has worked in the HR department of one company where they performed one HR function with limited exposure to other HR functions. These HR professionals therefore lack the knowledge and ability to work hand in hand with line managers and effectively penetrate into other parts of the organisation.

Although the aim of HR performing the work of a business partner and linking their work to business results is still far reaching, there is evidence of some SOEs attempting to align company business objectives and individual performance objectives with technical support from their HR departments (Vo, 2009). This can be considered an initial step towards establishing a link, or partnership, between the HR function and the organisation.

Key Factors Determining HRM Policies and Practices

Recent decades have witnessed the strong development of comparative institutionalism, which has shown how different forms of economic organisation have been established, reproduced and changed in different market economies. It focuses on macro-level societal institutions, in particular those that govern 'access to critical resources, especially labour and capital' (Whitley, 1999: 47). The effects of variations in businesses' institutional contexts on companies' behaviours are prominent, as a 'firm will gravitate towards the mode of coordination for which there is institutional support' (Hall and Soskice, 2001: 9). The influence of such social institutions is so strong that they can almost be regarded as additional factors of production that become the basis of competitive advantage or disadvantage (Maurice *et al.*, 1980; Lane, 1992; Porter, 1990). Using the institutionalist approach, this section aims to reach an understanding of the political and socio-economic configurations of Vietnam, which have strong influences in the shaping and implementation of HRM and IR policies and practices in Vietnam.

The Economy

Vietnam's economic reform has been gradual and homeopathic with overriding political power still remaining, as opposed to what is termed 'shock therapy' or 'big bang' in the context of East European economic reforms (Kerkvliet, Chan and Unger, 1999). The results of the economic reforms were remarkable. The GDP growth rate has increased since 1986. In the five years from 1992 to 1997, Vietnam achieved an average GDP growth rate of 8.8 per cent, with a peak of 9.54 per cent in 1995, which represents the longest period of sustained economic growth in Vietnam's recent history (*Vietnam Economic Times*, 2003). Vietnam's economy slowed down in the late 1990s, due to being affected by the Asian Financial Crisis. However, since the first quarter of 2000, the economy has witnessed some recoveries. In 2007, growth accelerated to 8.48 per cent, which marked seven consecutive years of increases (GSO, 2008). The growth rate of GDP in 2011 compared to that of 2010 was 5.89 per cent (GSO, 2012).

In spite of the recent economic successes, the fact remains that Vietnam is a poor country. The country is still healing the wounds from decades of wars,[1] and is in the process of recovering from decades of adopting distorted and ill-managed macro-economic policies. Vietnam is mainly an agricultural economy. It is estimated that in 2006, 16 per cent of the Vietnamese population were living below the poverty line (Joint Donor Group, 2007: 4). As far as population income is concerned, in 2010, Vietnam's Gross National Income per capita was $US2,910, classifying Vietnam as a 'lower middle-income' economy ($1,006 to $3,975) (World Bank, 2011). Meanwhile, foreign direct investment (FDI) is one of the most essential sources of investment (World Bank, 2011).

The Culture

Vietnam's cultural heritage is deeply rooted, having developed over 4,000 years with strong Confucius influences (Quang and Vuong, 2002). Confucians prioritise collective units, such as the group, family and community, over self-interest. They focus on order and hierarchy with senior members of the family and society exercising authority and expecting submission and obedience from younger members. Furthermore, according to the framework developed by Hofstede (1980), previous research on Vietnamese national culture describes it as high power distance, high collectivism, moderate uncertainty avoidance and high context (Quang, 1997; Ralston, Nguyen and Napier, 1999).

High power distance is reflected in family life where children are expected to have high levels of obedience to the heads of the family and within organisations where subordinate–superior relationships are clearly defined (Quang, 2002). Collectivism is another defining feature of the Vietnamese culture, where the role of the individual is recognised as being secondary to the group (Xingzong, 2000). Formal guidelines and tight social frameworks inform social interaction as a means of protecting a group's 'face' or reputation (Quang, 1997). The Vietnamese will generally avoid conflict; however, where it does arise, they strive for a win–win situation (Quang and Vuong, 2002). Quang and Vuong (2002) also suggests that Vietnamese culture is characterised by moderate levels of uncertainty avoidance. Ambiguity is largely regarded as a threat in the work environment, and is reconciled with greater job stability, the establishment of formal rules and the rejection of deviant ideas and behaviours.

Having manifested over several centuries, these beliefs are deeply entrenched in the Vietnamese value system and heavily influence how firms are managed in Vietnam. Respect for authority, hierarchical order, collectiveness, consensus, cooperation and long-term commitment characterise the traditional Vietnamese firm. In the workplace, many Vietnamese managers still display authoritarian and familial styles of management, particularly in the state sector (Quang and Vuong, 2002). This reflects the tradition of a centrally controlled system and is consistent with Vietnamese culture (Vo and Hannif, forthcoming).

The Role of the Party and the State

As in other socialist countries, the Vietnamese polity is characterised by extensive Party intervention in the affairs of state. It is very difficult, if not impossible, to separate the Vietnamese government's roles and functions from that of the Party. The Vietnamese political system is dominated by a sole political party – the Vietnamese Communist Party (VCP). Like other communist parties, the Vietnamese Party adheres to the principles of democratic centralism, which insists on unanimity at the top and unquestioning obedience from below (Riedel and Turley, 1999). Vietnam's zeal for *Doi Moi* has not been mirrored in its approach to political reform. Vietnam's ruling VCP has consistently rejected external calls for political reform, insisting that its self-appointed ruling elite can better serve the country than political pluralism. VCP and the government maintain a long-standing policy of not tolerating open dissent and of prohibiting independent political and labour organisations. All non-governmental Vietnamese organisations must belong to the VCP-controlled Fatherland Front. As with China, the communist party's rule is grounded in broad – although not unquestioning – popular support (Beresford, 1988). However, if the economic reforms and ideological shifts continue apace, the Party may find itself communist in name only (Ashwood, 1994; Beresford, 2008).

The nature and the role of the VCP have one major implication for the operation of HRM/IR. The Party maintains the ideology of a socialist society, imported from the former Soviet Union. This ideology respects the peaceful co-existence of different actors of the economy in a win–win relation: the state, the management and the employees/their legal representatives. This defines the nature of IR in Vietnam and the unions' stance towards management and it influences HRM policies and practices in firms. Furthermore, the Party's monopoly in the political arena and its close relationship with the State ensure that governments enjoy majority support and that policy initiatives have not usually been overturned after government changes. This creates a high degree of political stability, which contributes to the creation of a long-term framework for industrial decision making.

The Banking System

As in other countries, the banking system is a macro-economic tool to guide the economy. Prior to 1988, the Vietnamese banking system was characterised as a part of the centrally planned economy. It was under the direct control of the government with the sole task of financing the national budget and SOEs on a non-commercial basis (Wolff, 1999; Gates and Truong, 1992). Vietnam's first banking reform was initiated in early 1988. However, nowadays the banking system is still characterised by its small size and under-capitalisation. It is still under the strict control of the government.

The banking system is dominated by five large, state-owned commercial banks (SOCBs) that frequently operate on a non-commercial basis, with a culture of policy lending that is subject to government direction and interference. SOEs remain the main recipients of bank credit, typically borrowing on an unsecured basis at concessionary interest rates. Additionally, in 1997, the State Bank of Vietnam issued several directives to the SOCBs aimed at improving the availability of credit to SOEs. Having close ties with the SOCBs and being able to obtain credit fairly easily compared to other economic sectors discourages SOEs from being innovative and competitive in their operations in general and in management practices in particular.

The Education and Training system

In 2010, the population of Vietnam was approximately 86.93 million (GSO, 2012). In terms of its population, Vietnam ranks 13th in the world. With 89 per cent of the population under or of working age, the labour pool continues to increase by 1.1–1.3 million workers annually (GSO, 2008). The Vietnamese government is aware that an improvement of the human resource base is essential to underpin macro-economic reforms, where continued weakness in the education sector will result in a human resource bottleneck that will impede faster growth.

In the early 1990s, with the significant improvement of the economy, action was taken to renovate the education and training (E&T) system, for example ownership in education was diversified, more attention was paid to vocational training, the contents and methods of education and training were continuously renewed, and the standardisation of teachers was implemented at all levels (Ministry of

Education & Training, 1997a, 1997b). Although the reform in the E&T system achieved some encouraging results, such as increasing the number of enrolments and the number and type of educational institutions, the national E&T system's weaknesses are shown by an insufficient infrastructure, an irrelevant curriculum and under-qualified and under-paid teachers at all levels of education (ADB, 2000). Furthermore, even though mass education levels are high, Vietnam still suffers from a significant scarcity of highly skilled labour. It is estimated that 96 per cent of the Vietnamese population is literate and that 80 per cent graduate primary school. However, the skilled labour force accounts for only 8 per cent of the total labour force (MOLISA, 2002: 7). Management and people-related skills continue to be the weakness of Vietnamese employees (Vo, 2009). This leads to competition among companies for skilled managerial employees and an augmentation of salaries for this segment of the workforce.

The Vietnamese E&T system strongly emphasises Confucian values, which have greatly influenced the Vietnamese standards of social values and provided the background for Vietnamese political theories and institutions. The educational system upholds strict hierarchical orders, righteous behaviour in relationships and social harmony. Whitley (2000) makes the criticism that the Confucian values present in the teaching and learning style affect the nature of authority relations in the workplace. Paternalism in education and training leads to paternalism in employment relations where there is an imbalance in the employer–employee relation and the superiors are expected to give concrete directions and to act in the interests of subordinates. The Confucian values that govern personal relationships, such as respect for elders, loyalty to friends, benevolence on the part of superiors and so forth also influence the conduct of HRM/IR practices such as payment and performance appraisal practices in firms.

Business Networks

Embedded in an institutional environment that until 1986 did not encourage the development of the private sector, and where the allocation of input and distribution of output of the production process were centrally controlled, business associations in Vietnam have been historically weak. Currently, there are three main types of associations. First, the Vietnamese Chamber of Commerce and Industry (VCCI), which in the past was essentially responsible for foreign trade interests, represents business enterprises from all economic sectors and business associations in Vietnam. Second, separate from the VCCI are a small number of business groups representing specific domestic industries. Third, the Vietnam Union for Cooperatives and Small and Medium Enterprises emerged from the former association of cooperatives. None of these bodies have so far been particularly successful in representing their members in an economic sense. They are dependent on government contributions and finance their activities by qualifying for development aid resources and running their own enterprises. Alongside business networks of Vietnamese firms, many businesses from around the world have formed groups in Vietnam representing country and regional commercial interests.

The Vietnamese government, however, promotes inter-firm cooperation in strategic industries. In Vietnam's SOE conglomerates, inter-firm cooperation is utilised to stabilise output and prices. Elsewhere, inter-firm relationships have been very limited. Weak linkages among firms and industries are the main reason why Vietnamese firms tend to centre on traditional industries that require a low level of capital investment and focus on short-term profit maximisation. In terms of HRM, weak linkages among firms and industries augment the situation where poaching talents and job-hopping to accelerate salary are popular. In this context, firms are more hesitant to invest in the training and development of their staff members.

In brief, this section provided an overview of some key factors in the Vietnamese national business system, their vigorous reforms and the influences they have had on the HRM policies and practices at the workplace level. The main characteristics of the Vietnamese national business system are summarised in Table 9.1.

Table 9.1 The Vietnamese National Business System

	Characteristics
The Economy	• in the process of transferring from a centrally planned economy to a market-oriented economy • a developing, low-income, agricultural country • a very poor infrastructure • bearing great pressures from external forces and dependent on foreign capital.
Culture	• strong Confucian influences • high levels of power distance, high collectivism, moderate uncertainty avoidance and high context • respect for authority, hierarchical order, collectiveness, consensus, cooperation and long-term commitment • authoritarian and familial styles of management popular in SOEs.
The Party and the State	• monopoly in politics • stability in politics • centralised and interventionist.
The Financial and Banking System	• small in size and under-funded • the banking industry is almost monopolised by state-owned commercial banks, and under strict control of the government • state banks primarily serve SOEs.
The System of Education and Training	• a unitary system • large and inexpensive labour force, which enjoys a high level of mass education, but suffers from a considerable degree of scarcity of skilled labour.
Business Networks	• Business associations have been historically weak. • Business associations only play the role of a dialogue bridge to connect the business community and the government.

Source: adapted from Vo (2009: 59).

The Contemporary HRM/IR System in Vietnam

Recruitment and Selection

SOEs focus strongly on internal promotions and personal recommendations. To a much lesser extent, they also utilise advertisements in newspapers to attract more candidates. The selection criteria used are mainly based on educational qualifications and harmonious personal characteristics. Nepotism is still prevalent. A typical process for selecting white-collar and blue-collar workers is very simple and consists of reading a written application to make the first cut, and then interviews, health checks and a probation period for the newly recruited employee. For blue-collar workers, a manual dexterity test is also normally required. SOEs rely heavily on unstructured interviews as a selection method, which has a low level of reliability and validity, and thus is not a sufficient or appropriate method for identifying the best candidates. Furthermore, top-level positions are normally appointed rather than selected. This situation implies the need for objective selection criteria and sophisticated selection methods in the state sector.

Performance Management (PM)

PM in SOEs is in a gradual transition from a political-oriented bureaucratic assessment towards an equitable system that aims to break egalitarianism by linking performance to compensation and placing stronger emphasis on merit and achievements. The PM process has been separated from the intervention of mass organisations, although trade union representatives are still informed of the final performance-rating decisions. Employees can no longer take for granted that they will receive the same treatment regardless of their productivity. Instead, the new performance appraisal system places emphasis on competence and performance criteria, which are used to evaluate an employee's work effectiveness and real contributions to the organisation. Although solid attempts to link performance to payment have been recorded, it is evident that the old practice of egalitarianism still lingers. Vietnamese employees have a non-confrontational style of communication, as they try to minimise the loss of face and preserve harmonious relations. Negative feedback and areas for improvement are normally provided and recorded in vague terms only (for example, 'working attitude needs to be improved' or 'performance can be enhanced'). More detailed feedback is preferably given in informal talks in some private place out of working hours.

PM systems still serve more of an evaluation purpose rather than a developmental purpose. Although SOEs use PM systems to justify pay for performance and salary increases and to identify candidates for promotion, all of which are considered short-range goals, they do not use this tool to implement any long-range goals. It is evident that SOEs show more concern with the assessment of past performance than on planning future development. There is a very weak link, if any, between the results of an employee's performance appraisal and any training and development opportunities they may receive in the near future. In practice, career planning and development are hardly discussed during the performance appraisal process.

Reward System

In the wake of the *Doi Moi* period, the government has given special attention to the remuneration policies in order to reinvigorate the state sector. The government only imposed a floor income but not an income ceiling. Wage differentials within the state sector between skilled and unskilled workers have been increased. However, SOEs are not totally free to set their own remuneration system as the government still determines and promulgates minimum salary levels for each region and each industry (Labour Code 1994, Article 56) and stipulates the principles for formulation of wage scales, wage tables and labour rates (Labour Code 1994, Article 57).

The current salary system is criticised for being too complex and being burdened with too many salary schemes, grades and steps. Furthermore, employees can gradually proceed through salary schemes and ladders without the need to improve their performance, and thus seniority is strongly emphasised. More importantly, the SOE salary is notoriously insufficient for employees to maintain an average standard of living. In this situation, SOE employees must find other jobs to supplement their income, leading to low productivity and limited work stimulation in the state sector.

Unofficial income and related issues such as the generation of the unofficial income by enterprises and by employees in the state sector, is a phenomenon that emerged in the transition to a market economy in Vietnam (Vo, 2009). These issues are complex, controversial and closely connected to the present low salary, allowance and bonus system. There are no official statistics available on unofficial income. CEOs can receive gifts and under-the-table money as thanks or to ask for a favour. The amount in the envelope depends on the role of the receiver and the political and/or economic benefit the favour may bring. Employees in lower positions can also receive 'facilitation payment' in the forms of gifts or money for providing assistance in dealing with certain issues. Unofficial income paid by individuals is extremely hard to measure; however, it is an ongoing issue in SOEs. Lucrative unofficial income enjoyed by highly positioned employees is believed to be the real reason for them staying with the state sector, when their official income is as low as 10 times less than that of their colleagues in the foreign invested or private sectors.

Meanwhile, corruption is endemic in Vietnam. A 'Report of the Survey on Corruption in Vietnam' (2005) by the Vietnamese government reveals that 77 per cent of enterprises consider corruption to be the most significant socio-economic problem in Vietnam. However, according to the World Bank's Vietnam Development Report (2006), few companies rank corruption as a constraint on their business activities. One possible explanation for the relatively low importance attached by respondents to corruption is the very institutionalisation of bribes, which means that companies may have learned how to 'live with floods', to the point where they do not see it as a significant constraint on their activities.

Training and Development

After *Doi Moi*, workforces with low skill levels are still a common situation in SOEs. SOEs only invest limited resources on training and development for their managerial staff. Their activities suffer from limited financial resources, low-quality training, out-of-date training methods and a lack of systematic training systems. Workers are offered technical on-the-job training and are required to pass technical grade examinations, which are held every year. Management training courses are still primarily concerned with familiarising managers with the government's laws and regulations rather than offering opportunities to learn modern management concepts and methods. Finally, SOEs demonstrate a lack of a systematic approach to training with no analysis on training needs, poor training design and implementation and no training evaluation process. There is also a lack of commitment and involvement by senior management to the training processes.

Industrial Relations

Economic reform in Vietnam has had an enormous impact on the working conditions of employees. Recognising the necessity of adjusting to the changing labour situation, the Vietnamese government passed the new Trade Union Law in 1990, the Trade Union Constitution in 1993 and the Labour Law in 1994. These legislations, however, have not led to any fundamental changes in the IR system in Vietnam. After many decades under the shadow of the Party, trade union cadres are not equipped with the necessary knowledge to fulfil their roles properly and their organisation lacks the necessary resources to make use of their newly found autonomy and create their own power. As far as financial resources are concerned, officially the main financial source of unions has been their modest union fees. This amount is clearly insufficient to pay for the union's activities and to finance the salaries of the union cadres. In contrast to what is regulated and understood from labour-related laws, the trade unions' roles and activities in the workplace are limited to organising social activities and providing education to employees regarding labour law and work discipline, and as such have not exceeded the traditional roles and activities defined under the former centrally planned system.

The Transformation of the HRM/IR System in Vietnam

In order to achieve a meaningful discussion on the changes in the HR function in Vietnam, one main characteristic of the Vietnamese business system needs to be emphasised: the incoherent and transforming nature of the national business system. In the middle of a radical transformation process, the Vietnamese business system contains features of both a centrally planned economy and a market-oriented one. Moreover, the transformation of the country to a market economy itself is a learning and experimental process. The formation and implementation of new legislation, including regulations governing the status and operations of foreign firms, remains a major source of uncertainty. Institutional change in Vietnam is what Djelic and Quack (2002: 10) call a 'stalactite' model of change, in which national configuration is eroded and reshaped progressively through time.

The state sector, for the last 20 years or so, has witnessed this sector cruising through the *Doi Moi* storms. As never before, since the country's reunification

SOEs have had to change dramatically to survive and successfully retain their roles as the key economic instrument of the state in the socialist-oriented market economy. It is clear that the transformation process of Vietnamese SOEs, in terms of their structure and operations, is far from complete. In the centrally planned economy, SOEs placed the personnel function within the administration department. As SOEs operated as production units only, leaving the management side of things to the government, the administration department's roles were limited to keeping personnel records, processing payroll, benefits administration and recording employee status. However, following *Doi Moi*, administration departments assumed more strategic responsibilities pertaining to HRM, including but not limited to job analysis, HR planning, recruitment and selection, performance appraisals, compensation and benefits, and training and development. As enterprises progressively obtained control of their own managerial activities, they were able to implement more practical managerial strategies.

Vo (2009) argues that Vietnam HR is increasingly being viewed as having strategic and financial implications where competitive pressures will lead to the development of management systems along the lines of Western-style HRM policies and practices. However, organisational inertia, ideological legacies of socialism, the lack of financial resources and a general lack of knowledge about the 'modern' concept of HRM among those responsible for HR functions has resulted in a slow pace of change in SOEs' HRM systems. This argument conforms to the main findings made by a number of pieces of research. The best of these studies recognise that Vietnamese firms seem to still be in the period of 'learning and developing a HRM system' (Siengthai, 2004: 18) (see also Kamoche, 2001; Zhu, 2002; Thang and Quang, 2005).

Barriers and Challenges of Implementing Strategic HRM

At the macro level, weak and incoherent business systems have posed considerable constraints to the implementation of strategic HRM in Vietnamese firms. The environment for the operation of HRM is complex, chaotic and uncertain. The sub-systems (the economy, culture, the state, the financial system, the system of education and training, the network of business associations and the system of HRM/IR) are constantly under pressure due to change and innovation. Furthermore, although SOEs are provided with autonomy and self-responsibility for their business and HR operations, considerable red-tape still persists and HR procedures are under the control of at least a half dozen governmental bodies. The system is made more complicated by legislative duplication and incoherence, which might send confusing messages to firms and HR practitioners. This macro environment places great constraints on daily HR operations as well as any intention to introduce changes, as a new policy may not be relevant in the near future. HR managers therefore still rely heavily on government's regulations and guidelines.

At the miso level, the barriers and challenges of implementing strategic HRM come from the state sector itself. A few milestones in the development of SOEs since *Doi Moi* will show that this sector has experienced and will continue to experience turbulence in the years ahead. On 21 January 1981 the government enacted Decision 25 – CP that aimed to provide guidelines and measures to increase the initiatives and financial autonomy of SOEs in business operations. Decree 315/HDBT in 1990 realised the rationalisation and liquidation of SOEs. By the end of 1989, there were 12,297 SOEs in operation in Vietnam, with a total capital value of 34,216 billion VND (US$1.6 bn). By June 1993, the total number of SOEs had dropped to 7,060, with a total capital value of 44,965 billion VND (US$2.16 bn). Since 1994, SOE reform has become even more robust, targeted at reorganising SOEs, establishing General Corporations, and implementing the transformation of SOEs into joint-stock companies. Recently, the focus of reform was on speeding up the equitisation process. The number of SOEs continues to decline. In 2000, the number of SOEs was 5,759, decreasing to a total number of 3,706 at the end of December 2006 (GSO, 2008: 125). The transformation of Vietnamese SOEs is far from being complete. The number of SOEs is still large and there will be further reduction. These constant changes no doubt have created a very chaotic environment for HR operations. When uncertainty is present, inaction is preferred.

At the micro level, or organisational level, major challenges facing the implementation of strategic HRM include financial problems and inefficient management. SOEs still encounter financial difficulties and incur prolonged and unsettled debts. In 2000, the number of profitable enterprises accounted for just over 40 per cent, while break even enterprises fell to 31 per cent, and chronically loss-making enterprises accounted for 7.8 per cent (Tran, 2003: 4). In this context, HR departments are always in the situation where they lack the financial resources to make use of their newly found autonomy, given to them by *Doi Moi*. Furthermore, the management and operation of SOEs are said to be inefficient, compared to the foreign invested sector, and are burdened by bribery and corruption. HR managers are under pressure to introduce changes but are equipped with little knowledge of a market-oriented economy and far less business understanding. Attempts to attract a new generation of highly competent managers are still feeble and unsystematic.

Finally, at the HR-specific level, each HR function is facing a different set of constraints to its operation. As far as recruitment and selection is concerned, companies face an unbalanced labour market. A noticeable aspect of the Vietnamese labour market is the excess of non-skilled and semi-skilled labour co-existing with the shortage of highly skilled labour, even though companies continuously display a demand for skilled labour. It is estimated that in 2005 the size of the labour force that graduated from universities accounted for only 5.28 per cent of the total labour force – although this is the highest figure since 1996 (MOLISA, 2006: 160). Companies claim that the outputs of the educational system do not meet with the required inputs of their companies. This leads to tough competition among firms for skilled and managerial employees and an augmentation of salaries for this segment of the workforce. Interestingly, while multinational companies (MNCs) display a continuous and rising need for talent, SOEs' labour retrenchment means that they require minimum new labour input, with the exception of some newly found and expanding industries such as banking and finance and information technology. Shortage in the skilled labour supply leads to other problems such as high turnover rates of white-collar workers, rising salaries and job-hopping (to obtain a higher salary).

In terms of performance appraisal, certain cultural traits such as non-confrontation and a strict hierarchical order might hinder the practice. However, some studies pointed out that the transitional period in Vietnam, which has witnessed the fall of the centrally planned system and its promises, is receptive to new and seemingly contrasting practices. As argued by Gamble (2001), cultural traits such as attitudes to hierarchy are often complex and ambiguous, provoking different responses in different situations.

In terms of the reward system, the government regulates the state sector and foreign invested sector with two different sets of law. In the state sector, the government stipulates the principles for developing the salary system (employee specifications, salary scales and salary tables), minimum salary and salary ratio. Under the pressure of rising living costs and competition from the private and foreign invested sectors, in recent years the government has frequently increased the minimum salary level. Even with the new regulation, the minimum salary level in SOEs is lower than that of MNCs. The regulations on rewards is criticised as being rigid and always falling behind the real needs of employees and market changes. On the other hand, foreign invested companies claim that the Vietnamese personal income tax rates are very high and that they effectively place a barrier to the upward progression of Vietnamese employees as they desire to advance to positions of authority.

As far as training and development are concerned, the weak vocational training system has become a serious constraint to the development of the economy and poses a serious constraint to companies (Nguyen and Truong, 2007). Furthermore, there is a chronic mismatch between the output of the education system and the input of companies (Duoc and Metzger, 2007; Hargreaves *et al.*, 2001). Up to 80 per cent of graduate students have to be retrained by employers to match job requirements (Nguyen and Quang, 2007: 142). Due to the above mentioned weaknesses in the E&T system, the workplace is expected to be the other major source of skill formation and training in Vietnam. However, companies are faced with a dilemma – they could spend a fortune on training and developing their management staff only to see them leave the company (newly equipped with skills that make them more desirable in the marketplace) for higher-paying employers, in many cases a competitor company. As skills are scarce within and across industries, job-hopping to accelerate salary growth is popular. While some companies have a practical viewpoint on this matter, others think twice before determining their training budget.

Lastly, as far as IR is concerned, at the national level the new Trade Union Laws and new constitutions suggest that the VCP is willing to relax its hold on the labour unions, and that there is a strong legislative base for trade unions to step out of the Party and State's shadow and renew their organisation and activities to perform the function of workers' representatives in protecting their rights and interests. However, at the workplace level, organisational inertia and the government's eagerness to maintain labour peace and attract foreign capital make for an enormous gap between what is written on paper and the reality of what is implemented. After many decades under the shadow of the Party, trade union cadres are not equipped with the necessary knowledge and their organisation lacks the necessary resources to make use of their newly found autonomy to create their own power.

Future Development of the Vietnamese HRM System

As previously mentioned, the adoption of best practices in SOEs and the transformation of HRM/IR systems in Vietnam are weak. Instead of adopting best practices systematically, SOEs are still dependent on government guidelines and regulations, and tend to use fairly universalistic forms of common-sense management, experimenting, learning and copying pieces from foreign firms and/or other local firms in a haphazard and eclectic manner. The low degree of transformation may be attributed to the perceived lack of necessity and assumptions about the importance of particular HRM practices, lack of financial resources and a weak management team. There are cases where more advanced HRM models are available in joint ventures with foreign partners for 'imitation' or 'learning-by-watching', however SOEs choose to maintain their old and less effective models of management.

On the other hand, with *Doi Moi*, the Vietnamese government has sought industrialisation by embracing an 'open-door policy' towards foreign investment, thus welcoming an influx of newcomers to the economy in the form of MNCs. SOEs are facing fierce competition from MNCs, which have well-developed strategic management plans for their enterprises due to their historical exposure to the global market economy. A component of these plans is HRM policies and practices. Due to the comparatively advanced nature of MNC HRM development and the diffusion of these HRM policies, MNCs are in a stronger position than SOEs in regard to having well laid out strategic management plans for HRM. There is strong evidence that MNCs have successfully transferred their home country HRM to their Vietnamese subsidiaries, albeit with some adaptations to the local situation (see, for example, Vo, 2009; Vo and Stanton, 2011). These HRM policies and practices are advanced and sophisticated.

This chapter acknowledges positive spill-over effects (Tran, 2002; Le Thanh Thuy, 2007) from MNCs to SOEs. In her succinct summary of the literature on spill-over effects, Le Thanh Thuy (2007) argues that there are three important channels through which foreign direct investment (FDI) can benefit the innovation activity of domestic firms in the host country: demonstration, competition, and labour turnover (Le Thanh Thuy, 2007). By their presence in the domestic markets, foreign firms can inspire and stimulate local firms to innovate or develop new products and processes. The first source of potential competitive advantage for MNCs is at the parent company level and represents the unique bundle of assets and capabilities that the MNC has developed over its lifetime (Taylor, Beechler and Napier, 1996). If these factors are transferred to the subsidiaries, technical progress in industry in the host country is expected (Blomström,

1986). Domestic firms can observe foreign firms' actions, skills or techniques and 'imitate' them or make efforts to acquire these techniques and apply them, which results in production improvements. MNCs also can diffuse their superior technology to domestic firms through competition. Under the pressure of competition, domestic firms are more likely to introduce new technologies earlier than would otherwise have been the case. On the other hand, competition spurs further technology transfers to subsidiaries (Blomström, 1994). Finally, MNCs can create spill-over effects on domestic production through labour turnover. This effect occurs when employees employed in MNCs decide to move to domestic firms or open their own enterprises (Blomström and Kokko, 1996). Furthermore, foreign invested firms have helped to modernise management and corporate governance, and have helped to train a new group of young and dynamic managers. Some 300,000 workers, 25,000 technicians and 6,000 managers have been trained or re-trained partially abroad (Le, 2002 cited in Le Thanh Thuy, 2007: 16).

In Vietnam, the technology gap between foreign and domestic sectors is expected to create the spill-over effects from FDI. Furthermore, FDI flows into Vietnam during periods when the country is experiencing important structural reforms; hence, its impact in introducing new ideas, technology and know-how is likely to be higher compared to the cases of other countries. Le Thanh Thuy (2007) finds significant positive spill-over effects in Vietnam's industry during 1995–99 and, to a lesser extent, pullovers in 2000–02. However, it is noted that compared to technology spill over, the effects in terms of management technologies in Vietnam is subject to little research, with some exceptions such as Zhu (2002), Le and Truong (2005) and Napier (2005). In terms of HRM policies and practices, Le and Truong (2005) point out that foreign invested firms in general are more advanced in the adoption of some practices, such as selection, compensation, benefits, and training, compared to SOEs (see also Vo, 2009). Apparently, MNCs offer models of 'best practices' that local firms could choose to benchmark. Foreign-owned firms, without doubt, have important implications for the development of HRM practices in Vietnam. The way that human resources is managed in MNCs, especially those that attempt to transfer 'best practices' to their Vietnamese subsidiaries, is expected to impact on the way that other organisational forms (including SOEs and private enterprises) will be managed in the future.

Case Study

In this section, the HR system of a well-known, large state hospital located in Hanoi will be described. Four critical HRM functions will be explored: recruitment and selection; performance management; remuneration; and training and development.

The findings presented here are part of a qualitative study conducted in the health sector in Vietnam in 2009. Interviews were conducted with two groups of participants: internal to the hospital and external to the hospital. For the first group, in-depth interviews were held with the management of hospitals (including board of director members, the HR manager and middle and line managers), clinicians and trade union officials to compile information on the HRM system. The second group of participants included government officials at both the national and local level who are in charge of administering relevant laws, regulations and managing the activities of the hospitals. They provided the official and in some cases unofficial views of the government authorities that regulate and manage hospital activities such as the Ministry of Health, the Ministry of Labour, Invalids and Social Affairs. Nine individual interviews and two focus group interviews were conducted at this particular hospital. The interviews were supplemented by documentary analysis (internal documents regarding HRM policies and practices, company correspondence with local authority on HR issues, trade union meeting records, and so forth).

Recruitment and Selection

This function is still centralised and tightly regulated across the health care system. At the central level, a key regulation Decision No. 32/2006/ QD-BYT (legislated in October 2006 by the Ministry of Health (MoH)) governs the recruitment and selection activities of organisations under the control of the MoH. More specifically, the legislation regulates the human resource planning process, the principles of selection, the establishment of the selection committee and selection processes. Legislation also stipulates a yearly recruitment quota as established by the MoH. Each hospital will then work out a detailed recruitment plan, which needs to be submitted and approved by the MoH. The hospitals have two choices regarding the selection process: They can either organise the selection process themselves under the control and guidelines of MoH or MoH will conduct the process on their behalf. The case study hospital elected for the MoH to conduct the recruitment process. The selection criteria consisted of three clear criteria: academic grades; an interview mark; and a bonus mark. A bonus mark is given to those who belong to certain ethnic groups, volunteers who have served in remote areas, army heroes, labour heroes, veterans, children of veterans, those injured in war and children of those injured in war and those who have certain preferred degrees, such as medical degrees from prestigious medical schools. The influence of personal networks is strong and, in reality, the hospital gives priority to hiring their employees' immediate family members (parents, spouse and children) and relatives.

Performance Management

The hospital reported that performance appraisals are held once a year at fixed intervals. No individual performance objectives are officially set. However, 'impressions' of individual performance are established through daily interactions with supervisor and colleagues. Performance criteria consist of four broad areas: work achievement; work attitude and effort; collegial relationship; and potential for further improvement. An overall grading

– excellent, good, pass or poor – is required for the first three categories. It is evident that the old practice of the centralised communist system's egalitarianism still persists. Of the hospital workforce, normally about 70 to 80 per cent is rated as good through to excellent. Interviewed managers revealed that they are hesitant to criticise chronic low performers as they believe that this could disrupt a harmonious working environment. Further, the current state sector's employment system, which favours long-term employment, makes it very difficult for managers to dismiss low-performing employees.

Reward

Presently, salary in the hospital is calculated as follows:

$$\text{Salary} = \text{Minimal salary level} \times \text{Salary ratio}$$

Both minimal salary level and salary ratio are controlled by the central government. The salary ratio for an employee working in a hospital is determined by a complex matrix of salary ladders and salary schemes set out by the tate. A combination of a wide range of salary factors, such as an employee's educational background, work experience, seniority, the industry, the size of the enterprise that one works in, position titles, standards required by their occupied positions and working conditions determine the salary ratio.

Despite state determination of the salary regime and its uniform application in all SOEs, the government does allow SOEs some autonomy in salary allocation. The case studies show that while salary systems remain within the government's framework, there is evidence of the use of incentive mechanisms. Investigated state hospitals (SHs) have successfully developed and adopted a dual salary system consisting of two parts, namely a 'hard' salary, which strictly follows government's salary schemes, and a 'soft' salary, which is sensitive to the firm's performance and the individual's performance. The 'soft' salary enhances the effectiveness of the salary system. A 'soft' salary budget is earned by the number of 'service' beds that the hospitals allow to run and the number of extra patients that the hospital treats. The 'soft salary' budget is then distributed to employees according to their performance.

Besides salary, employees in the studied hospitals also enjoy several types of allowances, such as an area allowance; a mobility allowance; a responsibility allowance; a hazardous, difficult and dangerous allowance; night-shift allowances; extra shift allowances; surgical allowances; and disease prevention and control allowances. A fixed bonus is paid in the form of a Tet (Lunar New Year) bonus. The 13th month salary bonus is also applied in the studied SHs. However, this type of bonus is not fixed and is dependent on the hospitals' economic performance. Clinicians also have other significant incomes from their private practices.

Training and Development

Training and development functions have been centralised to MoH or the Provincial Health Office. The MoH and the Provincial Health Office co-ordinate the training activities of hospitals by gathering the training needs of hospitals and by organising training courses. Training programmes can be divided into two areas: medical training and general training. General training covers the following fields: business administration; government policy studies (for example, tax policies); English literacy; informatics; and political training. Training courses are not offered on a regular basis but are dependent on the availability of trainees, trainers and, most importantly, funding. Training is conducted by trainers from universities, external consultants or relevant governmental agencies (for example, tax policies courses are taught by the Tax Policy Research Institute, and business administration courses by the Vietnam Chamber of Commerce and Industry). The majority of these courses are reserved for department heads and high-level employees. Overseas training opportunities are very rare and generally restricted to directors and senior managers.

Link Between Strategic HRM and Employee Well-being, Quality of Patient Care and Hospital Effectiveness

Overall, employees felt dissatisfied with their remuneration, working conditions, training and development, and promotional opportunities. Among participants, remuneration and long working hours are the most cited reasons for job dissatisfaction. However, within this context job satisfaction has no bearing on employee turnover. As jobs in hospitals located in big cities are very difficult to obtain there is a zero turnover rate for medical staff recorded for many years. Clinicians reported that they perceived that this leads to the problems of low quality of patient care and hospital effectiveness.

Useful Websites

Asian Development Bank: Vietnam operations business plan (2009–11) www.adb.org/documents/viet-nam-country-operations-business-plan-2009-2011?ref=countries/viet-nam/documents

Asian Development Bank: Country planning documents 2012–14 www.adb.org/documents/viet-nam-country-operations-business-plan-2012-2014-vi?ref=countries/viet-nam/documents

CIA World Factbook www.cia.gov/redirects/factbookredirect.html

General Statistic Office: www.gso.gov.vn/default.aspx?tabid=217

Ministry of Labour – Invalids and Social Affairswww.molisa.gov.vn

Vietnam Chamber of Commerce and Industry:
http://vccinews.com

Vietnam News
http://vietnamnews.vnagency.com.vn

World Bank: Taking stock: An update on Vietnam's recent economic developments (June 2011)
http://www.wds.worldbank.org/external/default/WDSContentServer/WDSP/IB/2005/12/02/000160016_20051202141324/Rendered/PDF/34474φVN.pdf

World Bank: Vietnam Data and Statistics
http://data.worldbank.org/country/vietnam

Note

1 After the French and American war, the country fought the Chinese (over national boundaries), and the Khmer Rouge at different times from 1954 until 1989.

References

Ashwood, N. (1994) *Vietnam, a Business Guide*. London, UK: Graham and Trotman.

Asian Development Bank (ADB) (2000) *Country Economic Review: Socialist Republic of Viet Nam*, November 2000, www.adb.org/documents/CERs/CER_VIE_2000.pdf, last accessed 12 January 2003.

Blomström, M. (1986) 'Foreign investment and productive efficiency: The case of Mexico', *Journal of Industrial Economics* 15: 97–110.

Beresford, M. (1988) *Vietnam: politics, economics and society*. London: Pinter Publishers.

Beresford, M. (2008) 'Doi Moi in Review: The Challenges of Building Market Socialism in Vietnam', *Journal of Contemporary Asia* 38(2): 221–43.

Blomström, M. and Kokko, A. (1996) 'The impact of foreign investment on host countries: A review of the empirical evidence', The World Bank Policy Research Working Paper Series, No. 1745, World Bank, Washington, D.C.

Blomström, M, Kokko, A. and Zejan, M. (1994) 'Host country competition and technology transfer by multinationals', *Weltwirtschaftliches Archiv*,130: 521–33.

Che, T. N. (1995) 'The Sequence of Economic Reforms in the Industrial State-Owned Enterprises of Vietnam', Working Paper, AUSAID/NCDS Vietnam Economic Research Project, presented at Project Workshop, Hanoi.

Decision 25 – CP, issued on 21 January 1981 by the government, regarding several directions and measures to enhance the rights of industrial state enterprises to take initiative in production and business and in self-financing.

Decree No. 315/HDBT, issued on 1 September 1990 by the Vietnamese Council of Ministers, regarding reorganizing Production and Business in the Public Sector.

Djelic, M. L. and Quack, S. (2002) 'The missing link: Bringing institutions back into the debate on economic globalisation', Discussion Paper FS I 02-107, Wissenschaftszentrum Berlin für Sozialforschung.

Duoc, T. Q. and Metzger, C. (2007) 'Quality of Business Graduates in Vietnamese Institutions: Multiple perspectives', *The Journal of Management Development* 26(7): 629.

Fahey, S. (1995) 'Changing labour relations', in Kerkvliet, B J T (ed.), *Dilemmas of development: Vietnam update 1994*, Australia National University Department of Political and Social Change Research School of Pacific and Asian Studies, Canberra.

Gamble, J. (2001) *Transferring Business Practices from the United Kingdom to China: The limits and potential for convergence*, Paper presented to 'Multinational companies and human resource management: Between globalisation and national business systems' Conference, De Montfort University Graduate School of Business, Leicester.

Gates, C. L. and Truong, D. (1992) *Reform of a Centrally-managed Developing Economy: The Vietnamese perspective*, NIAS report No. 20, Nordic Institute of Asian studies, Copenhagen.

General Statistics Office (GSO) (2008) *Statistical Yearbook of Vietnam 2007*, Statistical Publishing House, Hanoi.

General Statistics Office (GSO) (2012) *Statistical Yearbook of Vietnam 2011*, Statistical Publishing House, Hanoi.

Hall, P. and Soskice, D. (2001) 'An introduction to varieties of capitalism', in P. Hall and D. Soskice (eds), *Varieties of Capitalism: The institutional foundations of comparative advantage*. Oxford: Oxford University Press.

Hargreaves, E., Montero, C., Chau, N., Sibli, M. and Thanh, T. (2001) 'Multigrade teaching in Peru, Sri Lanka and Vietnam: An overview', *International Journal of Educational Development* 21(6): 499–520.

Hofstede, G. (1980) 'Motivation, leadership, and organization: Do American theories apply abroad?', *Organizational Dynamics* 9: 42–63.

Joint Donor Group (2007) *Vietnam Development Report 2008: Social Protection*. Hanoi: The World Bank.

Kamoche, K. (2001) 'Human resources in Vietnam: The global challenge', *Thunderbird International Business Review* 43(5): 625–50.

Kerkvliet, B. J. T., Chan, A. and Unger, J. (1999) 'Comparing Vietnam and China: An introduction', in Chan, A., Kerkvliet, B. J. T., and Unger, J. (eds), *Transforming Asian Socialism: China and Vietnam compared*. Sydney: Allen and Unwin in association with ANU, pp. 1–14.

Labour Code 1994.

Lane, C. (1992) 'European business systems: Britain and Germany compared', in R. Whitley (ed.), *European Business Systems Firms and Markets in their National Contexts*. London: SAGE publications.

Le, C. T. and Truong, Q. (2005) 'Human Resource Management Practices in a Transitional Economy: A Comparative Study of Enterprise Ownership Forms in Vietnam', *Asia Pacific Business Review* 11(1): 25–47.

Le, D. D. (1997) 'Legal consequences of state-owned enterprise reform', in Yuen, N. C., Freeman, N. J. and Huynh, F. H. (eds), *State-owned Enterprise Reform in Vietnam: Lessons from Asia*. Singapore: Institution of Southeast Asian Studies, pp. 63–76.

Le Thanh Thuy (2007) 'Does foreign direct investment have an impact on the growth in labor productivity of Vietnamese domestic firms?', Research Institute of Economy, Trade and Industry (RIETI), IAA, Tokyo.

McCarty, A. (1993) 'Industrial Renovation in Vietnam, 1986–91', in M. Than, M and J. L. H. Tan, (eds), *Vietnam's Dilemmas and Options: The Challenge of Economic Transition in the 1990s* Singapore: Institute of Southeast Asian Studies, pp. 97–143.

Maurice, M., Sellier, F. and Silvestre, J. J. (1980) 'Societal differences in organizing manufacturing units: A comparison of France, West Germany and Great Britain', *Organization Studies* 1: 59–86.

Ministry of Education and Training (1997a) *Tong ket va danh gia muoi nam doi moi giao duc va dao tao (1986–1996): Bao cao tong hop va chi tiet* [Summarising and assessing the renovation of education and training in the 1986–1996 period: General and detailed report], Hanoi, Vietnam.

Ministry of Labor, Invalids and Social Affairs (MOLISA) (2002) *Statistical Yearbook of Labour-invalids and Social Affairs 2002*. Vietnam: Labour Social Publishing House.

Ministry of Labor, Invalids and Social Affairs (MOLISA) (2006) *Statistical Data of Employment and Unemployment in Vietnam 1996–2005*. Hanoi: The Publishing House of Social Labor.

Napier, N. K. (2005) 'Knowledge Transfer in Vietnam: Starts, Stops, and Loops', *Journal of Management Psychology* 20(7): 621–36.

Nguyen, V. H. and Tran, V. N. (1997) 'Government policies and state-owned enterprises', in Yuen, N. C., Freeman, N. J. and Huynh, F. H. (eds), *State-Owned Enterprise Reform In Vietnam, Lesson From Asia*. Singapore: Institute of Southeast Asian Studies.

Nguyen, N. T. and Truong, Q. (2007) 'International briefing 18: Training and development in Vietnam', *International Journal of Training and Development* 11(2): 139–49.

O'Connor, D. (1996) 'Labour Market aspects of state enterprise reform in Vietnam', Technical Papers No. 117, OECD development centre, Paris.

Porter, M. (1990) *The Competitive Advantage of Nations*. London/Basingstoke: MacMillan.

Quang, T. (1997) 'Conflict management in joint-ventures in Vietnam', *Transitions*, 38(1and2): 282–306.

Quang, T. and Vuong, N. T. (2002) 'Management Styles and Organisational Effectiveness in Vietnam', *Research and Practice in Human Resource Management* 10(2): 36–55.

Ralston, D. A., Nguyen, V. T. and Napier, N. K. (1999) 'A Comparative Study of the Work Values of North and South Vietnamese Managers', *Journal of International Business Studies* 30(4): 655–72.

Riedel, J. and Turley, W. S. (1999) 'The Politics and Economics of Transition to an Open Market Economy in Viet Nam', OECD Development Centre Working Papers 152, OECD Development Centre, Paris.

Siengthai, S. (2004) 'HR practices in Southeast Asia: an exploratory notes', An occasional paper, School of Management, Asian Institute of Technology, Thailand.

The Socialist Republic of Vietnam (2005) *Report of the Survey on Corruption in Vietnam 2005*, Government of the Socialist Republic of Vietnam, Hanoi.

Statistical Office of Ho Chi Minh City (1995) *Statistical Yearbook, 1995*. Ho Chi Minh City: City Statistical Office.

Taylor, S. Beechler, S. and Napier, N. (1996) 'Toward an integrative model of strategic international human resource management', *Academy of Management Review* 21(4): 959–85.

Thang, L. C. and Quang, T. (2005) 'Human resource management practices in a transitional economy: A comparative study of enterprise ownership forms in Vietnam', *Asia Pacific Business Review* 11(1): 25–47.

Tran, N. C. (2002) 'Learning Technological Capacities for Vietnam's Industrial Upgrading: Challenges of Globalization', Working Paper 165, National Institute for Science and Technology Policy and Strategy Studies and Stockholm School of Economics, Stockholm.

Tran, N. C. (2003) 'International cooperation in science and technology: some critical issues for Vietnam', paper presented at MOST-IDRC roundtable on international cooperation in science and technology, Hanoi, October.

Tran, V. H. (1997) (ed.) *Economic Development and Prospects in the ASEAN: Foreign investment and growth in Vietnam, Thailand, Indonesia, and Malaysia*. Basingstoke: Macmillan.

Vietnam Economic Times (2003) 26 May.

Vo, A. N. (2009) *The Transformation of Human Resource Management and Labour Relations in Vietnam*. Oxford: Chandos Publishing.

Vo, A. and Hannif, Z. (forthcoming) 'The Reception of Anglo Leadership Styles in a Transforming Society: The Case of American Companies in Vietnam', T*he International Journal of Human Resource Management*.

Vo, A. N. and Stanton, P. (2011) 'The transfer of HRM policies and practices to an transitional business system – the case of performance management practices in US and Japanese MNEs operating in Vietnam', *International Journal of Human Resource Management* 22(17): 3,513–27.

Vu, Q. N. (2002) 'State Owned Enterprises Reform in Vietnam', PhD Thesis, Australian National University, Canberra.

Whitley, R. (1999) *How and Why are International Firms Different?: The consequences of cross-border managerial coordination for firm characteristics and behaviour*, presented to sub theme 3 'Business System in their International Context' of the 15th EGOS Colloquium held at the University of Warwick, 4–6 July 1999.

Whitley, R. (2000) *Divergent Capitalisms: The social structuring and change of business systems*. Oxford: Oxford University Press.

Wolff, P. (1999) *Vietnam – the incomplete transformation*. London: Frank Cass Publishers.

World Bank (2006) 'Vietnam Development Report 2006', Report No. 34474-VN, www-wds. worldbank.org/external/default/WDSContentServer/WDSP/IB/2005/12/02/000160016_ 20051202141324/Rendered/PDF/344740VN.pdf, last accessed 3 April 2008.

World Bank (2011) *Country Classification – Data and statistics*. http://ddp-ext.worldbank.org/ ext/ddpreports, Accessed 2 January 2012.

Xinzhong, Y. (2000) *An Introduction to Confucianism*. Cambridge: Cambridge University Press.

Zhu, Y. (2002) 'Economic Reform and Human Resource Management in Vietnam', *Asia Pacific Business Review* 8(3): 115–35.

10 Human Resource Management in Malaysia

MARLIN ABDUL MALEK, ARUP VARMA
AND PAWAN S. BUDHWAR

Over the last 10 years or so, HRM in Malaysia has evolved from merely an abbreviation that HR personnel used to show that they are abreast of the current developments in the function around the globe, to a strategic function that is awarded due recognition. Indeed, the new-found respect for HRM is manifested in the establishment of the Ministry of Human Resources, in charge of all human resources related aspects and dedicated to producing a skilled, knowledgeable and competitive workforce through ongoing training. This ministry is also responsive to the current development of global HR practices through close ties with the employers and trade unions, and by encouraging and maintaining conducive and harmonised industrial relations between employers, employees and trade unions, for the nation's economic development and wellness of people. This chapter will continue from the previous edition by highlighting the challenges that Malaysia faces in light of stiff competition and shifting global human mobility – the by-products of globalization. We start with a discussion of the historical development of HRM in Malaysia, followed by the role of HR in most companies, key factors in determining HRM practices and policies and key challenges facing HRM in Malaysia. We also look ahead to the future and speculate how the HR function is likely to evolve over the next five years. We conclude with a short case study that showcases HR practices in Malaysia with a discussion of how these practices differ from HR practices around the world.

Human Resource Management (HRM) in Malaysia

In Malaysia, the history of Human Resource Development (HRD) can be traced back to the 1980s, although there are no clear documents noting the emergence of HRD in Malaysia. It is speculated that HRD may have started when the Commonwealth Secretariat began developing the Human Resources Development Group (HRDG) in 1983 with the intention of assisting the Association of Southeast Asian Nations' (ASEAN) countries in developing their human resources (Commonwealth Secretariat, 1993). This was followed, in 1984, by the ASEAN countries commencing their proposals to provide assistance in developing human resources, particularly in education, training and skills development for new technology (Hashim, 2000). On the other hand, it has also been argued that HRD in Malaysia could have started emerging during the mid-1970s when the government began developing the Bumiputras in businesses to improve economic disparities (Malaysia Government, 1971), or it may have started during the economic recession in 1985, as it was during this period that the government began its aggressive drive towards manufacturing and industrialisation (Malaysia Government, 1991). However, clear evidence of the emergence of HRD was seen when the Government of Malaysia began to include HRD strategies in the country's development plans and policies in 1991 in the Second Outline Perspective Plan (OPP2) and the Sixth Malaysia Plan (6MP). One of the main thrusts of these plans is to become a fully industrialised nation with a skilled and knowledge-based workforce by the year 2020 (Malaysia Government, 1991). Nevertheless, it could be argued that HRD could have started even before Malaysia's independence, when workers migrated from India to work in the tin-ore mining fields and oil palm plantations.

This chapter is designed to provide a general overview of the HRM practices and policies and a discussion of future challenges for HR practitioners in this country.

The Role and Importance of HR

At the outset, it is worth mentioning that while HRM has been around in the corporate sector of Malaysia for a while it has received limited academic attention. In this connection, Hazman Shah (1998) noted that Malaysian human resource managers tend to have little influence in the strategic management process, while Rowley and Saaidah (2007) have argued that the attention has always been on the politics and economy of Malaysia with little attention paid to its people management practices. These authors concluded that, in general, Malaysian people management would be better characterised as still tending to be more like the traditional 'personnel' function than the more current 'HR' management. Indeed it is often argued that management in Malaysian organisations tended to treat staff as a variable, rather than a fixed asset, and that HR issues were treated as being of secondary importance, as organisational priorities centred upon financial control and profit maximisation. Indeed, Hope-Hailey, Farndale and Truss (2005) have noted that one particular area of neglect in understanding the link between HRM and performance is the role played by the HR department. Chew (2005) concurred that although the HR role is gradually expanding in importance, the general notion is that the HR department still plays largely an administrative role. Consistent with Chew's argument, a more recent study involving 32 manufacturing companies in Malaysia by Long and Wan Khairuzzaman (2008) found that HR professionals are lacking in their capacity to play an important role as strategic partners and agents for change. Clearly, to improve the performance of the HRM department, HR managers need to devolve some of the HR activities (that is, operational activities) to the line managers as a move to become more strategic in their orientation. This is borne out in a study by Perry and Kulik (2008) which found that HR managers perceived that people management was more effective when HR staff were less tied up with routine activities. As is obvious, strategic activities are time consuming for HR managers and consequently they feel over-worked if they are still responsible for handling the operational tasks (Kulik and Bainbridge, 2006).

As such, it is imperative that Malaysian HR practices incorporate the flexibility and adaptability required in changing work environments such as those in multi-national companies, joint ventures or other types of organisations (Abdul Malek and Budhwar, 2010; Chiah-Liaw, Petzall and Selvarajah, 2003; Rozhan, Rohayu and Rasidah, 2001) in order to be more competitive in the wake of internationali-sation and globalisation.

In this connection, Musa (2007) noted that the Malaysian government has real-ised the importance of HR by emphasising HR and HR practices in policies, blueprints and development plans since the late 1980s. Other issues that HR authorities in the country need to look into are the changing demographics of the workforce as internalisation and globalisation not only brought in foreign companies to operate in the country but also brought in foreign workers to fill the need for white and blue collar workers. In Malaysia, the Ministry of Human Resources holds the responsibility for enacting a suitable work environment to enhance productivity and to ensure that the welfare of employees in the country is not neglected (Aminuddin, 1995). The Malaysian HR is governed by the Labour Law and the enforcement of legislation such as the Employment Act 1955, the Employees Provident Fund Act 1951, the Social Security Organisation Act 1969, the Trade Unions Act 1959, to name only a few. When Malaysia stepped into the 21st century, changing work patterns and the demographics of the workforce compelled the Ministry to update its policies to encompass foreign companies operating in Malaysia and foreign nationals working in Malaysia. The govern-ment also took it upon itself to create separate documentations for foreign work-ers and expatriates so as to create less confusion. In the following sections, we explore the various issues that could affect HRM in Malaysia.

Key Factors Determining HRM Practices and Policies

Intensifying Human Capital Development

First, it is well known that the quality of the Malaysian workforce is deteriorat-ing, with many of the new entrants to the labour force falling short in terms of the skills needed for the industry. Specifically, the new entrants are lacking mostly in analytical and problem-solving capabilities. In addition, there are deficiencies in language proficiency and social networking aptitude that hinder progress in the adoption of cutting-edge technology and modern teamwork processes needed for high-value added activities. The pivotal need is a radical revamp of the current education system, ranging from the primary to the tertiary levels, and requir-ing improvements at each level. This constant refrain is well recognised yet the attempted fixes have failed to yield the desired results. The education system must move beyond the 'nation building stage' to providing the tools and skills to compete in the global marketplace. Close partnership among all stakeholders, that is government, industry, academia, parents and non-governmental organisations (NGOs), and drawing from past and international experience will be the key to achieving the desired outcome. To address this issue, among others, the National Economic Advisory Council (NEAC) was set up by the prime minister of Malaysia in May 2009 with a mandate to formulate a New Economic Model (NEM) that is designed to transform Malaysia into a high-income economy by 2020. The NEAC completed its mandate officially on 31 May 2011, and has produced the *2011 New Economic Model Report* in which there is a summary of policy measures for intensifying human capital development (see Table 10.1).

Table 10.1 below depicts the policy measures that are needed to be implemented in order to transform the workplace and the workforce in line with Malaysia's aspiration to intensify its human capital development. Some of the policy measures are already in place and will be explored further in the later part of this chapter. The policy measures set forth by the NEAC are holistic in nature and aim to address the issue of lack of a talented workforce especially to cater to the high-technology industry and to attract better quality talent.

The country is in a race to deliver competent, highly skilled human capital to move the economy up the value chain but, ironically, Malaysia lacks one critical element to support its drive towards knowledge or a 'K' economy, a fact that the Economic Planning Unit (EPU) of the prime minister's department concedes – that the country lacks a creative and highly competent and skilled workforce to move the economy up the value chain. Although this issue has been revisited

Table 10.1 Summary of Policy Measures for Intensifying Human Capital Development

Workplace transformation

- Set up an expert group to modernise and align labour legislation and regulation consistent with international best practice, with the dual objectives of reduced costs to business of labour management and increased effectiveness of worker protection.
- Strengthen strategic human resources management.
- Enhance the workers' safety net through the introduction of unemployment insurance.
- Establish a National Wage Consultative Council (NWCC).
- Facilitate a Productivity-Linked Wage System (PLWS).
- Consider a minimum wage policy.

Workforce transformation
- Undertake a labour market forecast and survey programme.
- Up-skill and upgrade the workforce.
  - *Set overall strategy for upgrading the workforce.*
  - *Standardise certification of semi-skilled workers.*
- Leverage women's talents to raise productivity.

Source: National Economic Advisory Council (NEAC), Malaysia.

many times over, and especially so in recent years, as the year 2020 draws closer it has not managed to take centre-stage until recently (under the 10th Malaysia Plan, that is, 10MP). Referring to some statistics from the World Bank's previous report, one can perhaps gain a clearer picture of how urgent it is for Malaysia to produce a pool of innovative and highly skilled talent to realise its ambition to be a developed nation by 2020. According to the World Bank, only one quarter of Malaysia's workforce is considered to be highly skilled. This pales in comparison to high-income economies that tend to have more than one-third or half of their total workforce being highly skilled. The majority of Malaysia's workforce (about 75 per cent) has low skills, clearly indicating that most Malaysians have not been adequately equipped to handle high-value work. This pain is particularly acute within the engineering, life sciences, pharmaceutical, information and communications technology (ICT) and retail sectors.

The growing mismatch between the supply of skills and the requirements of various industries in the local market is a reflection of the inadequacy of the country's education system in producing the relevant human capital that can drive the country's economy in this globalised, new world order. Many quarters are of the opinion that the Malaysian education system needs to undergo a major reform at all levels. Education is certainly an important element of human capital formation. The curriculum needs to be revamped in order to produce knowledgeable graduates, with relevant and sophisticated skills, good attitudes, good analytical and interpersonal skills and good English proficiency in order to fit into the country's changing economic landscape. One has to only look at the growing preference for private education to show that there is lack of confidence in the country's public education system. However, it is not only the lack of talented students, the teachers should be better qualified to teach English and critical subjects such as mathematics and sciences. Thankfully, the government has demonstrated its willingness to spend money to attract well-trained and qualified teachers as part of its effort to improve the public education system.

Furthermore, there need to be better alternatives for school leavers who are not academically inclined to learn new skills that can contribute to the country's economy. For instance, the general academic stream equips one with general skills that may be more appropriate in a services-sector driven economy while vocational/technical training equips one with specific skills that are more responsive to technological change, and hence, more relevant to an industrialising economy. As such, one can contribute better in his or her chosen field and there is no question of being left out from being employed. In some Asian industrialised countries such as Japan, Singapore and South Korea, for example, vocational/technical education features prominently in schools, colleges and polytechnics. Some economists even attribute the industrialisation of these economies to their strong focus on vocational/technical training. In this connection, economists argue that vocational/technical education can cultivate a skill culture and contribute to the progress of an economy. In addition, such training can also help reduce unemployment and mitigate the challenges faced by school dropouts. Unfortunately, however, vocational/technical education is not yet well regarded by most Malaysians. Indeed, Malaysian society has a strong bent towards an academic culture and it seems that vocational/technical education has not garnered enough confidence to go mainstream. In light of this, the Economic Planning Unit (EPU) is reported to be working on looking for ways to encourage greater appreciation for vocational/technical skills in the society and can perhaps help to dispel the perception that those who are not academically inclined cannot contribute to the economy and nation. The government's seriousness in raising appreciation for vocational/technical education is evidenced in the injection of the related financial means to the establishment of 10 skills training institutes and the upgrading of 16 existing institutes under the 9th Malaysia Plan (9MP). This move has resulted in the rise of the number of trainees to 88,050, or a student intake growth of 1.5 per cent per annum from 2005 to 2009. Ironically, however, the number of graduates from vocational/technical institutions had decreased from 72,557 graduates in 2005 to 57,782 in 2009, and this slide needs to be stemmed.

Without an adequate talent pool, innovation-led growth can only be sub-optimal and it is imperative that for industries to move up the value chain there needs to be less dependence on unskilled or low-skilled foreign workers in the economy; instead there should be a growing reliance on a skilled or highly skilled workforce that can be tapped from the Malaysian diaspora and expatriates. Malaysia's over-dependence on low-cost, unskilled foreign workers is perturbing. Official estimates put the influx of low-skilled foreign labour in the country to more than double since 2000 to 1.9 million. Experts believe that a more sustainable solution lies in developing the domestic human resources at all levels as ultimately it is the human capital that is the greatest asset to the country's economy.

Brain Drain

In the recent issue of the World Bank's Malaysia Economic Monitor (2011), Malaysia was flagged as a country with a serious case of 'brain drain'. The World Bank defines 'brain drain' as the emigration of individuals aged 25 or over with an academic or professional degree. Apart from offering a thorough analysis of this issue, supported by an online survey of about 200 Malaysians studying or working overseas, as well as data from Malaysian government departments and other countries, the World Bank report makes several key points. First, human capital is the bedrock of any high-income economy. For Malaysia to be successful in its journey to high income, it will need to develop, attract and retain talent, but the sad truth is that talent seems to be leaving. According to the report, the brain drain represents about one-third of the unskilled and skilled men, women and children born in Malaysia but now living overseas. Conservatively estimated to total one million, the World Bank labels this group the Diaspora. Second, Malaysia's brain drain is the symptom, not the problem itself. This suggests that the government must address all the factors that caused the brain drain instead of focusing solely on persuading migrants to return, a challenging task that cannot be the sole responsibility of institutions like Talent Corp, established to tackle the issues of brain drain. Key factors that motivate Malaysians to move overseas include better salary levels, career prospects, access to high-quality education and quality of life issues that include safety and security.

Third, brain drain is a phenomenon that is inevitable. The World Bank report suggests several ways that Malaysia can tap this global pool of talent – for example, by employing more expatriates and encouraging a greater number of foreign students to study in local universities and to work in this country after graduation. Instead of fixating on persuading migrants to return to Malaysia, the report suggests they can help in other ways, for example, by acting as a bridge between foreign technology and markets and local entrepreneurs. In China and India, migrants have helped to develop high-tech industries and the same can be done in Malaysia. Fourth, Malaysia's brain drain intensity is high. For every 10 skilled Malaysians who were born in this country, one of them elects to migrate, which is a ratio double that of the world average. While these figures are comparable with Hong Kong and Singapore, the World Bank argues that their high numbers are typical for small and open economies.

Fifth, although the share of Malaysians with tertiary level education increased considerably from 16 per cent in 2001 to 22 per cent in 2008, during the same period the proportion of Malaysians with higher skill jobs changed only marginally from 18.4 per cent to 19.9 per cent. The report suggests two possibilities: because employment opportunities were insufficient to absorb people with higher education, these graduates were forced to take jobs with a lower skills requirement. Another possibility is that the higher education curriculum and market demand is misaligned. In short, the report implies that Malaysia's brain drain is not merely a human resource issue but a structural economic problem. And although the brain drain may be economic in origin, minimising or reversing it will require decisive political action as well as a sustained and steely political commitment.

Minimum Wage and Retirement Age Issues

Malaysia's minimum wage policy, which was announced on the 1 May 2012 sees starting salaries fixed at between RM800 and RM900. The National Wage Advisory Council (NWAC) stated clearly in its proposal that the minimum wage salary should be above RM740, which is the poverty line. Although some quarters are of the opinion that the salary should be above RM1,200, especially in the wake of the current economic conditions and the rising of the price of goods and services, the government has not managed to fix it at a higher rate due to other important financial commitments. The NWAC has been cautioned by the World Bank and other studies that any figure above RM1,200 could have some challenging impacts on the Malaysian economy. There are, of course, other complicated issues when salary is fixed at above RM1,200. These include the risk of unemployment, the risk of being non-competitive and the risk of inflation. While effort to introduce the minimal wage should be applauded, there are also those who are unhappy with the radical changes. Overall, however, this is definitely a step forward for Malaysia in emulating the practise of a minimum wage policy.

Next, the lifespan of Malaysians has increased from 55 to 65 and with better health facilities and improving lifestyles, Malaysia is in the middle of drafting a bill to actually fix a retirement age for the private sector, something that is currently left to individuals, although most employers use 55 as the retirement age. However, in the public sector retirement age is 60, and the private sector should align their retirement age accordingly, so as to give individuals five more productive years. This would help families, as well as the economy, and ensure that efficiency and productivity levels are maintained, which is critical to the growth of an organization. In addition, understanding and leveraging the differences between generational groups and their levels of experience is critical for organizations in order to get optimum performance outcomes. Before the retirement bill is passed, organisations will need to be prepared to integrate the culture within the generational workforce and design a systematic knowledge transfer programme between their ageing workforce and the incoming and younger workforce in order to maximise productivity.

In this connection, private employers surveyed want the bill to address all gaps and concerns well after in-depth study and consultation with stakeholders instead of having it amended simply based on employee concerns. One way to ensure that the workers remain productive after the age of 55 is that senior employees aged 55 should be re-employed under the retirement bill as per their current employment terms until they reach the age of 60. After 60, this pool of senior employees will be re-employed based on their capabilities and new terms of employment will be in place where they may be posted into new roles such as in training and mentoring programs for knowledge transfer to the younger generation. This will help to fully utilise their expertise while minimising redundancy. Of course, there needs to be a shift in the mindset before the policy can work its intended benefits. The teething phase may see some reluctance on the part of employers, who may remain reluctant to hire a potential candidate who is 50, compared to one in their 30s or 40s, but the government could play a pivotal role by offering subsidies or medical benefits for hiring older employees as an incentive, which is the case in Singapore where the upcoming budget proposes offering subsidies to employers who hire older workers. Most importantly, the bill should be passed with the view that older employees with the relevant skill sets and experience should have equal opportunity to be hired and should not be let go without valid reasons.

Acute Shortage in the Domestic Maid Sector

According to the Indonesian embassy, there are 300,000 Indonesian maids working in Malaysia, and according to the Deputy Human Resources Minister Datuk Maznah Mazlan, Malaysia needs some 200,000 domestic helpers. Whichever figure you choose to look at, it is an alarming one. The Indonesian government has already put up some resistance in the recruitment of their nationals to work as maids in Malaysia, given the reports of the cases of maid abuse. The fact remains that Malaysia is facing a problem that most developing nations face at this stage – a severe shortage of human power in the labor sector. Relatedly, the role of women as traditional providers of care for the family has evolved over the last three decades. In the past, women have been a key part of Malaysia's workforce and have been instrumental in its socio-economic growth. Over time, however, family structures have changed with more women having joined the labour market, either through choice or necessity, which means that households with both spouses at work need domestic help to either care for their children or their ageing parents, or both. As a result, there are many instances when female employees have to take 'emergency' leave due to not having people to look after their children while they are at work. In many countries, there are facilities and programmes in place to provide a favourable support system for families, specifi-cally for working mothers and families. Studies have shown that where childcare services have been integrated into a framework that involves local authorities, NGOs and even trade unions, the benefits are tremendous for families, society and the economy.

Clearly, there is an urgent need to reconcile the labour shortage and make child-care available for families. Efforts by all stakeholders – the government (includ-ing local councils and authorities), employers, employees, NGOs and trade unions – are required towards developing a policy for long-term solution. Gov-ernments in a number of countries, such as Australia, Singapore and the United Kingdom, specifically encourage and help employers to provide some form of childcare support, in some cases backed by incentives. For instance, besides crèches in workplaces, childcare centres, child-minder or nanny services should be made available in housing areas as part of the framework of national policies, or even local government policies or regulations. With policies covering child-care, it will also benefit the low-income groups, who form a big part of the labour market. Access to affordable, good-quality childcare goes beyond the welfare of individual children and their families because it works favourably in the social and economic development of the whole society. Among the societal benefits of childcare are promoting gender equality and the rights and development of children as well as contributing to the national economy. In fact, well-structured childcare support policies can pay for themselves: Without support, parents can face a more difficult time participating in the labour force, which can lead to 'higher welfare' expenditure, lost tax revenues, inhibited growth and wasted human capital.

Management Culture and HRM in Malaysia

About 60 per cent of Malaysians are Muslim. And similar to other Muslim socie-ties, management practices are influenced by key Islamic values and principles. However, more than 30 per cent of the population is Chinese or Indian, the former strongly influenced by Confucian values of collectivism (see Mansor and Ali, 1998). These authors argue that Malaysian management practices should be understood in the context of interposing Confucian, Islamic and Western values.

It is pertinent to note here that the former colonial power, Britain, deeply influ-enced organisational cultures, especially in the public sector, which was followed, in the 1970s, by an increasing Americanisation of workplace organisation, due to US dominance in management education. As noted, Japanese success led to the adoption of the Look East policy in the 1980s, coterminous with moves towards indigenisation. This interposition is, at times, contradictory. The persistence of religious and cultural difference has precluded any single cultural paradigm from gaining predominance; neither American nor Japanese managerial cultures have attained hegemony.

In terms of national culture, Malaysia is a collectivist society (Noordin, Williams and Zimmer, 2002), where social relations, self-sacrifice and family integrity are an important part of the social fabric. The Malay culture is essentially a cooperative society based on *kampung* (village) and *gotong royong* (mutual help) values (Taib and Ismail, 1982). Malaysian *kampungs* were self-sufficient, small and dispersed, and thus created a sense of community and need for collective work. Wolfe and Arnold (1994: 207) noted: 'Malays were socialised to place the needs of the *kampung* above their personal needs.' *Gotong royong* implies that people who offer help or services will expect the same service or help to be returned at some point (Taib and Ismail, 1982: 109). The *gotong royong* is underpinned by the Islamic concept of the *Ummah* (Islamic religious community) where each Muslim is responsible to his fellow Muslims. Taib and Ismail (1982: 109) noted: 'The unity of the Malay community thus rests on the *adat resam (*social customs), which include the institution of *gotong royong*, and the concept of *ummah* and *malu* (self-respect)." The Malay culture puts a strong emphasis on the importance of having and maintaining, 'face', an emphasis shared by many cultures in the Far East.

Further, Islamic values and teaching put strong emphasis on obedience to leaders. Beekun and Badawi (1999: 16) noted that in Islam 'at all times, the leader must be obeyed'. They added: 'Islam considers obedience to the leader so important that it views any kind of insubordination to be abhorrent unless in very specific circumstances.' The authority of the leader or manager is thus accepted as right and proper, and subordinates are expected to show respect and obedience to superiors. Beekun and Badawi (1999: 16) noted that although 'Islam emphasizes that followers should comply with the directives of their leader, it does not condone blind subservience'. That is, although the typical Muslim worker does respect his or her leader, the onus in most cases is on the leader to convince subordinates that his or her orders are worth obeying rather than imposing his or her will on others by administrative fiat. This is why, according to *Sharia*, Muslim leaders are asked to consult their subordinates before a decision is made. In addition, Islamic teachings put heavy emphasis on forgiveness, kind-heartedness and compassion. Atiyyah (1999) noted that Islamic values emphasise harmony, cooperation and brotherly relationships, and conflicts should be avoided or suppressed. The business leader, in turn, is expected to show responsibility for the quality of work life of employees and concern for their families and the surrounding society.

Not surprisingly, Wolfe and Arnold (1994) reported that the *kampung* headman received respect, obeisance and loyalty but was expected, in turn, to display generosity and *anakhuah*, a fatherly concern for the welfare of his subjects. Taib and Ismail (1982: 113) noted that in Malaysian schools, the power distance factor is further reinforced:

> Malay children are normally taught to consider teachers as a figure of authority, and as kings of the institution, to be respected and obeyed . . . and the end-product is an obedient and law abiding citizen, but not an independently thinking one.

> Taib and Ismail (1982: 113)

Wolfe and Arnold (1994: 208) argue that, in addition to the above, power distance is a product of the *kampung* values where there is a strict code of behaviour that applied to both leaders and followers. They noted that, 'recognising one's relative status and acting in accordance with one's station were the hallmarks of a *halus* person, the idealized member of society'. Further, Malays are socialised to be non-assertive and compliant, and humility, courtesy and tactfulness are strongly held values. The latter have strong impact on HRM policies and practices. For instance, Wolfe and Arnold (1994) noted that Malay values make direct discipline at work unacceptable because it leads to the loss of face. Over time, there has been a widespread diffusion of new management practices in Malaysia. These have taken the form of changes to the business culture and HRM policies and practices. They have invariably been accompanied by Western practices and sometimes by Japanese practices including quality control (QC), total quality management (TQM) and teamwork. The new business environment has shifted management culture from collectivist behaviour towards individualist practices, ever so slightly. This has led to the erosion of some of the old HRM practices and to attempts, especially by transnational corporations (TNCs), to Westernise HRM practices through the use of Western universalist best practices. In this context, there has been increasing interest in the effect of these economic and social changes on HRM practices. Indeed, there has been some speculation that HRM practices in Malaysia may be becoming more individualistic in their management practices. From this perspective, the new Western management practices can be seen as a direct threat to indigenous Malaysian practices. For instance, Lim (1998, 2001a, 2001b, 2002) found that while power distance in Malaysia is still high, and masculinity is still moderate, there is evidence to suggest that the levels of uncertainty avoidance and individualism in Malaysia have increased over the past few decades. However, others have argued that new forms of participation have done little to erode a tradition of autocracy and deeply entrenched managerial prerogatives (Elger and Smith 2001: 460).

Indeed, it has been suggested that the alleged drift to individualism does not necessarily lead to the eradication of traditional Malaysian practices; the impact of the individualisation of Malaysian managers should not be overstated. Noordin, Williams and Zimmer (2002: 46–47) note that individualism is most pronounced in the new middle class whereas the upper class pay attention to traditional collectivist values and social norms that secure and prolong their comfortable position in the society. Nonetheless, these authors suggest that at least one facet of individualism, an emphasis on global competitiveness, has infiltrated into the collectivist values held by Malaysians, but harmony and social behaviour still appear to be important for Malaysian managers as well as relationships, self-sacrifice and family integrity. However, while Malaysian managers remain inclined towards collectivism in situations involving in-groups, they appear to be individualistic in situations that involve out-groups, and the organizations they work for may fall into the latter category. Table 10.2 highlights Malaysia's scores on the Global Leadership and Organisational Behaviour Effectiveness (GLOBE) Study, a worldwide study on leadership attributes.

Human Resource Development Strategy

From the discussion above, it should be clear that if Malaysia is to become a developed nation by the year 2020, an educated multi-skilled, disciplined and productive workforce has to be created. Several critical factors demand this – the rapid transformation of the economy during the late 1980s and 1990s, the shift

Table 10.2 GLOBE Social Culture Dimension in Malaysia (highest 7–lowest 1)

Uncertainty avoidance	4.78
Future orientation	4.58
Power distance	5.17
Institutional collectivism	4.61
Humane orientation	4.87
Performance orientation	4.34
Group and family collectivism	5.51
Gender egalitarianism	3.51
Assertiveness	3.87

Adopted from Gupta *et al.* (2002).

from traditional to modern technological production processes, and the need for bold and innovative HRD strategies to meet the challenging skills requirements. To further encourage and stimulate the private sector to introduce training and development for its employees, the HRD Act 1992 requires organisations employing more than 50 employees to contribute 1 per cent of their monthly payroll to a fund to promote training. In turn, the fund aims to provide financial assistance to defray part of the allowable costs in training undertaken by employers. It acts as an incentive scheme whereby grants from the fund can be provided to employers to undertake and accelerate systematic training programmes to equip the workforce with high skills, knowledge and positive industrial attitudes. The fund was initially open only to the manufacturing sector but has since been expanded to the service sector.

The HR Ministry's Manpower Department and the National Vocational Training Department formulate the curriculum of training programs and supplying skilled and trained workforce to meet the needs of the economy. Their aim is to minimise skill mismatches and to conduct training to supply a multi-skilled, innovative and adaptive workforce, in order to facilitate the transition from labour-intensive to knowledge-intensive industries with a strong science and technology base.

The HRM Function

HRM is currently a rapidly growing field in Malaysia. Indeed, since the late 1980s Malaysian managers have increasingly used the term HRM instead of personnel management (Todd and Peetz, 2001; Yong, 1996). Yong (1996) argues that the diversity of the composition of the modern workforce in Malaysia requires more appropriate and imaginative HRM solutions than have hitherto been deployed. In 1990, the former Ministry of Labor adopted the new term and changed its name to Ministry of Human Resources in keeping with the international trend and 'need of recognizing people as a key resource for national development' (Yong, 1996).

Malaysian HRM departments are usually staffed by people who have general qualifications and usually substantial working experience in the field (Todd and

Peetz, 2001). Yong (1996) describes the typical HRM professional in Malaysia as 'a male with a social science degree plus qualifications in personnel management with five years experience and around 33 to 45 years old, able to communicate well, in Bahasa Malaysia, and English'. However, it is interesting to note that Todd and Peetz (2001: 1,373) found evidence of the increasing strategic integration of the HR function.

The Human Resource Ministry plays a key role in shaping HRM policies and practices in Malaysia. The government is responsible for developing labour administration policy, promoting workers' welfare (especially *bumiputras*) and promoting industrial harmony. More importantly, it plays the role of a coordinator with the private sector by maintaining the supply of a multi-skilled, disciplined (through controlling union activities) and efficient workforce.

Conclusions

Overall, Malaysia represents a success story in many respects. From an economy centred on the production of primary commodities, it has graduated to developing a significant manufacturing sector. In particular, the country has assumed an important role in the global consumer electronics industry. Moreover, from a predominantly poor, rural grouping, *bumiputras* have increasingly urbanised, and gained representation at the highest levels of industry. In some ways, the Malaysian experience highlights the continued relevance of state interventions – globalisation notwithstanding – and the possibilities of active industrial policy. At the same time, Malaysia's growth trajectory is fraught with contradictions. While official HRD initiatives have had some success – above all, in enhancing productivity – chronic skills shortages persist in certain areas. Moreover, both the kind of products that tend to be manufactured in Malaysia – mature standardised products, and components thereof – do not always readily lend themselves to be regarded as high value-added products. Further institutional barriers to a high wage–high skill scenario include an autocratic managerial tradition, with geographic, ethnic and regional barriers being deliberately erected between managers and workforces. This is not to suggest that in certain niche areas, Malaysia may retain global competitiveness on grounds other than cost. However, the diffusion of a culture of autocracy from the political centre would seem to mitigate against the emergence of a genuine culture of involvement and participation, unlocking the fullest potential of the country's human capital. In other words, HRM can only be developed if corporate and societal governance systems have the ability to support and follow through the necessary investments in physical resources and trust (see Marsden 1999: 268).

We would like to end on a positive note with a cautionary caveat – Malaysia has come a long way in the last two decades in terms of the growth of its economy, and the efforts put towards developing its workforce have clearly paid dividends. However, it is imperative that the government does not rests on its laurels – instead it needs to continue its efforts in partnership with all stakeholders, if the vision of 2020 is to be realised.

Case Study

John B was excited about going to Malaysia. Four days later, he would be in a country known for its friendly people. He had spent a lot of time learning about Malaysia from the Internet and from those who had spent time in the country, either on expatriate assignments or studying there. Malaysia, he thought to himself, seemed like straightforward country and he was confident that he had learnt enough to be able to adjust easily, especially because he had spent time in several universities around the globe. He was sure that he would enjoy his stay in Malaysia for the next two years, where he had accepted an assignment with a public university, which was hiring foreign nationals as part of the education sector's internationalisation strategy.

However, on the very first day, he was faced with some disconcerting facts – first, he felt that there was no sense of urgency among Malaysians. From those he met in the airport, to those he met on the way to his new work place, and then among his local colleagues, almost everyone seemed to be working on a different sense of time. The driver that was assigned to meet him at the airport was late and he had to wait in the blistering heat for 45 minutes. When the driver did arrive, he casually sauntered up to him, asked his name and said, 'Good, follow me,' without uttering a word of apology. He had to explain to the driver that he had no Ringgit Malaysia and wanted to go to the nearest American bank to cash his travellers' cheque. But the driver just said, 'No bank – bank close. Go on Monday.' It was Thursday, and Monday seemed rather far off, so he told the driver to bring him to his new office. He was irritated that the driver was smiling and chatting with almost everybody along the way. He heard words like '*orang baru*' or something like '*Mat Salleh*' being uttered by those around him. People were staring and giving shy smiles and stealing glances along the way. He was desperate to meet somebody that had a good command of the English language to help him.

He finally met up with the Dean who assured him that he will be fine, noting that Malaysians need some time to warm up to newcomers. In the first faculty meeting, he was surprised to note that the agenda was quite long. He was even more surprised when people sauntered into the meeting room 20 or 30 minutes late without any sense of contrition. As he looked around the meeting room he noticed that some were clearly engrossed in other things and were not paying attention to the chairperson. John lost his patience and mentioned to the chairperson that he should be more in control of the attendees.

When the chairperson asked for opinions on how best to increase foreign student enrolment and increase staff and student mobility, John felt that his Malaysian colleagues were offering 'polite and safe suggestions', as if they were afraid of saying 'politically incorrect' things, or simply because they were too respectful of their employer. John couldn't just sit there as a silent observer, so he shook his head and said, 'Look, the suggestions that were put forth were too conservative. To be the best, you need to be bold. You need to be aggressive and be a trendsetter. Just because everybody else does it, doesn't mean that you too have to do it. I don't understand the rationale of giving such crappy suggestions. This is just a waste of my time.' He then stormed off. Over the next few days, John had several uncomfortable encounters with colleagues, forcing him to wonder if he had erred in accepting the offer in Malaysia. During research presentations, he was surprised and somewhat irritated by people's defensive reactions when he offered suggestions or comments. To his way of thinking, John felt that the presenters should be grateful that he took the time to read their papers and offer constructive comments. One young colleague even cried when John commented, 'You are sure about this? What is your theory? This is rubbish, don't insult my intelligence!'

It didn't take very long before the Dean called John to his office and told him that he should be more tactful in offering his opinions. Needless to say, John was surprised – in his culture being upfront and direct was appreciated, and this had led him to believe that when feedback was sugar-coated, the recipients would not learn anything. What really surprised John in the meeting with the Dean was that he was also told that he dressed too informally for work. John always wore a short-sleeved linen shirt with chinos and sandals, which he deemed appropriate for the hot Malaysian weather. He just could not understand why the staff were subjected to wearing formal office clothes with neckties and covered formal shoes in the blistering humid weather. In addition, he found the practice of clocking in and out of the office rather surprising. He was used to a much more flexible attendance policy for academics at other universities – coming and going as they pleased, including working from home or wherever their creativity took them.

John tried to meet the senior officials at the university to express his concerns and share his views but found it very difficult to make an appointment with the Vice Chancellor (VC). It seemed to him that the VC was always somewhere doing something such as presenting certificates, attending dinners or officiating events. And when he finally managed to see the VC, his comments were duly heard but the replies were always the same: 'Give it time; things will change,' or 'Don't worry, you'll soon adapt'. John used to be able to write a new book every three months or send a paper for journals at least every two months but because he was preoccupied with attending the compulsory activities lined up for all staff, he had not managed to find time to do either.

Not so long after he showed up in Malaysia full of enthusiasm, John was sitting in his office one fine day trying to make sense of his experience and decide on his next steps. When he accepted the offer in Malaysia, he had thought that he could be happy there, but he was far from happy. In fact, he was miserable and had never felt so alone and isolated. He had worked in 10 universities before coming to Malaysia, but this was the first time that he was tempted to end his two-year contract prematurely and head home. John wasn't sure what to do – on the one hand he feels that he could contribute much to the betterment of this university, his new employer; however, on the other, he feels that he should be left to do things his own way. He has made an appointment to see the HR people. He does not know what to do and he feels this place is stifling his progress and he feels that he is alienated. Maybe he could find a middle ground and come to terms with his local colleagues. Whatever it is, time is running out and he feels that the longer he continues working with a heavy heart the more detrimental it will be to his career.

If you were John, what would you do?

Useful Websites

Human Resources Development Council, Malaysia
www.hrdnet.com.my

Industrial Relations Department Malaysia
http://61.6.32.133/jppm

Ministry of Human Resources, Malaysia:
http://mcsl.mampu.gov.my/english/fedgovt/Human_resc.htm

References

Abdul Malek, M. M. and Budhwar, P. S. (2010) 'Cultural intelligence as predictor of successful expatriate adjustment and performance', Paper Presented at the British Academy of Management, Sheffield, UK.

Aminuddin, M. (1995) *Human Resource Management*, 3rd edn. Shah Alam: Fajar Bakti.

Atiyyah, H. S. (1999) Public organisation's effectiveness and its determinants in a developing country, *Cross Cultural Management* 6(2): 8–21.

Beekun, R. and Badawi, J. (1999) *Leadership: An Islamic perspective*. Beltsville: Amana Publications.

Chew, Y. T. (2005) 'Achieving organizational prosperity through employee motivation and retention: A comparative study of strategic HRM practices in Malaysian institutions', *Research and Practice in Human Resource Management* 13(2): 87–104.

Chiah-Liaw, G., Petzall, S. and Selvarajah, C. (2003) 'The role of Human Resource Management (HRM) in Australian–Malaysian joint ventures', *Journal of European Industrial Training* 27(5): 244–62.

Commonwealth Secretariat (1993) 'Foundation for the future: Human resource development', Report of the Commonwealth Working Group on Human Resource Development Strategies, London: Commonwealth Secretariat.

Elger, T. and Smith, C. (2001) 'The global dissemination of production models and the recasting of work and employment relations in developing societies', in J. K. Coetzee, J. Graaff, F. Hendricks and G. Wood (eds), *Development: Theory, policy and practice*, pp. 449–463. Cape Town: Oxford University Press.

EPU (2001) Eighth Malaysia Plan. Kuala Lumpur: Economic Planning Unit.

EPU (2006) Ninth Malaysia Plan. Putra Jaya: Economic Planning Unit.

Gupta, V; Surie, G; Javidian, M. and Chhokar, J. (2002) Southern Asia Cluster: Where the Old Meets the New. *Journal of World Business*, 37: 16–27.

Hashim, F. Y. (2000) Pembangunan Sumber Manusia di Malaysia: Cabaran abad ke-21. Kuala Lumpur: Universiti Teknologi Malaysia. [Human Resource Development in Malaysia: Challenges in the 21st Century].

Hazman Shah, A. (1998) 'The level of participation and influence of HR managers in the strategic management process in Malaysian corporations', *Malaysian Management Review* 33(2): 47–60.

Hazman Shah, A. (2002) 'Sending HR to the line: Beyond the prescription', Paper Presented at the National Human Resource Management Conference, Penang, Malaysia.

Hope-Hailey, V., Farndale, E. and Truss, C. (2005) 'The HR department's role in organizational performance', *Human Resource Management Journal* 15(3): 49–66.

Kulik, C. T. and Bainbridge, H. T. J. (2006) 'HR and the line: The distribution of HR activities in Australian organizations', *Asia Pacific Journal of Human Resources* 44(2): 240–56.

Lim, L. (1998) 'Cultural attributes of Malays and Malaysian Chinese: Implications for research and practice', *Malaysian Management Review* 33(2): 81–88.

Lim, L. (2001a) 'Work-related values of Malays and Chinese Malaysians', *International Journal of Cross Cultural Management* 1(2): 209–26.

Lim, L. (2001b) 'Work-related values of Malaysians and Japanese: A re-examination of Hofstede's propositions', *Journal of Transnational Management Development* 6(3/4): 39–56.

Lim, L. (2002) 'Have work-related values of Malays and Chinese Malaysians changed over the last 30 years?', Paper Presented at the 12th International Conference on Comparative Management, College of Management, National Sun Yat-sen University Kaohsiung, Taiwan, ROC, 23–25 May 2002.

Long, C. S. and Wan Khairuzzaman, W. I. (2008) 'Understanding the relationship of HR competencies and roles of Malaysian human resource professionals', *European Journal of Social Sciences* 7(1): 88–103.

Malaysia Government (1971) First Outline Perspective Plan, 1971–1990. Kuala Lumpur: National Printing Department.

Malaysia Government (1991) Second Outline Perspective Plan, 1991–2000. Kuala Lumpur: National Printing Department.

Mansor, N. and Ali, M. (1998) 'An exploratory study of organizational flexibility in Malaysia: A research note', *International Journal of Human Resource Management* 9(3): 506–15.

Marsden, D. (1999) *A Theory of Employment Systems*. Oxford: Oxford University Press.

Musa, M. B. (2007) *Towards a Competitive Malaysia: Development challenges in the 21st Century*. Petaling Jaya: Strategic Information and Research Development Centre.

New Economic Model Report (2011) *National Economic Advisory Council (NEAC)*. Putrajaya.

Noordin, F., Williams, T. and Zimmer, C. (2002) 'Career commitment in collectivist and individualist cultures: A comparative study', *International Journal of Human Resource Management* 13(1): 35–54.

Perry, E. L. and Kulik, C. T. (2008) 'The devolution of HR to the line: Implications for perceptions of people management effectiveness', *The International Journal of Human Resource Management* 19(2): 262–73.

Rowley, C. and Saaidah, A.-R. (2007) 'The management of human resources in Malaysia: Locally-owned companies and multinational companies', *Management Revue* 18(4): 427–53.

Rozhan, O. and Poon J. M. L. (2000) 'What Shapes HRM? A multivariate examination', *Employee Relations 22(5)*: 467–84.

Rozhan, O., Rohayu, A. G. and Rasidah, A. (2001) 'Great expectations: CEO's perception of the performance gap of the HRM function in the Malaysian manufacturing sector', *Personnel Review* 30(1): 61–80.

Taib, A and Ismail, M Y. (1982) 'The social structure', in E. K. Fisk and H. Osman-Rani (eds), *The Political Economy of Malaysia*. Kuala Lumpur: Oxford University Press.

Todd, P. and Peetz, D. (2001) 'Malaysian industrial relations at century's turn: Vision 2020 or a spectre of the past?', *International Journal of Human Resource Management* 12(8): 1,365–82.

Wolfe, D. and Arnold, B. (1994) 'Human resource management in Malaysia: American and Japanese approaches', *Journal of Asian Business* 14(4): 80–103.

Yong, A. K. (1996) *Malaysian Human Resource Management*. Kuala Lumpur: Eagle Trading Sdn Bhd, Malaysian Institute of Management.

11 Human Resource Management in Singapore

KLAUS J. TEMPLER, DAVID T. W. WAN
AND NARESH KHATRI

Introduction

Singapore is an island- and city-state at the southern tip of the Malay Peninsula with a total population of 5.18 million as at the end of June 2011. Singapore is truly cosmopolitan: 3.26 million are Singapore citizens (with an ethnic composition of 74.1 percent Chinese, 13.4 percent Malay, 9.2 percent Indian, and 3.3 percent others), 0.53 million are foreigners with permanent resident status and 1.39 million are non-resident foreigners (Singapore Department of Statistics, 2011). The common language of business and daily parlance is English.

Since its independence in 1965, Singapore has achieved tremendous economic advancement. From earning a gross domestic product (GDP) of S$2.2 billion or US$0.7 billion in 1960 to a GDP of S$326.8 billion or US$259.8 billion in 2011 (Singapore Department of Statistics, 2012), Singapore is today one of the world's leading financial centers and a key trading center with one of the world's largest ports. Singapore has "a highly-developed and successful free-market economy. It enjoys a remarkably open and corruption-free environment, stable prices, and a per capita GDP higher than that of most developed countries" (Central Intelligence Agency, 2012). Singapore has a skilled workforce and an advanced and efficient infrastructure. For example, 23 percent of the Singaporean citizens who were employed in 2010 were university graduates, up from 14 percent in 2001 (Manpower Research and Statistics Department, and Singapore Department of Statistics, 2011). Over the same period, the percentage of those who were in professional, managerial, executive and technical jobs rose from 42 percent to 49 percent. In other words, one in two Singaporeans in the workforce is a professional. More than 7,000 multinational corporations from the United States, Europe and Japan, 1,500 from China and 1,500 from India are represented in Singapore. As of 2010, the stock of investment by US companies alone was more about US$106 billion (total assets) (US Department of State – Bureau of East Asian and Pacific Affairs, 2011).

The GLOBE study on 62 societies showed for Singapore high cultural practice scores on the dimensions future orientation, performance orientation, uncertainty avoidance, institutional collectivism and in-group collectivism (House *et al.*, 2004). Singapore has also been described as a tight society (Gelfand, Nishii and Raver, 2006; Triandis and Suh, 2002) with strong, clear and pervasive social norms. Whereas loose societies, such as the United States, tolerate deviations from social norms and have also fewer norms and rules for social situations, tight societies, such as Singapore, have many rules and strong social norms about behavior and a high degree of sanctioning (Gelfand, Nishii and Raver, 2006; Triandis and Suh, 2002).

The total labor force in Singapore in June 2011 stood at 3,158,900 with a breakdown for manufacturing, construction and services of 538,900 (17 percent), 400,700 (13 percent) and 2,199,500 (70 percent) respectively. The weekly total and overtime paid hours were 46.2 and 3.7. The average resignation rate was 2.1 percent with the highest turnover rate being in restaurants (4.7 percent) and the retail trade (4.3 percent). Whereas there were 55,900 job vacancies (74 percent of these from the services sector), the seasonally adjusted unemployment rate for residents was 3 percent (Manpower Research and Statistics Department Singapore, 2011a).

Historical Development and Key Factors Influencing HRM Practices in Singapore

Singapore obtained full independence in August 1965. In this relatively short period of time of national development, it has emerged as one of the world's most competitive economies. In just one generation, Singapore has progressed from Third World to First. One of the many reasons why the country could achieve its current economic status is the effective utilization of its human assets.

Singapore's economic strategy. There would be few, if any, countries today in which the government is not involved in one way or another in influencing and directing the country's economic development. Singapore's proactive government has been credited with its ability to quickly adapt policies (even "unpopular" ones) to meet new challenges, achieve public consensus and support for its economic/social policies (Wan and Hui, 2008).

Singapore has a unique wage system, which has evolved along with its economic strategy. In the period from 1965 to 1978, the economic strategy was to provide employment by attracting labor-intensive industries. To make Singapore more competitive than its neighbors, it put a restraint on wages. Singapore changed its economic strategy (1979 to 1984) from labor-intensive manufacturing to more skill- and capital-intensive manufacturing. This phase can be termed as wage correction. The government pushed for phasing out low-wage, labor-intensive industries and attracting high-wage capital-intensive and skill-based industries. The third phase of the economic strategy was to be more competitive in the face of increasing competition from the neighboring countries, especially Malaysia. This phase is called wage flexibility and it began in 1985. The flexible wage system has several components: (1) a basic fixed component reflecting the value of the job and to provide stability, (2) an annual wage supplement (AWS) of one month that can be adjusted under special circumstances, (3) a variable bonus based on a company's profitability and improved productivity, and (4) a service increment each year for loyalty, experience and length of service.

It is worth noting that the variable bonus in Singaporean companies varies significantly. It ranges roughly between the equivalent of one month's salary to six months' salary. Nowadays for bonuses and increments, the value placed on individual performance is more direct. Singapore has achieved one of the highest saving rates through employing a wage system in which a significant component is contributed by both employees and employers to the Central Provident Fund (CPF) scheme. The Central Provident Fund contributions (both from employee and employer) have been as high as 40 percent of each monthly salary. Lately, the focus is on improving national productivity and the sharing of productivity gains. The emphasis on productivity gain-sharing is logical given that Singapore aims to boost its yearly productivity growth to 2 to 3 percent over the next 10 years (Straits Times, 14 October 2011).

Singapore's administrative system. Singapore's administrative system is also unique. It can be said that Singapore has put in place one of the most elaborate management control systems. A neutral observer will find the Singaporean administrative system to resemble a military system. In fact, a number of senior officers in the military take up positions as head of a government ministry, department or corporation after their retirement from the military. Although sometimes exaggerated a bit too much in the Western media, there is some truth in Singapore's image of a controlled society. The positive side of it is that Singapore is one of the most disciplined societies in the world and it is one of the cleanest cities on earth.

The role of the Singapore government as a key player in the management of employment relations is clearly reflected in the administration of employment laws by the Ministry of Manpower; its assistance in the settlement of disputes; and participation in various tripartite organizations. In general, the government's expectations of the Singapore labor movement are multi-fold: to protect the interests of the workers at the workplace; to earn the trust and respect of workers and managers; to support the nation's development strategies; as well as to play an active role in shaping responsible work ethics. On the other hand, the employer organization is expected to support national goals and to be active in tripartite collaboration through various tripartite channels (Wan, 2010). Examples include: the Tripartite Committee on Union Representation of Executives (1999); the Tripartite Committee on Work–Life Strategy (2000); the Tripartite Committee on Portable Medical Benefits (2000); the Tripartite Committee on Employment of Older Workers (2005); the Tripartite Alliance for Fair Employment Practices (2006); the Tripartite Workgroup on Enhancing Employment Choices for Women (2007); the Tripartite Committee on Central Provident Fund and Work-Related Benefits for Low-Wage Workers (2007); and the National Tripartite Committee on Workplace Health (2008).

Multinational Corporations as Growth Drivers. Singapore has one of the most open, trade-oriented economies. It realized the importance of a pro-business environment in 1965, which its neighbors understood much later. Its government made a deliberate choice of attracting multinationals to be an engine of economic growth. Interestingly, Asian economies are pursuing three distinct economic strategies. While Japan and Korea have a few mega companies/conglomerates that control the bulk of their economic activity, Hong Kong and Taiwan have depended on small, entrepreneurial firms for their growth and development. Singapore and Malaysia chose still a distinct path. Both have relied heavily on multinational corporations for their economic growth.

Singapore's small, open economy is vulnerable to external shocks because the value of its exports is much larger than its GDP. The country has a good mix of multinationals from Europe, Japan and North America. This mix of multinationals is also reflected in a mix of human resource management practices in Singapore companies.

The strategy of attracting multinationals led to rapid growth in Singapore, which was not possible otherwise. Multinationals bring capital, the latest technology and diverse management practices, three of the most critical factors for business success. On the negative side, multinationals do not show any loyalty. If business conditions are not favorable, they move to other locations.

Countries in the region, such as Malaysia and Thailand, and now China, have realized the importance of a pro-business environment and the role of multinationals to achieve rapid growth. The neighboring countries have greater natural resources and cheaper labor. For example, competition from Malaysia has intensified. Malaysia has expanded its seaport infrastructure in the State of Johor—the southern-most part of mainland Malaysia. With a larger human resource pool, lower wages and cheaper land, the Johor seaport is now a serious competitor. Consequently, Singapore has to further enhance its competitive advantage. It has created a new niche in high-technology, bio-medical sciences and high-value added services to isolate it from the threat of competition.

China's emergence as an economic power provides both threats and opportunities. While China's economic potential makes it the largest recipient of foreign direct investment (FDI) (hence less investment flow for Southeast Asia), its growing middle class also presents a huge source of demand for goods and services. Singapore, with ample knowledge and expertise in hotel management and tourism, logistics, infrastructure, transportation and port management, education, consulting as well as other niche services, has intensified its presence in the mainland. At the same time, more and more Chinese firms are making use of Singapore's financial infrastructure and its close networks with the region to establish a foothold in Southeast Asia.

Role and Status of HRM in Singapore Companies

HRM functions and HRM practices in Singaporean companies are in transition. Many organizations have realized the importance of HRM, and salary surveys show that HR executives are among the best paid in Southeast Asia. HR that used to be part of the finance and accounts department in most organizations in the past is being configured as a standalone function. More HR managers are reporting directly to their CEOs, unlike in the past, when they used to report to the head of finance and accounts department. HR managers are also increasingly participating in strategic planning meetings, and the link between strategic planning and the human resource function has been getting stronger. The linkage of HR with strategic planning is thus growing.

Khatri and Budhwar (2002) interviewed 35 senior managers including CEOs of nine companies in Singapore and found that two factors, HR competencies and top management enlightenment, affect the status of HR function in an organization. HR managers felt that their competencies were important in gaining trust and strategic involvement in the organization. They also felt the need to convince the upper management that they were capable of managing the fundamental HR functions well before being invited to the strategic table. In addition, top management enlightenment (recognition by the top management that HR function can play a critical role in formulating and implementing organizational strategies) impacts on the role and status of the HR function in the organization.

As more and more companies realize the significance of the HR function, they are also placing more emphasis on the role of the human resource personnel in their firms. Practitioners in the Singapore HR profession from time to time see the need to uplift its image and reputation. Similar to what the accountants, engineers and other professions have done, the Singapore Human Resources Institute (SHRI) initiated an HR accreditation program in February 2006 to "enhance the standing of the HR profession and to provide a clear roadmap for HR competency and knowledge acquisition" (see the SHRI website). Three accreditation statuses are accorded: the Human Resource Associate (HRA), the Human Resource Professional (HRP) and the Senior Human Resource Professional (SHRP).

While the term Strategic HRM has been in use in Singapore for more than a decade, the (actual) strategic role of the HR personnel depends very much on their ability to anticipate new developments, embrace change and provide the needed leadership for organizational success. Questions that remain to be answered include: How do we define and measure HR performance? How can we make HR a strategic partner? How do HR professionals drive change and add value to organizational effectiveness? Basically, two sets of questions are being asked: what and how.

Key Challenges Facing HRM in Singapore

There are a number of HR challenges facing Singaporean companies. The chief among them include chronic employee turnover/job-hopping, a relatively low participation rate of females and older workers in the workforce, training and development, management of Singaporeans working abroad, and overhauling management systems and HR practices that can sustain a high-value added, knowledge-based service economy.

Turnover/Job-hopping. The labor shortage has been the main feature of the Singapore economy due to its small labor pool. A result is a chronic employee turnover problem. Khatri, Budhwar and Chong (2001) in their study of companies in three industries (retail, food and beverage, and marine and shipping industries) attempted to identify the root causes of turnover in Singapore. The authors found no evidence for the common myth that young and educated Singaporeans have developed a job-hopping attitude because of labor shortage and that they hop from one job to the other for a few extra dollars. Instead, turnover is caused by factors under the control of management. Especially, the authors found that companies were not doing enough to create a sense of belongingness and commitment in their employees and that their management practices were perceived lacking in fairness and transparency.

Achieving work–life integration is seen as one way to enhance morale and reduce employee turnover. Since the setting up of the tripartite committee on a work–life strategy, guidelines on Best Work–Life Practices and Family Friendly Workplace Practices have been issued and promoted. The idea is that employees must enjoy a fulfilling life by having a healthy lifestyle while working hard. The three are crucial to organizational survival because of increased business uncertainty, the need to improve productivity, reduction of human power costs and effective utilization of new technology. In practice, organizations do not restrict themselves to the use of one particular form of flexibility.

A possible response to the generally tight labor market is to develop more flexible work arrangements, such as flexi-hours, job sharing, part-time work and work from home. Part-time working in manufacturing and services is one of the many alternatives to relieve human power shortage in these sectors. While part-time work has become more common over the years, Singapore still lags behind other developed countries. Some employers in the manufacturing sector have reservations about employing part-time workers on the grounds that they need longer time to be trained. Employers also perceive that full-timers are more productive and more committed (Wan and Hui, 2008).

Participation of females in Workforce. The female participation in the Singapore labor force has risen over the years. The employment rate for women in the prime-working age bracket of 25 to 54 increased from 65.4 percent in 2001 to 75.7 percent in 2011 (Manpower Research and Statistics Department, 2011b). However, Singapore has a large pool of highly educated female workers aged 29 to 34 who take themselves out of the workforce temporarily to raise their children. These women have to struggle to find suitable jobs when they want to return to the workforce. HR managers need to tap the pool of highly educated, older women. Older women are likely to job-hop much less than other employees. Further, by understanding the needs of these employees and by providing them with job-sharing and flexible scheduling opportunities, it is possible to create a sense of commitment in them.

Participation of older employees in the workforce. Singapore's workforce, following the trend of many other developed countries, is ageing fast. By the late 1980s Singapore already had a larger proportion of its population aged 65 and above compared to its neighboring countries. By the year 2030, the number of those aged 65 and above is expected to rise to 20 percent, the highest percentage of aged persons in any ASEAN country (Committee on Ageing Issues, 2006). Increased life expectancy (79 years for men and 84 years for women) combined with a declining fertility rate prompted the government to increase the minimum retirement age from 55 to 60 in 1993. It was raised to 62 in January 1999 and the long-term target is 67. Since older workers are more vulnerable to retrenchment, the government has substantially reduced the employers' Central Provident Fund contribution for those aged 50 and above. Employer contribution rates are cut from age 50, and again at 55 and 60. Lately, the union movement called for a review of this decades' old CPF policy. The rationale is to entice older workers to stay in the workforce. Moreover, as more companies have moved away from a seniority-based pay system towards performance-based pay, older workers are not necessarily more costly to hire or retain.

The employment rate of older workers, aged 55 to 64, in the labor force in Singapore is 61.2 percent, which still lags behind other developed countries like Japan or Great Britain with an employment rate for older workers of about 65 percent (Heng, 2012). The older workers in Singapore are generally less educated, compared with the younger cohorts, because many of them have missed out on the limited opportunities that were available when they were young. However, future cohorts of older workers will be increasingly better educated.

Although older workers have a lower turnover compared to their younger counterparts, they are more vulnerable to job loss and longer unemployment spells. This can be attributed to the incorrect perceptions among employers that they are less productive and less receptive to change. In reality, older workers can perform better in many jobs, especially those involving service and human contact such as retail, counseling, social services and consultancy. Also in jobs that require a substantial amount of training and experience such as professional and highly technical work, older workers can maintain high levels of performance well into their 50s and 60s. The growing importance of the services industry in fact augurs well for the employment of older workers as the nature of work will be less dependent on physical stamina and requiring softer skills such as communication and service delivery.

The Singapore Tripartism Forum (2012) actively encourages the re-employment of older workers. On its website www.re-employment.sg it provides advice for employers and employees, and it showcases companies that have implemented age-friendly HR policies or practices.

Training and development (T&D). In general, training focuses on improving skills in the current job while development aims to improve the employee's skills and abilities on future jobs. The purposes of T&D are not restricted to removing performance deficiencies or increasing productivity. This HR function also acts as an important tool to attract good recruits and retain staff. For expanding enterprises, investment in human capital, in addition to recruitment, becomes crucial for the company's success.

In the last two decades, training consultants in Singapore have mushroomed. The emphasis on training is so much that some bigger companies have even created a standalone department on training along with the human resource management department. One wonders, however, if the current training programs with an emphasis on improving operational efficiencies are appropriate in the new economy that is increasingly knowledge-based. Most of the training programs at present are designed to support cost-reduction or quality-enhancement strategies. They do not necessarily support innovation strategy. As Singaporean companies attempt to move from a cost-quality combination to a quality-innovation combination, the nature of training programs has to change significantly.

Singapore's success can also be partly attributed to its well-established education system. Singaporeans enjoy a wide range of education opportunities. At the tertiary level, there are five universities: National University of Singapore; Nanyang Technological University; Singapore Management University; Singapore University of Technology and Design; and SIM University, which caters to the upgrading needs of working professionals. In addition, there is the Singapore Institute of Technology that caters for polytechnic graduates. The Ministry of Education has formed a Committee on University Education Pathways Beyond 2015 to examine how the university sector can better provide opportunities for Singaporeans to upgrade. The key considerations are economic relevance, quality education and cost effectiveness.

At the continuous education and training scene, the Workforce Development Agency (WDA) is at the forefront to promote adult learning. Its vision "Learning for Life, Advancing with Skills" highlights its mission to build capabilities and ensure the competitiveness and employability of the country's workforce.

Management of Singaporeans working abroad. An important HR issue in Singapore is the effective management of its employees sent as expatriates out of Singapore. Realizing that it has limited market and natural resources, Singapore has pursued a two-pronged economic strategy: (1) to go high-tech and (2) to regionalize. To actualize the second prong of its strategy, Singapore has been encouraging its companies to invest in regional countries. The fast-growing countries in Asia-Pacific provide ample opportunities to grow and expand. To manage the overseas operations of Singaporean companies requires capable and willing Singaporeans. Currently, there are many Singaporeans working in various countries.

There are a number of major issues involved in the management of Singaporean expatriates, such as training and appropriate compensation. In fact, repatriation has been the major concern of Singaporean expatriates, for example the re-integration of their children into the Singaporean school system. Other concerns are the living standards in third-world countries and whether to make the family join for a foreign assignment. Khatri (2000a), in a study of determinants of Singaporean expatriates in China, identified several key factors contributing to their greater performance/success. While many studies of American and European expatriates have found cultural competency as more important than technical competency, this study found that technical competency plays a more important role in the success of Singaporean expatriates in China. The second factor affecting the success of Singaporean expatriates was the nature of the assignment, which includes briefing the expatriates about their overseas assignment, explaining clearly to them their role in overseas operations, and giving them greater autonomy. Another factor affecting the success of Singaporean expatriates was related to the value of the assignment. Successful expatriates perceive that their overseas assignments open new career opportunities for them. They also value greatly the development of their skills during foreign assignments.

Unfortunately, at present there is still a dearth of qualified and professional HR managers in the region. In many organizations, the HR function is still not getting the attention from top management that it deserves. The ad hoc nature of HRM policies and practices in many companies in Singapore contributes significantly to the job-hopping phenomenon. As such, when HR managers lack the necessary skills to manage the HR function competently, line managers and executives take over some of the functions of HR managers. Khatri (2000b) noted that companies in Singapore do a poor job especially in the recruitment and selection of employees. Companies rarely use valid recruitment and selection strategies. The most common approach to selection was unstructured interviews, which are known to have low-predictive validity for performance. Performance management is also not a particularly well-managed function. Although there is great emphasis on training and development activities, they are often not aligned with organizational strategy and culture. Consequently, it is not clear how much value training and development programs are adding to organizational performance.

Companies in Singapore can be grouped into two broad categories in their management practices: (1) multinational corporations and their Singaporean subsidiaries headed mostly by senior managers from home country nationals or expatriates from other countries and (2) local Singaporean companies, government departments and government corporations headed by local Singaporean managers.

Practices and Challenges in Multinational Corporations and Their Singaporean Subsidiaries

As noted above, Singapore has a mix of multinational companies. These multinationals reflect the management philosophy and culture of their home countries. For example, Japanese multinationals emphasize "life-long" employment and use decision-making and compensation systems similar to Japanese organizations. Singaporean subsidiaries of American corporations tend to show greater goal-orientation and outcome-based management practices consistent with management practices observed in the United States (Khatri, 2000b).

Typically, middle and top managers of the Singaporean subsidiaries are non-Singaporeans, and junior managers and non-managers are Singaporeans, Malaysians and other foreign workers from the region. Multinationals have exploited this synergy between managerial abilities from home country nationals and disciplined and hard-working Singaporean workers to achieve a high level of performance and productivity.

As the Singapore economy continues to develop and open up, HR managers will have to recruit more and manage their global talents. Often, top managers, many middle managers and technicians who are specialists in their fields are foreign talent. Talent management and the effective management of diversity are crucial in the HR professional's agenda. As noted by Landau and Chung (2001: 210):

Anyone managing in Singapore must be attuned to its cultural complexity. The values, rules and norms may vary considerably, depending not only on the demographic make-up of the labour force, but also the culture of each organisation and the organisation's home country.

Templer (2010) found that relational leadership skills, cultural openness and adaptability, and job knowledge were related to expatriate success criteria, such as an expatriate manager's work adjustment, subordinate commitment, subordinate job satisfaction and unit performance. Most important was the personal attribute relational leadership skills, and it was the crucial success factor for expatriate managers' unit performance. On the other hand, if a subordinate of an expatriate manager held ethnocentric attitudes against foreign talent then the expatriate manager showed lower work adjustment.

Practices in Local Companies/Government Departments and Corporations

Practices in local companies and government departments and corporations are an amalgamation of administrative systems inherited from the British and Confucian work ethics, strong authority and power distance orientation of the Chinese/Asian culture. The result is a highly structured, authoritative management philosophy.

One salient feature of the Singaporean management style is an emphasis on micromanagement. In local companies and government departments, there is a strong tendency in managers to micromanage organizational activities. Even relatively minor routine decisions are taken to the enterprise's top for resolution.

Furthermore, voluntary feedback from the bottom is minimal. Subordinates are unwilling to openly express their opinions and disagreements due to fear of losing face or making someone else lose face. There exists a big chasm in communication between superiors and their subordinates because it is hard for subordinates to air their views to their senior managers. However, the education level of Singaporeans has increased steadily and they are also coming in contact with the outside world. Although they are used to taking orders and instructions from above, there is a growing sentiment/resentment against the authoritative management approach (Templer, 2003). It is not clear how the tussle between demand for more instruction from the top by Singaporeans and their need for greater say in decision making is going to be resolved.

HR in the next Five Years in Singapore

The economic development of Singapore has long been and still is heavily shaped by the role of the government. It is indeed an indispensable driving force in the strategic utilization of human resources in the country, accomplished through a well-established tripartite framework of government, employers and unions. The annual inflation rate in 2012 in Singapore was 4.6 percent (Singapore Department of Statistics, 2013). This figure may not sound much in comparison to many other countries; however, the impact on low-wage workers is of utmost concern to the tripartite bodies. While the long-term possibility of low-wage workers stuck at the bottom of the income hierarchy is real, this does not mean that the wages of low-wage workers should be substantially increased overnight. Any growth in wages must be backed by productivity gains.

For the immediate and medium term, the HR scene in Singapore will be dominated by three forces: first, the need to expand a capable and innovative workforce; second, the need to achieve continued productivity growth; and third, the need to ensure that the country's elder workforce gain meaningful employment.

One way to build up a capable workforce is through continued education, training and development. This will increase the country's pool of professionals and skilled workers and will nurture a life-long learning spirit among Singaporeans. This task has become more urgent because of Singapore's own economic restructuring, the increasing shortening of product lifecycles, rapid technological breakthroughs and keener competition from both developing and developed countries.

Raising the productivity effort is crucial because this will help counter rising business costs and human power shortage. It also enhances the chance of upgrading low-wage jobs. Attaining the long-term target of 2 to 3 percent growth a year will not be easy. It requires perseverance and sustained efforts on the part of the workers, the employers and the government. Employers need to show workers that productivity growth does not mean more work with the same pay.

The Retirement and Re-Employment Act has been in force since January 2012. The adjustment process and coping strategies of older workers who are re-employed after they turn 62, or not offered re-employment, will be closely monitored by the government, the employers and the unions alike. Although older workers have lower turnover compared to their younger counterparts, they are more vulnerable to job loss and longer unemployment spells. This can be attributed to the preconceived notion among employers that they are less productive and less receptive to change.

Maintaining a good employer–employee relationship in a period of economic uncertainty and constant organizational restructuring is a critical HR function, irrespective of whether a firm is unionized or not. With a well-tested tripartite framework and various institutional structures and procedures in place, for example, the National Wages Council, the Ministry of Manpower and the Industrial Arbitration Court, it is up to the employers and their employees to decide how they should work together. For example, in a rare show of disagreement, the National Trades Union Congress (NTUC) and the Singapore National Employers Federation (SNEF) made public their different views on the foreign workers issue. The labor movement's argument is that cheap foreign workers suppress the wages of locals, which discourages employers to recruit and grow locals (Toh, 2011). On the other hand, employers believe that sufficient measures and mechanisms are already in place to tackle this problem. Indeed, this is a highly sensitive issue in many other countries and, if not handled well, conflicts and industrial actions will result. In the Singapore context, policies/actions based on reasonable and pragmatic ideas will finally prevail.

There are changes taking place in the economy in the region. The twin cities of Hong Kong and Singapore prospered using pro-business economic strategies at a time when other countries and governments in the region relied upon socialist economic philosophies. However, other countries like Indonesia, Vietnam and Myanmar are following in their footsteps and opening their economies to foreign direct investment. The foreign direct investment that used to flow naturally to the two cities is not flowing at the same rate as before. Other countries are becoming more attractive because of size, natural resources and cheap labor. The Singapore government and policy makers do realize this challenge and are trying to create a niche (the Singapore brand) and looking for ways on how to have as big a slice as possible of the ever-bigger-growing economic pie in the Asia-Pacific.

Many of the guiding fundamentals adopted by the government since independence are still relevant to the present-day context – good government, an efficient infrastructure, a strong emphasis on education, open competition, pragmatism, high savings rate, fiscal prudence, a conducive business climate and international orientation. Not only do these contributing factors help explain the fast recovery from previous recessions, they continue to play a crucial role in shaping the country's future.

Case Study on Singapore Airlines (SIA)

SIA is an international carrier that serves 40 countries and more than 90 destinations. Over the years, it has evolved into one of the leading airlines in the world and indeed one of the most respected travel brands. The company's success can be attributed to its management's vision, strategic choices, core competencies, internal organization, resource deployment, service excellence, innovative offerings and effective people management (Heracleous, Wirtz and Pangarkar, 2009).

For a company that proudly claims to be a "great way to fly," SIA relies heavily on state-of-the-art aircrafts, inflight facilities and dedicated employees (pilots, cabin crews, engineers and front-line staff) to deliver sustained customer care and service excellence. It has invested strategically in one of the youngest, most advanced, and fuel-efficient planes—the average age of its 101 passenger aircrafts is six years and eight months (Singapore Airplanes, 2013).

SIA's subsidiaries include the short-haul carrier SilkAir, the package-travel company Tradewinds, SIA Engineering Company, SIA Cargo and the ground-handling provider Singapore Airport Terminal Services (SATS). Given such a huge organization, it is no wonder that more than one employee organization represents its very diverse groups of workers. As expected, the five employee organizations differ in terms of membership profile, union goals and union strategies.

Heracleous, Wirtz and Pangarkar (2009: 141) reported that five interrelated elements seem to underline the company's pro-human resource strategy:

(i.) stringent selection and recruitment processes; (ii.) extensive investment in training and retraining; (iii.) high-performance service delivery teams; (iv.) empowerment of front-line staff to control quality; as well as (v.) motivation through rewards and staff recognition.

SIA's relationship with its unions, especially Alpa-S, provides an interesting case study on the occasional uneasiness and tensions created by the economic downturn, high oil prices and heightened competition brought about by the entry of budget airlines across Asia and the strengthening position of other arch rivals like British Airways, Emirates, Qantas and Cathay Pacific. Indeed, intense competition from the budget airlines in this part of the world has forced SIA to launch its own budget carrier (Scoot) that now flies on Asian short- to long-haul routes. The question that will always remain high when severe cost-cutting is needed is this: Can the five pillars of SIA's human resource strategy cushion short-term difficulties and ensure the continued success of the airline?

Useful Websites

Department of Statistics, Singapore: www.singstat.gov.sg

Ministry of Education (MOE), Singapore: www.moe.gov.sg

Ministry of Manpower (MOM), Singapore: www.mom.gov.sg

National Trade Union Congress (NTUC): www.ntuc.org.sg

Singapore Human Resource Institute (SHRI): www.shri.org.sg

Singapore National Employers Federation (SNEF): www.sgemployers.com

Singapore Tripartism Forum: www.tripartism.sg

Singapore Workforce Development Agency (WDA): www.wda.gov.sg

Tripartite Alliance for Fair Employment Practices: www.fairemployment.sg

References

Central Intelligence Agency (2012) *World Factbook – Singapore*, www.cia.gov/library/publications/the-world-factbook/geos/sn.html#Econ, accessed 29 April 2012.

Committee on Ageing Issues (2006) *Report on the Ageing Population*. Singapore: Ministry of Community Development, Youth and Sports.

Gelfand, M. J., Nishii, L. H. and Raver, J. L. (2006) "On the nature and importance of cultural tightness-looseness," *Journal of Applied Psychology 91*: 1,225–44.

Heng, J. (2012). "Silver workforce dulled by reality." *The Straits Times*, 30 July, p. A20.

Heracleous, L., Wirtz, J. and Pangarkar, N. (2009) *Flying High in a Competitive Industry*, 2nd edn. Singapore: McGraw Hill.

House, R. J., Hanges, P. J., Javidan, M., Dorfman, P. W. and Gupta, V. (eds) (2004) *Culture, Leadership, and Organizations: The globe study of 62 societies*. Thousand Oaks: Sage.

Khatri. N. (2000a) "Determinants of expatriate success in China," In Chung-Ming Lau, Kenneth S. Law, David K. Tse and Chi-Sum Wong (eds), *Asian Management Matters: Regional Relevance and Global Impact*. London: Imperial College Press.

Khatri, N. (2000b) "Managing human resource for competitive advantage in Singapore: A study of companies in Singapore," *International Journal of Human Resource Management 11*(2): 336–65.

Khatri, N. and Budhwar, P. S. (2002) "A Study of Strategic HR Issues in an Asian Context," *Personnel Review 31*(2): 166–88.

Khatri, N. Budhwar, P. S. and Chong, T. F. (2001) "Explaining Employee Turnover in an Asian Context," *Human Resource Management Journal, 11(1)*: 54–74.

Kor, K. B. and Toh, Y. C. (2011) "NTUC: Pay workers more for productivity," *Straits Times*, 14 October, pp. A1, A6.

Landau, J. and Chung, Y. K. (2001) "Singapore," in M. Patrickson and P. O'Brien (eds), *Managing Diversity: An Asian and Pacific Focus*. Singapore: Wiley, pp. 191–212.

Manpower Research and Statistics Department, and Singapore Department of Statistics (2011a) *Singaporeans in the Workforce*, www.mom.gov.sg/Publications/mrsd_singaporeans_in_the_workforce.pdf, accessed 29 April 2012.

Manpower Research and Statistics Department (2011b) *Labour Market, Second Quarter 2011*. Singapore: Ministry of Manpower.

Manpower Research and Statistics Department (2011c) *Report on Labour Force in Singapore, 2011*. Singapore: Ministry of Manpower.

Singapore Airlines (2013) *The Singapore Airlines Fleet*, www.singaporeair.com/en_UK/about-us/sia-history/sia-fleet, accessed 22 February 2013.

Singapore Department of Statistics (2011) *Population Trends 2011*. Singapore: Ministry of Trade and Industry.

Singapore Department of Statistics (2012) *Time Series on Annual GDP at Current Market Prices*, www.singstat.gov.sg/stats/themes/economy/hist/gdp2.html, accessed 29 April 2012.

Singapore Department of Statistics (2013) *Time Series on CPI & Inflation Rate*, Singapore: Ministry of Trade and Industry, www.singstat.gov.sg/stats/themes/economy/hist/cpi.html, last accessed 22 February 2013.

Singapore Tripartism Forum (2012) *Re-employment of Older Employees' Portal*, www.re-employment.sg, accessed 29 April 2012.

The Straits Times. Singapore's leading newspaper.

Templer, K. J. (2003) "Dimensions of power distance in organizations and their effects on subordinates' commitment and job satisfaction," in C. Akaborworn, A. Osman-Gani and G. McLean (eds), *Human Resource Development in Asia: National policy perspectives*. Bangkok: NIDA, pp. 741–48.

Templer, K. J. (2010) "Personal attributes of expatriate managers, subordinate ethnocentrism, and expatriate success: A host-country perspective," *The International Journal of Human Resource Management 21(10)*: 1,754–68.

Toh, Y. C. (2011) Govt, bosses, unions—things to get "noisier," *The Straits Times*, 1 November, p. A6.

Triandis, H. C. and Suh, E. M. (2002) "Cultural Influences on Personality," *Annual Review of Psychology 53*: 133–60.

US Department of State—Bureau of East Asian and Pacific Affairs (2011) *Background Note: Singapore*, www.state.gov/r/pa/ei/bgn/2798.htm, accessed 29 April 2012.

Wan, D. T. W. (2010) "Singapore industrial relations system in the globalization era," in Sununta Siengthai *et al.* (eds), *The Multi-dimensions of Industrial Relations in the Asian Knowledge-based Economies*. Oxford, UK: Chandos Publishing, pp. 125–40.

Wan, D. T. W. and Hui T. K. (2008) "Changing face of HRM in Singapore," in Chris Rowley and Saaidah Abdul-Rahman (eds), *The Changing Face of Management in South East Asia*. London, UK: Routledge, pp. 129–54.

12

Human Resource Management in Australia

MARILYN CLARKE AND MARGARET PATRICKSON

Introduction

Although the land area of Australia, almost 8 million square kilometres, is roughly equivalent to that of the continental United States and about twice that of the European union, its population is comparatively low, being only about 22 million, 80 per cent of whom live and work within 100 kilometres of the coastline, and over half of whom live on the eastern seaboard. Yet despite only about 6.5 per cent of the land area being arable, the country exports a wide range of agricultural products as well as mineral ores and selected manufactured goods. Being the world's 13th largest economy, Australia enjoys a high standard of living, political freedom based on universal franchise, and relative economic stability having been better able to withstand the recent ravages of the global financial crisis given its high preponderance of mineral deposits.

By far the majority of residents are first or second generation immigrants, dominated by British or Irish ancestry. With two out of every seven residents born overseas according to the 2001 census, the government has elected to follow an official policy of multiculturalism, which, despite a few hiccups, appears to be working well. In common with other Western countries the population is ageing. Culturally the country reflects this largely Anglo-Saxon heritage as evidenced by its legal and governance systems, the dominance of the English language, its media programs, and its religious affiliations being largely Christian, despite observable poor church attendances. More recently, Asian cultures are gradually replacing southern European cultures as the second major influence on the local scene as more people begin to explore the benefits of healthy lifestyles.

Compared with its major trading partners, wage levels are comparatively high and this has led industrial policies to assume a central location in business practices. Awards exist for the majority of jobs that specify a bottom benchmark for individually negotiated wages and conditions. Workplace agreements, negotiated directly between employers and employees, now form the basis of employment in most large organisations, and salaries for the most senior staff often significantly exceed those of others. Health and Safety levels at work are high. It is within such a context that the recent developments in HR management are discussed more fully below. The chapter unfolds by initially looking at contextual factors such as economic and political conditions that determine labour force demand and supply before moving on to address how these factors have influenced the development and operation of HR practices. Next it examines key issues at the forefront of current HR practice such as employee engagement, work–life balance and cultural diversity before finally considering how the future for HR may unfold in terms of strategic developments and internationalism.

Developments in HRM

The evolution of HRM in Australia mirrors that of other developed countries. That is, HRM has moved from welfare to personnel and then to a more strategic partner role within organisations. These changes are primarily in response to structural changes in the economy, as discussed below, which have created the need for a more professional approach to people management. This is particularly the case in service industries, which are populated largely by well-educated, skilled employees. The journey towards a more professional approach to HRM began in 1992 when IPMA (the Federal Institute of Personnel Management of Australia) was rebadged as AHRI (Australian Human Resource Institute), the professional body for HR practitioners. AHRI aims to lead the direction and foster the growth of the HR profession by actively setting standards and building capability through relevant and accessible education, professional development and networking opportunities (Australian Bureau of Statistics, 2012b). Members of AHRI must complete an AHRI-accredited or relevant undergraduate qualification, or be able to demonstrate equivalent knowledge, skills and experience in the HR industry. In 2011 AHRI had in excess of 17,500 members thus indicating continuing rising numbers of tertiary qualified staff being employed within the discipline. HR departments, in turn, reflect this increasing professionalism and no longer take such a back seat in staff management activities. They have broadened their responsibilities, raised their profile and their salaries, and have begun to contribute to strategic forward planning. Positions advertised indicate that their improved status is recognised and reflected in higher offering salaries.

Key Factors Determining HRM Practices and Policies

The National Context

Domestic consumption in Australia is heavily geared towards the service sector with total household expenditure on goods and services comprising 18 per cent of total income while food and other consumables represents a further 16 per cent of the total (ABS, 2010a). In August 2010, there were 9.8 million employees. Of these, 70 per cent were full-time employees in their main job (ABS, 2010b).

In August 2011 average weekly earnings were about US$1,300 (ABS, 2011a). Unemployment was steady at 5.1 per cent with an overall workforce participation rate of 65.6 per cent (ABS, 2011b). Over the past twenty-five years workforce skill requirements in Australia have gradually changed as comparatively lower wages in China and India have made many locally manufactured goods comparatively expensive for consumers and forced the export of associated manufacturing jobs abroad. In turn the local economy has responded towards developing its service sector. There are now few unskilled jobs in the workforce, and few jobs that do not demand computer literacy. Employees are more highly skilled than at any time in the past with relatively unskilled job-seekers finding it hard to secure steady employment. At the same time there have been changes in retirement age, with more working individuals electing to remain in the workforce, at least casually, if they can (ABS, 2012b).

A key characteristic of the labour force is that over recent decades there has been a gradual, long-term trend away from 'standard' full-time jobs to various forms of part-time work. From 1979 to 2009 the proportion of employed people working part time increased from 16 per cent to 29 per cent. While part-time work tends to be more prevalent among women, its increase over the past 30 years has been evident for both men and women. The proportion of employed women working part time increased from 34 per cent in 1979 to 45 per cent in 2009, compared to 5 per cent and 16 per cent, respectively, for men. The increased availability of part-time work has expanded opportunities for people to balance work with family responsibilities, to participate in education, or to make the transition to retirement. The majority of people who work part-time do not want to work more hours, or would not be available to work more hours even if the extra hours were available (ABS, 2010c). This trend is further exemplified by the high percentage of casual or temporary employees. Under Australian industrial agreements casual employees generally do not have access to the same rights and conditions as full-time or part-time employees. For example, they do not qualify for sick leave, holiday leave, carers' leave or long-service leave (Burgess and Baird, 2003). In recognition of this exclusion from standard employment benefits they are often compensated through an additional hourly payment or 'loading' of somewhere from 15 per cent to 25 per cent. In 2006 the casual workforce, estimated to be about 26.9 per cent of the total, comprised both full-time and part-time casual employees (Burgess, Campbell, and May, 2008). Casual employment is found across all industries and all sectors but is generally inversely related to skill levels.

Reasons for such a high level of casualisation include the desire for more flexible employment on the part of employees, structural demand for seasonal, short-term or 'at call' labour, changes to employment regulations that facilitate and promote casual employment, and changes to labour use practices. While growth in the part-time, temporary and casual workforce has provided both organisations and employees with much greater flexibility it has also created new and more complex challenges for HR managers. Within this context HRM must deal with issues such as attraction and selection of employees with relevant skills and experience, training employees who may only stay for a short period, and the management and transfer of organisational knowledge (Watson, 2008).

Economic Factors

In the last 50 years the Australian economy has undergone significant structural transformations moving from an agricultural base to a predominantly manufacturing base and then more recently to a highly urbanised economy based primarily on the provision of services (Connolly and Lewis, 2010). In recent years there has also been a significant resurgence in the mining sector driven largely by demand for raw materials from growing economies such as China and India.

Structural change has been supported, and in some cases driven, by economic reforms at the federal government level including deregulation of a range of service industries (such as banking) and the lowering of tariffs for manufacturing and agriculture. Policies designed to foster greater competition and increase efficiencies have been pursued by successive governments in an attempt to assure Australia's position in a global economy (Connolly and Lewis, 2010).

One outcome of these structural changes is that from a labour market perspective Australia is now facing what some commentators refer to as a two-speed economy (Garton, 2008): 'fast speed' and 'low speed'.

The 'fast-speed' economy is associated with the mining sector, which is capital-intensive and comprises a relatively small but highly skilled blue-collar and professional workforce. Wages and other benefits in this sector are well above average in order to attract workers to remote locations either on a permanent or fly-in/fly-out basis. Importantly this has meant that jobs growth and wage dispersion has been concentrated in regions where there are large mineral deposits (Salary Survey, 2008).

The 'slow-speed' economy includes industry sectors such as services and manufacturing. Significant job growth has occurred in the burgeoning services sector in areas such as health, education, finance and business services. Service industries tend to be less capital-intensive but generally more labour-intensive with a high demand for skilled and well-educated employees (Connolly and Lewis, 2010). Growth in the services sector reflects societal changes, particularly an increase in the number of families where both parents work. This has led to the outsourcing of many household service activities such as child care, home maintenance and aged care (Connolly and Lewis, 2010). A less positive employment outcome has been the tendency for companies to send their business process operations offshore to countries such as India where wages are still much lower than in Australia (Russell and Thite, 2008). In addition, a significant proportion of jobs growth has been in part-time and casual positions (Burgess, Campbell and May, 2008). Many service sector employees, particularly those employed on casual contracts within the hospitality industry, perceive themselves to be underemployed, a situation that impacts on employee engagement and job satisfaction. From a HRM perspective this creates issues for training, development, performance management and career development. The future of manufacturing remains uncertain, although clearly there will need to be further major structural changes if this sector is to compete globally.

The Political Context

An important factor in any analysis of Australian HRM is the underlying industrial relations context, which has shaped the way in which employer–employee relations have evolved. Until 1983 Australia had an adversarial labour system regulated by a centralised conciliation and arbitration process. The system operated through permanent quasi-judicial tribunals, employer tribunals and union representation of employees. Employment contracts were framed by state and federal awards that specified minimum terms and conditions of employment, such as hours of pay, minimum pay and leave allowances (Kramar, Bartram and De Cieri, 2011).

From 1983 to 1996 gradual changes were implemented in an attempt to reduce the number of industrial disputes and to move to a more collaborative industrial relations environment. The driving force for these changes was an increasing awareness that Australia needed to become internationally competitive through a more neo-liberal policy regime based on market forces. The key change in this period was an innovative approach to incomes policy known as 'The Accord', an agreement between the Labour government and the trade unions to modify demands for wage increases in exchange for government commitments to advance economic and social policy issues (Kramar, Bartram and De Cieri, 2011).

By 1993 Australia had shifted from a centralised wage setting model to an enterprise bargaining model. The Industrial Relations Reform Act (Cwth) 1993 provided for decentralisation of employee relations through enterprise level negotiations over wages and working conditions and collective agreements between employer and employees rather than through trade unions. These changes set the scene for the next decade. When the conservative government won power in 1997 neo-liberal policies were further enforced through a shift to individual contracts, known as Australian Workforce Agreements (AWAs). A key outcome was that managerial prerogative was expanded and the role of trade unions was increasingly marginalised as the government sought to break what it believed to be a union stranglehold over many industries. The shift to the right culminated in the passing of the Workplace Relations Amendment (Work Choices) Act 2005, which offered significantly greater power to employers in negotiating wages and conditions.

To some extent this may have contributed to the conservative government losing power to the Labour party in 2007 after an election campaign that was fought largely on the issue of workers' rights. By 2009 the Workplace Relations Amendment (Work Choices) Act had been replaced by the Fair Work Act (Kramar, Bartram and De Cieri, 2011), which provided the framework for a shift back to more collective bargaining, the re-introduction of safety net provisions through National Employment Standards (minimum levels), stronger unfair dismissal laws and bargaining in good faith provisions. Workers' rights are protected through the 10 National Employment Standards covering areas such as maximum weekly hours, annual leave, parental leave, requests for flexible working arrangements and termination of employment.

Although trade unions continue to play a role in Australia their influence has been weakened in the last two decades as a result of the shift to enterprise bargaining and a decline in manufacturing. From 1990 to 2008 the proportion of employees who were trade union members in their main job decreased from 41 per cent to 19 per cent (ABS, 2009). Modernisation of the award system through a reduction in the number of awards from 4,053 in 2005 to just 122 in 2010 has also weakened the power of unions in the negotiation process. Both changing legislative frameworks and a decline in union membership have resulted in a significant decrease in the number of strikes and other forms of industrial action.

The Impact on HRM

In recent years economic and political changes have impacted on the HR function in a number of critical areas. Modernisation of the award system and the shift to enterprise bargaining have increased employer flexibility in terms of wages and salaries thus enabling organisations to pursue more competitive compensation strategies (Gollan, 2009). For example, in areas of skills shortages, such as accounting, engineering and information technology, the market has become more flexible but at the same time wage costs have increased. Many organisations are taking a skill-based pay approach in which pay rates are determined by the skills that employees acquire and their capacity to use those skills. This approach is well suited to an environment characterised by ever-changing technological advancements (De Cieri et al., 2009).

As Australia moves from manufacturing to service, mining and high-tech industries there is an urgent need to up-skill and re-skill its workforce and this has been aided by a range of government- and industry-sponsored education and training initiatives. ABS data shows that 9 per cent of large organisations, 70 per cent of medium-sized and 39 per cent of small organisations provide some form of structured training to their employees including in-house training, outsourced training or support towards gaining additional qualifications (ABS, 2003). About 80 per cent of employers claim to be providing training with about 50 per cent of workers taking part in formal training and 70 per cent receiving on-the-job training. Vocational training is largely provided by the Vocational Education and Training (VET) Sector, which offers qualifications ranging from Certificate I up to Advanced Diploma. These qualifications are based on training packages that set out qualifications, competency standards and assessment guidelines for particular industries and occupations (Smith and Smith, 2007). A major component of the VET system is apprenticeships and traineeships, which combine on-the-job and off-the-job training for skilled trades and which are based on industry competency and qualification standards. Vocational, work-skills related training is critical to the future of the Australian economy and thus the recruitment and management of VET trainees is often an important task for HR departments in medium and large organisations.

The tertiary education sector is also expanding with recent forecasts that by 2025 40 per cent of Australians aged from 25 to 34 years will be university educated, which will produce an additional 217,000 graduates (IBISWorld Industry Report, 2011). International education is Australia's third largest export industry, generating US$18 billion in exports in 2009. It is 50 per cent larger than tour-ism–related travel, and has grown by 94 per cent since 2004. In 2009, there were 629,918 international students in Australia, of whom 203,324 were in higher education, 232,475 attended a VET provider and 135,141 were on an English lan-guage course (Phillimore and Koshy, 2010). Recent changes to student visa regu-lations will allow those with tertiary qualifications from a university to apply for a two-year working visa and then subsequently to apply for permanent residency, a strategy designed to help alleviate skill shortages in a range of professional areas (Sainsbury, 2011).

Remuneration

Compared to other countries in the region, particularly major trading partners such as China and India, Australians enjoy high wages and benefits. In the 10 years to 2011 wages rose on average by 57 per cent (ABS, 2011a). Changes in mean weekly earnings were affected not only by changes in the rate of pay, but also by changes in the composition of the Australian workforce, including diversity of employment arrangements, number of hours worked, the extent of part-time and casual employ-ment; and mix of industries and occupations (ABS, 2010b). For HR managers, wages pose two competing challenges: the need to offer competitive salaries to attract and retain quality employees but, at the same time, the need to contain wage costs in order to remain competitive in both local and global markets.

One controversial area in relation to pay is executive remuneration. In the previ-ous edition the authors noted that the relationship between CEO rewards and organisational performance had yet to be determined (Patrickson and Sutiyono, 2004). Recent reviews of the state of executive pay in Australia note that little has changed and that advice and data from remuneration consultants has been much more influential in determining executive packages than the views of sharehold-ers, board members or industry associations (Peetz, 2009). While executive pay is not considered to be especially high in comparison to international standards, and not extreme in comparison to the United States (Fels, 2010), in Australia there is still a perception, often perpetuated by the media, that executive pay is excessive. A 2005 survey sponsored by the Australian Institute of Company Directors showed that the majority of those surveyed believed CEOs to be over-paid (Buffini and Pheasant, 2005) even though salaries are largely determined by market rates and the need to remain competitive, which is unlikely to change in the immediate future (Peetz, 2009).

Role and Importance of the Business–HR Partnership

HRM is now recognised as critical to gaining and maintaining a competitive advantage through the recruitment, development and rewarding of competent staff even though there is still some discrepancy between the ideal and the actual practice (Guzman, 2011). A 1995 survey showed that the typical responsibilities of HR professionals included traditional personnel-related roles such as recruit-ment and selection, performance management, compensation and reward management, health and safety, employee services, and job design and analysis as well as more strategic activities including staff planning, performance evaluation and diversity management (SHRM-BNA Survey, 1995). Recent Australian surveys indicate that both the scope and depth of HR responsibilities have increased and suggest that the majority of HR managers are responsible for broad policy development in areas as diverse as recruitment, performance appraisal, selection, occupational health and safety (OHS), work–life balance, family-friendly policies and career planning (Sheehan, Holland and De Cieri, 2006). Significantly, there has been an increase in the number of HR managers reporting directly to the CEO or board of directors. Accompanying these changes, in recent years there has been an increase in relative salaries of 5 to 10 per cent for competent HRM professionals (Fenton-Jones, 2008).

In keeping with international trends, Kulik and Bainbridge (2006) reported the continued devolution of HRM functions to line managers with HR professionals retaining responsibility for negotiations with unions and other regulatory agencies and line managers dealing with day-to-day activities such as coaching, performance management and disciplinary issues.

Progress may be slow but in a number of organisations there are also positive signs that the business–HRM relationship is becoming stronger. For example, in a recent restructure the Australia and New Zealand Bank decided to bring non-HR people into HR roles. Staff from all over the business were slotted into HR roles so that they could help educate HR professionals on the harder side of operations while at the same time developing better people management skills (Gettler, 2009). Similarly, at National Australia Bank HR people have been placed into operational roles while operational leaders have been put into roles normally associated with HR (Gettler, 2009). Another area where HR is making a stronger contribution is in the area of employee metrics. One organisation recently reported that it had collated a unique set of HR metrics in the form of a dashboard so that senior executives could see the direct relationship between employee costs and strategic issues in the business (Ross, 2011). The company's Chief Executive HR claimed that the metrics were like 'putting a human capital lens on our competitiveness' (Ross, 2011: 23).

However, despite the rhetoric that HRM is now a strategic business partner, in practice there is considerable variation across organisations, and in many cases HR has not yet taken its place on the board. For example, data from a 1995 study of more than 800 organisations showed that 55 per cent had no HR representation on the Board of Directors, yet by 2005 (in a sample of more than 1,000 organisations) this had fallen to 42 per cent, which, although it indicates a strengthening of the HR function, nevertheless shows that there is still considerable scope for improvement (Sheehan, Holland and De Cieri, 2006). A 2007 survey by AHRI of almost 2,000 managers found that while most respondents believed HRM to be a critical function many did not fully understand the role of HR or feel that it was effective in serving the needs of the business (Sardo and Begley, 2007). Clearly there still remains a challenge to educate senior management on potential HRM contributions as well as the need for practitioners themselves to increase their competence in broader managerial functions.

Key Changes and Challenges for HRM

In the first edition of this text one factor considered to be a key driver in the uptake of HRM was the need to coordinate and manage high levels of downsizing and restructuring (Patrickson and Sutiyono, 2004). At that time HR practitioners, primarily in larger public and private sector organisations, worked closely with senior managers in downsizing activities such as planning workforce reductions, counselling retrenched staff and handling the restructuring process. However, in recent years there has been a marked shift in thinking with regards to the wisdom and effectiveness of embracing downsizing as an HR strategy.

After successive waves of downsizing in the 1980s and 1990s, many organisations discovered that they had lost key skills, corporate knowledge and experience. Studies from the United States also indicated that although downsizing may lead to short-term improvements in financial performance, in the longer term the effects were likely to be minimal (Cascio, Young and Morris, 1997). In the latest economic downturn downsizing has been far less prevalent than at the end of the twentieth century. Australian organisations have looked for creative ways to retain employees rather than using job cuts to manage immediate financial problems. Organisations now recognise that in a climate of skill and labour shortages there is much to be gained from keeping experienced employees. For example, in the automotive industry shorter shifts, reduced working weeks and enforced annual leave were used to contain costs while retaining workers until the economy improved (Clarke, 2011).

Managing the Workforce

In common with many developed countries, Australia is facing significant changes in relation to its demographic profile. A report by demographer Bernard Salt estimated that from 2010 to 2050 the proportion of Australians aged 65 and over will increase from 14 per cent to 23 per cent (Huntley and Salt, 2010). At the same time, it is estimated that by 2025 only 50,000 new workers will enter the workforce each year (which is less than the number who will leave), a sharp drop from the heyday of the baby boomer generation when the figure was around 200,000 per annum (Critchley, 2004). The implication of these demographic shifts is that in the future a key challenge for Australian organisations will be to attract and retain a workforce with the necessary skills and experience to meet organisational requirements. One approach for dealing with skill and labour shortages that has been discussed quite broadly at a policy level is to target older workers as a source of ongoing labour.

Research indicates, however, that Australians prefer to retire before they reach 65 years of age (Shacklock, Brunetto and Nelson, 2009) and that organisations continue to focus more on younger workers as the solution to their staffing problems. To address this problem organisations are being encouraged to develop innovative ways to retain older workers (Patrickson, 2011). Both governments and organisations will need to offer retraining to older workers so that they can continue to make an effective contribution in the later part of their working lives

(Parker, 2011). At a policy level this is also being addressed. In 2009 the federal government announced a gradual increase in the age at which individuals can access government pensions so that by 2023 it will be 67 years rather than the current 65 years of age (DHS, 2009).

Another challenge for organisations is to find ways to transfer knowledge from older to younger workers so that corporate memory is retained. Many larger organisations have introduced mentoring programs as one way of assisting knowledge transfer while at the same time supporting career development for employees in the early stages of their careers. To assist in this process AHRI offers mentoring programs that link younger employees with more experienced staff as well as professional development networks for recent graduates (*HR Monthly*, 2007).

Employee Engagement

In a labour market characterised by skill and labour shortages workforce attraction and retention will become a key challenge for HR managers but so too will employee engagement. The next generation of employees will be better educated, will have higher expectations and are predicted to be more mobile than the current cohort of baby boomers. At the same time, as noted previously, organisations will need to find ways to engage the baby boomer generation to avoid losing much needed knowledge and experience (Quine, 2006). In this context employee engagement has become a critical issue and a key challenge for organisations. Employee engagement has been found to result in lower absenteeism and turnover as well as higher profits and higher levels of customer satisfaction. Engaged employees are important for gaining competitive advantage and maintaining overall organisational success (Ross, 2009).

Organisational approaches to employee engagement range from participation in programs such as the annual Australian AHRI Awards or seeking accreditation as an Aon Hewitt Best Employer, also referred to as 'employer of choice' (Kramar, Bartram and De Cieri, 2011). Increasingly having an Employer of Choice endorsement is seen as a major source of competitive advantage in attracting quality employees, although a 2007 workplace survey found that 52 per cent of job-seekers reported that they were rarely or never attracted to a company by such claims. By contrast 93 per cent of organisations surveyed considered it to be important and, of those who had not yet been accredited, more than 50 per cent stated that they planned to seek accreditation within the next two years (Chandler Macleod's Workplace Barometer Report, 2007). Surveys by Aon Hewitt have indicated that for the employer of choice branding to be successful employer promises needed to be matched with action in areas such as looking after or valuing employees, career development and progression, the provision of challenging and engaging work and work–life balance or employee benefits (Chandler Macleod's Workplace Barometer Report, 2007).

A recent survey indicated that there has been some improvement in employee engagement levels in recent years but there were still some worrying trends (Mercer Consulting, 2011). The survey found that one in five Australian employees were not happy with their job but were not planning to leave while four out of ten were thinking of leaving their organisation with those aged 25–34 most likely to be looking for alternate employment. Sixty per cent of older workers believed that their organisation had not provided sufficient opportunities for growth and development; females were less satisfied with career opportunities than men.

Given recent movements towards casualisation in the private sector and the lessening of union power it is not surprising that for many employees the public sector is emerging as an employer of choice given its relatively high salaries, the promotion opportunities, comparatively stable employment, flexible working hours and interesting job responsibilities (ABS 2012a). However, while it would appear that a number of Australian organisations are moving towards practices that support employee engagement there is still room for improvement in terms of delivering on promises.

Work–Life Balance

In common with many developed countries, the issue of work–life balance is increasingly on the HRM agenda. Although there has been steady growth in part-time and casual employment ironically there has also been a shift towards longer working hours for both full-time and part-time workers. In most Organisation for Economic Co-operation (OECD) countries the trend has been towards a shorter average working week yet in Australia the average full-time employee now works 42 hours per week, up from an average of 38 hours in 1982 (Rasmussen and Burgess, 2007). There has also been a significant increase in the number of people working 50 hours or more per week, often as unpaid overtime (Buchanan *et al.*, 2006). Over this same period there has been a steady increase in the number of women in the workforce. In August 2010, there were 9.8 million employees, of whom 5.2 million were males and 4.6 million were females (ABS, 2011b). These changes provide the context for growing calls from employees for a better work–life balance. Recent ABS Social Trends' figures indicate that 2.2 million workers believe that they are over-employed and want to work fewer hours. Reasons cited included wanting to spend more time with their family, more time to take care of children and more time for recreational and social activities (ABS, 2011c).

The HRM response has been to look for creative ways to match organisational and employee needs. Results of a 2005 study of more than 1,000 organisations found that work–life balance initiatives were being developed in 55 per cent of the organisations surveyed while 49 per cent had implemented family-friendly policies (Sheehan, Holland and De Cieri, 2006). Australian organisations are recognising that by offering flexibility, family-friendly benefits and generous maternity leave conditions they can gain a competitive advantage that may in fact determine their long-term survival. That is, with an ageing population and with skills shortages across many sectors there is a need to retain experienced employees. Yet, despite recognising employee retention as a major source of competitive advantage and despite significant progress in work–life balance policies in recent years, many women still leave the workforce after having children due to the pressures of finding suitable and affordable childcare, the difficulties associated with juggling the work–non-work interface, and male work cultures that may effectively discourage the take-up of flexible work options (Still, 2006). Redressing these issues will be a key challenge for organisations in general and more specifically for HR managers in the next decade.

Cultural Diversity

Australia is culturally diverse and becoming increasingly so. In the period up until World War II the majority of migrants came from the United Kingdom and thus were culturally very similar to Australians. After the war Australia experienced a wave of migration from Mediterranean countries, such as Italy and Greece, followed in more recent years by migrants from Middle Eastern, African and Asian countries. By 2006 approximately 25 per cent of Australia's workers were born overseas with 15 per cent originating from non-English speaking background (NESB) source countries (DIMA, 2006).

Current immigration policy reflects growing concern as to how Australia will remain productive in the future given a relatively low birth rate and a rapidly ageing population. However, preference is still given to English-speaking migrants with either specific skills or professional qualifications in areas of workforce shortages. As a consequence Australia is still predominantly English speaking and still holds to primarily British values and attitudes. Australians tend to be wary of cultural differences and at times openly hostile to migrants from Islamic or Arabic backgrounds. There are indications that these issues are often left unaddressed in the workplace (James and Heathcote, 2002). The management of cultural diversity is a low priority for Australian organisations and is often limited to legal compliance (Bertone and Leahy, 2001). As a consequence there is very little evidence of an integrated approach that takes into account race, ethnicity and religion (Syed and Kramar, 2010). There is also an under-representation of cultural diversity in higher level positions, a situation that perpetuates the over-representation of the views of mainstream employees at the expense of minority groups (Syed and Kramar, 2010).

Gender

More than a decade after the introduction of equal opportunity legislation (Equal Opportunity for Women in the Workplace Act 1999) and despite numerous affirmative action programs at state and federal level, women have still not managed to break through the glass ceiling to the executive ranks in Australian companies (Clarke, 2011b). Although women comprise 45 per cent of the workforce (with 55.9 per cent holding a tertiary qualification) women still make up only 2 per cent of chief executives of ASX200 (Australian Stock Exchange) companies, 8 per cent of board members of ASX 200 companies, 10.7 per cent of senior executives in ASX 200 companies and 37 per cent of senior public service roles (Equal Opportunity for Women in the Workplace Agency 2012). There are indications, however, that some organisations are taking pro-active measures to redress gender balance. For example, the accounting firm KPMG has increased its female managers by 6 per cent to 51 per cent since 2005 through a diversity program that includes paid parental leave, paid ad hoc childcare, family days and links to diversity networks such as Women on Boards. In the 2009 financial year, 40 per cent of its staff accessed one or more of the firm's flexible work options (Ross, 2010).

Women also continue to experience wage inequality despite efforts from the late 1960s onwards to remedy the imbalance through both legislation and the centralised wage fixing system (Short and Nowak 2009). While some of the gap can be explained by the existing social/cultural values that impact on women's ability to gain promotion or higher paid jobs there is also evidence that 'women's work' (that is, in caring or service organisations) is not as highly valued and therefore attracts lower remuneration than jobs traditionally regarded as 'men's jobs' (Short and Nowak, 2009). As more and more educated women enter the workforce HR has a critical role to play in gender equality through, first, identifying gaps in current practice and then, promoting voluntary actions to ensure that women take their place in leadership and management positions (Charlesworth, 2010).

Changes Expected in HR Functions in the Next Five Years

HRM in Australia has begun the transition to a recognised profession. In the next five to ten years people working in HRM are more likely to have appropriate qualifications and are more likely to be involved in strategic decision-making processes at senior levels in the organisation. In terms of qualifications, one study reported that in 2006 46 per cent of HRM professionals had completed some form of relevant graduate degree, an increase from 23 per cent in 1995 (Sheehan, Holland and De Cieri, 2006). A major shift, however, is needed in terms of career experience. Currently career paths tend to be via direct entry into HRM rather than through other business functions such as accounting, finance or sales/marketing. The implication is that many HR professionals lack broad strategic business experience or the skills and knowledge to contribute on an equal footing with other recognised professions (Sheehan, Holland and De Cieri, 2006). For HR professionals to increase their credibility they will be under pressure to gain experience across all areas of business, not just human resources.

Another major issue in the next five years will be the continued delegation of many HRM roles and functions to line managers (Kulik and Bainbridge, 2006). While this will reduce the amount of time that HR professionals spend on day-to-day administrative activities it will increase the need for training, coaching and mentoring of line managers to help them develop the requisite soft skills. It will also require an overarching strategy on the part of HR to ensure that delegated functions have a good fit with the organisation's overall mission, vision and policies.

At a more strategic level the future of HRM in Australia will require a focus on two key areas: international HRM and the integration of HR management into the overall strategy of the firm. Australia has been described as a small, late internationalising economy (Johnston and Menguc, 2007) with a future increasingly tied to global markets and multinational enterprises (MNEs). The Mayne Report (www.maynereport.com) 2010 found that 250 foreign-owned companies generate revenue of more than AU$250 million (US$250 million) in Australia. There are also about 80 Australian-owned firms that generate more than AU$200 million (US$200 million) revenue offshore. The recent AT Kearney confidence index (2010) ranked Australia as the seventh most attractive destination for foreign direct investment (FDI) and third for primary and retail sector investors. This data indicates that Australia is a significant contributor and an attractive destination as a host and source of multinational investment. Given anticipated growth in global markets over the next five years the focus for human resource managers will need to include international HRM. That is, HRM will need to expand its portfolio of skills to include expatriation and repatriation, industrial relations and employee relations across different countries, an understanding of HR practices in MNEs in Australia, and centralisation versus localisation. Staffing will include global talent management, a critical issue given current skills and labour shortages (McDonnell, Stanton and Burgess, 2011).

The second key focus will be on integrating HRM into the overall strategy of the firm and then demonstrating exactly how this adds value through its contribution to the triple bottom line (Compton, 2009). In other words, HR will need to provide tangible, quantitative evidence to support the argument for greater investment in human capital as a source of competitive advantage (Lundgaard, 2009; Ross, 2011). It will need to show how it supports key stakeholders – employees, line managers, key customers and shareholders (Ulrich, 2006). It will need to show that it can manage the 'big five' – managing cultural change, having personal credibility with business managers, demonstrating effectiveness in the traditional areas of HR, good business knowledge and the use of IT to support delivery of HR outcomes (Keen, 2004). This in turn will require the development of clear measures of HR activities that offer useful and meaningful data to assess and evaluate HRM's overall contribution to business outcomes (Ross, 2010).

At this stage it seems that the challenges have been identified but the nature of the best response is still a little unclear. There are signs that HR is moving in the right direction towards becoming a full business partner. The question of where to go from here has several options and lacks convergence between those employed in the service industries, the mining sector or not for profit organisations given their present differences. Both between countries in Asia (Budhwar and Yaw, 2009) and between industrial sectors within any specific country in this region there is evidence of multiple pathways and Australia is no exception to this increasing level of complexity. Clearly Australia has to confront the issue of wage discrepancies between its income earners here and abroad, and within its own economy. It also has to address issues of individual differences such as race, ethnicity, culture and gender within its workforce. It needs to develop policies and practices that steer a delicate balance between the demands of its stakeholders. Such pressures add significantly to the complexities of the HR manager's role and add further to the pressures both for professionalism in HRM and for understanding its broader impact on other business functions.

Brief Case Scenarios

One feature of modern Australian employment is the continuing transition from an earlier workforce scenario with a large manufacturing component to one now dominated by service industries. The manufacturing industry, where demand for these skills is waning as their products can no longer compete, has been especially hard hit. Two contemporary scenarios below illustrate the different situations facing two sets of workers, the first indicating special incentives offered to attract individuals to apply for jobs that have been difficult to staff in either the mining or service sector and the second indicating the difficulties faced by those whose skills are in waning demand. Industries (such as mining) have struggled with the recruitment and retention of staff in remote locations. To overcome this problem companies have been forced to offer high wages, extra amenities and family benefits in order to attract suitable employees (Price Waterhouse Coopers 2012). Similarly service industries, especially those in remote areas, or in less popular fields such as aged care, have responded by offering special incentives such as bonuses on job acceptance, assistance with family care responsibilities, flexible hours and the supply of job-related tools (Agrifood Careers 2011). Manufacturing continues to shed excess staff as the sustained high Australian dollar over the last two years makes it even more difficult for Australian enterprises to compete with their competitors from lower-wage countries abroad. This is illustrated in a recent incident (April 2012) where 350 workers were made redundant on a single day in one of the local car assembly plants, a practice that led to massive media coverage and public condemnation but with falling local sales the company could no longer maintain its payroll. Yet, on the same day, a large insurance company announced that it was introducing a new paid parental leave scheme that offers women a 'welcome back to work' payment. The company already provides 14 weeks' paid leave, but will now double the salaries of women for their first six weeks back at work, in effect raising their maternity leave to 20 weeks at full pay as a strategy designed to retain experienced employees and reduce expenditure on recruitment and training costs.

References

Agrifood Careers (2011) www.agrifoodcareers.com.au accessed 21 September 2011.

Aon Hewitt Best Employers Accreditation Program Australia and New Zealand, http://was2.hewitt.com/bestemployers/anz/pages/index.htm accessed 4 February 2013

AT Kearney. (2010) *Investing in a rebound: The 2010 AT Kearney Confidence Index*. Virginia: AT Kearney Inc.

Australian Bureau of Statistics (2003) *Employer Training Expenditure and Practices*. Canberra: AGPS.

Australian Bureau of Statistics (2009) *Employee Earnings, Benefits and Trade Union Membership Australia*. Catalogue No. 6310.0. Canberra: AGPS.

Australian Bureau of Statistics (2010a) 6530.0m – *Household Expenditure Survey*. Australia: Summary of Results, 2009–10.

Australian Bureau of Statistics (2010b) 6310.0 – *Employee Earnings, Benefits and Trade Union Membership*. Australia, August 2010.

Australian Bureau of Statistics (2010c) 1370.0 – *Measures of Australia's Progress*. 2010.

Australian Bureau of Statistics (2011a) 6302.0 – *Average Weekly Earnings*. Australia, May 2011.

Australian Bureau of Statistics (2011b) 6202.0 *Labour Force*. Australia, August 2011

Australian Bureau of Statistics (2011c) 4102.0 *Australian Social Trends*. June 2011

Australian Bureau of Statistics (2012a) 6306.0 *Employee Earnings and Hours*. Australia, May 2012.

Australian Bureau of Statistics (2012b) 6291.0.55.001 *Labour Force, Australia*, September 2012. Australian Human Resources Institute, www.ahri.com.au, accessed 12 August 2011.

Australian Human Resources Institute (AHRI): www.ahri.com.au, accessed 28 August 2011.

Bertone, S. and Leahy, M. (2001) 'Social equity, multiculturalism and the productive diversity paradigm: reflection on their role in corporate Australia' in S. Philips (ed.) *Everyday Diversity: Australian Multiculturalism and Reconciliation*, pp. 113–144. Melbourne: Common Ground Publishing.

Buchanan, J., Bretherton, T., Considine, G., and van Wanrooy, B. (2006) 'Longer and Irregular Hours: Employers, Decentralised Bargaining and Working Time Standards in Australia since the late 1970s', Paper presented at *Conference on New Standards for New Times: The Eight Hour Day and Beyond*, Centre for Social Research, RMIT University, Melbourne, 22–23 June.

Budhwar, P. and Yaw, D. (2009) 'Future research on Human Resource Management systems in Asia', *Asia Pacific Journal of Management* 26, 197–218.

Buffini, F. and Pheasant, B. (2005) 'By order of the board: CEOs are overpaid', *Australian Financial Review*, 8 September 2005: 5

Burgess, J. and Baird, M. (2003) 'Employment entitlements: Development, assess, flexibility and protection', *Australian Bulletin of Labour* 29(1): 1–13.

Burgess, J., Campbell, I., and May, R. (2008) 'Pathways from casual employment to economic security: The Australian experience', *Social Indicators Research* 88: 161–178.

Cascio, W., Young, C. and Morris, J, (1997) 'Financial consequences of employment-change decisions in major US corporations', *Academy of Management* 40(5): 1,175–1,189.

Chandler Macleod's Workplace Barometer Report (2007) 'Employer of choice: A reality cheque', *Chandler Macleod Consulting*, Sydney, Australia.

Charlesworth, S. (2010) 'The intersections of gender equality and decent work: Progress and prospects in Australia', *IIRA European Congress 2010*, 28 June–1 July 2010, Copenhagen, Denmark.

Clarke, M. (2011a) 'Downsizing practices for sustainable HRM', in Clarke, M. (ed.) *Readings in HRM and Sustainability*, pp. 100–116, Victoria: Tilde University Press.

Clarke, M. (2011b) 'Advancing women's careers through leadership development programs', *Employee Relations* 33(5): 498–515.

Compton, R. (2009) 'Towards an integrated model of strategic Human Resource Management – An Australian case study', *Research and Practice in Human Resource Management* 17(2): 81–93.

Connolly, E. and Lewis, C. (2010) 'Structural Change in the Australian Economy', *Bulletin*, September Quarter, Reserve Bank of Australia.

Critchley, R. (2004) *Doing Nothing is Not an Option: Facing the Imminent Labor Crisis*. South Western, Mason, Ohio.

De Cieri, H, Kramar, R. Noe, R.Hollenbeck, J.R. Gerhart, B., and Wright, P. (2008) *Human Resource Management in Australia: Strategy, People, Performance* (3rd edn). Sydney, NSW: McGraw-Hill.

Department of Human Services (2009) *Secure and Sustainable Pension Reforms.* www.centrelink.gov.au/internet/internet.nsf/publications/co597.htm, accessed 15 September 2011

Department of Immigration and Multicultural Affairs (DIMA) (2006) *The Evolution of Australia's Multicultural Policy.* Canberra: DIMA. www.immi.gov.au/facts/06evolution.htm accessed 12 August 2011.

Equal Opportunity for Women in the Workplace Agency (2012) *Annual Report 11/12.* Sydney, NSW. www.wgea.gov.au/Information accessed 4 February 2013.

Fels, A. (2010) 'Executive remuneration in Australia'. *Australian Accounting Review* 52(20): 76–82.

Fenton-Jones, M (2008) 'HR skills shortage lifts salaries', *Australian Financial Review,* 6 June 2008, p. 54.

Freyens, B. P. (2010) 'Managing skill shortages in the Australian public sector: Issues and perspectives', *Asia Pacific Journal of Human Resources* 48(3): 262–286.

Garton, P. (2008) 'The resources boom and the two-speed economy', *Economic Roundup Issue 3.* http://archive.treasury.gov.au/ , accessed 12 September 2011.

Gettler, L. (2011) 'When the only way is up', *HR Monthly,* April 2011: 12–15.

Global Business Policy Council (2010) *Investing in a Rebound: The 2010 AT Kearney Confidence Index,* Vienna, Virginia: AT Kearney Inc.

Gollan, P. J. (2009) 'Australian industrial relations reform in perspective: Beyond Work choices and future prospects under the Fair Work Act 2009', *Asia Pacific Journal of Human Resources* 47(3): 260–269.

Guzman, G. (2011) 'Human resource roles: Ideal versus practiced: A cross country comparison among organizations in Asia', *International Journal of Human Resource Management* 22(13): 2,665–2,682.

Huntley, R. and Salt, B. (2010) *Future Focus.* Melbourne, Australia: Ipsos Australian Pty Ltd and KPMG International.

IBIS World Industry Report N8431 (2011) *University and Other Higher Education in Australia,* 10 August 2011, http://clients.ibisworld.com.au, accessed 12 September 2011.

James, D. and Heathcote, A. (2002) 'Race gets the silent treatment', *Business Review Weekly*: 70–73.

Jerums, G. (2011) 'The special relationship', *HR Monthly,* February: 10–14.

Johnston, S. and Menguc, B. (2007) 'Subsidiary size and the level of subsidiary autonomy in multinational corporations: A quadratic model investigation of Australian subsidiaries', *Journal of International Business Studies* 38(5): 787–801.

Keen S. (2004) 'The HR skills that really matter', *HR Monthly,* October: 20–25.

Kramar, R. Bartram, T. and De Cieri, H. (2011) *Human Resource Management: Strategy, People, Performance* (4th edn). North Ryde, NSW: McGraw-Hill.

Kulik, C. and Bainbridge, H. T. J. (2006) 'HR and the line: The distribution of HR activities in Australian organisations', *Asia Pacific Journal of Human Resources* 44(2): 240–256.

Lundgaard, W. (2009) 'What gets measured gets done', *HR Monthly,* April: 28–31.

McDonnell, A. Stanton, P. and Burgess, J. (2011) 'Multinational enterprises in Australia: Two decades of international human resource management research reviewed', *Asia Pacific Journal of Human Resources* 49(1): 9–35.

Mercer Consulting (2011) 'Inside Employees' Minds: Navigating the new rules of engagement', Australian Survey Summary, September 2011, Mercer LLC, www.mercer.com.au, accessed 23 September 2011.

Michael Page International (2008) Engineering & Manufacturing Salary Survey, Michael Page International, Sydney, NSW.

Parker, D. (2011) 'Older but willing to carry on', *The Weekend Australian,* 20–21 August, p. 4.

Patrickson M (2011) 'Balancing the Competing Demands of Work and Retirement: Work Life Balance for Older Workers', paper presented to the Industrial and Organisational Psychology Conference, Brisbane.

Patrickson, M. and Sutiyono, W. (2004) "HRM in Australia", in Budhwar, P. (ed.) *Managing Human Resources in Asia-Pacific*. pp. 239–252. London: Routledge.

Peetz, D. (2009) *Submission to Productivity Commission Inquiry into Regulation of Director and Executive Remuneration in Australia*, May 2009.

Phillimore, J. and. Koshy, P (2010) *The Economic Implications of Fewer International Higher Education Students in Australia*. Curtin University, Perth WA: The John Curtin Institute of Public Policy, Curtin University.

Price Waterhouse Coopers (2012) *Mind the Gap: Solving the skills shortages in resources*, June 2012, www.pwc.com.au/industry/energy-utilities, accessed 4 February 2013.

Quine, S. (2006) "Australian baby boomers' expectations and plans for their old age". *Australasian Journal on Ageing* 25(1): 3–7.

Rasmussen, E. and Burgess, J. (2007) "Too much of a good thing: Longer working hours in Australia and New Zealand", Proceedings of the 21st AIRAANZ Conference February 7–9, Auckland, New Zealand.

Ross, E. (2009) "Creating a buzz", *HR Monthly*, October 2009: 22–26.

Ross, E. (2010) "Mind the gap", *HR Monthly*, April 2010: 18–23.

Ross, E. (2011) "Going metric", *HR Monthly*, April 2011: 22–25.

Russell, B. and Thite, M. (2008) "The next division of labour: Work skills in Australian and Indian call centres", *Work Employment and Society* 22(4): 615–634.

Sainsbury, M. (2011) "China crisis averted by student visa changes", *The Australian, Higher Education Supplement*, 28 September, p. 25.

Sardo, S. and Begley, P. (2007) 'Extreme makeover: Does HR need to improve its image?', HR Pulse Research Report, *Australian Human Resources Institute 1(1)*: 1–11. Society for Human Resource Management – Bureau of National Affairs Survey No. 60, 1995.

Shacklock, K. Brunetto, Y., and Nelson, S. (2009) "The different variables that affect older males' and females' intentions to continue working", *Asia Pacific Journal of Human Resources* 47(1): 79–101.

Sheehan, C. (2006) "A model of HR change", *Personnel Review* 34(2): 192–209.

Sheehan, C. Holland, P. and De Cieri, H. (2006) "Current developments in HRM in Australian organisations", *Asia Pacific Journal of Human Resources* 46(2): 132–152.

Short, C. and Nowak, M. (2009) "Persistent Australian gender wage inequality from 1990 to 2003: Stakeholders' views of why and how", *Journal of Industrial Relations* 51(2): 262–278.

Smith, A. and Smith. E. (2007) "The role of training in the development of Human Resource Management in Australian organisations", *Human Resource Development International* 10(3): 263–279.

Society for Human Resource Management-Bureau of National Affairs (SHRM-BNA) Survey No. 60, *Human Resource Activities, Budgets and Staffs: 1994–95*, bulletin to management, Bureau of National Affairs Policy and Practise Series, 29 June 1995, Bureau of National Affairs, Washington DC.

Still, L. (2006) "Where are the women in leadership in Australia?", *Women in Management Review* 21(3): 180–194.

Syed, J. and Kramar, R. (2010) "What is the Australian model for managing cultural diversity?", *Personnel Review* 39(1): 95–115.

The Mayne Report (2008) "Foreign companies generating more than 20 million", www.maynereport.com/articles/2008/02/04-1045-248.html accessed 5 February 2013.

Ulrich, D. and Brockbank, W. (2005) *The HR Value Proposition*. Boston, MA: Harvard Business Press.

Watson, I. (2008) "Skills in use: Labour market and workplace trends in skills use in Australia", Jobs Australia National Conference, Brisbane, 8 September 2008.

Websites

Aon Hewitt
http://was2.hewitt.com/bestemployers/anz/pages/index.htm

Australian Human Resources Institute
www.ahri.com.au

Equal Opportunity for Women in the Workplace Agency
www.eowa.gov.au

Fair Work Australia
www.fwa.gov.au

Mercer Consulting
www.mercer.com.au/home

13

Human Resource Management in the Fiji Islands

SUWASTIKA NAIDU, R. D. PATHAK AND ANAND CHAND

Introduction

The human resource management (HRM) environment of the Fiji islands has changed a lot since its independence in the 1970s and has undergone rapid changes in the recent decade. Both endogenous and exogenous environmental factors are closely knitted to the dynamism in the HRM environment. In Fiji, personnel management is practised by micro and small businesses, HRM practices are adopted by medium enterprises and strategic human resource management (SHRM) practices are practised in large organisations (Naidu, 2011b). This chapter is divided into seven sections. This first section of this chapter outlines the historical development of personnel management, industrial relations, employment relations, HRM and SHRM in the Fiji islands. The second section outlines the role of various institutions such as the state, trade unions, employer associations, non-government organisations (NGOs), donor agencies and trade agreements in the HRM environment. The third section outlines the endogenous and exogenous environmental factors that affect HRM practices. The fourth section discusses key changes in the HRM functions. The fifth section examines the key challenges and the future of HRM in the Fiji islands. The final section provides a case study of Paradise Manufacturers Fiji Limited within the context of the SHRM environment present in the Fiji islands.

Throughout this chapter, the discussions are designed to effectively distinguish the personnel management, HRM and SHRM in the micro and small businesses, medium and large enterprises and public sector organisations. The HRM practices within these sectors are homogenous; however, the HRM practices across these sectors are heterogeneous.

Historical Development of Personnel Management, Industrial Relations, Employment Relations, HRM and SHRM

The industrialisation process can be traced back to the 1870s, when the indentured labourers came to the Fiji islands to work on the sugarcane plantations (Prasad, Hince and Snell, 2002). In total, 60,965 workers were transported from India to the Fiji islands (Gillion, 1962). The indentured labourers from India brought with them a new culture, new norms and values and new ways of performing tasks. This marked the start of the era of personnel management adopted by the British Colonial rulers. During the era of personnel management, the indentured labourers were harshly treated and made to work on the sugarcane plantations for long hours (Gillion, 1962). There was a five-year contract between the indentured labourers and the British rulers and this contract was known as the *girmit*. Women were usually molested and harassed by the British rulers and the indentured male labourers, subsequently resulting in high suicide and illegal birth rates (Gillion, 1962). Throughout the colonial period, the Colonial Sugar Refinery (CSR), an Australian monopoly, controlled all the economic resources of the sugar industry. The monopolistic position of the CSR, coupled with brutal British rulers, further degraded the working conditions of the indenture labourers (Prasad, Hince and Snell, 2002). For instance, the management of labourers by the CSR was a challenging task. This company tried to keep the wages of the labourers as low as possible in order to increase the profits and return to the investors. The personnel administration model of the CSR emphasised dividing the workers based on caste structures, importation of labourers from India and harbouring of racist attitudes (Snell, 2000).

Similar to the sugar industry, the other sectors such as gold, manufacturing and agricultural were also constrained with staggering labour conditions and corporal punishments from the British rulers. In the gold mining industry, the Emperor Gold Mines Ltd, also an Australian monopoly, began operations in Vatukoula in 1954 by drawing labour from all 14 provinces of the Fiji islands (Prasad, Hince and Snell, 2002). The working conditions at the Emperor Gold Mines Ltd have been poor and dangerous for the workers, resulting in deaths, injury, industrial conflicts and loss of productivity.

Workers started organising and forming trade unions in the sugar and public services in the 1930s. This marked the start of an era of industrial relations (Prasad, Hince and Snell, 2002). In the 1920s, trade unions started emerging in the sugar and later on in the mining and manufacturing sectors. With the enactment of the Industrial Association Act, formal trade unions started arising by the late 1940s. In 1951, all the trade unions were consolidated into one single umbrella body known as the Fiji Industrial Workers' Congress (FIWC). The FIWC is currently known as the Fiji Trades Union Congress (FTUC). A major industrial dispute between the Oil and Allied Workers Union and the oil companies in 1959 clearly demonstrated the urgency to strengthen the labour legislation and institutions in the Fiji islands (Prasad, Hince and Snell, 2002). For instance, in the mining sector, there was increasing bitterness among the trade unions and the Emperor Gold Mines Ltd from 1950 to the 1960s. This contributed to widespread industrial sector unrest (Leckie, 2003) resulting in a decline in productivity, worker morale and economic growth. As a result of this conflict, the Fiji Employers' Consultative Association (FECA) was formed.

In 1960, the trade unions were able to exert pressure on the Colonial government in order to develop proper law and labour practice in the Fiji islands. This marked the start of employment relations. During the 1960s, key reforms of labour legislation were initiated and collective bargaining agreements were extended to the private enterprises (Prasad, Hince and Snell, 2002). The establishment of the Fiji National Provident Fund (FNPF) in 1968 brought together the employers, employees and the government in a tripartite forum for the overall management and administration of this scheme. For instance, in FNPF, the Board of Directors (BOD) is a tripartite body, with two trade union representatives, two employer representatives and two government representatives, and the chairman of is the Permanent Secretary for Finance (ILO, 2010). Similarly, the Training and Productivity Authority (TPAF) was established as a tripartite organisation to provide training to workers and to upgrade workers' skills.

On 10 October 1970, the Fiji islands gained independence from British rule and adopted the Westminster system of political democracy (Prasad, Hince and Snell, 2002). The independence of the Fiji islands marked a major change from personnel management to HRM in large organisations. The HRM model from the 1970s to the late 1990s was based on the principles postulated and enacted under the following nine pieces of labour legislation: Employment Act 1965, Trade Unions Act and Trade Unions (Recognition) Act 1998, Trade Union Disputes Act and Trade Union Disputes (Amendment) Decree 1992, Sugar Industry Act 1984, Health and Safety at Work Act 1996, Wages Council Act 1985, Shop (Regulation of Hours and Employment) Act 1964, Industrial Associations Act and Factories Act 1971. In the case of micro and small businesses, these legislations were poorly implemented while in the case of medium and large enterprises (including multi-national corporations), these legislations were properly implemented (Naidu, 2011b). The personnel management model in micro and small businesses are largely determined by the discretion of the owner or manager. In the majority of instances the micro and small business owners or managers have policies for annual leave and hours of work, but the effective implementation of these policies is dependent on the owner or manager. For instance, the majority of the restaurants in Fiji are small in nature and are family owned. According to the owners or managers of these restaurants, implementing employment law may not be cost effective and economically viable for these businesses due to their smallness and their limited access to resources (Naidu, 2011b).

After the 1980s, large organisations began to change their practice from personnel management to HRM and since the 1990s, as a result of the influence of HRM from Australia and New Zealand, SHRM began in the Fiji islands. In order to survive in the dynamic environment, organisations from both the private and public sectors are aligning their HRM policies and practices with the goals, missions and objectives of the organisations. Furthermore, from 2007, the SHRM model of the Fiji islands evolved around the Employment Relations Promulgation (2007) (ERP 2007). The ERP (2007) is an employment act that is based on the following five guiding principles (Naidu, 2012a):

- creating the labour standards that are equally fair to both employers and employees
- eliminating discrimination from the workplace
- providing the structure for collective bargaining and dispute resolution for employers and employees
- establishing institutions such as the Employment Relations Tribunal and the Employment Relations Court for dispute resolution
- fostering labour management consultation and cooperation.

Employers in Fiji are required to adhere to the ERP (2007) as it establishes the minimum standards for industrial relations and HRM policies and practices. The HRM policies and practices of organisations in Fiji have to be aligned to the ERP (2007). Once the HRM policies and practices have been aligned to the ERP (2007), then the next step is aligning HRM policies and practices with the goals, missions and objectives of the organisation. This employment law emphasised equality, integrity, transparency, teamwork, consultation and cooperation among the HRM partners. The ERP (2007) is properly implemented in the public and some sections of the private sector. In the case of the micro and small businesses in the private sector, the ERP (2007) is poorly implemented, whereas in the case of medium and large enterprises, the ERP (2007) is properly implemented (Naidu, 2011b; Naidu, 2012a; Naidu 2012b). A major change in the SHRM model occurred during September 2011 when the Essential National Industries (Employment) Decree was implemented by the military-led interim government. This decree requires existing trade unions to re-register as trade unions, trade union representatives to be workers of the designated corporations that they represent, and all existing collective bargaining agreements to be null and void 60 days after the implementation of the decree (Ministry of Labour Fij, 2011). This decree also has a provision for re-negotiation of the collective bargaining agreements if the employer is suffering from operating loss for two consecutive years. For instance, the employers have more avenues for aligning the HRM practices towards the goals and objectives of the organisation because the newly implemented Essential National Industries (Employment) Decree has more employer benefits as compared to the employee benefits (Naidu, 2011a, 2011b, 2012a, 2012b).

Figure 13.1 shows the historical development of HRM from personnel administration (PA)/industrial relations (IR)/employment relations (ER). It has been organised in chronological order. In summary, Figure 13.1 shows that from 1870 to 1929 personnel administration was practised in Fiji followed by industrial relations, employment relations, HRM and SHRM. The transition from personnel administration to SHRM occurred in a lapse of more than 100 years.

More specifically, the transition from industrial relations to employment relations and later to HRM and SHRM occurred on an average of 10 to 20 years. However, the transition from personnel administration to industrial relations took 59 years. For example, during the personnel administration period, Fiji was under British rule, hence it was challenging for the personnel administration model to evolve to industrial relations as the British rulers used brutal employee management practices.

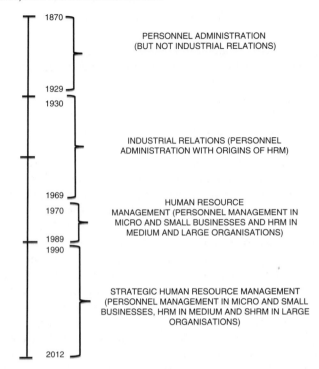

Figure 13.1 Timeline for Historical Development of Personnel Administration, Industrial
Relations, Employment Relations, Human Resource Management (HRM) and
Strategic Human Resource Management (SHRM)

Source: Council of Labor Affairs, Executive Yuan, *Yearly Bulletin of Labor Statistics*, various years

HRM Partnership

There are six key national actors in the HRM partners in the Fiji islands. These
six actors are the state, trade unions, employers, non-government organisations,
donor agencies and trading partners. Out of the six key actors, the state is the
most important. The other five have equal importance in determining the HRM
model of the Fiji islands. The following sections will provide an overview of the
role of each of the actors.

State: The state's primary role is to design and implement essential labour legislations. The Fiji islands' contemporary HRM model is largely influenced by
the Essential National Industries (Employment) Decree 2011 (see section 2.0).
Some of the sections of the ERP (2007) are still in force while other sections
have been abrogated by the implementation of the Essential National Industries
(Employment) Decree 2011. The state also ensures that institutions (Employment
Relations Court and Employment Relations Tribunal) are established in order to
provide effective dispute resolution machinery. In addition to this, the state also
establishes the minimum benchmark for HRM policies and practices for employment leave, compensation, employment benefits and grievance procedures.
Another essential role of the state in HRM partnership is the role of surveillance

and monitoring. The state through the Ministry of Labour ensures that labour legislation is effectively implemented. For instance, the Ministry of Labour carries out training for employers on employment law that is implemented in the country. This ministry also monitors organisations to ensure that employment law is effectively implemented in the country (Naidu, 2012a).

Trade unions/Employees: There are two trade union umbrella bodies: the Fiji Trades Union Congress (FTUC) and the Fiji Island Council of Trade Union (FICTU) in the Fiji islands. Initially, the members of the FICTU were members of the FTUC. A total of 15 trade unions who were disenchanted with FTUC combined to form the rival body of FTUC known as FICTU (Prasad, Hince and Snell, 2002). The officials of FTUC usually participate in tripartite forums that are involved in the design and implementation of labour laws. Other roles of trade unions include the representation of employee interests, influencing government on issues affecting employees and negotiating collective bargaining agreements (Elek, Hill and Tabor, 1993). The implementation of the Essential National Industries (Employment) Decree 2011 had major impact on the powers of trade unions. The trade unions are currently influencing the government to re-instate the powers that it had under the ERP (2007). For example, the National Secretary of FTUC is unhappy on the implementation of the Essential National Industries (Employment) Decree 2011 and emphasised that FTUC is currently working on protecting the trade union rights and reinstatement of ERP (2007) in all sectors of the economy (Anthony, 2011).

Employers/Employer associations: Currently, there is a single employer association in the Fiji islands known as the Fiji Employers and Commerce Association (FECA), formerly known as the Fiji Employers Federation. The FECA was formed in 1960 with 11 employers after the dispute between the oil industry and the Oil and Allied Workers Union (Prasad, Hince and Snell, 2002). The primary aim of FECA is to foster free trade and commerce activities for economic sustainability. Other activities of FECA include (Fiji Employers and Commerce Association, 2011: 1–2):

- providing a tripartite forum for consultation and collaboration on issues affecting employers
- establishing interdependent networks among employers
- promoting training of members.

For example, the CEO of FECF stated in a press statement that FTUC should engage in dialogues with the government rather than engaging in destructive lobbying with international trade unions, in order to solve the trade union crises that have aroused from the implementation of the Essential National Industries (Employment) Decree 2011. Any industrial actions by international trade unions will affect trade and communications as well as travel and the tourism industry (Chaudhary, 2011).

Non-government organisations (NGOs): NGOs such as the Fiji Women's Rights Movement (FWRM), the International Labour Organisation (ILO), United Nations Human Rights (UNHR), United Nations Children's Fund (UNICEF) and Save the Children Fund have an impact on the HRM partnership. These NGOs influence the government on child labour and equal employment opportunity legislations. Together with the state, the ILO plays a key role in providing capacity building to the tripartite constituents, technical assistance for the review of employment law, the implementation of programmes aimed at human resource development, and in tackling child labour issues via education of children. Currently, Fiji has ratified 31 labour conventions, out of which 28 are in force. For example, before an employment law is gazetted in Fiji, it is discussed at the ILO meeting by the representatives from the government, employers and the employees. Once all parties have reached mutual agreement, the employment law is gazetted and implemented in Fiji (ILO, 2012).

Donor agencies: The major donor agencies giving funds to Fiji are Australian Aid (AusAid), New Zealand Aid (NZAid), the European Union (EU), Japan and China. The aid programmes of these donor agencies are primarily directed towards delivery of essential social services, rural development, improving access to financial services, improving livelihoods and supporting sustainable development of the developing countries for the optimistic drive towards achieving Millennium Development Goals (MDGs) (Chand and Naidu, 2010). These donor agencies influence the government on laws, policies and practices towards the focus area of aid programmes. For example, the 2005 to 2010 NZAid policy still remains in force even though the partnership between the NZ and the Fiji government is frozen after the political turmoil of December 2006. The current NZAid policy is focused on promoting democracy and assisting people in squatter and non-squatter settlements in Fiji (ILO, 2010).

Trade agreements: Trade agreements such as the Melanesian Spearhead Group (MSG), the Pacific Island Countries Trade Agreement (PICTA), the Interim Economic Partnership Agreement (IEPA), the South Pacific Regional Trade and Economic Cooperation Agreement (SPARTECA) and the Pacific Agreement on Closer Economic Relations (PACER) have an impact on the HRM partnership in the Fiji islands. These economic agreements are based on conditions and rules of origin that influence employers and government to take a certain course of action in order to benefit from the trade agreements. For example, under the rules of origin of the SPARTECA agreement, Australia and New Zealand offer duty free, unrestricted or concessional access for all products originating from Fiji. The garment investors from China in Fiji produce the garments in Fiji at a higher cost as compared to China and export the garments to Australia and New Zealand in order to benefit from SPARTECA. These investors are not allowed to ship the garments produced in China to Fiji and re-ship these garments to Australia and New Zealand. In order to reduce the cost of production and increase profits, the Chinese garment factories import the Chinese workers to Fiji and make them work under very restrictive working conditions (Chand, 2011). Another example is the suspension of Fiji from the Pacific Islands Forum (PIF), which had a devastating impact on the PACER-Plus negotiations. Fiji was suspended from the PIF due to the deteriorating human rights issues in the country after the December 2006 coup (PIF, 2009).

Factors Determining HRM Practices

Similar to other small island developing states in the Oceania region, the HRM practices in the Fiji islands are largely affected by endogenous and exogenous factors. Endogenous factors include those variables that are determined by other variables in the system while exogenous factors include those variables that are determined by other variables outside of the system (Pathak *et al.*, 2005; Schuler and Jackson, 2007). The exogenous factors include political, social and economic conditions and the endogenous factors include the characteristics of the work-force, competitive dynamics and characteristics of the company. The exogenous and endogenous factors that affect the HRM practices are all interdependent with one another (Budhwar and Debrah, 2001; Budhwar and Sparrow, 2002). The fol-lowing section will provide an overview of the endogenous and the exogenous factors that affect the HRM factors.

Economic factors: Out of all the endogenous and exogenous factors discussed below, economic factors have the most severe impact on the HRM practices. The primary motive of the private sector is to maximise profits, hence the adoption of HRM practices is dependent on the economic situation of the company. Over the last five years, the annual growth rate of Gross Domestic Product (GDP) has been negative; hence employers are adopting cost-cutting and rigid HRM prac-tices. When the economy tightens up, the employers focus more on unilateral decision making, reducing the power of trade unions and cutting down on general employment benefits. The global economic shocks from the Greece and Italy debt crises and the slowdown of the European Union and American economies are also having an adverse impact on the HRM practices adopted by organisations in the Fiji islands. For example, the global financial crisis has had a major impact on the tourism industry of Fiji, clearly indicated by the decline in tourist num-bers. According to Reddy (2010), the global financial crisis affected the tourism industry of Fiji, evidenced by tourist numbers declining from 585,031 in 2008 to 542,186 in 2009. This resulted in micro and small tourist operators closing down or cutting down on labour costs. Cutting down on labour costs was in the form of making workers redundant or suppressing employees' wages (Sziraczki, *et al.*, 2009).

Political and legal factors: The state is the major player in the political and legal environment because they establish the benchmark for the HRM practices in both the private and public sectors. Political and legal affairs such as government stability, international relations of the government and labour laws have a direct impact on the HRM practices adopted by organisations in the Fiji islands. For instance, in large multi-national corporations, such as British American Tobacco (BAT), the ERP (2007) and the Essential National Industries (Employment) Decree 2011 has an impact on the HRM practices adopted by the Fiji-based sub-sidiary. The Fiji-based BAT subsidiary provides maternity and paternity leave to employees. Maternity leave is a requirement under the ERP (2007); however, there is no mandatory requirement for paternity leave. As BAT is a United King-dom-based MNC operating in Fiji, the company uses UK standards of manag-ing employees (providing paternity leave) while at the same time adhering to the local labour standards (providing maternity leave). Another example is the case of hotels in Fiji. The hotels have to hire 5 per cent of the graduates from the National Employment Centre (NEC) even though the preference of the employers is University of the South Pacific (USP) graduates. The military regime has made it mandatory for all the employers in Fiji that have more than 50 workers to employ *attachés* from NEC on a ratio of 5 per cent of the total workers employed in the company (Government of the Republic of Fiji, 2009).

Societal factors: The societal factors such as the culture, values, norms, ethics, good governance and societal expectations all have an impact on the HRM practices adopted by organisations. In order to survive in the dynamic environment, most large organisations commit to wider corporate social responsibility to gain public support, an optimistic corporate image and to attract talented employees. For instance, J Hunter Pearls Fiji Ltd employs villagers from the Savusavu community and maintains good relationship with the indigenous people to improve sales and to improve the quality of the products. This company uses a consultative and cooperative approach to deal with sensitive societal issues. Another example is Jacks Fiji Ltd that has become the leader of handicrafts in Fiji by purchasing the handicrafts directly from the villagers. Jacks Fiji Ltd is able to maintain authenticity of the handicrafts while its competitors are unable to. Jacks Fiji Ltd also hires staff that are able to effectively communicate with the village handcrafters. When there is a death in one of the villages, this company takes part in the funeral and financially supports the families of the handcrafters' (White, 2007).

Characteristics of the workforce: Workforce characteristics such as education level, male to female ratio and ethnic background have an impact on the HRM practices adopted by organisations. In the micro and small businesses, employers usually employ casual workers and focus more on unilateral decision making because the workers are not well educated and aware of their rights in the workplace. For instance, the garment workers are ill-treated because of lack of understanding on the part of the workers about their fundamental rights in the workplace. In the case of medium, large and public sector organisations, the workers are well educated about their rights in the workplace, hence they are empowered and motivated to perform. For example, in the hotels sector of Fiji, the turnover rate of the workers in the cleaning, food and beverage division is usually high and the staff turnover at the front office is very low. Workers in the cleaning, food and beverage division are less motivated to perform as compared to the workers at the front office. The managers in the hotels sector of Fiji rate front office staff as more important than the cleaning, food and beverage staff. As a result of this, the front office staff are highly motivated by the managers to perform and the cleaning, food and beverage staffs are ignored to some extent. This has resulted in higher absenteeism and a higher turnover rate of the cleaning, food and beverage staff as compared to the front office staff (White, 2007).

Competitive intensity: The higher the competitive intensity in the market, the lower the market share and profits, resulting in more rigid HRM practices adopted by organisations. In the case of technical industries, the effect is opposite as organisations try to employ the best workers and grab employees from the competitors to gain sustainable competitive advantage. For instance, Vodafone was enjoying a monopoly in the mobile market in Fiji until recently, that is, before Digicel entered Fiji's market. The competitive intensity caused both of the organisations to compete for the best technical staff in the market. Similarly, in the hotels sector in Fiji, due to intense competition in the workplace, employers engage in poaching of the senior employees to gain a sustainable competitive advantage over the other hotels. In order to tackle this issue the companies are implementing flexible HRM strategies to retain as many competent employees as possible (White, 2007).

Characteristics of the company: Company characteristics such as type of industry, ethnic background of the owner and size and country of origin of the owner have an impact on HRM practices adopted by organisations in the Fiji islands. As mentioned above, micro and small businesses have poor HRM practices while medium, large and public sector organisations have a proper HRM department with proper implementation of HRM practices. Organisations whose country of origin is a developing country such as China and India usually exploit labour in Fiji (the garment industry) while companies whose country of origin is a developed nation such as the United Kingdom (BAT) and the United States have proper standards for motivating and compensating workers. For example, Ghim Li Fiji was a Chinese-based garment company operating in Fiji. This company used to employ a high volume of female staff and engaged in sweatshop conditions to squeeze the maximum out of the workers (Storey, 2004).

Key Changes in the HRM Function

The HRM function of Fiji is changing and is largely dependent on the organisation's economic status. As already mentioned above, large organisations in Fiji are focusing on aligning the HRM practices and policies towards the goals, objectives and mission statement of the organisation and moving to SHRM. Unlike the traditional approach, whereby HRM was involved only in recruiting and retaining competent and knowledgeable employees and motivating these employees to perform, the contemporary focus of HRM in Fiji is more strategic in nature. Some of the key aspects of the HRM function that have changed include the following:

Understanding the Individual Needs of the Employees

Under the traditional approach of HRM, the main function of HRM involved understanding the individual needs of the employees and career goals. Currently, the SHRM function involves identifying individual needs and aligning these needs to the profit-maximisation goal of the organisation. For instance, in large organisations in Fiji such as Goodman Fielder, Carpenters Group and Reddy Group, employees are only rewarded if their department is performing well or the company's overall financial position is improving. In cases when the company is not performing well, employees are motivated to increase their efforts in debt collection and so forth so that they could be rewarded based on their productive efforts (Naidu, 2012b).

Ensure EEO for all Groups Irrespective of Gender, Ethnicity and Race

The traditional approach to HRM involves maintaining balance between the employees from different genders, races and ethnicities. Under the contemporary function of SHRM, organisations are largely focusing on recruiting employees that are competent and can perform the required tasks and at the same time are concerned with maintaining balance with gender, ethnicity and race. For example, at the Fiji Electricity Authority (FEA), in the maintenance and field work section, more males are employed as compared to the females because the nature of the job requires considerable physical effort. To get the maintenance and fieldwork done by the female staff may not be productive for FEA (Naidu, 2011b).

Providing Training and Development for the Employees

The traditional approach to HRM requires organisations to provide training and development for employees. Under the modern SHRM approach, large organisations in Fiji are carrying out proper training needs' analysis before training is provided to employees. For example, at the Fiji Sugar Corporation (FSC), proper training needs' analysis is carried out by the training department in conjunction with the HRM department before the training is provided to the employees (Naidu, 2011b). The content of the training is usually aligned with the goals and objectives of the organisation.

Employee Empowerment

Under the traditional approach to HRM, employees are empowered so that they feel a sense of belongingness and accountability towards the organisation. Under the contemporary SHRM approach to HRM, only those employees are empowered in large organisations that are performing and working towards the goals and objectives of the organisation. For instance, at the Australia New Banking Corporations branch in Fiji, the managers that are good advocates and ambassadors of the organisation are empowered to improve the company's profitability while the trouble makers are punished (through suspension) and non-performers have to work under the strict supervision of the supervisors (Naidu, 2012a).

Effectively and Efficiently Addressing Employee Grievances

The traditional approach to HRM requires efficiently and effectively meeting employee grievances. Under the modern approach to SHRM, employees are required to solve the grievance keeping in mind the organisation's quality (reputation and image) and profitability. For instance, at the Reddy Group of companies, more specifically at the Tanoa International Hotel, employees have to be nice and humble towards the tourists and the local customer even though the customers may be wrong sometimes (Naidu, 2011b).

Objective Performance Management System

The traditional approach to HRM requires a performance appraisal system to be objective in nature. Under the new SHRM approach to managing employees in Fiji, organisations are ensuring that the performance appraisals are objective and the outcome of the appraisal should be directed towards the goals, mission and objectives of the organisation. For example, at the Reddy Group of Companies, the 360-degree performance appraisal is conducted by a centralised HRM department to ensure the accuracy, reliability and transparency of the appraisal. The HR manager ensures that the outcome of the performance appraisal should increase the company's profitability.

Key Challenges Facing HRM

The HR managers are finding their role as employee champions and management advocates very demanding. Some of the main challenges facing the HRM include:

Implementing Proper HRM Information Systems in Order to Effectively Manage and Make Informed Decisions

Generally, the implementation of HRM information systems in Fiji is poor. There is no HRM information system in small organisations and in large organisations the HRM information system is implemented with a lack of skilled labour to manage the system. For instance, in small businesses the employees are casually hired, hence the employers do not see a necessity to implement a HRM information system. In large organisations, there is lack of specialised and skilled labour to implement proper HRM information systems (Naidu, 2012a).

Aligning the HRM Practices with the Goals, Objectives and Mission Statements of the Organisation

Aligning the HRM policies and practices to the goals, objectives and mission statements of the organisation is a very challenging task. The HR managers are faced with various difficulties in undertaking this task. For instance, the primary goal of any organisation in Fiji is to maximise its returns to the shareholders but HR managers are faced with difficulties as they have to implement policies that minimise the labour cost and at the same time motivate employees to perform (Chu and Siu, 2001).

Economic, Political and Legal Crisis

Managing human resources in the context of economic, political and legal crises is difficult as these environmental factors are dynamic and are continuously changing. Pressures from the global economic crisis, local and international politics and the legal crisis are imposing challenges on HRM. For instance, the implementation of the Essential National Industries (Employment) Decree 2011 is making managing HR very challenging because this decree has created a labour turmoil and this has largely affected the management of human resources in organisations. The implementation of the Essential National Industries (Employment) Decree 2011 has resulted in labour unrest and trade unions are strategising to take industrial action in conjunction with the international trade unions (Anthony, 2011).

Lack of Financial Budget for Training and Development

Lack of financial budget for training and development is a major issue for micro, small and medium organisations in Fiji. The main aim of the micro, small and medium enterprises is to survive in the dynamic internal and external environment. For instance, according to the majority of the business operators in the tourism sector, survival has become a concern due to a decline in tourist numbers. Currently, the tourism business operators do not have sufficient funds to invest in training and development (Naidu, 2011b).

Lack of Awareness of Employees about their Fundamental Rights at the Workplace

Employees in Fiji lack awareness and knowledge about their fundamental rights in the workplace. This is simply because a large majority of the workforce in Fiji are not well educated. For instance, employees in the garment industry are not well aware of their rights under the ERP (2007). This is the major reason that they are exploited in the workplace (Naidu, 2011b).

The Future of the HRM Function in the Fiji islands

The future of the HRM function in the Fiji islands is unpredictable. The development of the HRM function is closely knitted to the economic, political and legal situation of Fiji. Generally, the development of the HRM function in the Fiji islands can be divided into two functional categories. The first category includes the pessimistic approach to the future development of the HRM function. This approach foresees a worsening of Fiji's economy. If Fiji's economy worsens then it could come to a stage that HRM may be eliminated from some sectors of the economy and gets replaced by the traditional methods of managing employees. The following changes will be eminent.

Increase in Labour Unrest and Employee Grievances

If the economy of Fiji contracts then employers will pressure the government to implement labour laws that are employer-friendly so that labour costs could be lowered and the maximum could be squeezed out from the workers. This will result in an increase in labour unrest and employee grievances. For instance, the implementation of the Essential National Industries (Employment) Decree 2011 has resulted in labour unrest and trade unions are strategising to take industrial action in conjunction with the international trade unions (Anthony, 2011).

Elimination of SHRM from some Sectors of the Economy

The SHRM model (Figure 13.1) may be eliminated from the essential industries of Fiji such as the financial industry (Australia and New Zealand Banking Corporation, Bank of Baroda, Bank of South Pacific, Westpac Banking Corporation and Fiji Revenue and Customs Authority), the telecommunications industry (Fiji International Communications Ltd, Telecom Fiji Ltd, Fiji Broadcasting Corporation Ltd), the Civil Aviation Industry (Air Pacific Ltd) and the Public Utilities Industry (Fiji Electricity Authority, Water Authority of Fiji) if the economic, political and legal conditions of Fiji further worsen. These are all the essential industries gazetted by the military government. For instance, the deterioration of the economic, political and legal condition of Fiji will initiate a major reform of the existing labour laws. The new labour laws that will be implemented will deteriorate the employees' working conditions and rights in the workplace, hence making it impossible for employers to implement the SHRM model (Naidu, 2012b).

Replacement of Strategic Human Resource Management with Personnel Management

If Fiji's situation further worsens then it is likely that the existing SHRM model (the SHRM model presented in this paper) will be replaced by personnel management. The employment conditions in Fiji may worsen if more employment decrees are implemented that do not have the support of trade unions, donor agencies and THE ILO. As a result of this, there will be a drastic increase in 'brain drain'. For instance, a large bulk of the educated workforce will migrate to countries such as New Zealand and Australia for greener pastures (Naidu, 2011b).

The second category includes the optimistic approach to the future development of HRM. The following changes will occur in the HRM function if there is a positive outlook for Fiji's economy.

Investment in Cross-Functional and International HRM

If there is a positive outlook for Fiji, employers will be required to invest in cross-functional HRM in order to gain a sustainable competitive advantage. In future, the business environment will become more complex and dynamic, hence there will be a need for HR managers that are well versed in marketing, operations and finance but not just in HRM. Parallel to the argument of institutional theory, the HR managers will be required to understand the different functions of the organisation so that they are able to effectively and efficiently manage employees from different departments. Organisations will expand, hence there will be a need to invest in international HRM. For example, as Flour Mills of Fiji and Punjas spreads its operations across the Pacific islands, the HR managers of each of these companies have to invest in managing employees from different islands in the Pacific because there is significant variability in culture (Naidu, 2011b; Chu and Siu, 2001).

Computerisation of HR Functions

Organisations will have to spend more resources in computerising HR functions. HR processes have to be computerised in order to achieve efficiency and effectiveness. New software will be developed for managing the different HRM practices. For example, currently Fiji does not have sufficiently talented employees to manage the HR information systems. The tertiary institutions are not providing specialised courses on HR information systems. All these factors will create challenges for managing HR information systems and organisations will have to implement strategies to counter these challenges (Naidu, 2011b).

Case 1: Paradise Manufacturers Fiji Limited (PMFL)[1]

Paradise Manufacturers Fiji Limited (PMFL) is a tobacco manufacturing United Kingdom-based MNC that started its operations in the Fiji islands in 1951. The PMFL has 45 cigarette companies in 39 countries worldwide. This company's vision is to establish higher standards of leadership in Fiji's tobacco industry under the guiding principles of strength, diversity, open-mindedness, freedom through responsibility, and enterprising spirit. On the packet of every cigarette that is sold in Fiji there is clear indication of the average level of nicotine and tar that each cigarette will deliver. The PMFL is affected by high taxation and stringent regulation of the tobacco market. Serious health warnings on tobacco packets, smoking being restricted in public places, and a ban on advertising of tobacco-related products are some of the issues that PMFL has to deal with.

On the HRM side, the Occupational Health and Safety of the employees is a primary concern to the company. There are stringent guidelines and notices placed in the manufacturing area regarding employee safety. One of the most important HRM policies of this company is that employees have their safety gear on while they are in the manufacturing area. Employees who do not adhere to this policy have to face stringent penalties. For instance, workers that do not have safety equipment on while on site have to face the disciplinary committee who decide on the penalty for the crime committed by the employee. The HRM policies on fundamental principles and rights at work; employment relations advisory board; appointments, powers and duties of officers; contracts of service; protection of wages; holidays and leave; hours of work; equal employment opportunities; children; maternity leave; redundancy for economic, technological or structural reasons; employment grievances; registration of trade unions; rights and liabilities of trade unions; collective bargaining; employment disputes; strikes and lockouts; protection of essential services, life and property; institutions and offences are all guided by the Employment

---

Relations Promulgation (2007) and the Essential National Industries (Employment) Decree 2011. The PMFL uses its own discretion in managing labour employed from other countries. This company also gives priority to team work, employee empowerment and quality circles to improve the quality of the products. The PMFL workers are unionised and dispute resolution machinery is effectively set out in the collective bargaining agreement. This company is trying its level best to effectively manage employees in the light of the economic downturn that it is currently facing. Some of the factors that have shaped the HRM practices adopted by the PMFL include economic factors, political factors, societal factors, the characteristics of the workforce, competitive intensity and the characteristics of the company. Currently, the global economic pressures from the Italy debt crisis and the political instability of Fiji are having considerable impact on the earnings of the PMFL.

Primarily, the workers employed by the PMFL can be divided into two categories. The first category consists of those who are highly educated and skilled. These workers are the core employees of the organisation and they are motivated for best performance. The second group of workers are from the uneducated category. As PMFL is an MNC with cohesive and internationally recognised labour practices, the company treats the uneducated group of workers as being as important as the educated group of workers. This company also believes that profits could be improved if synergy could be achieved between both groups of workers.

Recently, many changes have occurred in the HRM function of PMFL. In particular, the implementation of the Essential National Industries (Employment) Decree 2011 has resulted in key mandatory changes to the HRM policies and practices. Some of these changes include re-registering of the existing registered trade unions under the Employment Relations Promulgation (2007), replacement of all existing collective bargaining agreements and suspension of the majority of trade union activities such as job actions, strikes, slowdowns and any form of financially harmful activity. These new clauses of the Essential National Industries (Employment) Decree 2011 make it obligatory for PMFL to change the collective bargaining and grievance handling function of the HRM.

According to the HR manager, the contemporary legal, political and economic pressures are making the task of managing employees in the PMFL very challenging. The HR manager also indicated in his interview that the future of HRM at the PMFL is very strong for the employees. Employees are the key asset to the company and managing employees effectively and efficiently is one of the priority concerns for PMFL.

Discussion Questions

1. Why is Occupational Health and Safety (OHS) a primary concern for the PMFL? Explain with examples.
2. Describe the employee management model practiced by PMFL. Explain with examples.
3. Explain some of the factors that are affecting the HRM function of PMFL.
4. Explain the impact of the newly implemented Essential National Industries (Employment) Decree 2011 on the employee management practices at PMFL.
5. Why is managing employees a challenging task for PMFL?

Conclusion

This chapter has discussed the HRM environment in the Fiji islands. The first section of this chapter outlined the historical development of personnel management, industrial relations, employment relations, HRM and SHRM in the Fiji islands. The second section of this chapter outlined the role of the state, trade unions, employer association, non-government organisations (NGOs), donor agencies and trading partners in the HRM environment. The third section outlined the endogenous and exogenous environmental factors that affect HRM practices. The fourth section discussed the key changes in the HRM function. The fifth section examined the key challenges and the future of HRM in the Fiji islands. The final section provides the case study of PMFL.

Useful websites

www.usp.ac.fj/editorial/jpacs_new/Snell.PDF

https://ojs.lib.byu.edu/spc/index.php/PacificStudies/article/viewFile/9853/9502

www.asu.asn.au/media/all-airlines-bulletin14-110919-factsheet.pdf

www.fijitimes.com/story.aspx?id=175648

www.fijitimes.com/story.aspx?id=175648

www.stuff.co.nz/world/south-pacific/5621934/Top-NZ-lawyer-criticises-Fijis-suppression

www.ilo.org/global/about-the-ilo/lang--en/index.htm

www.ilo.org/public/english/bureau/program/dwcp/download/fiji.pdf

http://news.smh.com.au/breaking-news-world/new-fiji-decree-hits-unions-20110809-1ikja.html

Note

1 This is a pseudonym and not the real name. The real identity of the company is not revealed as this was one of the conditions attached by the company when permission was granted to study the HRM practices.

References

Anthony, F. (2011) *Regime Enforces Repressive Decree*, Fiji Trades Union Congress. Fiji Islands: Des Vouex Road Suva.

Australian Council of Trade Unions (2011) *Union Condemn Fiji's Continued Attack on Work Rights*, Press Release, 12 September. Australia: ACTU.

Baljekal, R. (2010) *Building Human Capital: A strategic perspective*, Leaders' Forum, 29 March, Statham Campus. Fiji: University of the South Pacific.

Budhwar, P. S. and Debrah, Y. (2001) 'Rethinking comparative and cross national human resource management research', *The International Human Resource Management Journal* 12(3): 497–515.

Budhwar, P. S., and Sparrow, P. R. (2002) 'An integrative framework for understanding cross national human resource management practices', *The International Human Resource Management Journal* 12(3): 377–403.

Chand, A. (2011) *Global Supply Chains in the South Pacific Region: A study of Fiji's garment industry*. New York: Nova Science Publishers.

Chand, A., and Naidu, S. (2010) 'The Role of the state and Fiji Council of Social Services in service delivery in Fiji', *International NGO Journal* 5(8): 185–93.

Chaudhary, F. (2011) 'Threat worry', *Fiji Times*, 21 July, p. 1.

Chu, P., and Siu, W. (2001) 'Coping with the Asian economic crisis: The right sizing strategies for the small and medium sized enterprises', *The International Journal of Human Resource Management* 12(5): 845–858.

Commonwealth Secretariat (2009) *Small States: Economic review and basic statistics*. London: Commonwealth Secretariats Publication House.

Elek, A., Hill, H. and Tabor, S. R. (1993) 'Liberalisation and diversification in a small island economy: Fiji since 1987 coups', *World Development*, 21(5): 749–69.

Fiji Employers and Commerce Association (2011) *Fiji Employers Federation Research Report*, Press Release, 25 October. Fiji: FEF.

Gillion, K. L. (1962) *Fiji's Indian Migrants: A history to the end of indenture in 1920*. Melbourne: Oxford University Press.

Ministry of Labour Fiji (2011) *Essential National Industries (Employment) Decree*. Government Printers: Fiji Islands.

Government of the Republic of Fiji (2009) *National Employment Centre Decree: 2009*. Suva. Fiji Islands.

ILO (2010) *Decent Work Country Programme: Fiji*. Switzerland: Geneva.

ILO (2012) *About the ILO*. Switzerland: Geneva.

Irvine, H. J. (2004) *Sweet and Sour: Harbouring for South Sea islanders labour at the North Queensland Sugar Mill in the 1800's*, Working Paper, Faculty of Commerce. Australia: University of Wollongong.

Leckie, J. (2003) 'Trade union rights, legitimacy, and politics under Fiji's post coup interim administration', *The Journal of Pacific Studies* 16(3): 87–113.

Naidu, S. (2011a) 'Economic challenges imposed by employment relations promulgation (2007) on the private sector of Fiji', *Asia Pacific Journal of Research in Business Management* 2(11): 82–98.

Naidu, S. (2011b) *Employers Awareness on the Employment Relations Promulgation (2007): Challenges for contemporary and future employment relations*. Germany: Lambert Academic Publishing.

Naidu, S. (2012a) 'The economic impact index of the employment relations Promulgation (2007) on the Fiji Islands', *International Journal of Business Growth and Competition* 2(2): 152–64.

Naidu, S. (2012b) 'The nexus between human resource management practices and employment law in the Fiji Islands: A study of the employment relations promulgation', *International Journal of Entrepreneurship and Small Business* (in press).

Naidu, S., and Chand, A. (2012) 'A comparative study of the financial obstacles faced by the micro, small and medium enterprises in the manufacturing sector of Fiji and Tonga', *International Journal of Emerging Markets* 7(3) (in press).

Naidu, V. (2004) *Violence of Indenture in Fiji*. Fiji Islands: Institute of Applied Science.

Pacific Islands Forum (PIF) (2009) *2009 Statement to Pacific Island Forum Trade Ministers Regarding Deliberations on Potential PACER-Plus Negotiations*. Suva: Fiji Islands.

Pathak, R. D., Budhwar, P. S., Singh, V. and Hannas, P. (2005) 'Best HRM practices and employees' psychological outcomes: A study of shipping companies in Cyprus', *South Asian Journal of Management* 12(4): 7–24.

Pathak, R. D., Chauhan, V. S., Dhar, U. and Gramberg, B. V. (2009) 'Managerial effectiveness as a function of culture and tolerance of ambiguity: A cross cultural study of India and Fiji', *International Employment Relations Review* 15(1): 74–90.

Prasad, S., Hince, K., and Snell, D. (2002) *Employment and Industrial Relations in the South Pacific: Samoa, the Cook Islands, Kiribati, Solomon Islands, Vanuatu, Fiji Islands*. Australia: McGraw-Hill.

Reddy, S. (2010) *The Future of Fiji's Economy*, Presentation to the Fiji Institute of Accountants. Fiji Islands: Suva.

Schuler, R. S., and Jackson, S. E. (2007) *Strategic Human Resource Management*, 2nd edn. USA: Blackwell Publishing.

Snell, D. (2000) 'Globalisation and workplace reforms in two regional agri-Food industries: Australian meat processing and Fiji's sugar mills', *The Journal of Pacific Studies* 24(1): 51–76.

Storey, D. (2004) *The Fiji Garment Industry*. Oxfam. New Zealand.

Sziraczki, G., Huynh, P. and Kapsos, S. (2009) *The Global Economic Crisis: Labour market impacts and policies for recovery in Asia*, ILO Asia Pacific Working Paper. Switzerland: Geneva.

White, C. M. (2007) 'More authentic than thou: Authenticity and othering in Fiji tourism discourse', *Tourism Studies* 7(1): 25–49.

Human Resource Management in New Zealand

ANN HUTCHISON AND NOELLE DONNELLY

Introduction

On the surface, the development of human resource management in New Zealand follows a similar path to that of other Anglo-American countries, especially those with shared colonial pasts. However, deeper examination reveals several distinguishing aspects. This chapter begins with an overview of HRM's historical development within New Zealand. It then outlines the political, economic and cultural context within which HRM practices have emerged. Finally the chapter examines the current and future challenges facing HRM in New Zealand.

New Zealand is a small country situated far south in the Pacific Ocean. It comprises two islands, the 'North Island' (population approximately 3.3 million) and the 'South Island' (population approximately 1.1 million). While the North Island hosts the largest city, Auckland (population approximately 1.1 million), and the capital, Wellington (population approximately 400,000), the South Island is sparsely populated, known for its rugged beauty. The country's peaceful, clean image makes it one of the most visited places in the world by international tourists and immigrants alike. Furthermore, New Zealanders enjoy a high standard of living, with the country having been rated third on the United Nations' Human Development Index (United Nations Development Program, 2010).

The country itself is isolated, with its closest neighbour, Australia, being at least a three-hour flight away. Only 4.4 million people inhabit a land size that is similar to the United Kingdom (population approximately 61.8 million). This 'smallness' gives New Zealand a lower global profile than its Anglo-American counterparts; and, while multinational enterprises (MNEs) are represented on its shores, the majority of New Zealand's businesses are small to medium sized. In fact, 97 per cent of its businesses employ less than 20 employees (Statistics New Zealand, 2011a), making the small-to-medium enterprise (SME) the norm, and lending a particular flavour to the nation's HRM practices.

Although New Zealand shares a colonial history with the United Kingdom and Australia, it is culturally distinct, in that its indigenous Māori heritage makes a strong contribution to its national identity. Indigenous Māori comprise 14.6 per cent of the population (Statistics New Zealand, 2006), and their representatives visibly contribute to government policy, social commentary and business activity. This visibility traces back to the founding document, the 1840 'Treaty of Waitangi', signed by Māori leaders and the British crown (King, 2007). An important and sometimes contested part of New Zealand's historical context, that treaty today symbolises the importance of New Zealand's indigenous heritage and renders cultural diversity an important HRM consideration.

Historical Development of HRM

Phase I: The Early Years: A 'Very' British Heritage

The development of HRM in New Zealand has been shaped by historical ties with the 'mother country', Britain (Ransom, 1966), resulting in the mirroring of British HRM practices. Like other Anglo-American countries, HRM progressively shifted from an administrative to a strategic business function, while concurrently pursuing a professionalization agenda, requiring qualifications and specific expertise among its members (Toulson and DeFryn, 2006).

Not only can the development of HRM in New Zealand be traced back to British welfarist notions, elements of which remain today (Toulson and DeFryn, 2006), but a clear administrative focus is also evident in its early development (Rudman, 2010). The first personnel officers arrived in New Zealand with large overseas MNEs, their role being to administer head office policies. Employment relationships at that time were tightly regulated through a number of laws beginning with the Trade Unions Act 1878, the Factories Act 1891, 1894, the Employment of Females Act 1873, the Industrial Conciliation and Arbitration Act 1894 and the Public Service Act 1912. As a result, personnel administrators had a straightforward role to play in labour management (Bryson, 2006; Toulson and DeFryn, 2006).

That picture changed with World War II, which led to labour shortages and attraction and retention challenges (Toulson and DeFryn, 2006). It was at this time that MNEs started to enter the country, further exacerbating those difficulties. Personnel officers started to play a bigger role, using health and safety to attract and retain staff, tackling issues such as absenteeism and on-site welfare (Bryson, 2006). These activities, although basic, heralded the beginnings of the HRM profession and by the 1950s businesses had started to recruit specialist personnel experts (Toulson and DeFryn, 2006).

Phase II: The Path to Professionalism

From the mid-1950s the HR profession in New Zealand began to evolve, with HRM practices such as development, performance management and reward becoming more innovative (Cleland, Pajo, and Toulson, 2000; Toulson and

DeFryn, 2006). Early attempts to professionalise began with the 1956 formation of the Personnel Managers Association, which eventually grew into the New Zealand Institute of Personnel Management (NZIPM), under the governance of the New Zealand Institute of Management (NZIM). The first two decades of the NZIPM were directed towards growing membership and setting professional performance standards. In 1985 the Institute of Personnel Management (NZ) set itself up as an independent national organization, and its focus grew to encompass continuing professional development. By 1999 it was rebranded as the Human Resources Institute New Zealand (HRINZ), the professional body that remains today. From a membership base of 220 in 1986, HRINZ has grown to 3,900 members in 2010, representing 52 per cent of the known HR workforce in New Zealand (HRINZ, 2011a).

Phase III: Embracing All Things Strategic

The 1980s represented a turning point, with a 'new' philosophy espousing HRM's strategic value widely touted (Beer *et al.*, 1984; Fombrun, Tichy, and Devanna, 1984; Guest, 1989). The ascendency of strategic HRM principles raised HRM professionals' awareness of their potential contributions, and called for them to demonstrate their role's value to employers (Toulson and DeFryn, 2006). New Zealand also began to experience extensive economic and political change, businesses were downsizing, and there was a need for increasingly thoughtful HRM (Toulson and DeFryn, 2006), all of which led to higher pro-activity among HRM professionals. Despite pro-active intentions, however, HRM professionals reported struggling credibility, lamenting that they were 'firefighting' rather than adding value (Cleland, Pajo and Toulson, 2000; Toulson and DeFryn, 2006). Only one-third of HRM professionals reported to the chief executive (Gilbertson, 1984), suggesting that HRM was still not being given substantial influence.

During the 1990s, the HRM profession gained a slightly higher strategic profile in New Zealand, shown by Stablein and Geare's (1993) survey and Cleland, Pajo and Toulson's (2000) exploration of that period. HRM professionals increased in number over this decade and New Zealand's universities started to offer HRM education, resulting in a dramatic increase in the percentage of HRM professionals who were tertiary qualified, from 37 per cent in 1990 to 85 per cent in 1998. By 2000, 48 per cent of HR professionals reported taking a more strategic focus than previously, and 34 per cent reported an increasingly value-added focus (Cleland, Pajo and Toulson, 2000).

The Level of Business–HR Partnership

The level of business–HR partnership can be seen in the extent to which HRM (a) is represented at a senior management level, (b) contributes to business strategy, and (c) is devolved to line managers, so that HRM professionals can focus on strategic decision making (Lawler and Mohrman, 2003). On the first matter, it would appear that New Zealand's largest organisations have an HR executive reporting to the chief executive, although Rasmussen, Andersen and Haworth (2010) have found that only 40 per cent of small, medium and large organizations had an HRM expert in their senior management team and other surveys have found similar figures for board representation (Cleland, Pajo and Toulson, 2000; Johnson and Mouly, 2002).

In terms of strategy, HR professionals appear to be operating at a reasonably strategic level. Rasmussen, Andersen and Haworth (2010) reported that 79 per cent of organizations have HR contributions to corporate strategy, although the extent of involvement varies and that 60 per cent have a written HR strategy. Rasmussen *et al.*'s data comes from a wider global survey, known as the Cranet survey (www.cranet.org), and the data mirrors other Western countries' findings, suggesting that New Zealand's level of HRM–business partnership is not particularly unusual. Interestingly, however, the same Cranet survey was conducted in New Zealand in 1997, and produced very similar results (Johnson, 2000; Johnson and Mouly, 2002), leading to the question of whether New Zealand's business–HR partnerships have peaked in the last decade.

Devolution in New Zealand also indicates a reasonably strong HRM–business partnership. Rasmussen *et al.* (2010) show that most organizations devolve HRM activities to line managers, with the exception of employment relations issues, which tend to be more centralised. Overall, then, it seems that New Zealand's HRM profession is reasonably engaged in business partnership. However, since the above surveys, New Zealand has been through an economic crisis (Reserve Bank of New Zealand, 2011), which will have inevitably shifted the foci of HR professionals towards downsizing and other business-survival activities. Further research is now needed to explore how recent factors have affected HRM-business partnership.

Key Factors Determining HRM Practices and Policies

Political Factors

Understanding New Zealand's HRM practices requires a deeper look at the political frameworks that govern employment relationships and, in particular, the historical development behind today's political system. Some of the first employment laws, implemented by British settlers, reflected a traditional British approach to class conflict, perpetuated by the New Zealand government's efforts to control employment relationships (Bryson, 2006; Deeks and Rasmussen, 2002). New Zealand's industrial relations were dominated by a national system of compulsory conciliation and arbitration for most of the twentieth century (Deeks and Rasmussen, 2002). Along with Australia, New Zealand was distinctive in adopting this system of labour regulation, but even more unique in adopting it almost a centenary earlier than Australia.

While the introduction of the Industrial Conciliation and Arbitration Act 1894 was designed to facilitate the settlement of industrial disputes, it also became a mechanism for the control and constraint of wage policy (Barry and Wailes,

2004). Furthermore, it strengthened the role of trade unions, ensured that settlements were legally binding and limited the use of strike action and lockouts (Rasmussen, 2010). The impact was 'primarily one of centralisation, state involvement and a legalistic, adversarial approach to employment relations' (Deeks and Rasmussen, 2002: 54). In short, until 1984 the industrial relations system was characterised by government intervention.

The year 1984 is regarded as a 'watershed' year in New Zealand politics (Allen, Brosnan, and Walsh, 1999; Bray and Walsh, 1998). A change of government led to one of the most radical deregulation programmes across the Organisation for Economic Co-operation and Development (OECD). Almost overnight New Zealand abandoned protectionism, opening its economy to the full force of global competition. The New Zealand 'experiment', as it became known, resulted in the deregulation of financial markets, currency flotation and the privatization of state services (Allen, Brosnan, and Walsh, 1999; Barry and Wailes, 2004).

A major cornerstone of the reform programme was the restructuring of government structures. Through the State Sector Act 1988 and the State-Owned Enterprises Act 1986 significant HRM changes in the public sector were introduced. New Zealand became a 'world leader' in its adoption of New Public Management (NPM) principles to 'modernise' its public sector by introducing private sector management practices and strategic HRM into a public sector environment (Whitcombe, 2008).

A change in government in 1990 saw a response to mounting pressure from employer groups. With the introduction of the Employment Contracts Act (ECA) 1991 almost 100 years of conciliation and arbitration were removed. That act made unionism voluntary and gave all employees access to grievance procedures and rights to individual bargaining, representing a shift from collectivism to individualism (Rasmussen and Lamm, 2005). The political thinking was that such changes would promote higher productivity. The ECA resulted in what some refer to as a regulatory avalanche, giving rise to personal grievances and a shift toward individual contracts (Cullihane and Donald, 2000).

The most recent legislative shift came with the election of a centre-left government in 2000. With the introduction of the Employment Relations Act (ERA) 2000, that government tried to institute a return to collectivism (Rasmussen, 2010), giving greater support to unions, adding employment contracting constraints and encouraging 'good faith bargaining'. Interestingly, however, despite this shift, union density has remained static. Having dropped in the 1990s, it now sits at about the 20 per cent mark (Blumenfeld and Ryall, 2011). Despite attempts to revive union rights, the expectations of the ERA have yet to materialise (Rasmussen, 2010). If anything, the support for collectivism has paradoxically resulted in a decline in collective agreement coverage in the private sector. Recent commentators suggest that the legacy of the 1990s remains, with a rise in individual employee rights and individualised employment relationships (Rasmussen and Lamm, 2005).

Now, New Zealand's government is led by the centre-right National Party, elected in 2008. That government has retained the ERA, but made a number of changes to employment legislation, diminishing employee protection and union support, and further strengthening the individualistic focus (the Employment Relations Amendment Act 2010; Holidays Amendment Act 2010). The current legislation seeks to strike a balance between protecting employee rights and allowing organisations' freedom, taking the form of various protective legal requirements that stipulate minimum workers' rights (the Holidays Act 2003, the Human Rights Act 1993, the Privacy Act 1993, and the Health and Safety in Employment Act 1992).

Economic Context

Over recent decades the New Zealand economy has transformed from a protected agrarian economy, dependent on preferential trading arrangements with Britain, to an open, industrialised, free-market, mixed economy (New Zealand Treasury, 2010). The preferential trading arrangement with Britain, for the exporting of agricultural products, contributed to high standards of living during the 1950s (Bryson, 2006). However, when Britain joined the European Economic Community in 1973, New Zealand lost its main export market. In 1955 65.3 per cent of New Zealand's exports went to Britain, by 1973 that figure had declined to 26.8 per cent and today stands at 2.9 per cent (Statistics New Zealand, 2010). While economic independence led to a greater focus on national identity and sustainability (Toulson and DeFryn, 2006), it also led to a decline in productivity from the 1950s onwards. Recognising the need to compete globally, the newly elected government in 1984 set about liberalising the economy, as noted earlier, with the introduction of the New Zealand experiment (Hawke, 1985).

Concurrently, the government sought to increase its international engagement in the pacific through a number of free trade agreements and the building of its 'closer economic relations' with Australia where there is free trade in goods and most services between the two countries. These agreements have rendered the nation's businesses vulnerable to off-shore competition and have enabled overseas businesses to play an active role in local commerce. Importantly for HRM, the increase in global trade has increased the need for New Zealand to develop the skills to do business in the Asia-Pacific region.

Today the New Zealand economy is based on an export-oriented primary sector (agriculture, farming, forestry and fisheries), a relatively small manufacturing sector and a fast-growing services sector (Statistics New Zealand, 2011b). It relies heavily on its agricultural exports, which comprise half of the total exports sent to Australia, China, Japan and the United States (New Zealand Treasury, 2010). Despite this emphasis on goods and agriculture, however, the Department of Labour (2010) notes that New Zealand's knowledge economy has the potential to raise productivity, suggesting that New Zealand needs to be increasing its research and development skills, innovation, and managerial professionalism.

Overall, New Zealand's economy is comparatively advanced. However, similar to many Western economies, New Zealand went into recession in 2008 for five successive quarters. Although the economy has recovered, productivity remains of concern, being among the lowest in the OECD (Sloman and Malinen, 2010; Statistics New Zealand, 2011b). The government believes that skills development holds the key to improvement, but also notes that the nation has serious skills shortages (Sloman and Malinen, 2010), thus raising the importance of human resource development initiatives within organisations, industries and professions. HRM's role in enhancing productivity was borne out in a recent report that examined the performance of New Zealand manufacturing firms relative to their global counterparts. The research, undertaken by the London School of Economics and McKinsey and Co., found that New Zealand firms did indeed have lower productivity than their counterparts, and that a poor approach to 'people management' appeared to be the main differentiating factor. The report recommended that New Zealand firms pay particular attention to building management capability, particularly around HRM practices (Green and Agarwal, 2011).

Despite signs of economic recovery, recent reports suggest that the outlook remains fragile with recovery shallower than anticipated (Nicholls, 2012). Such tight economic conditions continue to exert downward pressure on wages, particularly within the public sector (Blumenfeld, Kiely and Ryall, 2011; *New Zealand Herald*, 2012a). Furthermore, cost-containment strategies have seen some firms adopt 'harder' approaches to performance management, and more recent attempts to renegotiate collective agreements have resulted in a number of strikes and lockouts (Edwards, 2012). Despite the need to retain and attract staff, it appears that the economic climate is simply constraining the ability of organisations to take 'softer' approaches to HRM.

Business Environment

The demographic landscape of New Zealand businesses is largely populated by small to medium enterprises, with a smaller population of multinational enterprises (foreign- and domestic-owned) and indigenous Māori-owned firms. This large representation of SMEs within New Zealand presents HRM challenges, as the visible and resource-intensive practices in large MNEs may not be appropriate for smaller businesses, given their need for flexibility (Gilbert and Jones, 2000). Recent research into the HRM practices of SMEs revealed that most operate informal HR practices that they see as facilitating employee engagement and loyalty (Massey *et al.*, 2006).

There are few economies where geographic location is more of an issue than New Zealand. While many point to the need to overcome 'the tyranny of distance' (Gyngell, Skilling and Thirlwell, 2007), others suggest that New Zealand businesses have a relative advantage in being located closer to key Asian markets (Donnelly and Dowling, 2010). In an attempt to overcome their relative isolation, New Zealand businesses have increasingly begun to offshore and outsource key aspects of their operations, closer to overseas consumers.

Many of New Zealand's businesses are owned off-shore, particularly those in the banking and retail sectors (Boxall & Frenkel, 2012), and for Australian-owned companies, the New Zealand operation tends to take the form of a regional office, with policies dictated by the Australian head office. Numerous MNEs have small offices in New Zealand and operate centralised approaches to HRM. Such practices can be sub-optimal, however, if not tailored to the New Zealand context.

Quite separately, Māori-owned businesses, owned by Māori tribes or collectives, make a substantial contribution to the nation's economy, particularly in terms of tourism, fishing and forestry. Such businesses, although profit-seeking, tend to focus more heavily on social goals rather than on mainstream businesses, and Māori values, such as collectivity and inclusiveness, feature heavily in their objectives. While further research is needed to explore HRM practices in Māori businesses, it is likely that pay, staffing and development in those organisations look quite different to the mainstream.

In general the demography of New Zealand businesses presents a particular set of challenges for their respective HRM functions: For SMEs there is a need to understand and evaluate the more sophisticated practices of larger organisations; for domestic MNEs the role of HRM in managing the dilemma of global integration and local differentiation is key; for the subsidiaries of foreign-owned MNEs the issue of localising to the New Zealand context is imperative; and, finally, for Māori businesses the adaptation of HRM practices to collective values is key.

Cultural Factors

Although the blend of British and Māori heritage has led some to label New Zealand 'bicultural' (Jones, Pringle, and Shepherd, 2000, p. 367), 'multicultural' is a more widely used term, given that 9.2 per cent of the population is Asian, and 6.9 per cent come from the Pacific Islands, in addition to 14.6 per cent being Māori (Statistics New Zealand, 2006). Ultimately, this multiculturalism makes diversity an HRM challenge. It is questionable, for example, whether New Zealand's Anglo-American models of management, such as performance management practices that are geared around individual achievement, are suitable for Māoris and Asians, who typically hold collectivist values (Haar and Delaney, 2009; Hofstede, 2005).

New Zealand also has one of the world's lowest scores in power distance (Hofstede, 2005), meaning that it is common to see managers behave in ways that are informal and egalitarian (Inkson, Henshall, and Marsh, 1986). Compared to organisations in the United States and in the United Kingdom, New Zealand workers report higher levels of management consultation and employee discretion (Boxall, Haynes, and Macky, 2007)

The increase in New Zealand's cultural diversity, and the unique characteristics of the Asian and Māori cultures in particular, render diversity-management practices important, not only at the policy level, but also in the practices that managers adopt to interact, coach and manage different ethnicities in the workplace.

Review of HRM Practices

We now present four core areas of HRM practice that best capture New Zealand's points of HRM difference. These areas are staffing (that is, recruitment and selection), development, performance management, and reward. We acknowledge that there are other HRM activities, but it is these four broad functions that form the 'core' of HRM practice in New Zealand, and when combined, it is these four that have the greatest potential to address New Zealand's skills shortages and productivity issues.

Staffing

New Zealand's skills shortages have intensified the need for effective staffing practices, with almost half of employers reporting difficulties in filling positions (Hudson, 2011). Literature is sparse, however, on whether employers in the current economic climate are investing in recruitment innovations to tackle these shortages.

Certainly, organisations in the public sector do display care in recruitment and selection, as the State Sector Act 1988 requires documented practices, clear policies, panel interviews, structured interview questions and reference checks. That said, the ultimate purpose in setting such constraints is that public sector organisations will be 'good employers'. Whether these processes are as effective as they could be for attraction and retention is unclear.

An obvious strategy for attracting skilled staff would be to cast the recruitment net globally, particularly to Australia, whose citizens do not need work permits to work in New Zealand. Historically, this has been the case to some extent; Johnson (2000) has reported that one-fifth of SMEs and one-third of large organisations have deliberately targeted the overseas labour market (Johnson, 2000). The Internet presents a good opportunity to reach the global labour market, but based on a study of 1,229 employers across diverse industries, Clark *et al.* (2001) reported that only 26 per cent were recruiting staff online. Our observation suggests that online recruitment has since increased, although recent data on this practice do not appear to be available.

The 1997 Cranet data showed that internal recruitment was a more popular staffing strategy than overseas recruitment (Johnson, 2000). In that sample, about 70 per cent of employers invested in internal development to meet skill needs, with 72 per cent recruiting middle managers from within. However, internal development was not working well for filling leadership positions, as most employers (70 per cent) were using executive search or recruitment agencies for senior roles.

In fact, the recruitment industry has developed in recent years, becoming more widely used (HRINZ, 2011b), and innovative. For example, recruitment consultants have embraced psychometric testing, with 89 per cent conducting personality tests during selection, and 64 per cent conducting cognitive ability tests (less common than usage within organisations; Taylor, Keelty and McDonnell, 2002). Furthermore, 37 per cent use assessment centres in their selection processes – more so than organisations themselves (10–14 per cent) – indicating a move towards innovative practices on the parts of consultants.

Despite the recruitment industry's move towards value-adding activities, New Zealand's selection practices lag behind what research shows to be effective. While the largest organisations tend to use more panel interviews, psychometric assessments and a larger variety of selection techniques than other nations (Ryan *et al.*, 1999), only 9 per cent of organisations (large, medium and small) structure their reference checks, only 43 per cent use behavioural or situational interview questions (a finding supported by Hudson, 2011, and Johnson, 2000), only half of assessment centres are conducted by a well-trained assessor, and only 50 per cent of organisations and 10 per cent of consultants rate applicants in a structured way during selection (Taylor et al., 2002). In fact, when asked which methods had the greatest predictive validity, most HR professionals and recruitment consultants did not know (Taylor, Keelty and McDonnell, 2002), suggesting that, although so-called 'best practice' is used in New Zealand, selection practices may not be implemented as thoughtfully as they could be.

Furthermore, some practices are completely absent. In Taylor *et al.*'s (2002) study of 200 organisations and 30 recruitment consultants, none said that they conduct a systematic job analysis based on critical incidents prior to recruitment, although some do use existing position descriptions to shape their selection practices. Also, none reported that they use personality data in a way that is tailored towards the specifications of a given role, despite research that shows how important this is (for example, Hogan and Holland, 2003).

Human Resource Development

Human resource development (HRD) is seen by the government as critical in helping New Zealand address skills shortages and raise its productivity (Sloman and Malinen, 2010). On a national level, however, HRD tends to be deregulated, happening very much at the organisational level. This is different to, say, Europe, which has a stronger emphasis on government-regulated apprenticeships and vocational training (Winterton, 2007). That said, New Zealand does have industry training organisations (ITOs), which develop accredited training programmes for certain industries and go some way towards raising skill levels (see www.itf.org. nz for further details of how these organisations operate).

At the organisational level, employers spend an average of 2.5 per cent of salary on HRD, which is slightly higher than in Europe (2 per cent) (Johnson, 2000). Furthermore, it seems that, through the global economic crisis, and despite inevitable budgetary constraints, employers have sought to retain an emphasis on HRD (EEO Trust, 2009). Nevertheless, although HRD investment is occurring, wider methods of development beyond traditional training are somewhat lacking, which perhaps reflects a lack of resources and expertise among SMEs.

The Cranfield data, for example, showed that only one quarter of employers used development methods besides training, with only 26 per cent of employers conducting succession planning, 25 per cent doing developmental job rotation, 22 per cent using formal career plans, 17 per cent using expatriate assignments, 14 per cent using high-flier schemes and 10 per cent using assessment centres (Johnson, 2000). Since then, HRD practices do not appear to have changed substantially. Bothwell (2010) reported that 51 per cent of organisations do not have a professional development strategy and that needs assessments happen purely by scanning performance appraisals (84 per cent), responding to line managers' requests (78 per cent), and employee requests (67 per cent). In fact, only about one half of employers used business-plan-based training at the time of the 1997 Cranet survey (Johnson, 2000). Furthermore, although most employers (75 per cent) try to measure their HRD effectiveness, none evaluate it comprehensively, using *all* of Kirkpatrick's (1998) four measures (reaction, learning, behaviour, and results). Finally, it appears that investments are not extending substantially to leadership and management development. Bothwell (2010), for example, surveyed 75 HR professionals about their organisations' practice and found that only 48 per cent of organisations have leadership development programs and 60 per cent spend less than NZ$2,000 (US$1,672) per manager on development. Admittedly this is a relatively small sample, but the results do suggest that New Zealand's HRD practices are perhaps not as innovative as academics may hope, and they have not moved substantially beyond traditional training.

Performance Management

Overall, research on performance management advocates a shift from traditional form-filling performance appraisal to more strategy-driven and continuous ways of defining, measuring and encouraging performance (Latham, *et al.*, 2005), but is this shift actually happening in New Zealand? Certainly, our observation suggests that larger organisations are trying to take thoughtful, systematic and integrated approaches to performance management, but once again, anecdotally it appears that resources constrain the practices of smaller organisations.

Generally, traditional performance appraisal is widely implemented, with only 10 per cent of organisations reporting that they do not conduct regular appraisals, and organisations frequently reporting that they use multi-source data (that is, data from peers, subordinates and/or customers) in their appraisal processes (Johnson, 2000). Usually, the employee has the opportunity to contribute to their appraisal and participate actively in the process (Johnson, 2000), which is perhaps reflective of the participative management approach noted earlier in the chapter.

Beyond traditional methods, however, New Zealand research shows that some organisations are moving towards more innovative approaches to performance management. Most notably, Walsh, Bryson and Lonti (2002) conducted a study to explore the HRM practices of New Zealand's most successful companies. They found that strategy-driven performance management was a factor that characterised these successful organisations. Most notably, these organisations deliberately used performance management to enhance agility and flexibility, focusing on values and desired behaviours instead of constraining employees to particular duties (Walsh, Bryson and Lonti, 2002). This reinforces the earlier argument that strategy-driven approaches to performance management are desirable, but whether these approaches are reaching New Zealand's smaller businesses is unclear, and further research is needed to explore the national prevalence of innovative performance management.

Rewards

The global economic crisis has raised the need for organisations to develop prudent salary budgets, and will have inevitably affected their ability to use rewards as an attraction and retention tool. Supporting this, very little movement was seen in remuneration levels over 2009 and 2010, with only marginal increases of about 1 per cent (Department of Labour, 2011a). Over that period, wage freezes and chief executive pay cuts were common (Doughty, 2010; Strategic Pay, 2011).

Under normal circumstances, these cuts and freezes may have affected job satisfaction and retention. However, New Zealand's reward consultancies have reported a concurrent shift in employees' priorities, with employees reporting acceptance of pay freezes in the current economic environment, and a gratitude for job security (Strategic Pay, 2009), and perhaps reward has become less salient for employees than in buoyant times. Now that the economy is seeing moderate improvement, however, employers are forecasting moderate pay increases once again (Doughty, 2010), which may prompt shifts in employees' priorities.

We observe that innovative approaches to reward in New Zealand have been encouraged by several local, boutique reward-consultancies, all of whom have used practitioner literature, local conference presentations and widely marketed workshops, to raise the awareness of approaches like broad banding and competency-based pay. That said, traditional approaches are still alive and well. For example, job evaluation remains popular, with the Hay scheme having a strong and loyal customer base. In the public sector especially, job evaluation is common, forming part of the *State Sector Act's* centralised approach (Walsh et al., 2002).

To our knowledge, there is no literature to confirm the incidence of the various approaches to reward. However, local reward consultants state that variable pay is on the increase. Even in 2000, two-thirds of employers used performance-related pay of some sort; with 80 per cent of employers using merit pay, 30 per cent using group bonuses, 20 per cent using individual commission, 22 per cent using profit sharing, and 18 per cent of organisations using stock options despite the small size of the New Zealand stock market (Johnson, 2000). Consultants' observations that variable pay has increased further will mean that it is a strong feature of reward practices in New Zealand.

In terms of benefits, 25 per cent of organisations use flexible benefits plans, incorporating the usual range of benefits – including cars, healthcare and pension schemes. However, childcare allowances and career break schemes tend to be rare, in the order of 5 per cent (Johnson, 2000). Interestingly, a recent survey of 1,139 New Zealand workers found that flexible working hours are the most desired non-monetary job perk (New Zealand Management, 2011).

Key Challenges Facing HRM and the Future of HRM

Demographic Shifts

The HRM profession faces several challenges within New Zealand, many of which relate to projected demographic shifts. While New Zealand has long been a 'substantial hub for migrants' (Inkson and Maani, 2011: 1), in recent years the composition of those migrants has changed. While most

(67.7 per cent) New Zealanders identify themselves as European, the fastest-growing ethnic group is Asian (Department of Labour, 2008). Census figures reveal that the Asian population increased by 104 per cent from 1996 to 2006 (Statistics New Zealand, 2006). It is anticipated to increase to 15 per cent by 2026 (Badkar and Tuya, 2010). This anticipated growth in the Asian work-force represents a significant future source of skilled labour (Badkar and Tuya, 2010), but also requires greater understanding of the diverse work approaches of different ethnic groups.

The New Zealand labour force has also become older and is projected to continue ageing over the next 20 years, due to increases in life-expectancy, declines in fertility rates and the ageing of the baby-boomer generation (Stephenson and Scobie, 2002). By 2020 one in four workers will be 55 years or over (Department of Labour, 2009). Similar to the Asian population, older workers are a potential source of knowledgeable labour, but as they retire they will leave gaps in the workforce. Representative groups of older workers have called on organisations to provide flexible work arrangements, opportunities to up-skill, and suitable workplace ergonomics in the employment of older workers (Department of Labour, 2009).

Globalisation

For a small open economy like New Zealand, exposure to the costs and benefits of globalisation is heightened. Some of those costs became visible with the global financial crisis, which hit New Zealand hard and inevitably had an impact on HRM. Employers became less able to invest in innovative HRM practices, but still needed to retain high-performing staff in preparation for the inevitable, but unpredictable, upturn – calling for innovative, but minimal-cost HRM tactics.

One benefit of globalisation, however, is the opportunity for organisations to integrate their production or service provision systems, and outsource and offshore those operations, thus saving costs and locating closer to key markets (Skilling and Boven, 2006). Such a model allows businesses to expand in a low-cost manner and to overcome skill shortages. With cheaper labour nearby, in emerging economies, it is now possible for New Zealand organisations to outsource high-value work. The outsourcing and offshoring of production systems raises significant HRM challenges in terms of international management.

Another outcome of globalisation is the international mobility of labour. Alongside the large numbers of migrants entering New Zealand, there is concern about the large number of skilled people leaving New Zealand. This outward migration of skilled labour has resulted in much discussion about the 'brain drain', or 'talent flow'. In 2006 it was reported that a quarter of a million New Zealand-born people were working in Australia (Haig, 2010), and that higher income levels are the driving force behind the decision of many New Zealanders to migrate to Australia. Using 2006 census figures, average incomes were estimated to be 25 per cent higher in Australia than in New Zealand (Haig, 2010), presenting retention challenges for New Zealand organisations.

Skills Challenges

In the next 10 years it is expected that New Zealand will face skills challenges or 'supply constraints', especially for professional roles (Department of Labour, 2010, p. 2). Higher levels of outward migration, an ageing population and increased reliance on knowledge work, all contribute to skills challenges that New Zealand organisations face.

Skills shortages persisted even through the recent recession (EEO Trust, 2009), and will worsen once baby boomers start to retire, leaving gaps in the middle management and senior executive ranks. Although certain industries are particularly susceptible, the skills shortage is seen across all industries. While government initiatives have focused on training, academics have argued that the solution really lies in greater organisational investment in managerial coaching, peer-group learning and less formal approaches to learning (Sloman and Malinen, 2010). It is here that HRM professionals can really add value.

Investment in skills is futile, however, if those skills are not retained, so development efforts have to be matched by retention efforts. Interestingly a 2011 survey of workers by Hudson showed that about 50 per cent of people are actively or passively seeking another job, meaning that they are at least thinking of changing roles, even if they are not taking proactive steps to do so (Hudson, 2011). Employees are now becoming far more discerning and mobile, reference-checking employers, as well as vice versa (HRINZ, 2011b), requiring interesting work, and being willing to leave if that interesting work is not provided (Boxall, Macky, and Rasmussen, 2003). Over the next five years, then, intensified skills shortages will probably force organisations to be more innovative in their staffing, development and retention methods.

Changing Nature of Work

A quite separate factor has also called for quick and innovative HRM responses, and that is the fact that the nature of work has substantially changed in recent years, due to the sheer pace of technological advancement and subsequent increases in the speed and capacity to transfer information (Department of Labour, 2008).

In keeping with developments overseas, the demand for flexible working arrangements (FWAs) among New Zealand workers is significant (Fursman and Zodgekar, 2009). For organisations the benefits of FWAs are manifold: improvements to the attraction and retention of key staff, employee commitment and an ability to respond more effectively to labour market changes (Kelliher and Anderson, 2008). Within New Zealand, recent legislative changes have sought to mandate the provision of workplace flexibility. These changes include the Parental Leave and Employment Protection (Paid Parental Leave) Amendment Act (2002), the Employment Relations (Flexible Working Arrangements) Amendment Act (2007) and the Employment Relations (Breaks, Infant Feeding, and Other Matters) Amendment Act (2008). Similar to provision within the United Kingdom and Australia, employees with caring responsibilities are given the statutory 'right to request' FWAs and employers have a 'duty to consider' such requests. Recent research into women's experiences of flexible working point, however, to a number of factors that limit the uptake. Workloads, time pressures, fears of job insecurity and 'not wanting to burden their co-workers' were key reasons why FWAs were not taken up by women workers (Proctor-Thomson, Donnelly and Plimmer, 2010). The implication for HR practitioners is that the uptake of FWAs is complex and dependent on workplace contexts.

Case Study: Kiwibank

Kiwibank is a home-grown success story. Started as a government-led initiative in 2002 by the national postal service provider, New Zealand Post, its aim was to provide better value than the existing Australian-owned banks, by being a 'bank that provides real value for money, that has Kiwi values at heart, and that keeps Kiwi money where it belongs—right here, in New Zealand' (Kiwibank, 2013). Using existing Post Shops as premises, the bank trained existing shop staff to provide front-line services, quickly resulting in more branches than any other bank in New Zealand. Not only did it achieve fast growth in its customer, lending and deposit portfolios, it also won a string of awards that reflected superior customer service, value and innovation.

Why was Kiwibank so successful? Innovation, a visible part of its ethos, played a strong part throughout. For example, the bank states that it was the first to introduce customer texting, online international transfers, and weekend opening, among other things. The chief executive, Peter Brock, argues, however, that the critical success factor behind these innovations was the bank's deliberate and thoughtful HRM practices.

From the start, HRM was represented at a senior level and contributed to business strategy. A balanced scorecard approach was used to translate strategic objectives into departmental objectives, and a clear 'people plan' was implemented. Instead of using New Zealand Post's existing HRM practices, the bank recognised that its small business context and unique culture called for a different approach, developing a basic competency framework to capture the required behaviours and ethos. These competencies then guided selection and performance management, and were even communicated to a preferred recruitment agent, who assisted the bank with all staffing needs. Some 600 existing post-shop staff were given rigorous front-line training, so that they were certified to 'open shop' and train others within the business. Brock believes that this combination of formal and on-the-job training resulted in immediate increases in customers, and, using HRM metrics, he estimated the return on investment (ROI) to be 187 per cent.

Key Point

Kiwibank is a prime example of HR business partnership playing a critical role in organisational success. The case also illustrates the fact that the HRM practices of larger corporates are not always suitable for New Zealand's small businesses.

Discussion Questions

1. How have the human resource management practices supported Kiwibank's strategic position?
2. What do you think are the 'required behaviours and ethos' that Kiwibank have identified as being compatible with their business culture and context?
3. What do you see are the future HRM challenges for Kiwibank?

Sources: Brock (2011); Kiwibank (2013).

Useful Websites

Business New Zealand: www.businessnz.org.nz

Department of Labour: www.dol.govt.nz

EEO Trust: www.eeotrust.org.nz

Employers and Manufacturers Association: www.ema.co.nz

Equal Employment Opportunities Trust: www.eeotrust.org.nz

Human Resources Institute of New Zealand: www.hrinz.org.nz

The Human Rights Commission: www.hrc.co.nz

Industry Training Federation: www.itf.org.nz

New Zealand Institute of Management: www.nzim.co.nz

New Zealand Trade Development Board: www.nzte.govt.nz

NZ Council of Trade Unions: www.union.org.nz

Office of the Privacy Commissioner: www.privacy.org.nz

State Services Commission: www.ssc.govt.nz/hrframework

References

Allen, C., Brosnan, P., and Walsh, P. (1999) 'Human resource strategies, workplace reform and industrial restructuring in Australia and New Zealand', *International Journal of Human Resource Management* 10: 828–41.

Badkar, J., and Tuya, C. (2010).*The Asian Workforce: A critical part of New Zealand's current and future labour market.* Wellington, NZ: Department of Labour.

Barry, M., and Wailes, N. (2004) 'Contrasting systems? 100 years of arbitration in Australia and New Zealand', *Journal of Industrial Relations* 46: 430–47.

Beer, M., Spector, B., Lawrence, P., Quinn Mills, D., and Walton, R. (1984). *Managing Human Assets*. New York, NY: Free Press.

Blumenfeld, S., and Ryall, S. (2011) 'Unions and union membership in New Zealand: Annual review for 2008', *New Zealand Journal of Employment Relations* 35: 84–96.

Blumenfeld, S., Kiely, P. and Ryall, S. (2011) *Employment Agreements: Bargaining trends and employment law update 2010/2011*, Victoria University of Wellington, Industrial Relations Centre, New Zealand.

Bothwell, J. (2010) 'University of Otago professional development survey: Summary report', www.hrinz.org.nz/Site/Resources/Research/Research_Participation_Information_and_Results.aspx, accessed 26 October 2011.

Boxall, P. and Frenkel, S. (2012) 'Models of human resource management in Australia and New Zealand'. In C. Brewster and W. Mayrhofer (Eds), *Handbook of Research on Comparative Human Resource Management*, pp. 644–662. Cheltenham: Edward Elgar.

Boxall, P., Haynes, P., and Macky, K. (2007) 'Employee voice and voicelessness in New Zealand', in R. B. Freeman, P. Boxall, and P. Haynes (eds), *What Workers Say: Employee voice in the Anglo-American workplace*, pp. 145–165. Ithaca, NY: ILR Press.

Boxall, P., Macky, K., and Rasmussen, E. (2003) 'Labour turnover and retention in New Zealand: The causes and consequences of leaving and staying with employers', *Asia Pacific Journal of Human Resources 41:* 195–214.

Bray, M., and Walsh, P. (1998) 'Different paths to neo-liberalism? Comparing Australia and New Zealand', *Industrial Relations* 37: 358–86.

Brock, P. (2011) 'Why HR has been integral to Kiwibank's success', *Human Resources*, August/September: 8–10.

Bryson, J. (2006) 'Human resource management in New Zealand', in A. Nankervis, S. Chatterjee, and J. Coffey (eds), *Perspectives of Human Resource Management in the Asia Pacific*, pp. 111–142. Sydney, Australia: Pearson.

Clark, D., Bowden, S., Corner, P., Gibb, J., Kearins, K., and Pavlovich, K. (2001) *Adoption and Implementation of E-business in New Zealand: Empirical results*, Research Report, University of Waikato Management School.

Cleland, J., Pajo, K., and Toulson, P. (2000) 'Move it or lose it: An examination of the evolving role of the human resource professional in New Zealand', *International Journal of Human Resource Management* 11: 143–60.

Cullihane, J., and Donald, D. (2000) 'Personal grievances,' in J. Burgess and G. Strachan (eds), *Research on Work, Employment and Industrial Relations*, Proceedings of the 14th AIRAANZ Conference, Newcastle, 2–4 February, pp. 52–60.

Deeks, J., and Rasmussen, E. (2002) *Employment Relations in New Zealand*. Auckland, NZ: Pearson.

Department of Labour (2008) *Workforce 2020: Forces for change in the future labour market of New Zealand*. Wellington, NZ: Department of Labour.

Department of Labour (2009) *Understanding the job mobility and employability of older workers – synthesis report*. Wellington, New Zealand: Department of Labour.

Department of Labour (2010) *Skills Challenge Report: New Zealand's skills challenges over the next 10 years*. Wellington, NZ: Department of Labour.

Department of Labour (2011) 'Wage growth – June 2011 quarter', 2 August, www.dol.govt.nz/publications/lmr/lmr-wage-growth.asp, accessed 6 October 2011.

Donnelly, N., and Dowling, P. (2010) 'Managing globalisation and IHRM', in J. Connell and S. Teo (eds), *Strategic HRM: Contemporary issues in the Asia Pacific Region.* Victoria, Australia: Tilde University Press.

Doughty, S. (2010) 'Remuneration and rewards in 2010', *Employment Today* May: 146 42.

Edwards, B. (2012) 'Political round up: 6 March', *New Zealand Herald*, 6 March, www.nzherald.co.nz/best-of-political-analysis/news/article.cfm?c_id=1502734&objectid=10790186, accessed 6 March 2012.

EEO Trust (2009) 'People management in tough economic times: Employers' responses to the recession', November, www.eeotrust.org.nz/content/docs/reports/People per cent-20management per cent20in per cent20tough per cent20economic per cent20times per cent202009.doc, accessed 1 August 2011.

Fombrun, C., Tichy, N., and Devanna, M. (1984) *Strategic Human Resource Management*. New York, NY: Wiley.

Fursman, L., and Zodgekar, N. (2009) 'Making it work: The impacts of flexible work arrangements on New Zealand families', *Social Policy Journal of New Zealand* 35: 43–54.

Gilbert, J., and Jones, G. (2000) 'Managing human resources in New Zealand small businesses', *Asia Pacific Journal of Human Resources* 38: 55–68.

Gilbertson, D. W. (1984) 'Personnel's path to organizational effectiveness', Proceedings of the National Conference of the New Zealand Institute of Personnel Management, October, 48–51.

Green, R. and Agarwal, R. (2011) 'Management matters in New Zealand: How does manufacturing measure up?', *Ministry of Economic Development Occasional Papers 11/03*.

Guest, D. (1989) 'Human resource management: Its implications for industrial relations and trade unions', in J. Storey (ed.), *New Perspectives on Human Resource Management*. London, UK: Routledge.

Gyngell, A., Skilling, D., and Thirlwell, M. (2007) 'Australia and New Zealand in a globalising world', *Lowry Institute Perspectives*, www.lowyinstitute.org, accessed 28 October 2011.

Haar, J., and Delaney, B. (2009) 'Entrepreneurship and Māori cultural values: Using "Whanaugatanga" to understanding Māori business', *New Zealand Journal of Applied Business Research* 7: 25–40.

Haig, R. (2010) *Working Across the Ditch – New Zealanders Working in Australia*. Wellington, NZ: Department of Labour.

Hawke, G. (1985) *The making of New Zealand: An economic history*. UK: Cambridge University Press.

Hofstede, G., (2005) *Cultures and Organisations: Software of the mind*. New York, NY: McGraw-Hill.

Hogan, J., and Holland, B. (2003) 'Using theory to evaluate personality and job-performance relations: A socioanalytic perspective', *Journal of Applied Psychology* 88: 100–12.

Hudson (2011) *Next Generation Recruitment: Battle strategies for the talent war*, Report published by Hudson Highland Group Inc.

Human Resources Institute New Zealand (HRINZ) (2011a) 'The history of the human resources institute of New Zealand', www.hrinz.org.nz/Site/About/history.aspx, accessed 26 October 2011.

Human Resources Institute New Zealand (HRINZ) (2011b) 'HR practice in New Zealand', www.hrinz.org.nz/Site/Resources/hrm_in_nz.aspx, 26 October 2011.

Inkson, K., Henshall, B., Marsh, N., and Ellis, G. (1986) *Theory K: The key to excellence in New Zealand management*. Auckland, NZ: Bateman.

Johnson, G. (2000) 'The practice of human resource management in New Zealand: Strategic and best practice?', *Asia Pacific Journal of Human Resources* 38: 69–83.

Johnson, G., and Mouly, S. (2002) 'The human resource function in New Zealand organisations: The Cranfield survey', *New Zealand Journal of Human Resources Management* 2: 1–15.

Jones, D., Pringle, J., and Shepherd, D. (2000) '"Managing diversity" meets Aotearoa/New Zealand', *Personnel Review* 29: 364–80.

Kelliher, C., and Anderson, D. (2008) 'For better or for worse? An analysis of how flexible working practices influence employees' perceptions of job quality', *International Journal of Human Resource Management* 19: 419–31.

King, M. (2007) *The Penguin History of New Zealand Illustrated*. London, UK: Penguin.

Kirkpatrick, D. L. (1998) *Evaluating Training Programs: The four levels.* San Francisco, CA: Berrett-Koehler.

Kiwibank (2013) 'Kiwibank: more about us', www.kiwibank.co.nz/about-us/more-about-us, accessed 7 February 2013.

Latham, G. P., Almost, J., Mann, S., and Moore, C. (2005) 'New developments in performance management', *Organizational Dynamics 34:* 77–87.

Lawler, E., and Mohrman, S. (2003) *HR as a Strategic Partner: What does it take to make it happen?* University of Southern California: Center for Effective Organizations.

Massey, C., Lewis, K., Cameron, A., Coetzer, A., and Harris, C. (2006) *It's the People that you Know: A report on SMEs and their human resource practices.* Massey University: New Zealand Centre for SME Research.

(2012a) 'Political round up: 6 March', www.nzherald.co.nz/best-of-political-analysis/news/article.cfm?c_id=1502734&objectid=10790186, accessed 6 March 2012.

New Zealand Herald (2012b) 'Wage inflation speeds up in private sector, slows for public', 7 February 2012, www.nzherald.co.nz/business/news/article.cfm?c_id=3&objectid=10783900, accessed 7 March 2012.

New Zealand Management (2011) 'Bend it like a kiwi', *New Zealand Management* 58(3): 8.

New Zealand Treasury (2010) 'New Zealand economic and financial overview', www.treasury.govt.nz/economy/overview/2010/nzefo-10-1.pdf, accessed 30 October 11.

Nicholls, P. (2012). Tracking the economy. *National Business Review,* 16 March 2012, www.nbr.co.nz/article/tracking-economy-113196, accessed 7 February 2013.

Proctor-Thomson, S. B., Donnelly, N., and Plimmer, G. (2010) *Constructing Workplace Democracy: Women's voice in the New Zealand public service.* Wellington: Public Service Association (PSA) and Industrial Relations Centre, Victoria University of Wellington.

Ransom, S. W. N. (1966) 'Background of management', in G. Hanley (ed.), *Personnel Management in New Zealand.* Wellington, NZ: Sweet and Maxwell.

Rasmussen, E. (2010) *Employment Relationships: Workers, unions and employers in New Zealand.* Auckland, NZ: Auckland University Press.

Rasmussen, E., Andersen, T., and Haworth, N. (2010) 'Has the strategic role and professional status of human resource management peaked in New Zealand?', *Journal of Industrial Relations* 52: 103–18.

Rasmussen, E., and Lamm, F. (2005) 'From collectivism to individualism in New Zealand employment relations', Paper presented at the 15th AIRANNZ Conference, 9–11 February, University of Sydney.

Reserve Bank of New Zealand (2011) 'New Zealand economic and financial chronology, 2011–1993', www.rbnz.govt.nz/about/whatwedo/1613129.html, accessed 15 September 11.

Rudman, R. (2010) *Human Resources Management in New Zealand.* Auckland, NZ: Pearson.

Ryan, A., McFarland, L., Baron, H., and Page, R. (1999) 'An international look at selection practices: Nation and culture as explanations for variability in practice', *Personnel Psychology* 52: 359–91.

Skilling, D., and Boven, D. (2006) *The Flight of the Kiwi: Going global from the end of the world.* Auckland, NZ: The New Zealand Institute.

Sloman, M., and Malinen, S. (2010) 'One size doesn't fit all: The skills debate and the New Zealand economy', *New Zealand Journal of Human Resource Management,* 10(2): 83–98.

Stablein, R., and Geare, A. (1993) 'Human resource management in New Zealand: Profession and practice', *Asia Pacific Human Resource Management* 31: 26–38.

Statistics New Zealand (2006) 'QuickStats about culture and identity: 2006 census', www.stats.govt.nz/Census/2006CensusHomePage/QuickStats/quickstats-about-a-subject/culture-and-identity.aspx, accessed 26 October 2011.

Statistics New Zealand (2010) *New Zealand Business Demography Statistics: At February*

2010, October 2010, www.stats.govt.nz/browse_for_stats/businesses/business_characteristics/BusinessDemographyStatistics_HOTPFeb10.aspx, accessed 7 February 2013.

Statistics New Zealand (2011a) 'New Zealand in profile', January 2011, www.statistics.govt.nz/browse_for_stats/snapshots-of-nz/nz-in-profile-2011.aspx, accessed 15 August 2011.

Statistics New Zealand (2011b) 'Economic development indicators', www.statistics.govt.nz/browse_for_stats/economic_indicators/productivity/development-indicators/2011-indicators.aspx, accessed 15 August 2011.

Stephenson, J., and Scobie, G. (2002) *The Economics of Population Ageing*, New Zealand Treasury Working Paper 02/05.

Strategic Pay (2009) 'Credit crisis hits employees in the back pocket', www.strategicpay.co.nz/Portals/0/Documents/Press%20Release%200109.pdf, accessed 26 October 2011.

Strategic Pay (2011) 'CEO pay to go backwards?', www.strategicpay.co.nz/Portals/0/Documents/CEO%20pay%20to%20go%20backwards.pdf, accessed 26 October 2011.

Taylor, P., Keelty, Y., and McDonnell, B. (2002) 'Evolving personnel selection practices in New Zealand organizations and recruitment firms', *New Zealand Journal of Psychology* 31: 8–18.

Toulson, P. K., and DeFryn, M. K. (2006) 'The development of human resource management in New Zealand', *Human Resource Management* 52: 75–103.

United Nations Development Program (2010) 'Human development report 2010', November 2010, http://hdr.undp.org/en/media, accessed 26 October 2011.

Walsh, P., Bryson, J., and Lonti, Z. (2002) '"Jack be nimble, Jill be quick": HR capability and organizational agility in the New Zealand public and private sectors', *Asia Pacific Journal of Human Resources* 40: 177–92.

Whitcombe, J. (2008) 'Contributions and challenges of "new public management": New Zealand since 1984', *Policy Quarterly* 4: 7–13.

Winterton, J. (2007) 'Training, development, and competence', in P. Boxall, J. Purcell, and P. Wright (ed.), *The Oxford Handbook of Human Resource Management.* UK: Oxford University Press.

15 Human Resources in Asia-Pacific: Agenda for Future Research and Policy

ARUP VARMA AND PAWAN S. BUDHWAR

Introduction

Since the publication of the first volume (see Budhwar, 2004), there has been continued interest in studying the human resource (HR) practices in the Asia-Pacific region. Not surprisingly, countries in the region have followed different trajectories in their growth paths. This is to be expected as the socio-cultural, economic, political and legal frameworks (among others) guide and often determine national HRM policies and practices (Budhwar and Debrah, 2009). For example, China follows a one-party political framework that makes decision making relatively easier. On the other hand, India has a multi-party democracy that often makes decision-making excruciatingly difficult, thus one often hears that it takes China just six months to build a bridge, while India may take six years to just plan the building of the bridge. This is not to say that one system is better than the other, instead it is critical that a country's policies and practices be understood in context.

In keeping with this line of thought, the chapters in this book have been designed to explore the countries' HR practices in relation to their contextual realities. While we would have liked to have covered many more countries in the Asia-Pacific region in this volume, practical realities limited the final number. However, we are very pleased with the final list, as it provides a comprehensive coverage of countries in the region.

As the readers would have noticed, each of the preceding chapters followed a general framework designed to help the readers compare and contrast the HR practices of each country. In addition, the unique contextual factors of each country are presented so that readers may interpret the HR practices in light of those realities. For example, the Islamic work principles in Malaysia result in very unique practices that stand in stark contrast to the multi-ethnic and multi-religious Indian society, where work practices are still guided by laws and regulations established by the British.

In addition, each chapter also provides a discussion of the possible future challenges faced by each of the nations included in this volume. For example, the tremendous growth of the Indian economy (spurred, to a large extent, by the arrival of Business Process Outsourcing (BPO)/call centres) resulted in job opportunities for college students. This meant that a new class of employee was created, which had a significant impact on the socio-economic fabric of the Indian society. At the same time, the influx of the multi-national corporations has led to a sharp increase in the number of options available to the working professional with the result that job-hopping has become commonplace. This thus requires HR departments to devise strategies for employee attraction and retention.

As such this book was designed to present a comprehensive overview of HRM practices in key Asia-Pacific countries, with one caveat. Obviously not all countries of the region are covered in this volume; however, we believe that the list of countries included presents a diverse range of nations, each with their own unique social, cultural and political reality, thus allowing the reader to interpret the prevalent HRM practices in conjunction with the relevant context. Such an approach helps to highlight the context-specific nature of HRM and to explore the unique practices of the countries that directly or indirectly affect HRM strategy and practices in the countries (also see Schuler, Budhwar, and Florkowski, 2002). So, for example, China's one-child policy has a direct bearing on labour supply. At the same time the one-child policy has led to better standards of living, thus leading to increased demand for consumer goods, in turn leading to increased labour demand. Similarly, the tremendous growth of the Indian economy has resulted in increased opportunities for management professionals, leading to severe job-hopping. Given that the management schools in India are unable to produce anywhere near the number required, organisations in India find themselves competing for the same pool of management professionals. As one may expect, this situation has a direct effect on how organisations set up their compensation strategies as well as their recruitment and selection strategies.

HRM Challenges of the Asia-Pacific Region

Even though the various chapters in this book are dedicated to the unique and specific realities of each of the countries, it is not difficult to see some common threads running across all of them. For example, the continuing globalisation forces all nations to react appropriately and design policies and strategies to take advantage of globalisation while at the same time trying to protect against any negative fallout. For example, Japan's continued insistence on restricting inward migration, coupled with an ageing workforce, has resulted in the need to come up with creative solutions for the labour shortage, thus new policies offer incentives to retirees to rejoin the workforce.

Perhaps one of the biggest changes seen in the business world since the publication of the first edition is the clear shift of balance of power from North America and Europe to Asia. As is well known, China is now considered a clear economic global leader with India not so far behind. Interestingly, while these two countries are neighbours, their social, cultural and political environments are very different, resulting in unique advantages and disadvantages for each. For example, while India's multi-party democracy often results in a lot of debate but few results, China's one-party system allows it to plan and execute developmental projects at tremendous speed. Similarly India's history of British rule has resulted in English being taught across the country and is almost always the language of business. On the other hand, China is only now beginning to introduce English at the primary school level.

In this connection, it is important to note that one of the key factors that led to the increased importance of China and India was the shift of manufacturing and BPO jobs to these countries. This requires HR departments of companies in these two countries to re-calibrate their HR strategies to address the new reality. Indeed, this is a common theme across all the countries; that is, the continuing development of the industrial sector in these countries calls for HR departments to continually stay one step ahead and pro-actively address the changing needs of their respective workforces. In the following section we present the key challenges faced by the countries covered in this volume.

Talent Acquisition and Retention

As one may expect, the influx of companies to the Asian region has resulted in a marked shortage of quality talent. While one often hears that countries like China and India have huge populations, this does not automatically translate to having a qualified workforce. Indeed, several authors have noted the problems with recruiting and retaining talent in China (for example, Dickel and Watkins, 2008) and India (Budhwar and Varma, 2011). Both China and India produce millions of university graduates each year, however most of these graduates lack soft skills and are often considered unemployable. As an alternative, many companies (mostly MNCs, although some local companies too) have tried to hire foreign-returned graduates, however, this has met with little success as these graduates often lack local knowledge that is crucial in industries such as real estate, consultancy, legal affairs, finance and banking. Sadly, the shortage of qualified professionals leads to poaching of talent, as well as unreasonable expectations from individuals. In the short run, this often means that individuals change jobs frequently in an effort to gain higher salaries, leading to a loss of intellectual capital for organisations and higher turnover and replacement costs. Indeed, as a result of this shortage, organisations are sometimes forced to offer job candidates job titles, salaries and responsibilities well beyond what they deserve based on their experience and potential (Cooke, 2012).

Other countries in the Asia-Pacific region are also struggling with attracting and retaining talent, albeit for different reasons. In Taiwan, the skills shortage issue manifests itself differently; here the growth of technology has resulted in a polarisation of the labor force, with the result that Taiwanese companies are struggling to find a sufficient number of qualified people to fill their vacancies. Several different initiatives are being implemented to address this gap (San, 2011), including attracting foreign workers to join the workforce. However, a lack of succession planning and strategic talent management tend to exacerbate the talent problem, with the primary reason for the high turnover of mid-level managers being a lack of career-development programs, which is precipitated by the fact that most Taiwanese businesses are family owned and thus fail to implement succession management.

On the other hand, Australia is at the precipice of an interesting situation, whereby it is estimated that the number of new workers entering the workforce will steadily go down in comparison to those leaving the workforce (Critchley, 2004), creating an increasing demand–supply gap. Similarly, Korean organisations are responding to the war for talent by aggressively devising and implementing attraction and retention strategies (Kim and Bae, 2004), such as sign-on bonuses and stock options.

It should be clear from the above discussion that one of the most serious challenges facing HR departments in the Asia-Pacific region is how to attract and retain talent. What is also clear from the examples above is that there is no 'one-size-fits-all' strategy that will work for all of the countries. Thus, HR departments in all of these countries will have to pro-actively identify and implement appropriate talent acquisition and retention strategies, so as to be able to support their business strategy. In addition, given the dynamic nature of business and talent in the current environment, HR professionals will need to realise that such strategies are likely to prove to be a moving target at best, and they need to continually re-visit, re-evaluate and re-tool their strategies as necessary.

Training and Development

On a related subject, organisations are faced with a difficult choice, that is, to train or not to train their employees. On the one hand, they often end up hiring employees who are not job-ready, and thus require training, yet on the other hand, this very training leads to turning the employees into employable commodities, easily poached by competitors. Various other issues result in making this a complicated issue. For example, the Vietnamese workforce has an excess supply of non-skilled and semi-skilled labour while there is a continuing shortage of skilled labour, making it imperative that training is provided, either in-house or externally. It should be pointed out, however, that while in-house training has to be weighed against cost–benefit concerns, external training needs to be evaluated against corporate needs and for quality. Singapore is an interesting case, which has seen a huge growth in the number of training consultants over the last two decades or so, yet it is not clear if they are able to support organisations appropriately. While many of these training outfits (and in-house training) programmes emphasise operational efficiencies and cost-reduction strategies, what the economy seems to really need is a different kind of skill (for example, innovation), given that the new economy is increasingly knowledge-based. On the other hand, Thailand is facing a different, although related, problem. As technology and automation lead to re-structuring of organisations and jobs, numerous individuals (especially older workers who have lower or no technology skills) are likely to be laid off or forced into retirement. Again, this means that re-training may be needed to keep the workers gainfully employed.

Work–Life Balance

The growth of the economies in the Asia–Pacific region has given rise to an important concern – work–life balance. As individuals attempt to cash in on the increased opportunities, there is always the danger of going overboard and ignoring family in the pursuit of economic success. In fact, the impact of this is already being felt in various circles. In India, increasing numbers of applicants are seeking companies that offer work–life balance while Korean firms are pro-actively addressing the issue by adopting family-friendly policies, such as designating every Wednesday as a family day, and switching all lights off at 6 p.m., so employees are not tempted to work late, and instead go home to be with their families.

The issue of work–life balance is also becoming an important agenda item for the Australian HR professionals. A steady shift towards longer working hours for both full-time and part-time workers has led to a longer working week with the average full-time employee now working 42 hours per week, up from 38 hours in 1982, with many working 50 hours or more each week (Van Wanrooy *et al.*, 2006).

Changing Workforce Demographics

One difficult issue that HR departments in the region are struggling with is the changing nature of the workforce demographics. For example, in Taiwan, the average age of the population has been increasing (from 34 years old in 2001 to 43 years old in 2011). This change has a direct affect on the supply of young workers while at the same time the ageing workforce requires HR departments to devise relevant HR policies that address such key issues as life-long learning, opportunities for atypical employment and medical-care systems. Singapore and Hong Kong also face similar situations, that is, their workforce is ageing fast.

In addition, the rate of participation of females in the workforce has been steadily rising, with the result that the employment rate for females in Singapore has grown from 65.4 per cent in 2001 to 75.7 per cent in 2011. However, Singapore is also characterised by a unique phenomenon—a large pool of highly qualified females (typically in their early 30s) who voluntarily withdraw from the workforce temporarily to raise families. Ironically, while the government has enacted policies to motivate older workers to stay in the workforce (thus reducing the need for immigrants), not much has been done to address the issue of females rejoining the workforce after the time taken to raise families.

Interestingly, in both India and China the young workforce is often credited as one of the key reasons for their tremendous economic success. However, this advantage has an obvious downside where many in this young workforce think little of issues like loyalty and long-term commitment. In other words, turnover rates are skyrocketing, leading to higher replacement costs for organisations.

Culture

Any discussion of HR issues must necessarily address the role of culture in all its complexities. As Gamble (2001) noted, cultural traits such as attitudes to power distance are difficult to predict and often evoke different responses depending on the context. Given the complex societies that make up the Asia-Pacific, it is not sensible to try to develop a single model that would help researchers and practitioners better understand the role that culture plays. However, several trends are clearly emerging and need to be addressed pro-actively, so the countries may capitalise on the opportunities presented by the shift in economic focus from the West to the East, so to say. First, most of the Asia-Pacific region has been known to display collectivistic tendencies. Here, the introduction of Western models of performance and rewards can often be in direct contrast to the cultural leanings of the individuals. For example, Chinese socialistic values promote paternalism and egalitarianism, thus requiring employers to take care of the employees in a just manner. In Korea, the introduction of performance-based management and evaluation systems has seemingly led to the erosion of traditional cooperative behaviours, as individual employees are focusing more on individual behaviours and rewards. In India, employees seem to be moving away from the traditional expectation of paternalistic management, and are expressing increased individuality and desire for autonomy. On the other hand, this shift is seen to a limited degree in Malaysia, where only the new middle class seems to be displaying increased individualism while the so-called upper class continue to subscribe to traditional collectivist values, perhaps because this helps secure their position in the society.

Australia is experiencing the evolution of culture in a somewhat different fashion – while the majority of migrants prior to the 1950s came from the United Kingdom, subsequent waves of immigrants have come from culturally diverse countries such as Italy and Greece, followed by those from the Middle East, Africa and Asia. The introduction of these new waves of immigrants has brought myriad cultural values and beliefs distinctly different from the Anglo-Saxon mores of the initial immigrants. Australia's neighbour, New Zealand, has also seen an influx of migrants from Asia and the Pacific islands, thus making it imperative for HR departments to move away from traditional Anglo-Saxon models of management and devise policies and practices that address the cultural leanings of the new members of the workforce. For example, performance management systems must incorporate the collectivistic norms of Asian immigrants.

Conclusion

Overall, it is clear that the Asia-Pacific countries have seen tremendous change over the last decade or so, and this speed of change is not likely to abate any time soon. Clearly, HR departments need to pro-actively address these changes and treat their policy manuals as living, breathing, documents that are able to incorporate strategies that can address the numerous challenges faced by these nations. From addressing issues such as managing contingent workers to partnering with governments to enact appropriate employment-related legislation, HR departments have a tremendous opportunity to become strategic partners of industry.

At the same time, the academic community needs to ramp up its research efforts to focus on this region and investigate its complex issues. As we noted in the introduction, there is some research focusing on cultural values, which emphasised the importance of adapting and/or developing indigenous management practices in Asia-Pacific organisations. However, given the limited number of research publications on the subject, it is critical that scholars focus their attention on this region. As we noted earlier, the extant literature lacks a systematic framework, which reduces its generalisability and applicability. We are happy to be able to present this volume, which offers a framework for future research.

References

Budhwar, P. (2004) *Managing Human Resources in Asia Pacific.* London: Routledge.

Budhwar, P. and Debrah, Y. (2009) 'Future research on human resource management systems in Asia'. *Asia Pacific Journal of Management,* 26: 197–218.

Budhwar, P. and Varma, A. (2011) 'Emerging HR management trends in India and the way forward', *Organizational Dynamics* 40(4): 317–25.

Cooke, F. L. (2012) *Human Resource Management in China: New trends and practices.* London: Routledge.

Critchley, R. (2004) *Doing Nothing is Not an Option: Facing the imminent labor crisis.* Ohio: South Western.

Dickel, T. and Watkins, C. (2008) 'To remain competitive in China's tight labour market, companies must prioritize talent management and track compensation trends', *China Business Review* July–August: 20–23.

Gamble, J. (2001) 'Introducing Western-style HRM practices to China: Shop-floor perceptions in a British multinational,' *Journal of World Business* 41(4): 328–43.

Kim, D. and Bae, J. (2004) *Employment Relations and HRM in South Korea.* London: Ashgate.

San, G. (2011) 'Retrospect and prospect of Taiwan's human resources planning', *Yan Kao Shuang Yue Kan* 35(2): 71–93 (in Chinese).

Schuler, R. S., Budhwar, P. and Florkowski, G. W. (2002) 'International human resource management: Review and critique', *International Journal of Management Reviews* 4(1): 41–70.

Van Wanrooy, B., Bretherton, T., Considine, J. and Buchanan, J. (2006) 'Longer and irregular hours: Employers, decentralised bargaining and working time standards in Australia since the late 1970s', *Conference on 8 Hour Day and Beyond,* RMIT, Melbourne.

Index

Note: Page numbers followed by 'f' refer to figures and followed by 't' refer to tables.